THUNDERBOLTS

VOLUME 5

PUNISHER VS. THE THUNDERBOLTS

THUNDERBOLTS

VOLUME 5

PUNISHER VS. THE THUNDERBOLTS

WRITERS
BEN ACKER & BEN BLACKER

#27
PENCILER
CARLO BARBERI
INKER
CARLOS CUEVAS
COLORIST
ISRAEL SILVA

#28
ARTIST
GERARDO SANDOVAL
COLORIST
ISRAEL SILVA

#29, #31-32
ARTIST
KIM JACINTO
COLORIST
ISRAEL SILVA

#30
ARTIST
JORGE FORNÉS
COLORIST
ISRAEL SILVA

ANNUAL #1
PENCILER
MATTEO LOLLI
INKER
SEAN PARSONS
COLORIST
JAMES CAMPBELL

LETTERER
VC'S JOE SABINO

COVER ARTISTS
DAVID YARDIN AND CARLO BARBERI & EDGAR DELGADO

ASSISTANT EDITOR
FRANKIE JOHNSON
EDITOR
JORDAN D. WHITE

THUNDERBOLTS VOL. 5: PUNISHER VS. THE THUNDERBOLTS. Contains material originally published in magazine form as THUNDERBOLTS #27-32 and ANNUAL #1. First printing 2014. ISBN# 978-0-7851-8983-1. Published by MARVEL WORLD WIDE, INC., a subsidiary of MARVEL ENTERTAINMENT, LLC. OFFICE OF PUBLICATION: 135 West 50th Street, New York, NY 10020. Copyright © 2014 Marvel Characters, Inc. All rights reserved. All characters featured in this issue and the distinctive names and likenesses thereof, and all related indicia are trademarks of Marvel Characters, Inc. No similarity between any of the names, characters, persons, and/or institutions in this magazine with those of any living or dead person or institution is intended, and any such similarity which may exist is purely coincidental. Printed in the U.S.A. ALAN FINE, EVP - Office of the President, Marvel Worldwide, Inc. and EVP & CMO Marvel Characters B.V.; DAN BUCKLEY, Publisher & President - Print, Animation & Digital Divisions; JOE QUESADA, Chief Creative Officer; TOM BREVOORT, SVP of Publishing; DAVID BOGART, SVP of Operations & Procurement, Publishing; C.B. CEBULSKI, SVP of Creator & Content Development; DAVID GABRIEL, SVP Print, Sales & Marketing; JIM O'KEEFE, VP of Operations & Logistics; DAN CARR, Executive Director of Publishing Technology; SUSAN CRESPI, Editorial Operations Manager; ALEX MORALES, Publishing Operations Manager; STAN LEE, Chairman Emeritus. For information regarding advertising in Marvel Comics or on Marvel.com, please contact Niza Disla, Director of Marvel Partnerships, at ndisla@marvel.com. For Marvel subscription inquiries, please call 800-217-9158. Manufactured between 10/24/2014 and 12/1/2014 by R.R. DONNELLEY, INC., SALEM, VA, USA.

0 9 7 6 5 4 3 2 1

COLLECTION EDITOR: ALEX STA
ASSISTANT EDITOR: SARAH BRUN
EDITORS, SPECIAL PROJECTS: JENNIFER GRÜNWALD & MARK D. BEAZLEY
SENIOR EDITOR, SPECIAL PROJECTS: JEFF YOUNGQUIST
SVP PRINT, SALES & MARKETING: DAVID GABRIEL
BOOK DESIGN: NELSON RIBEIRO

EDITOR IN CHIEF: AXEL ALONSO
CHIEF CREATIVE OFFICER: JOE QUESADA
PUBLISHER: DAN BUCKLEY
EXECUTIVE PRODUCER: ALAN FINE

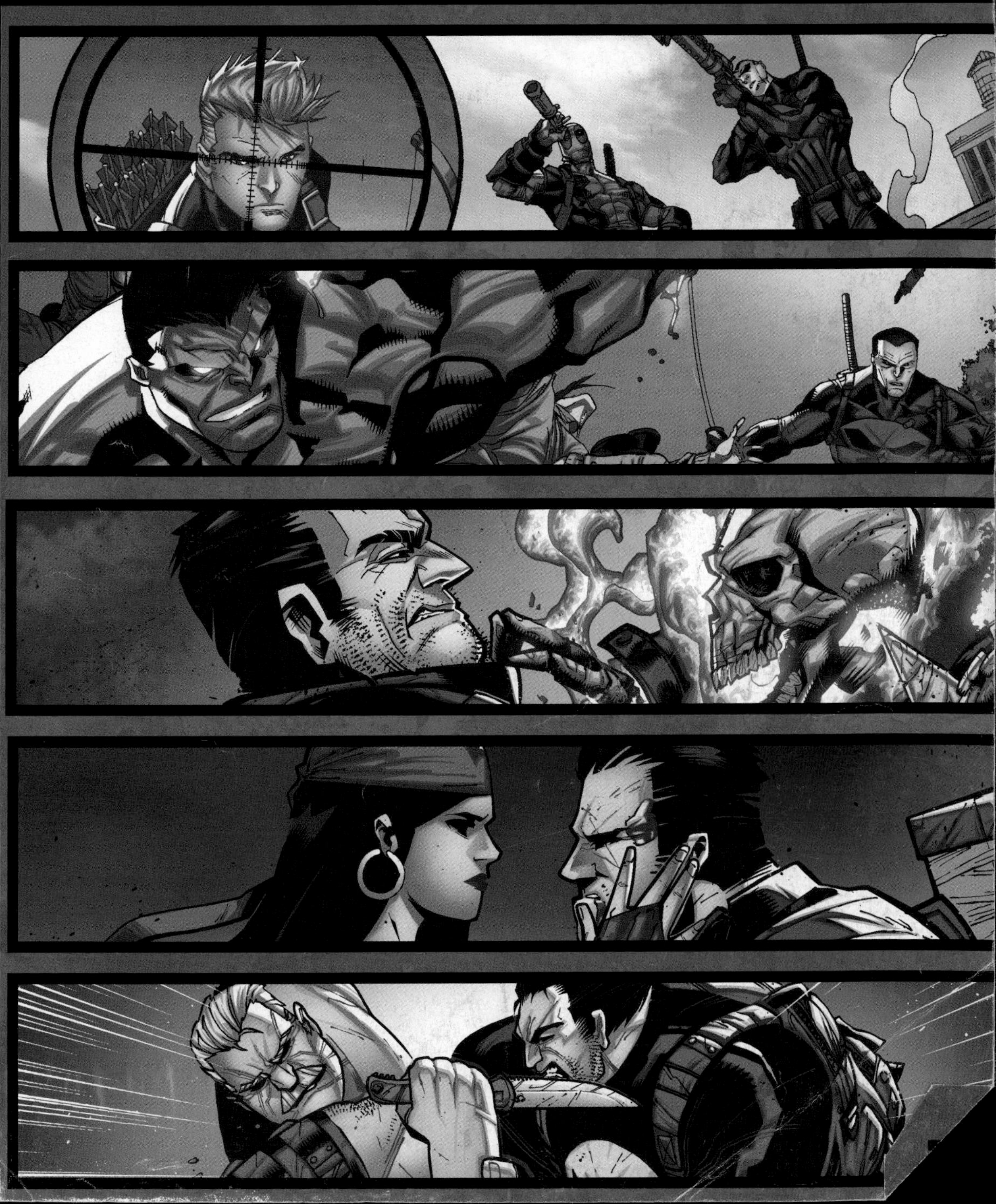

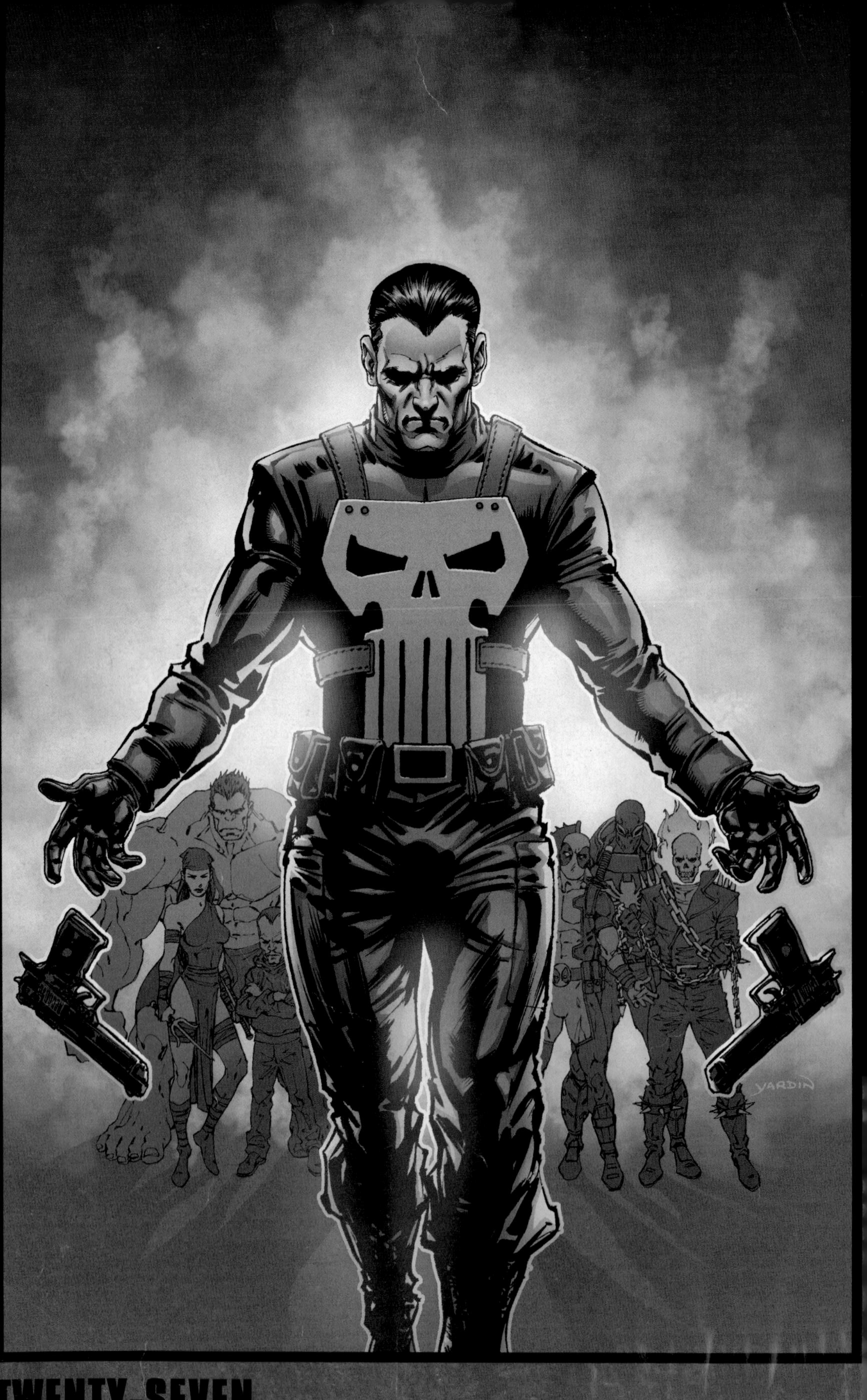
YARDIN

TWENTY-SEVEN

ED HULK
UNISHER
LEKTRA
HOST RIDER
EADPOOL
ED LEADER

General Thaddeus "Thunderbolt" Ross--The Red Hulk--has assembled a team inte cutting out the cancer of evil that infects this world. By his side are a handpicked g of like-minded individuals--former loners bound together to accomplish what might have been out of reach on their own. Frank Castle, aka Punisher, vigilante executioner. Johnny Blaze, aka Ghost Rider, Spirit of Vengeance. Wade Wilson, aka Deadpool, regenerating psychopath. Elektra Natchios, aka Elektra, ninja assassin. Re-powered former gamma-villain genius Samuel Sterns, aka Red Leader. Together, they are the...

THUNDERBOLTS

General "Thunderbolt" Ross—also known as the Red Hulk—formed the Thunderbolts as a way to fight for good against evil. Knowing that sometimes the greatest good must be accomplished by any means necessary, his team would use any tactics at their disposal, without concern for conventional ideas of morality. This way, his team would do what the Avengers and X-Men could not: fight evil on its own terms.

Ross, Elektra, the Punisher, Deadpool, Johnny Blaze, and the deceptively cunning Red Leader have managed to work together to accomplish their goals--but can members of a team with no moral code really trust each other?

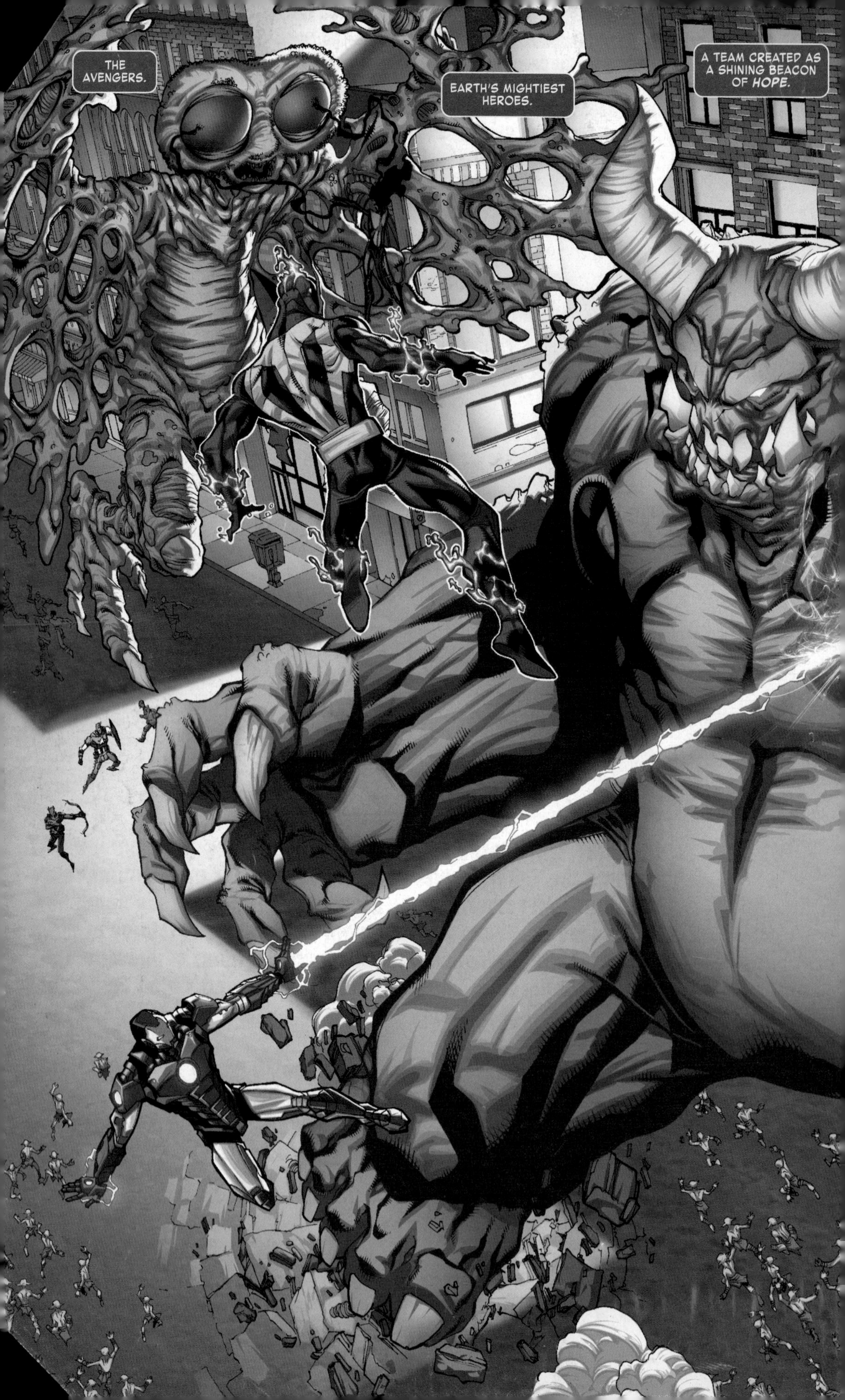
THE AVENGERS.
EARTH'S MIGHTIEST HEROES.
A TEAM CREATED AS A SHINING BEACON OF *HOPE*.

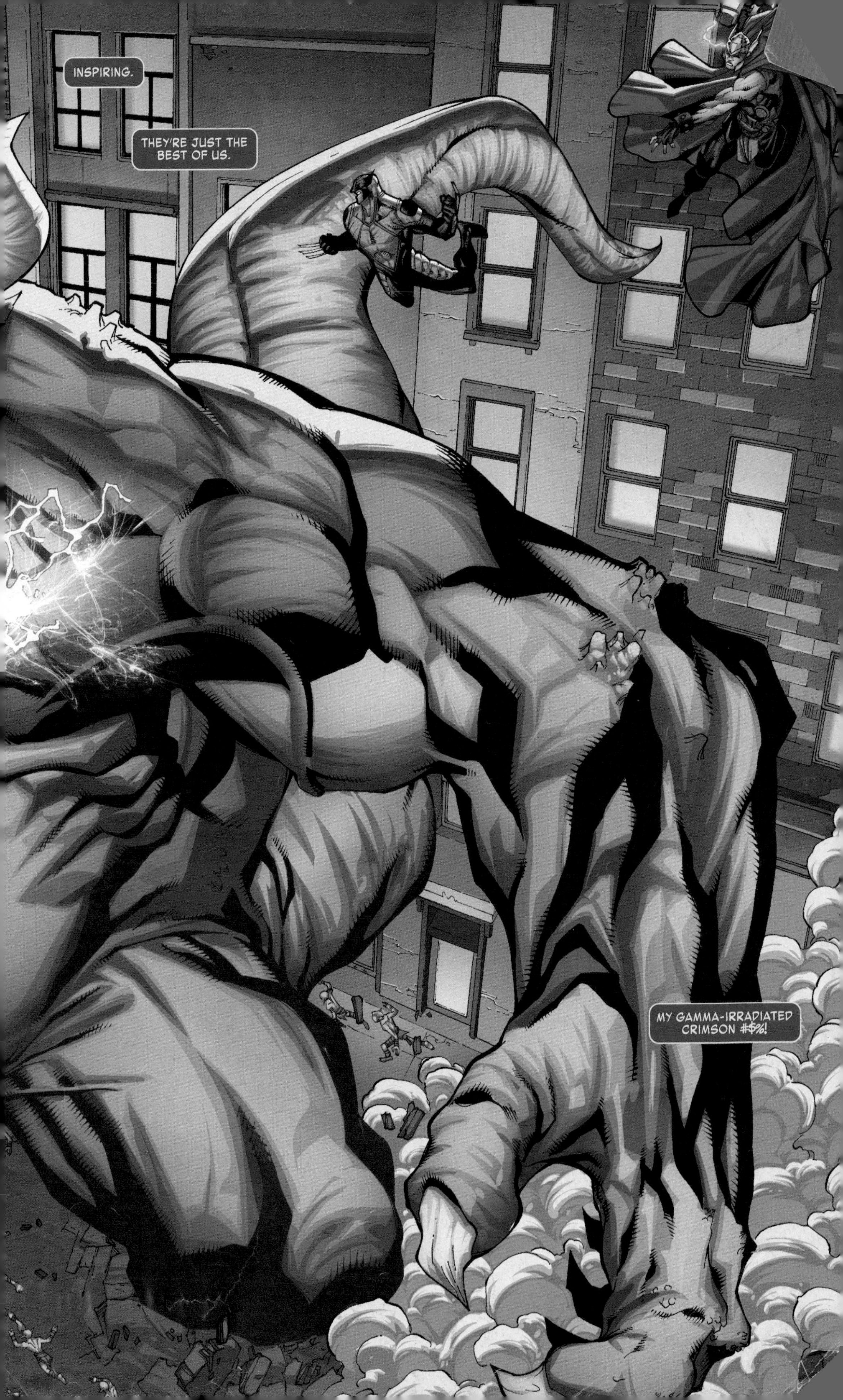

INSPIRING.
THEY'RE JUST THE BEST OF US.
MY GAMMA-IRRADIATED CRIMSON #$%!

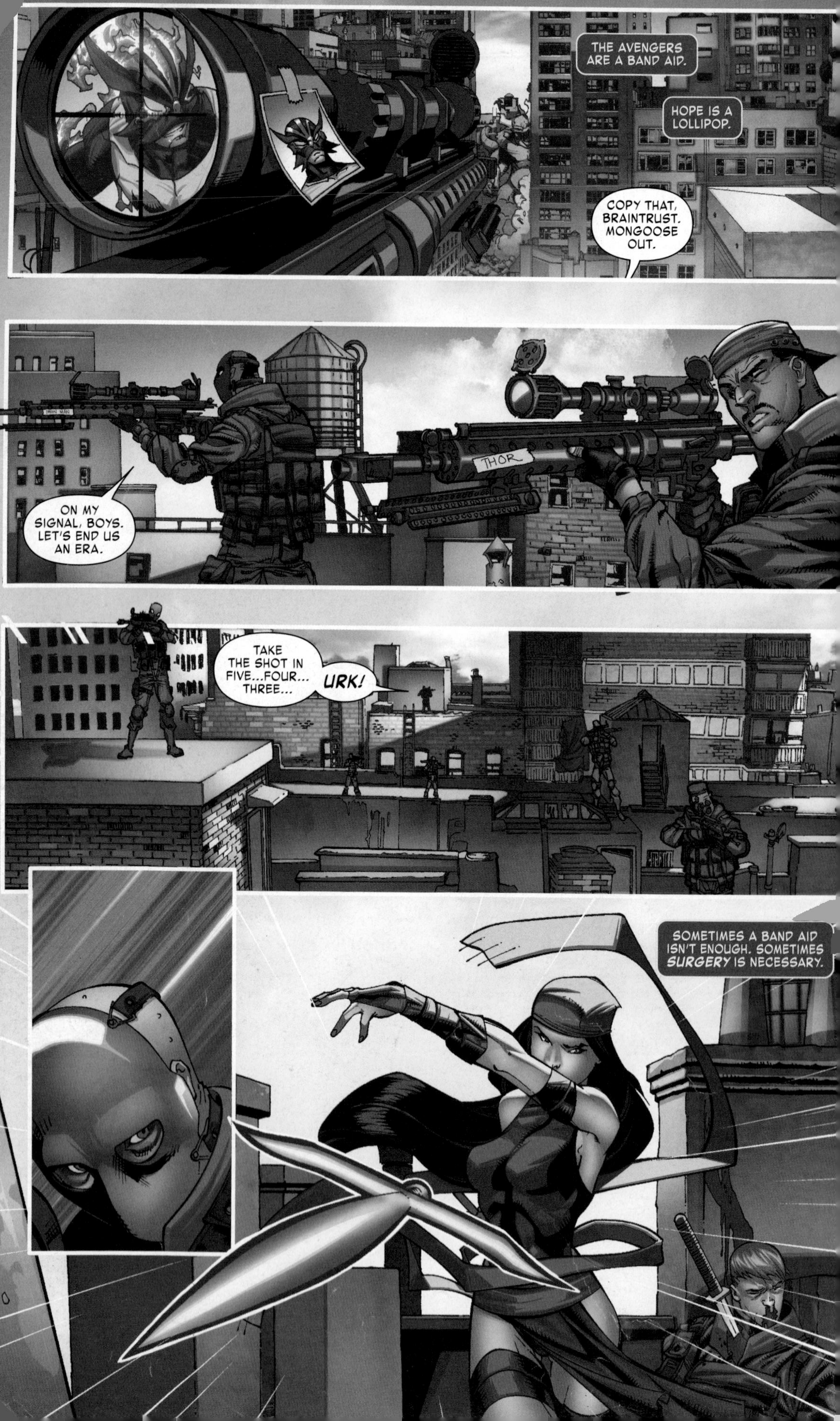
THE AVENGERS ARE A BAND AID.
HOPE IS A LOLLIPOP.
COPY THAT, BRAINTRUST. MONGOOSE OUT.
IRON MAN
THOR
ON MY SIGNAL, BOYS. LET'S END US AN ERA.
TAKE THE SHOT IN FIVE...FOUR... THREE...
URK!
SOMETIMES A BAND AID ISN'T ENOUGH. SOMETIMES SURGERY IS NECESSARY.

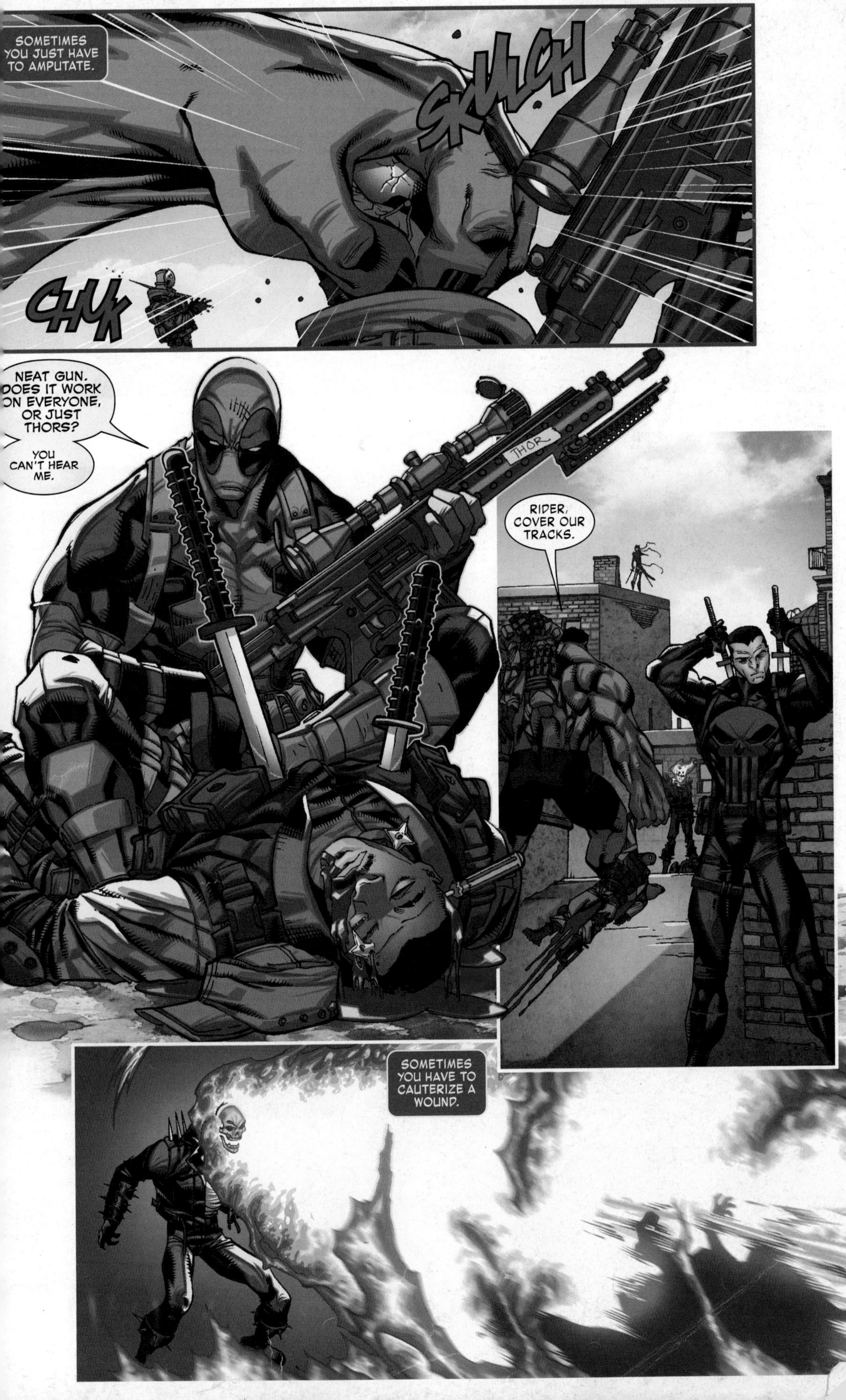
SOMETIMES YOU JUST HAVE TO AMPUTATE.
SKULCH
CHUK
NEAT GUN. DOES IT WORK ON EVERYONE, OR JUST THORS?
YOU CAN'T HEAR ME.
THOR
RIDER, COVER OUR TRACKS.
SOMETIMES YOU HAVE TO CAUTERIZE A WOUND.

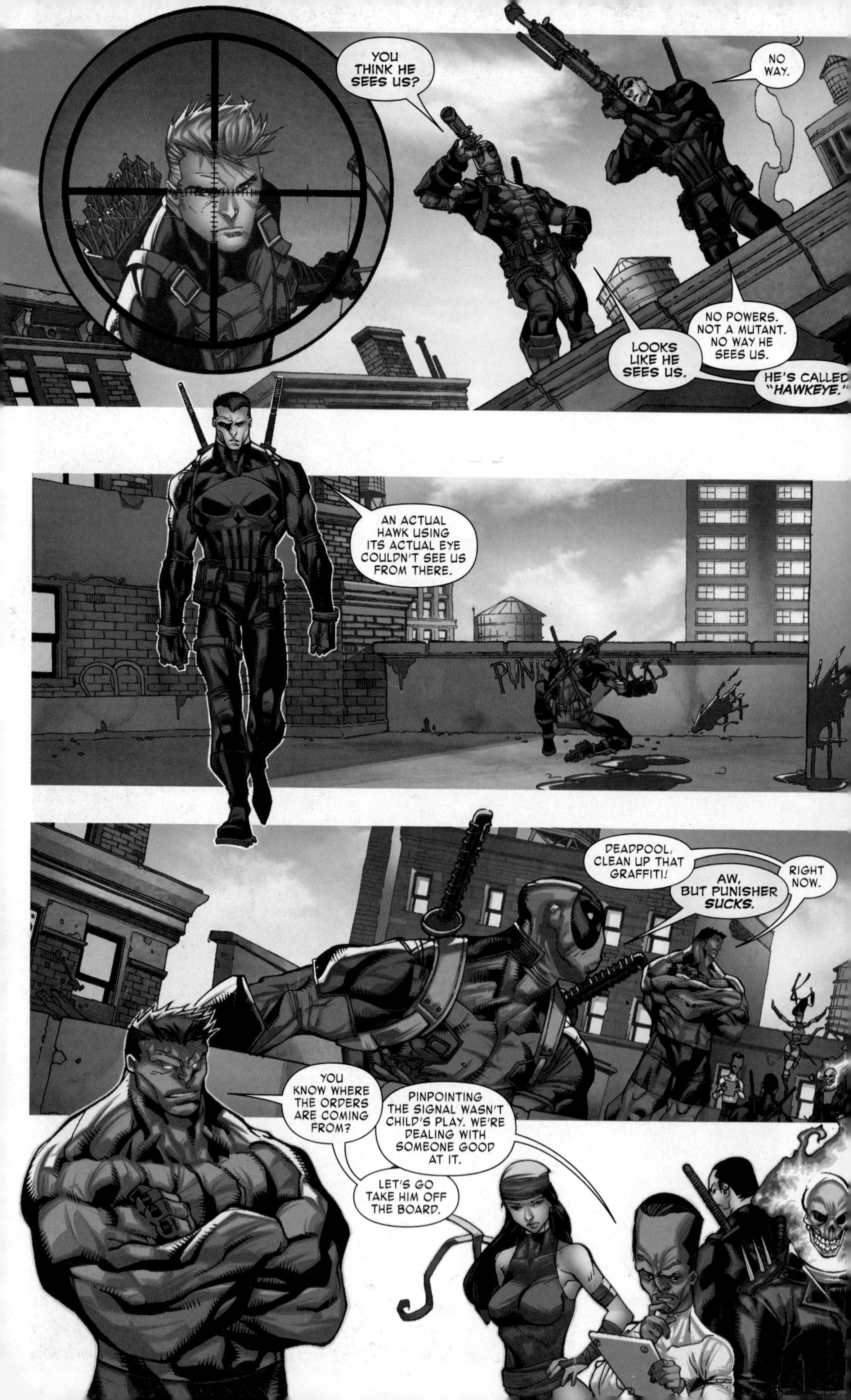
YOU THINK HE SEES US?
NO WAY.
LOOKS LIKE HE SEES US.
NO POWERS. NOT A MUTANT. NO WAY HE SEES US.
HE'S CALLED "HAWKEYE."
AN ACTUAL HAWK USING ITS ACTUAL EYE COULDN'T SEE US FROM THERE.
PUNIS SUCKS
DEADPOOL, CLEAN UP THAT GRAFFITI!
RIGHT NOW.
AW, BUT PUNISHER SUCKS.
YOU KNOW WHERE THE ORDERS ARE COMING FROM?
PINPOINTING THE SIGNAL WASN'T CHILD'S PLAY. WE'RE DEALING WITH SOMEONE GOOD AT IT.
LET'S GO TAKE HIM OFF THE BOARD.

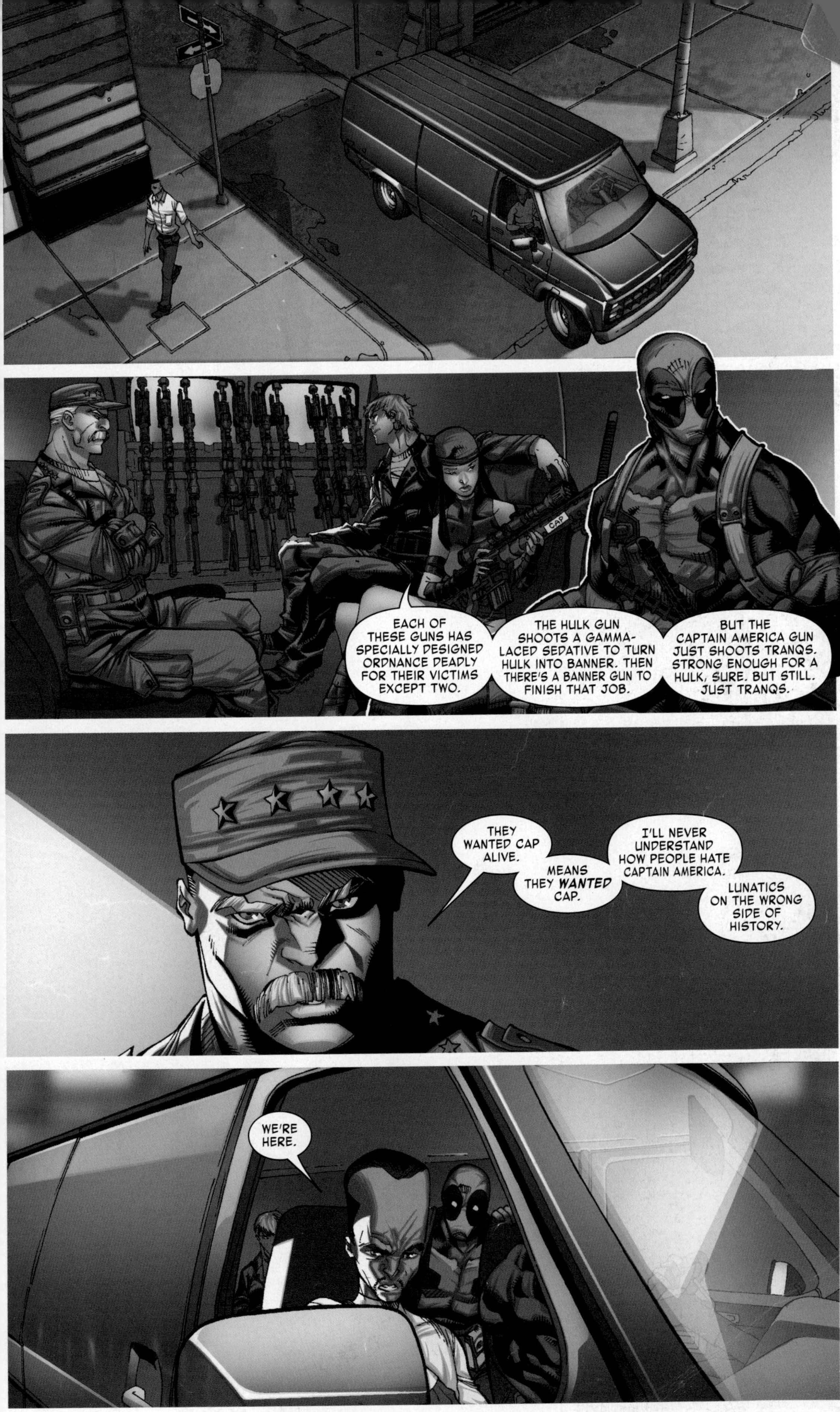

EACH OF THESE GUNS HAS SPECIALLY DESIGNED ORDNANCE DEADLY FOR THEIR VICTIMS EXCEPT TWO.
THE HULK GUN SHOOTS A GAMMA-LACED SEDATIVE TO TURN HULK INTO BANNER. THEN THERE'S A BANNER GUN TO FINISH THAT JOB.
BUT THE CAPTAIN AMERICA GUN JUST SHOOTS TRANQS. STRONG ENOUGH FOR A HULK, SURE. BUT STILL. JUST TRANQS.
CAP
THEY WANTED CAP ALIVE.
MEANS THEY *WANTED* CAP.
I'LL NEVER UNDERSTAND HOW PEOPLE HATE CAPTAIN AMERICA.
LUNATICS ON THE WRONG SIDE OF HISTORY.
WE'RE HERE.

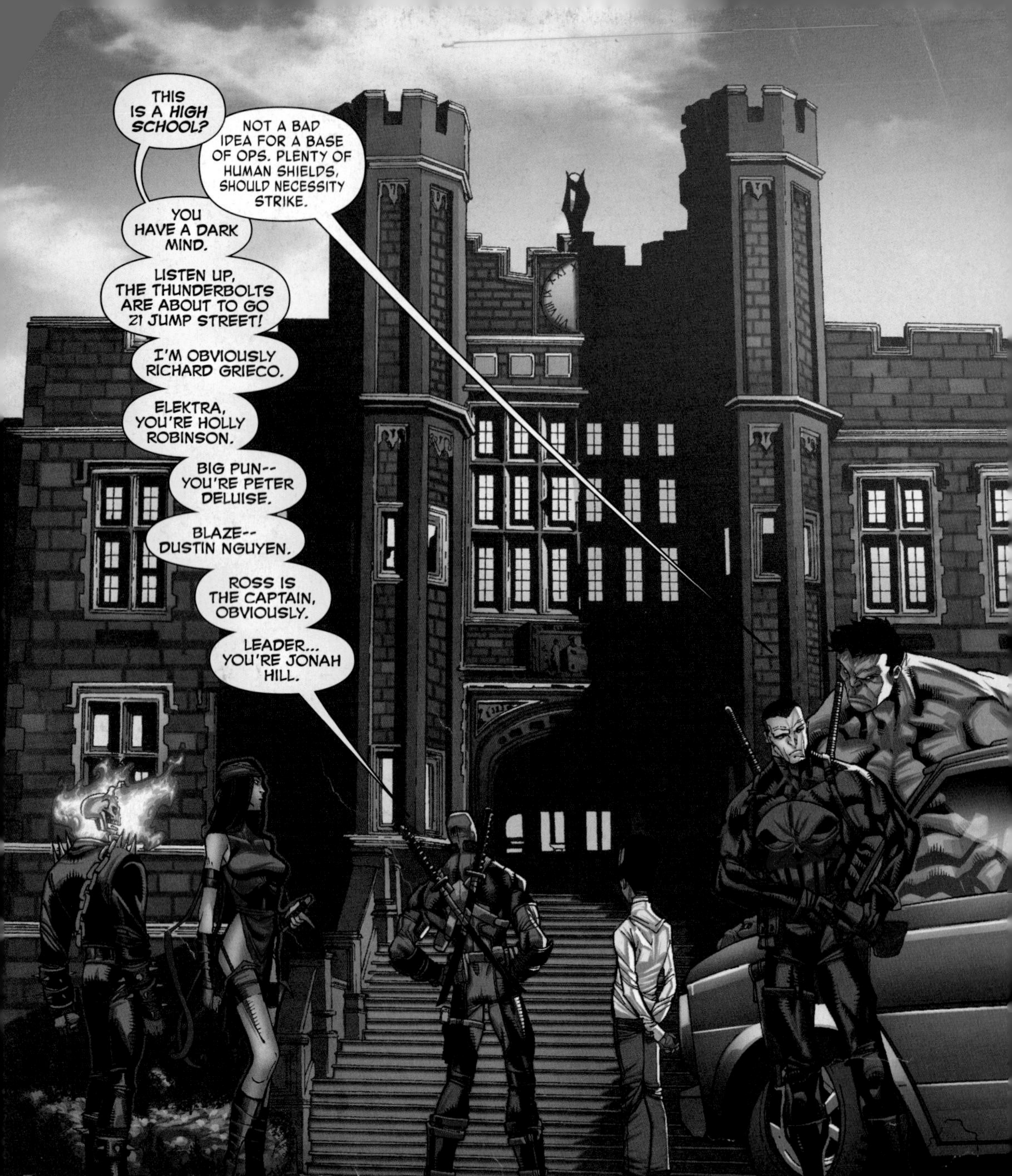
THIS IS A *HIGH SCHOOL?*
NOT A BAD IDEA FOR A BASE OF OPS. PLENTY OF HUMAN SHIELDS, SHOULD NECESSITY STRIKE.
YOU HAVE A DARK MIND.
LISTEN UP, THE THUNDERBOLTS ARE ABOUT TO GO 21 JUMP STREET!
I'M OBVIOUSLY RICHARD GRIECO.
ELEKTRA, YOU'RE HOLLY ROBINSON.
BIG PUN-- YOU'RE PETER DELUISE.
BLAZE-- DUSTIN NGUYEN.
ROSS IS THE CAPTAIN, OBVIOUSLY.
LEADER... YOU'RE JONAH HILL.

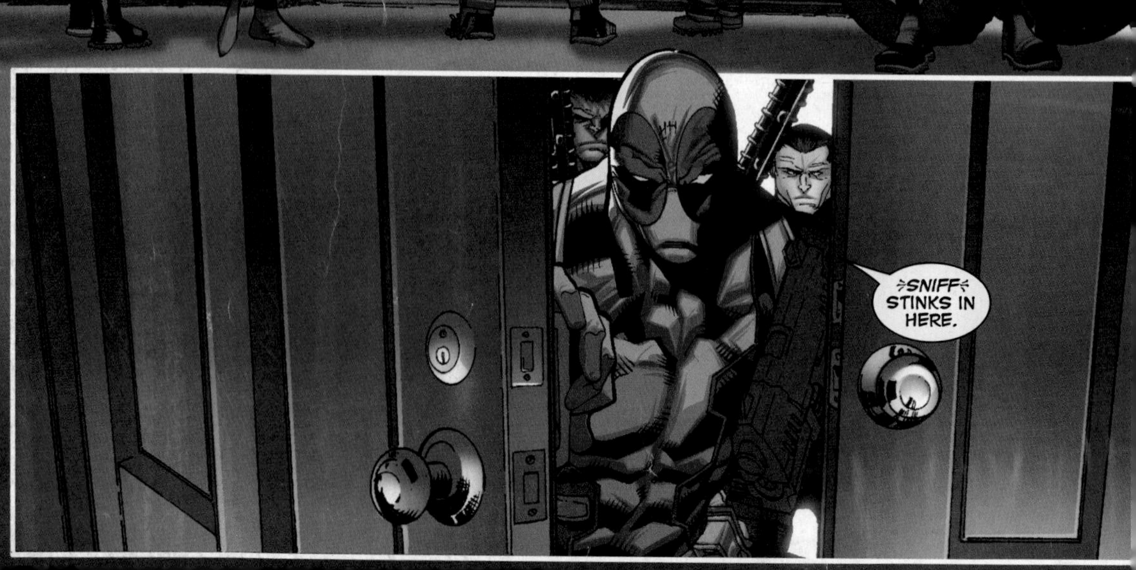
SNIFF STINKS IN HERE.

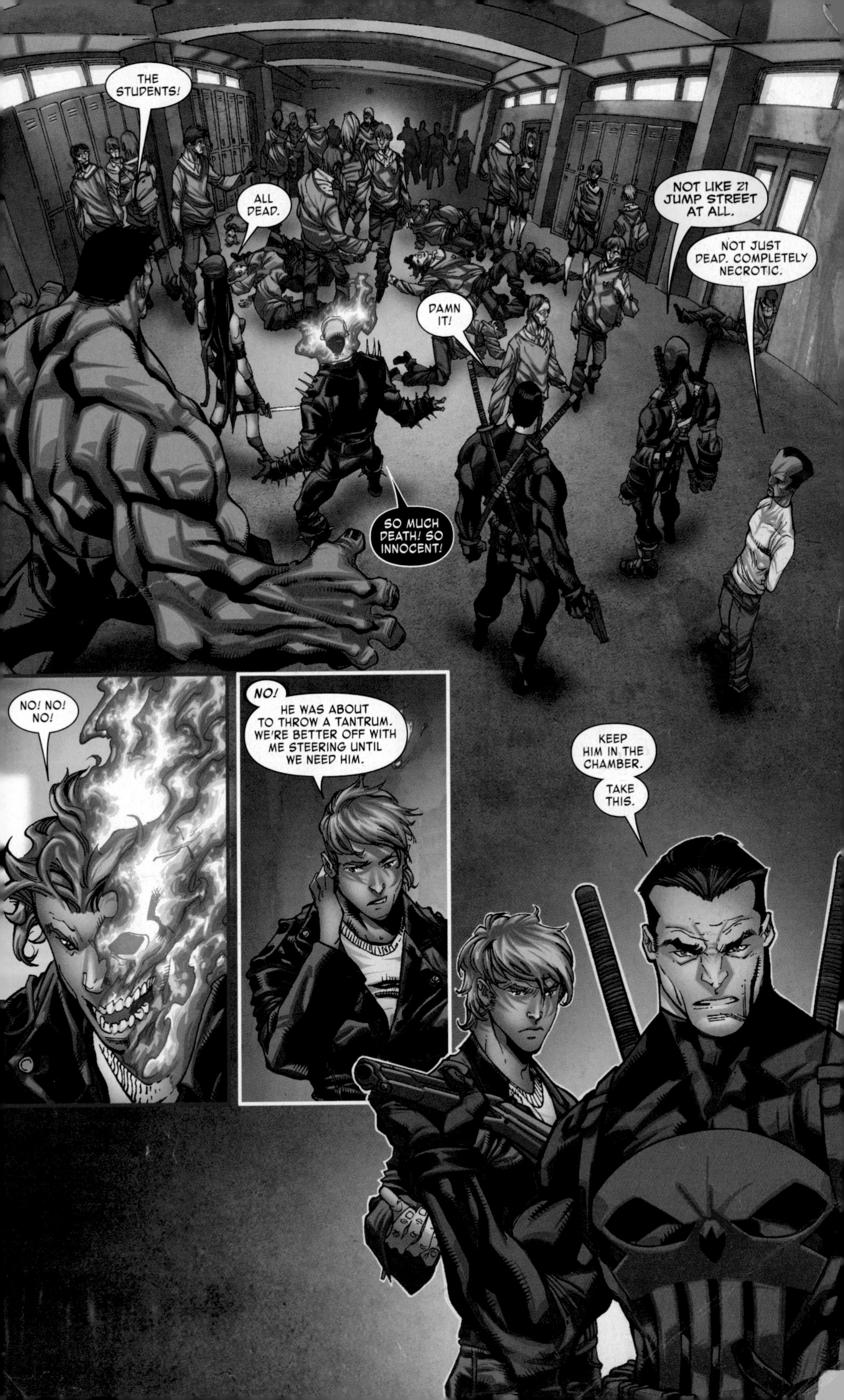
THE STUDENTS!
ALL DEAD.
DAMN IT!
NOT LIKE 21 JUMP STREET AT ALL.
NOT JUST DEAD. COMPLETELY NECROTIC.
SO MUCH DEATH! SO INNOCENT!
NO! NO! NO!
NO!
HE WAS ABOUT TO THROW A TANTRUM. WE'RE BETTER OFF WITH ME STEERING UNTIL WE NEED HIM.
KEEP HIM IN THE CHAMBER.
TAKE THIS.

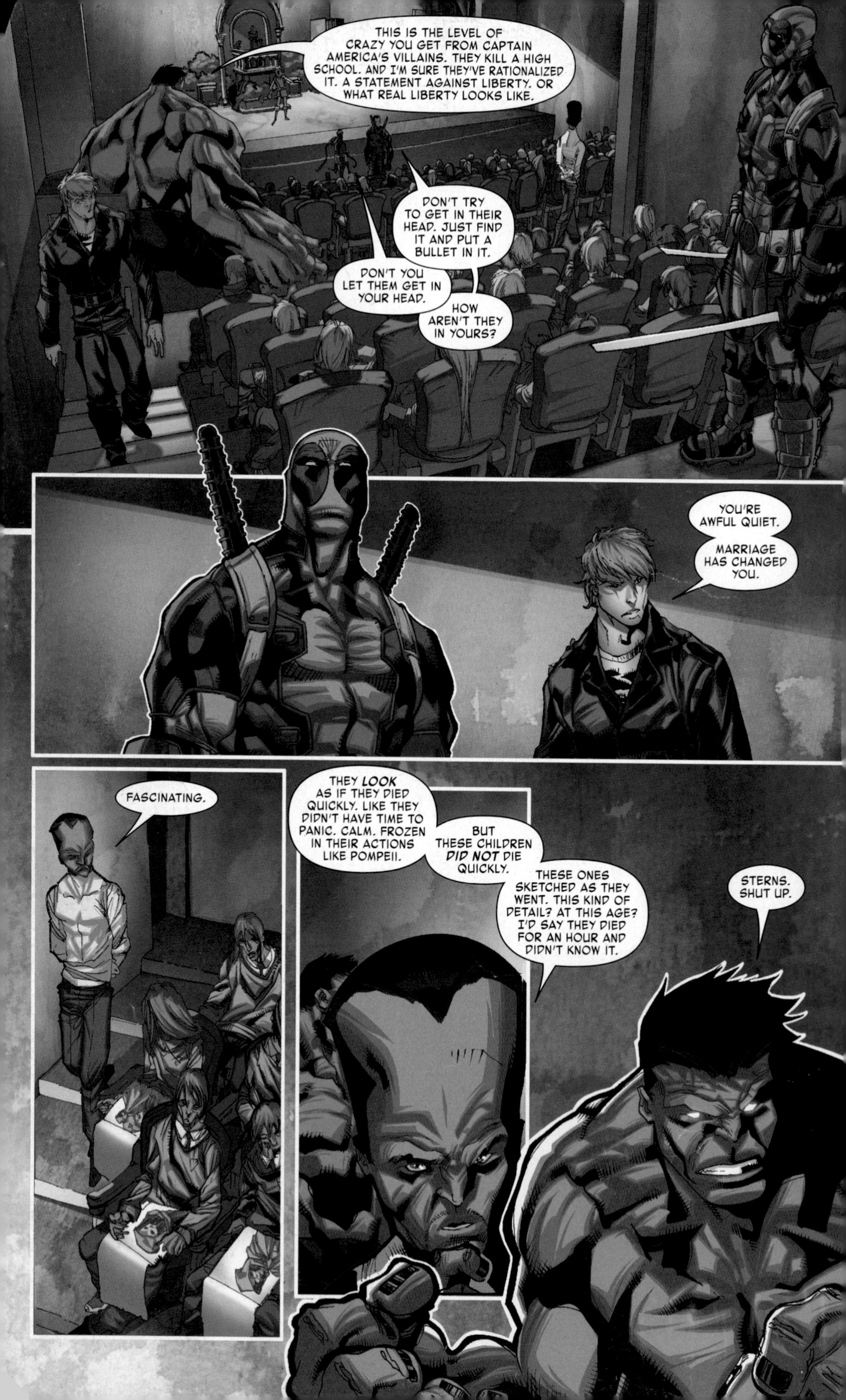
THIS IS THE LEVEL OF CRAZY YOU GET FROM CAPTAIN AMERICA'S VILLAINS. THEY KILL A HIGH SCHOOL. AND I'M SURE THEY'VE RATIONALIZED IT. A STATEMENT AGAINST LIBERTY. OR WHAT REAL LIBERTY LOOKS LIKE.
DON'T TRY TO GET IN THEIR HEAD. JUST FIND IT AND PUT A BULLET IN IT.
DON'T YOU LET THEM GET IN YOUR HEAD.
HOW AREN'T THEY IN YOURS?
YOU'RE AWFUL QUIET.
MARRIAGE HAS CHANGED YOU.
FASCINATING.
THEY LOOK AS IF THEY DIED QUICKLY. LIKE THEY DIDN'T HAVE TIME TO PANIC. CALM. FROZEN IN THEIR ACTIONS LIKE POMPEII.
BUT THESE CHILDREN DID NOT DIE QUICKLY.
THESE ONES SKETCHED AS THEY WENT. THIS KIND OF DETAIL? AT THIS AGE? I'D SAY THEY DIED FOR AN HOUR AND DIDN'T KNOW IT.
STERNS. SHUT UP.

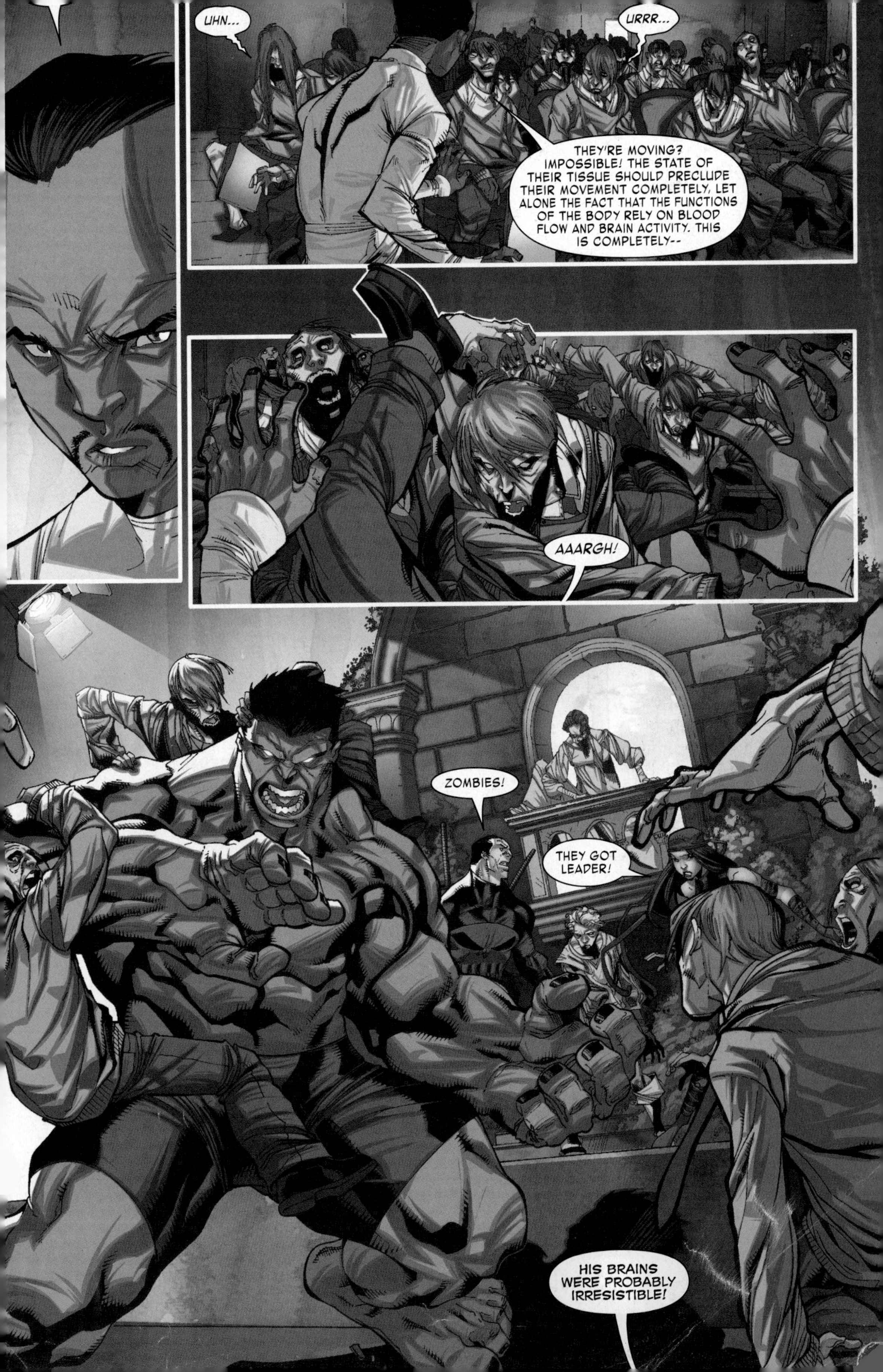
UHN...
URRR...
THEY'RE MOVING? IMPOSSIBLE! THE STATE OF THEIR TISSUE SHOULD PRECLUDE THEIR MOVEMENT COMPLETELY, LET ALONE THE FACT THAT THE FUNCTIONS OF THE BODY RELY ON BLOOD FLOW AND BRAIN ACTIVITY. THIS IS COMPLETELY--
AAARGH!
ZOMBIES!
THEY GOT LEADER!
HIS BRAINS WERE PROBABLY IRRESISTIBLE!

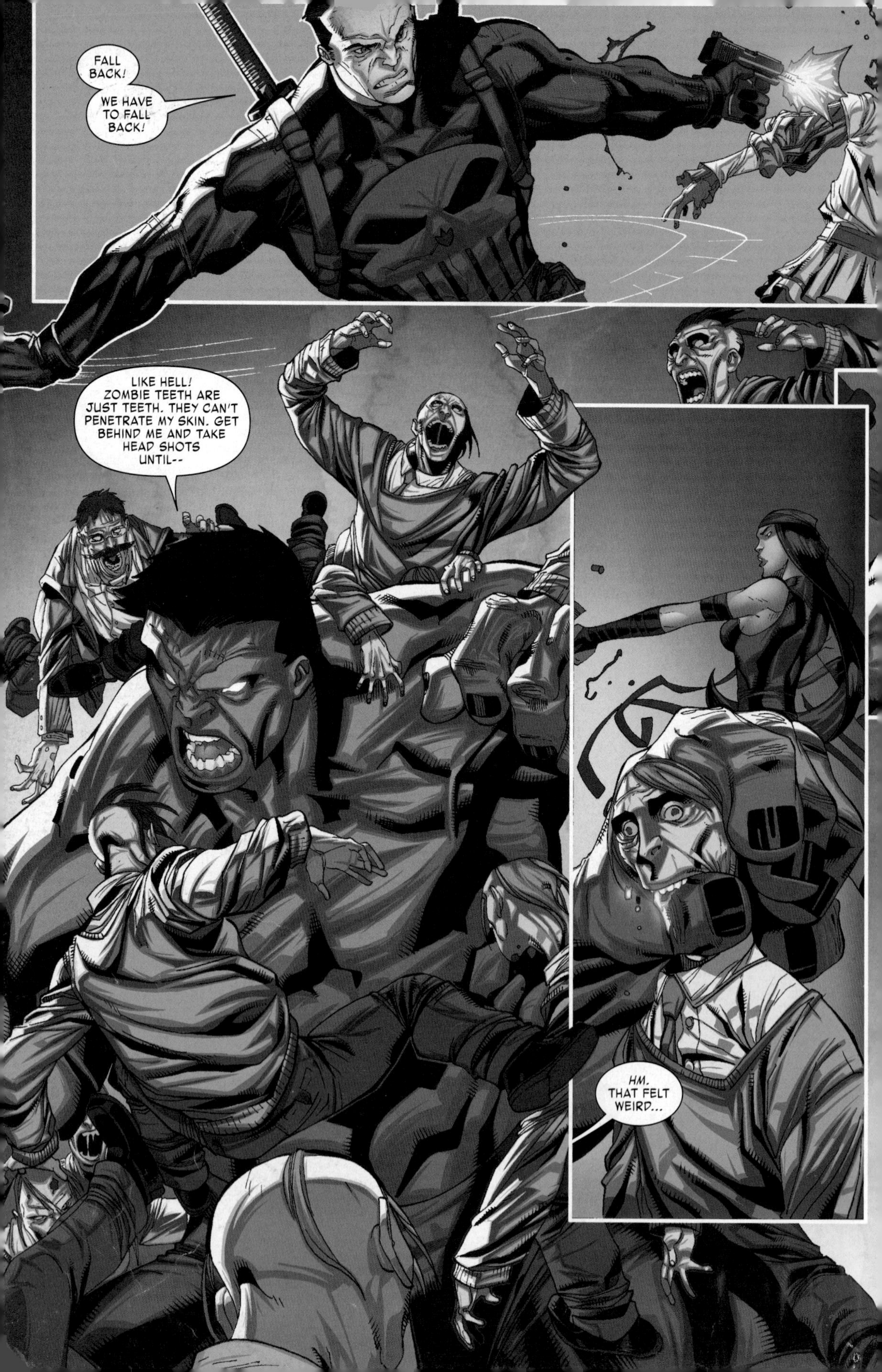
FALL BACK!
WE HAVE TO FALL BACK!
LIKE HELL! ZOMBIE TEETH ARE JUST TEETH. THEY CAN'T PENETRATE MY SKIN. GET BEHIND ME AND TAKE HEAD SHOTS UNTIL--
HM. THAT FELT WEIRD...

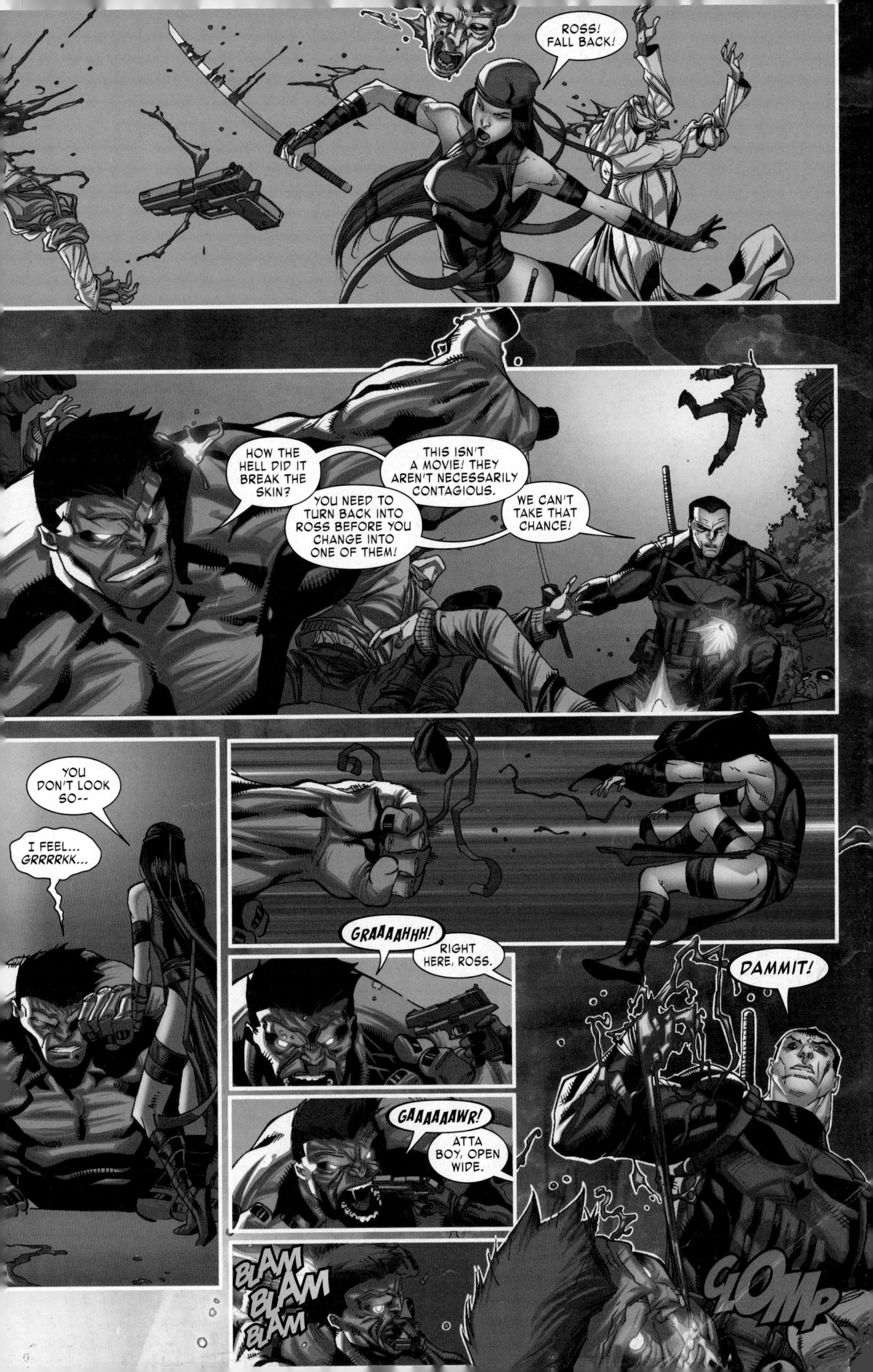

ROSS! FALL BACK!
HOW THE HELL DID IT BREAK THE SKIN?
THIS ISN'T A MOVIE! THEY AREN'T NECESSARILY CONTAGIOUS.
YOU NEED TO TURN BACK INTO ROSS BEFORE YOU CHANGE INTO ONE OF THEM!
WE CAN'T TAKE THAT CHANCE!
YOU DON'T LOOK SO--
I FEEL... GRRRRKK...
GRAAAAHHH!
RIGHT HERE, ROSS.
GAAAAAAWR!
ATTA BOY, OPEN WIDE.
BLAM BLAM BLAM BLAM
DAMMIT!
GLOMP

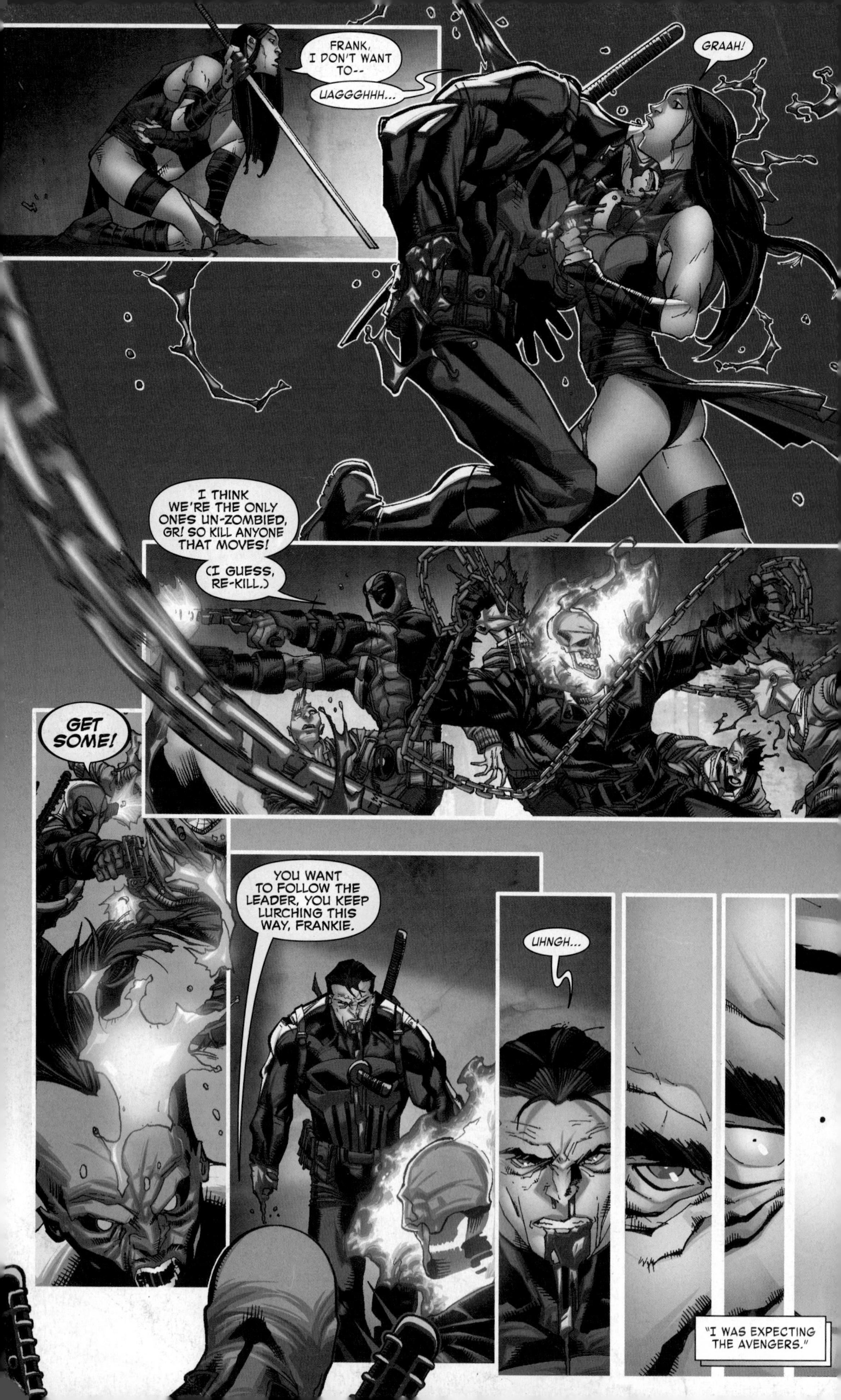

FRANK, I DON'T WANT TO--
UAGGGHHH...
GRAAH!
I THINK WE'RE THE ONLY ONES UN-ZOMBIED, GR! SO KILL ANYONE THAT MOVES!
(I GUESS, RE-KILL.)
GET SOME!
YOU WANT TO FOLLOW THE LEADER, YOU KEEP LURCHING THIS WAY, FRANKIE.
UHNGH...
"I WAS EXPECTING THE AVENGERS."

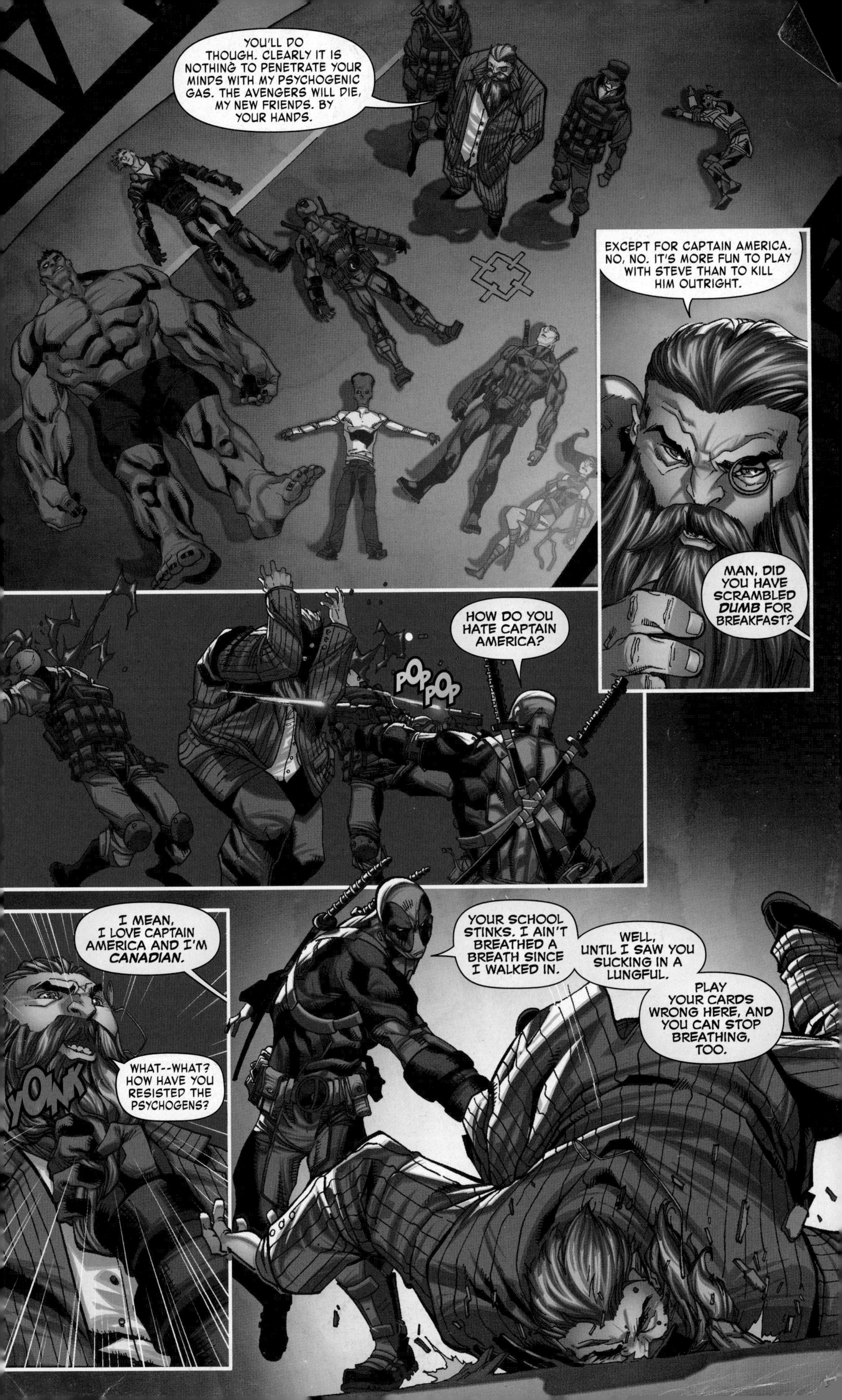
YOU'LL DO THOUGH. CLEARLY IT IS NOTHING TO PENETRATE YOUR MINDS WITH MY PSYCHOGENIC GAS. THE AVENGERS WILL DIE, MY NEW FRIENDS. BY YOUR HANDS.
EXCEPT FOR CAPTAIN AMERICA. NO, NO. IT'S MORE FUN TO PLAY WITH STEVE THAN TO KILL HIM OUTRIGHT.
MAN, DID YOU HAVE SCRAMBLED DUMB FOR BREAKFAST?
HOW DO YOU HATE CAPTAIN AMERICA?
POP POP
I MEAN, I LOVE CAPTAIN AMERICA AND I'M CANADIAN.
YOINK
WHAT--WHAT? HOW HAVE YOU RESISTED THE PSYCHOGENS?
YOUR SCHOOL STINKS. I AIN'T BREATHED A BREATH SINCE I WALKED IN.
WELL, UNTIL I SAW YOU SUCKING IN A LUNGFUL.
PLAY YOUR CARDS WRONG HERE, AND YOU CAN STOP BREATHING, TOO.

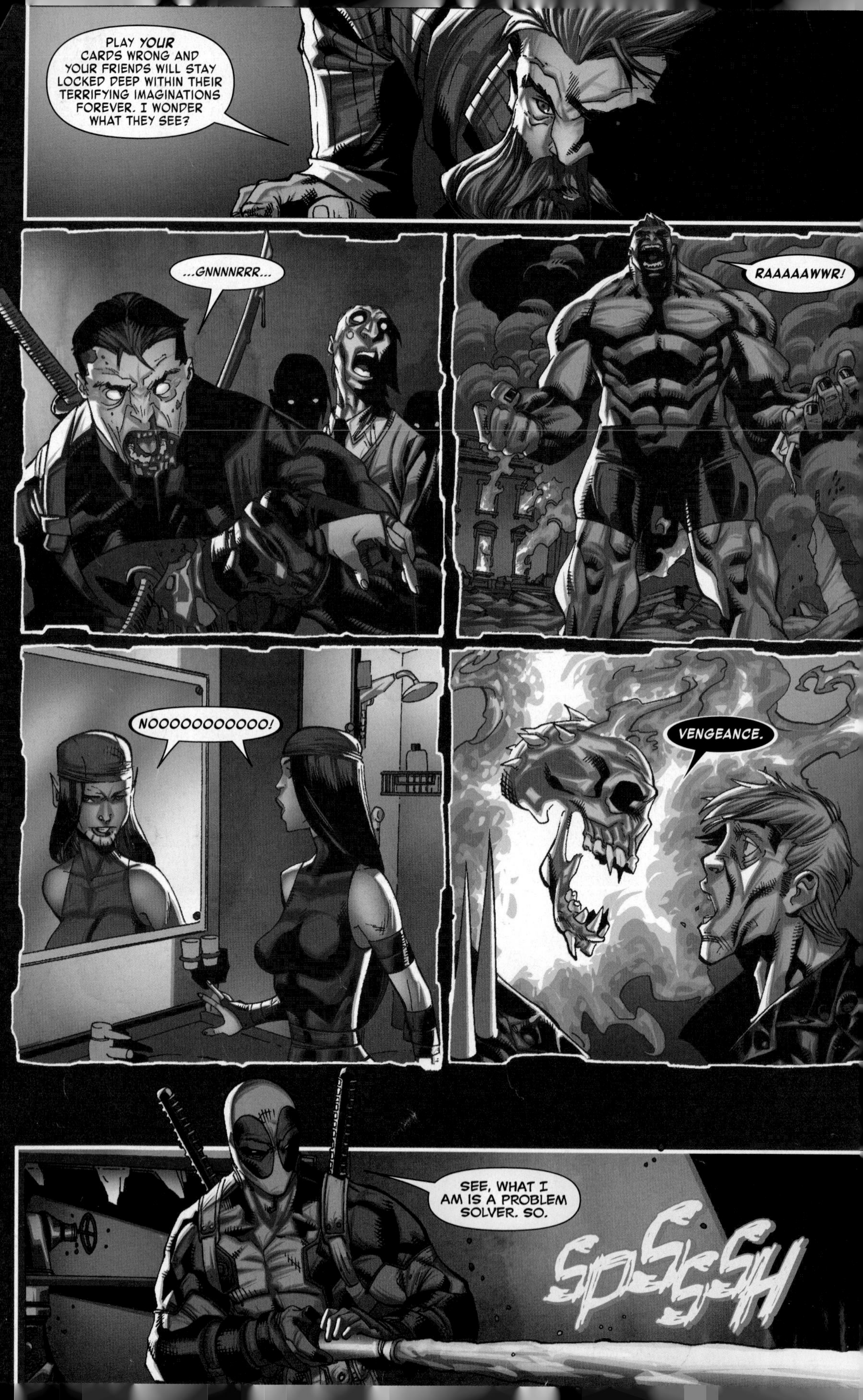

PLAY YOUR CARDS WRONG AND YOUR FRIENDS WILL STAY LOCKED DEEP WITHIN THEIR TERRIFYING IMAGINATIONS FOREVER. I WONDER WHAT THEY SEE?
...GNNNNRRR...
RAAAAAWWR!
NOOOOOOOOOOO!
VENGEANCE.
SEE, WHAT I AM IS A PROBLEM SOLVER. SO.
SPSSSH

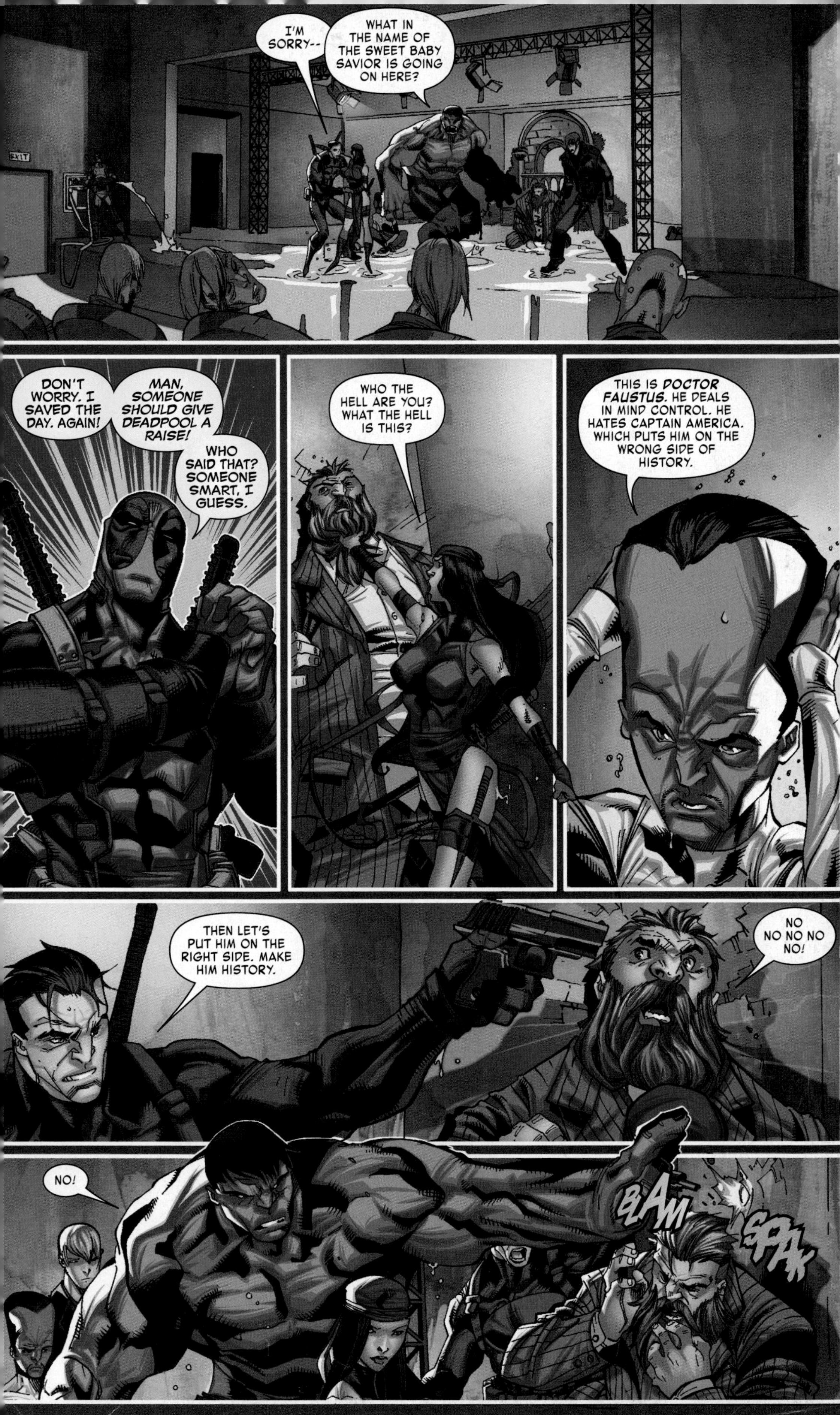

I'M SORRY--
WHAT IN THE NAME OF THE SWEET BABY SAVIOR IS GOING ON HERE?
DON'T WORRY. I SAVED THE DAY. AGAIN!
MAN, SOMEONE SHOULD GIVE DEADPOOL A RAISE!
WHO SAID THAT? SOMEONE SMART, I GUESS.
WHO THE HELL ARE YOU? WHAT THE HELL IS THIS?
THIS IS DOCTOR FAUSTUS. HE DEALS IN MIND CONTROL. HE HATES CAPTAIN AMERICA. WHICH PUTS HIM ON THE WRONG SIDE OF HISTORY.
THEN LET'S PUT HIM ON THE RIGHT SIDE. MAKE HIM HISTORY.
NO NO NO NO NO!
NO!
BLAM
SPAK

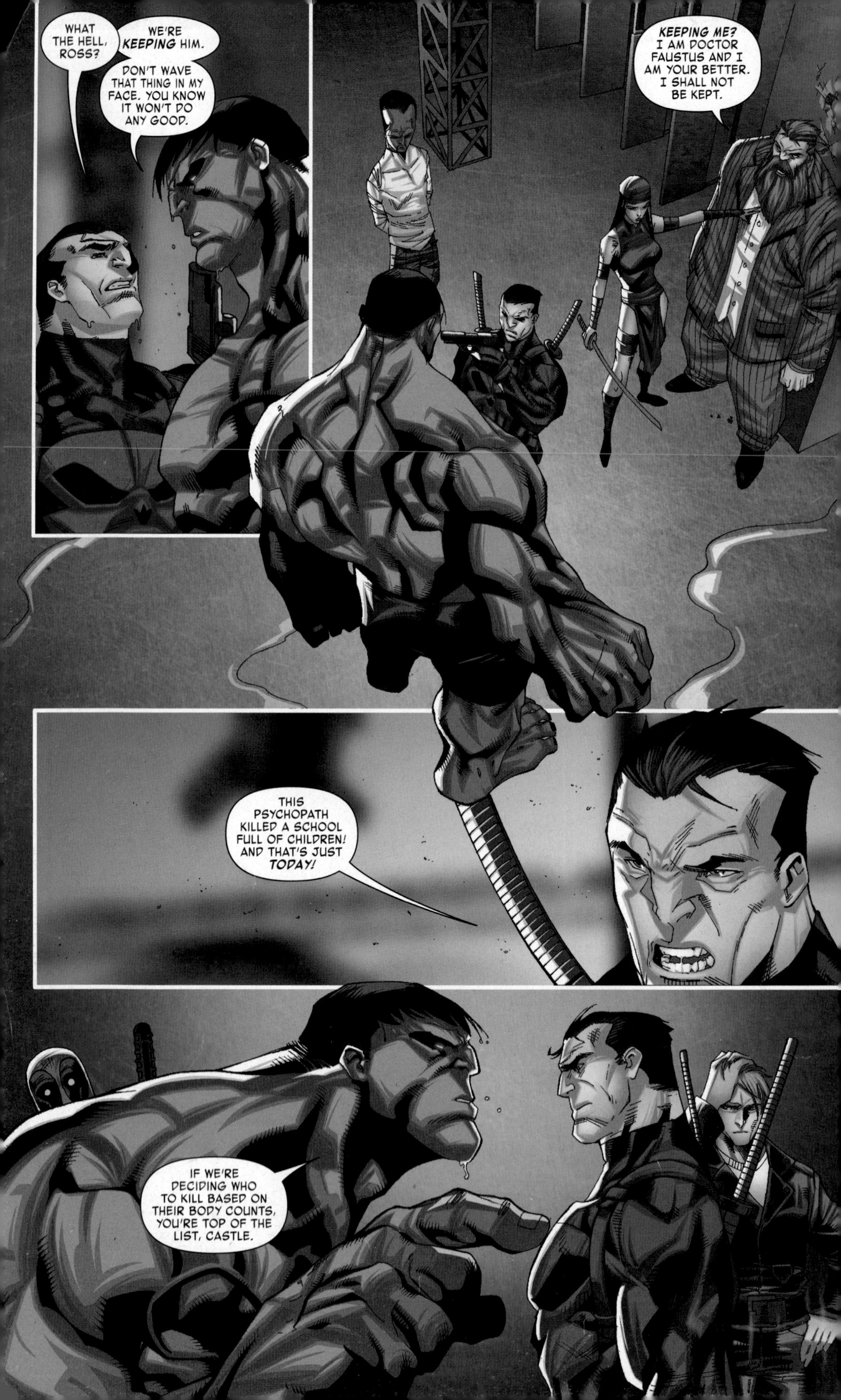
WHAT THE HELL, ROSS?
WE'RE KEEPING HIM.
DON'T WAVE THAT THING IN MY FACE. YOU KNOW IT WON'T DO ANY GOOD.
KEEPING ME? I AM DOCTOR FAUSTUS AND I AM YOUR BETTER. I SHALL NOT BE KEPT.
THIS PSYCHOPATH KILLED A SCHOOL FULL OF CHILDREN! AND THAT'S JUST TODAY!
IF WE'RE DECIDING WHO TO KILL BASED ON THEIR BODY COUNTS, YOU'RE TOP OF THE LIST, CASTLE.

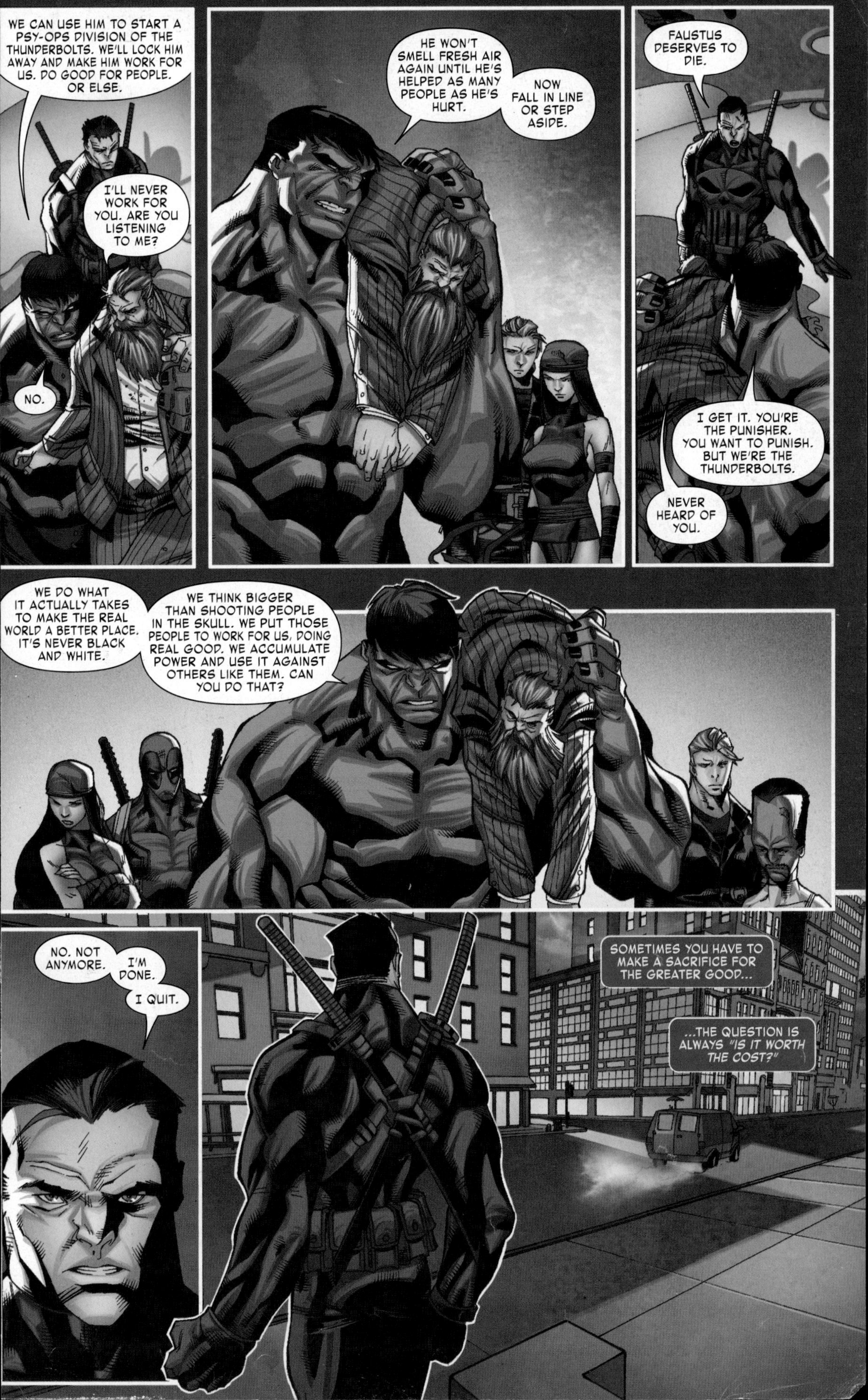

WE CAN USE HIM TO START A PSY-OPS DIVISION OF THE THUNDERBOLTS. WE'LL LOCK HIM AWAY AND MAKE HIM WORK FOR US. DO GOOD FOR PEOPLE. OR ELSE.
I'LL NEVER WORK FOR YOU. ARE YOU LISTENING TO ME?
NO.
HE WON'T SMELL FRESH AIR AGAIN UNTIL HE'S HELPED AS MANY PEOPLE AS HE'S HURT.
NOW FALL IN LINE OR STEP ASIDE.
FAUSTUS DESERVES TO DIE.
I GET IT. YOU'RE THE PUNISHER. YOU WANT TO PUNISH. BUT WE'RE THE THUNDERBOLTS.
NEVER HEARD OF YOU.
WE DO WHAT IT ACTUALLY TAKES TO MAKE THE REAL WORLD A BETTER PLACE. IT'S NEVER BLACK AND WHITE.
WE THINK BIGGER THAN SHOOTING PEOPLE IN THE SKULL. WE PUT THOSE PEOPLE TO WORK FOR US, DOING REAL GOOD. WE ACCUMULATE POWER AND USE IT AGAINST OTHERS LIKE THEM. CAN YOU DO THAT?
NO. NOT ANYMORE.
I'M DONE.
I QUIT.
SOMETIMES YOU HAVE TO MAKE A SACRIFICE FOR THE GREATER GOOD...
...THE QUESTION IS ALWAYS *"IS IT WORTH THE COST?"*

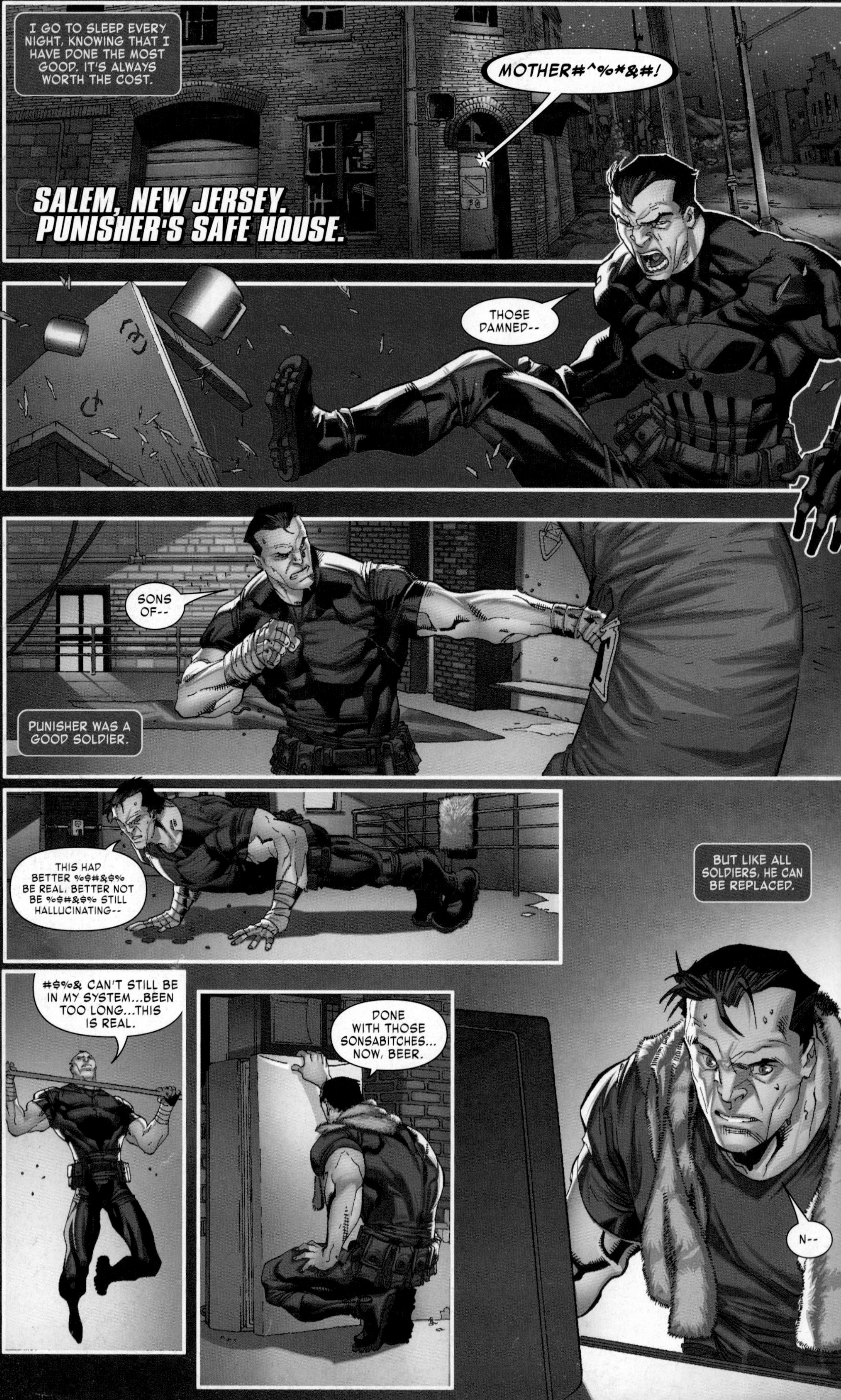
I GO TO SLEEP EVERY NIGHT, KNOWING THAT I HAVE DONE THE MOST GOOD. IT'S ALWAYS WORTH THE COST.
MOTHER#^%*&#!
SALEM, NEW JERSEY. PUNISHER'S SAFE HOUSE.
THOSE DAMNED--
SONS OF--
PUNISHER WAS A GOOD SOLDIER.
THIS HAD BETTER %$#&$% BE REAL, BETTER NOT BE %$#&$% STILL HALLUCINATING--
BUT LIKE ALL SOLDIERS, HE CAN BE REPLACED.
#$%& CAN'T STILL BE IN MY SYSTEM...BEEN TOO LONG...THIS IS REAL.
DONE WITH THOSE SONSABITCHES... NOW, BEER.
N--

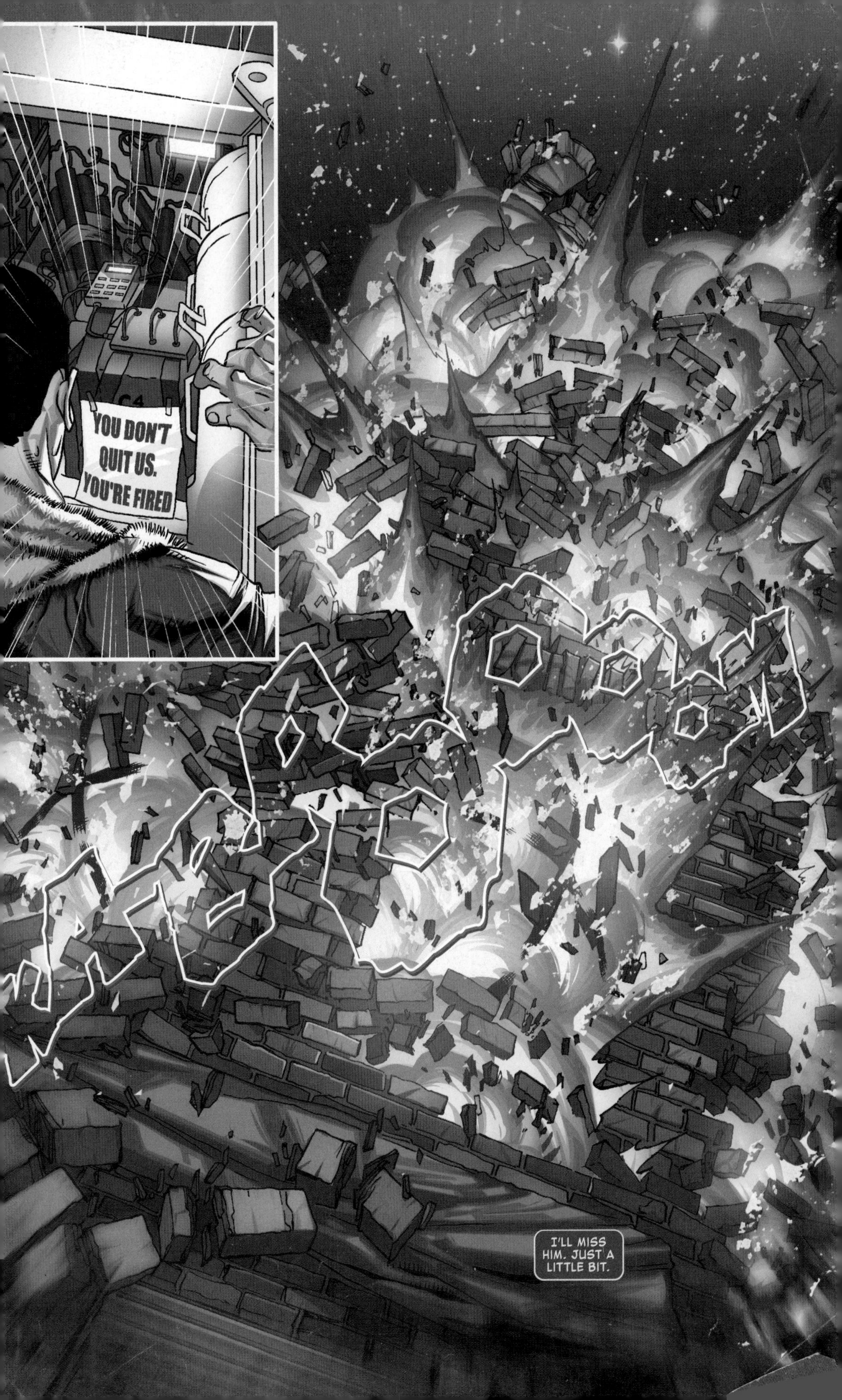
YOU DON'T QUIT US. YOU'RE FIRED
I'LL MISS HIM. JUST A LITTLE BIT.

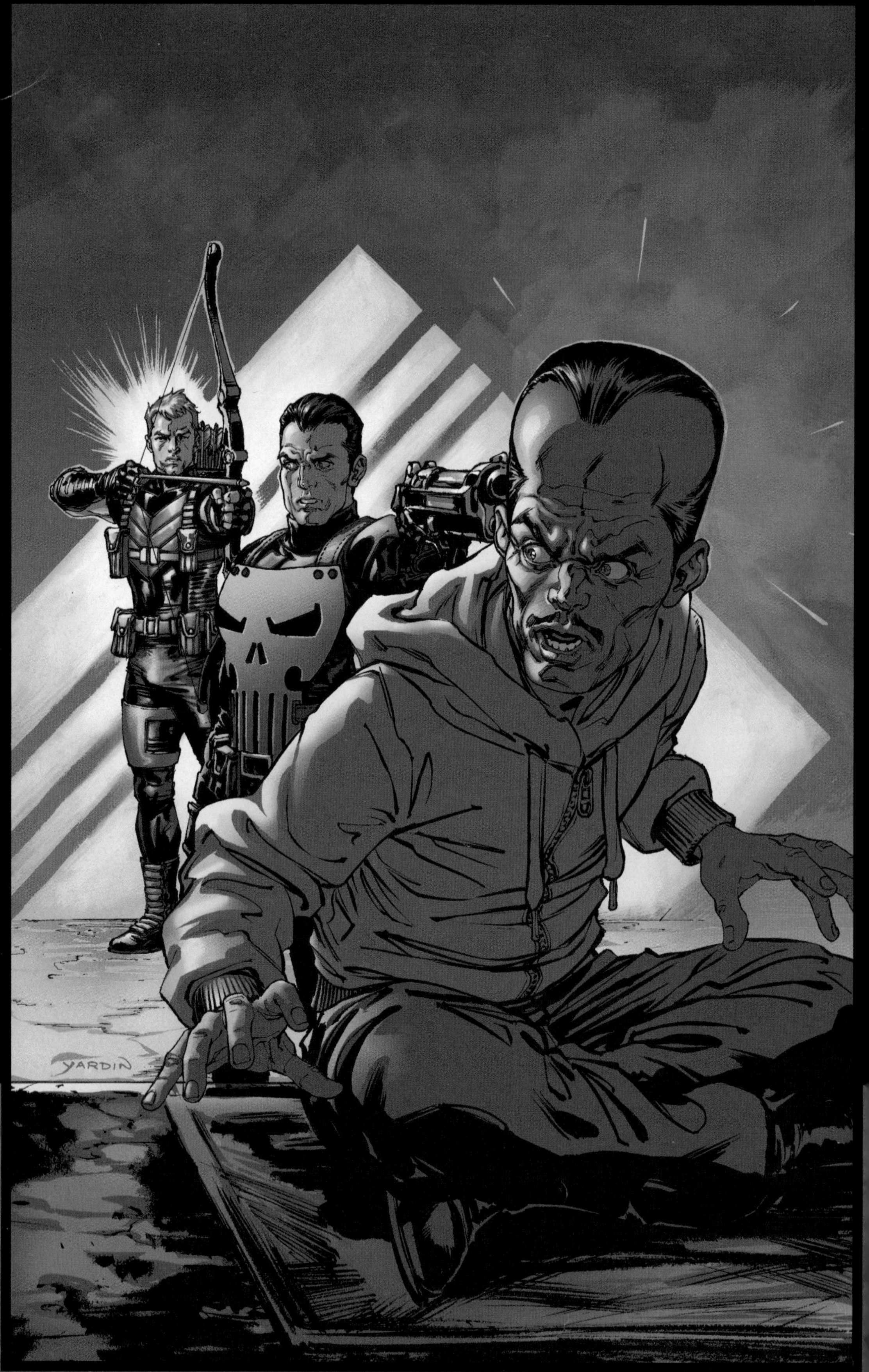
YARDIN

TWENTY-EIGHT

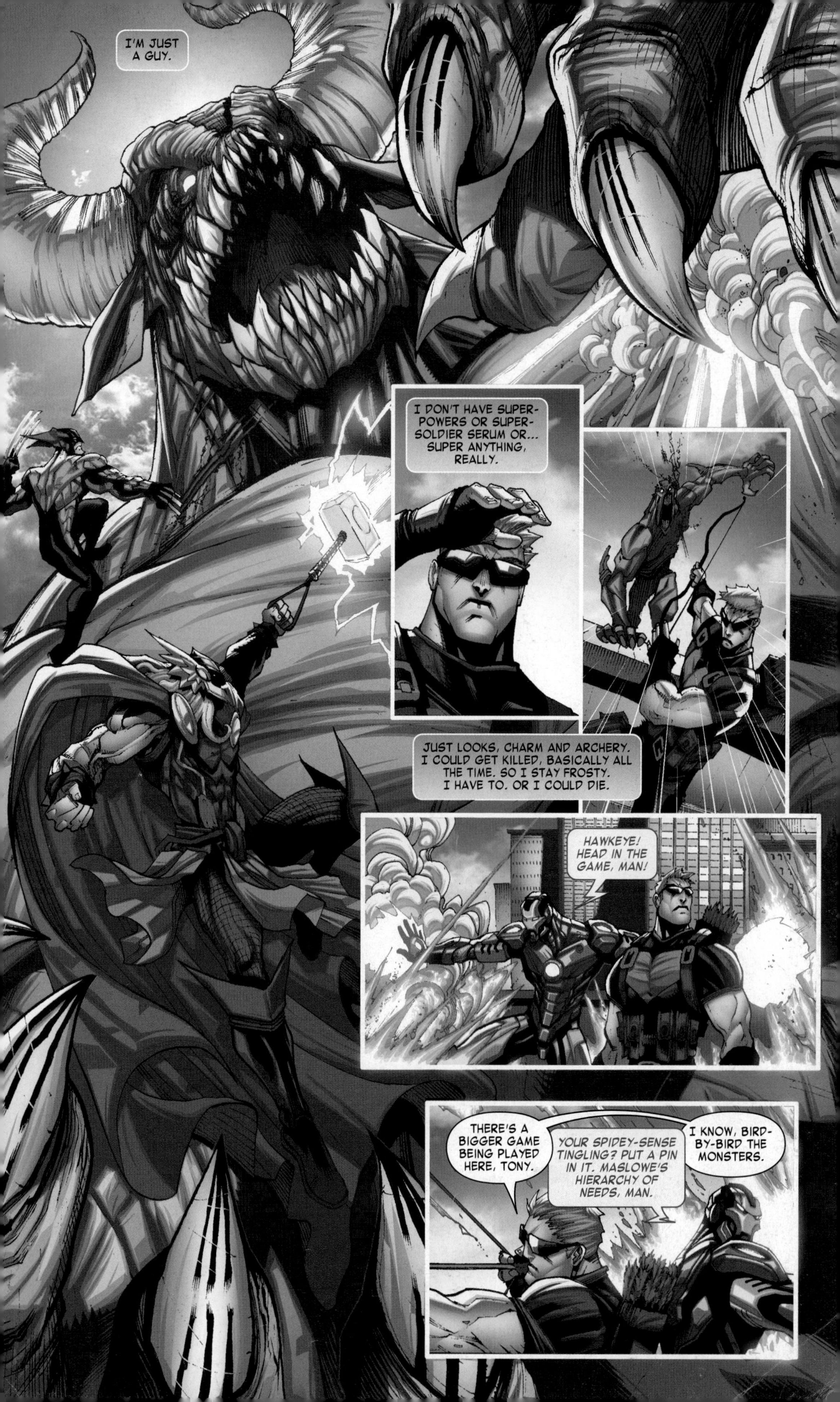
I'M JUST A GUY.
I DON'T HAVE SUPER-POWERS OR SUPER-SOLDIER SERUM OR... SUPER ANYTHING, REALLY.
JUST LOOKS, CHARM AND ARCHERY. I COULD GET KILLED, BASICALLY ALL THE TIME. SO I STAY FROSTY. I HAVE TO. OR I COULD DIE.
HAWKEYE! HEAD IN THE GAME, MAN!
THERE'S A BIGGER GAME BEING PLAYED HERE, TONY.
YOUR SPIDEY-SENSE TINGLING? PUT A PIN IN IT. MASLOWE'S HIERARCHY OF NEEDS, MAN.
I KNOW, BIRD-BY-BIRD THE MONSTERS.

CAUGHT A FLASH OF **SOMETHING** UP THERE.

CAN'T SHAKE THE FEELING THAT THE MOLEMAN MONSTERFIGHT WAS JUST A DISTRACTION.

UP THERE...

BUFFALO BORE AMMO. AND BLOOD EVERYWHERE. THAT'S GOT PUNISHER WRITTEN ALL OVER IT.

KNOW WHAT ELSE HAS PUNISHER WRITTEN ALL OVER IT?

THIS WALL. IN BLOOD. SEE? YOU WERE LOOKING CLOSE AT STUFF WITH YOUR HAWKEYE EYES, SO MAYBE YOU COULDN'T SEE WHERE SOMEONE WROTE "PUNISHER."

THERE ARE SOME SCORCH-MARKS AND ASH BUT MY AUTOSCAN ISN'T DETECTING ANY ACCELERANT IN THE CHEMICAL COMPOSITION.

PHOSPHATE 47.5% CALCIUM 25.3% SULPHATE 30.00% POTASSIUM 3.69% SODIUM 1.12% CHLORIDE 1.00% SILICA 0.9% ALUMINUM OXIDE 0.72%

UNKNOWN/UNIDENT...
HUMAN REMAINS...
UNKNOWN/UNIDE...
=FZZZZT=

THEY'RE DETECTING HUMAN REMAINS AND--WAIT, "ELEMENTS UNKNOWN?" CROSS CHECK WITH PRETENDIUM INTEL.

"PRETENDIUM" IS HOW I FILE THOR, DR. STRANGE, HERCULES AND THAT SORT OF STUFF. TAKES A MINUTE. HARD TO SCAN.

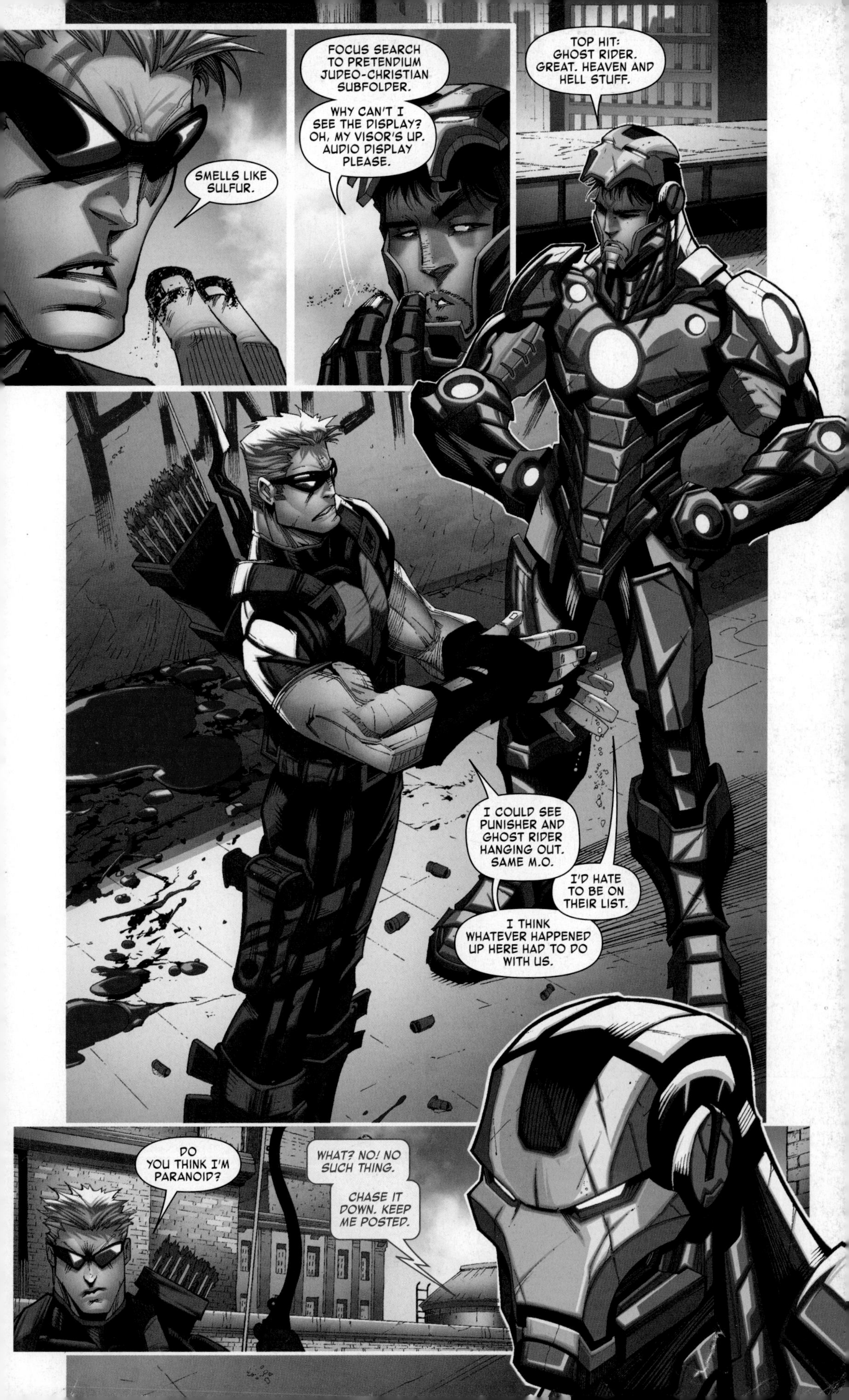
SMELLS LIKE SULFUR.
FOCUS SEARCH TO PRETENDIUM JUDEO-CHRISTIAN SUBFOLDER.
WHY CAN'T I SEE THE DISPLAY? OH, MY VISOR'S UP. AUDIO DISPLAY PLEASE.
TOP HIT: GHOST RIDER. GREAT. HEAVEN AND HELL STUFF.
I COULD SEE PUNISHER AND GHOST RIDER HANGING OUT. SAME M.O.
I'D HATE TO BE ON THEIR LIST.
I THINK WHATEVER HAPPENED UP HERE HAD TO DO WITH US.
DO YOU THINK I'M PARANOID?
WHAT? NO! NO SUCH THING.
CHASE IT DOWN. KEEP ME POSTED.

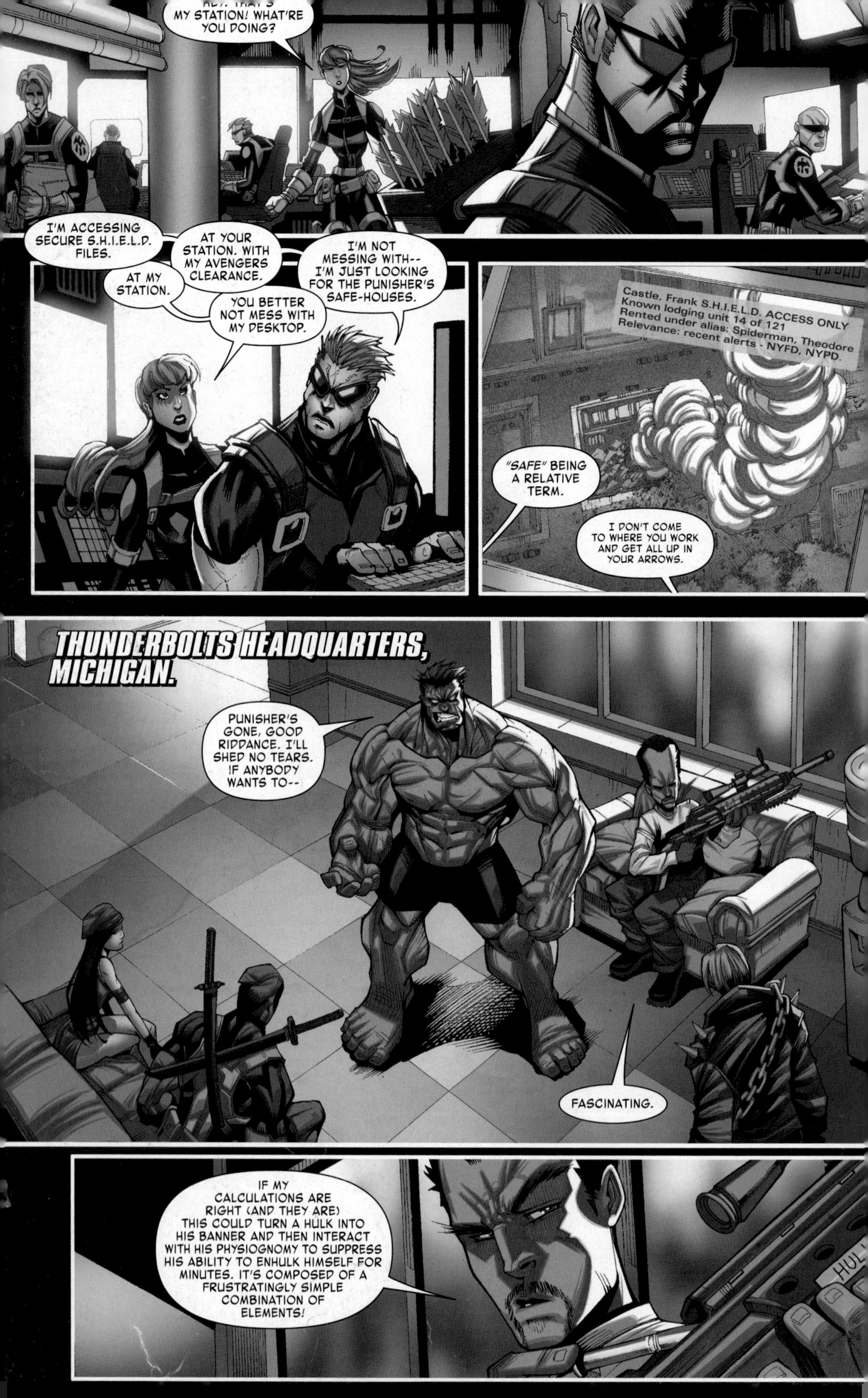

MY STATION! WHAT'RE YOU DOING?
I'M ACCESSING SECURE S.H.I.E.L.D. FILES.
AT MY STATION.
AT YOUR STATION. WITH MY AVENGERS CLEARANCE.
YOU BETTER NOT MESS WITH MY DESKTOP.
I'M NOT MESSING WITH-- I'M JUST LOOKING FOR THE PUNISHER'S SAFE-HOUSES.
Castle, Frank S.H.I.E.L.D. ACCESS ONLY
Known lodging unit 14 of 121
Rented under alias: Spiderman, Theodore
Relevance: recent alerts - NYFD, NYPD.
"SAFE" BEING A RELATIVE TERM.
I DON'T COME TO WHERE YOU WORK AND GET ALL UP IN YOUR ARROWS.
THUNDERBOLTS HEADQUARTERS, MICHIGAN.
PUNISHER'S GONE, GOOD RIDDANCE. I'LL SHED NO TEARS. IF ANYBODY WANTS TO--
FASCINATING.
IF MY CALCULATIONS ARE RIGHT (AND THEY ARE) THIS COULD TURN A HULK INTO HIS BANNER AND THEN INTERACT WITH HIS PHYSIOGNOMY TO SUPPRESS HIS ABILITY TO ENHULK HIMSELF FOR MINUTES. IT'S COMPOSED OF A FRUSTRATINGLY SIMPLE COMBINATION OF ELEMENTS!

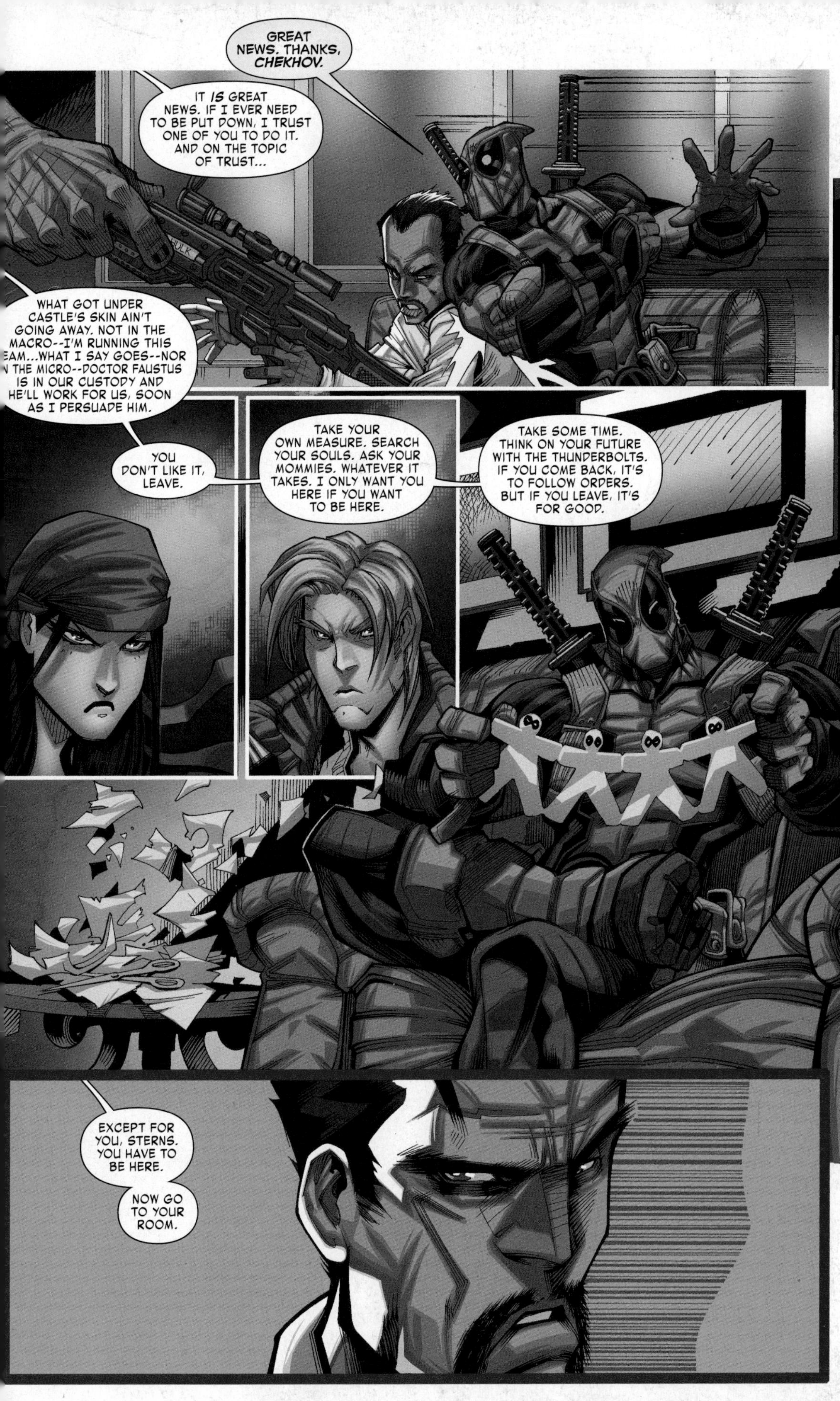

GREAT NEWS. THANKS, CHEKHOV.
IT IS GREAT NEWS. IF I EVER NEED TO BE PUT DOWN, I TRUST ONE OF YOU TO DO IT. AND ON THE TOPIC OF TRUST...
HULK
WHAT GOT UNDER CASTLE'S SKIN AIN'T GOING AWAY. NOT IN THE MACRO--I'M RUNNING THIS EAM...WHAT I SAY GOES--NOR N THE MICRO--DOCTOR FAUSTUS IS IN OUR CUSTODY AND HE'LL WORK FOR US, SOON AS I PERSUADE HIM.
YOU DON'T LIKE IT, LEAVE.
TAKE YOUR OWN MEASURE. SEARCH YOUR SOULS. ASK YOUR MOMMIES. WHATEVER IT TAKES. I ONLY WANT YOU HERE IF YOU WANT TO BE HERE.
TAKE SOME TIME. THINK ON YOUR FUTURE WITH THE THUNDERBOLTS. IF YOU COME BACK, IT'S TO FOLLOW ORDERS. BUT IF YOU LEAVE, IT'S FOR GOOD.
EXCEPT FOR YOU, STERNS. YOU HAVE TO BE HERE.
NOW GO TO YOUR ROOM.

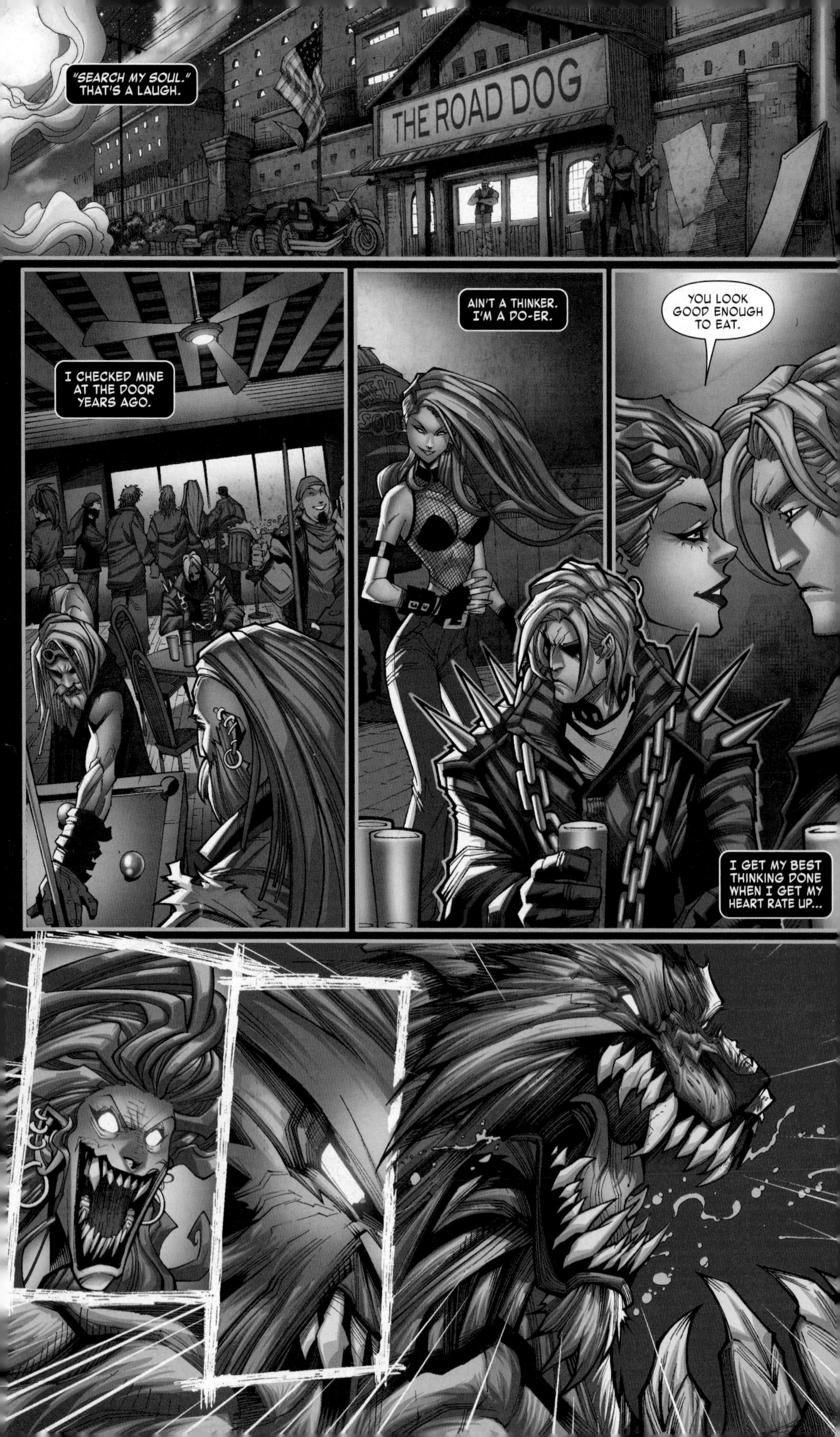
"SEARCH MY SOUL." THAT'S A LAUGH.
THE ROAD DOG
I CHECKED MINE AT THE DOOR YEARS AGO.
AIN'T A THINKER. I'M A DO-ER.
YOU LOOK GOOD ENOUGH TO EAT.
I GET MY BEST THINKING DONE WHEN I GET MY HEART RATE UP...

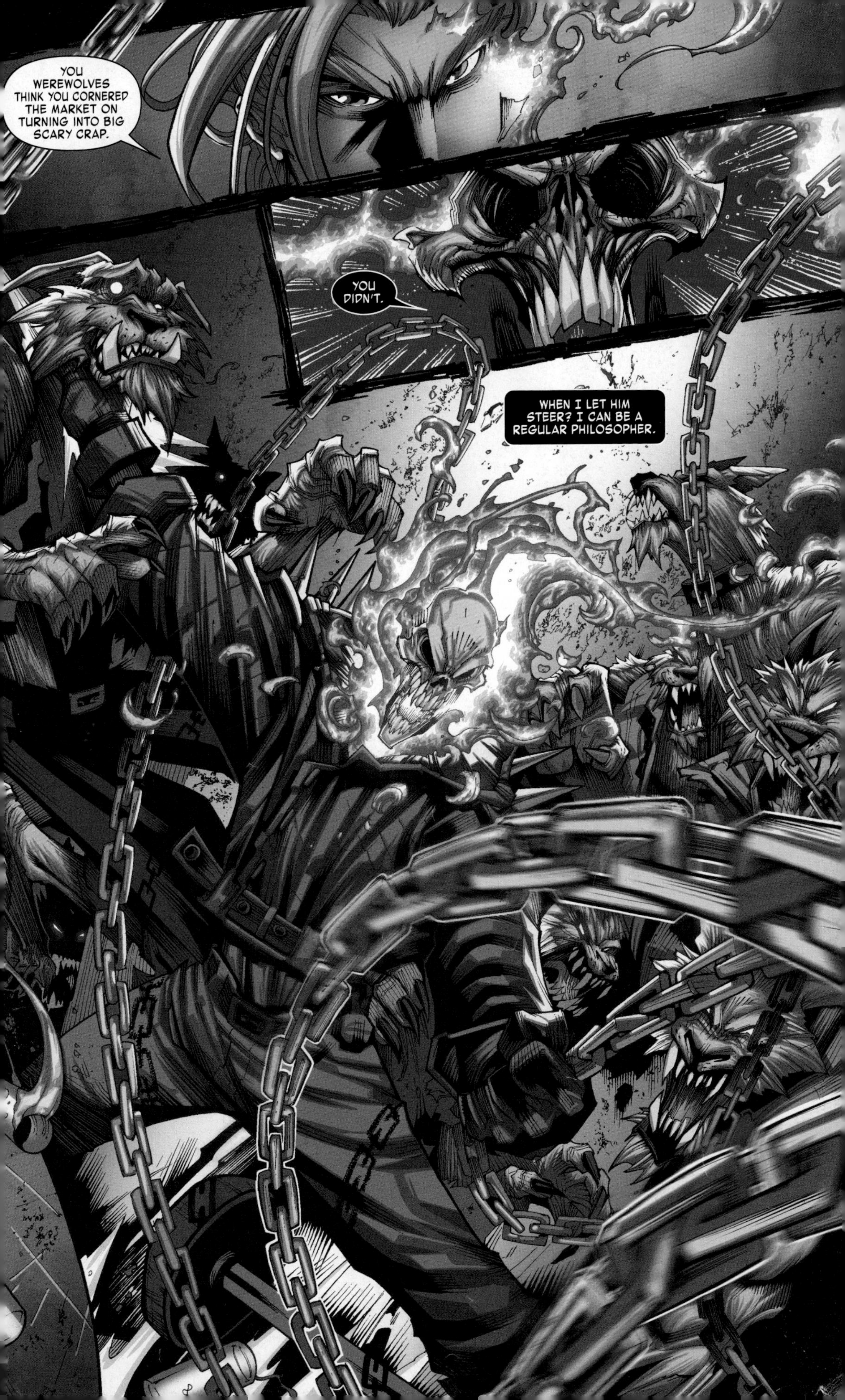
YOU WEREWOLVES THINK YOU CORNERED THE MARKET ON TURNING INTO BIG SCARY CRAP.
YOU DIDN'T.
WHEN I LET HIM STEER? I CAN BE A REGULAR PHILOSOPHER.

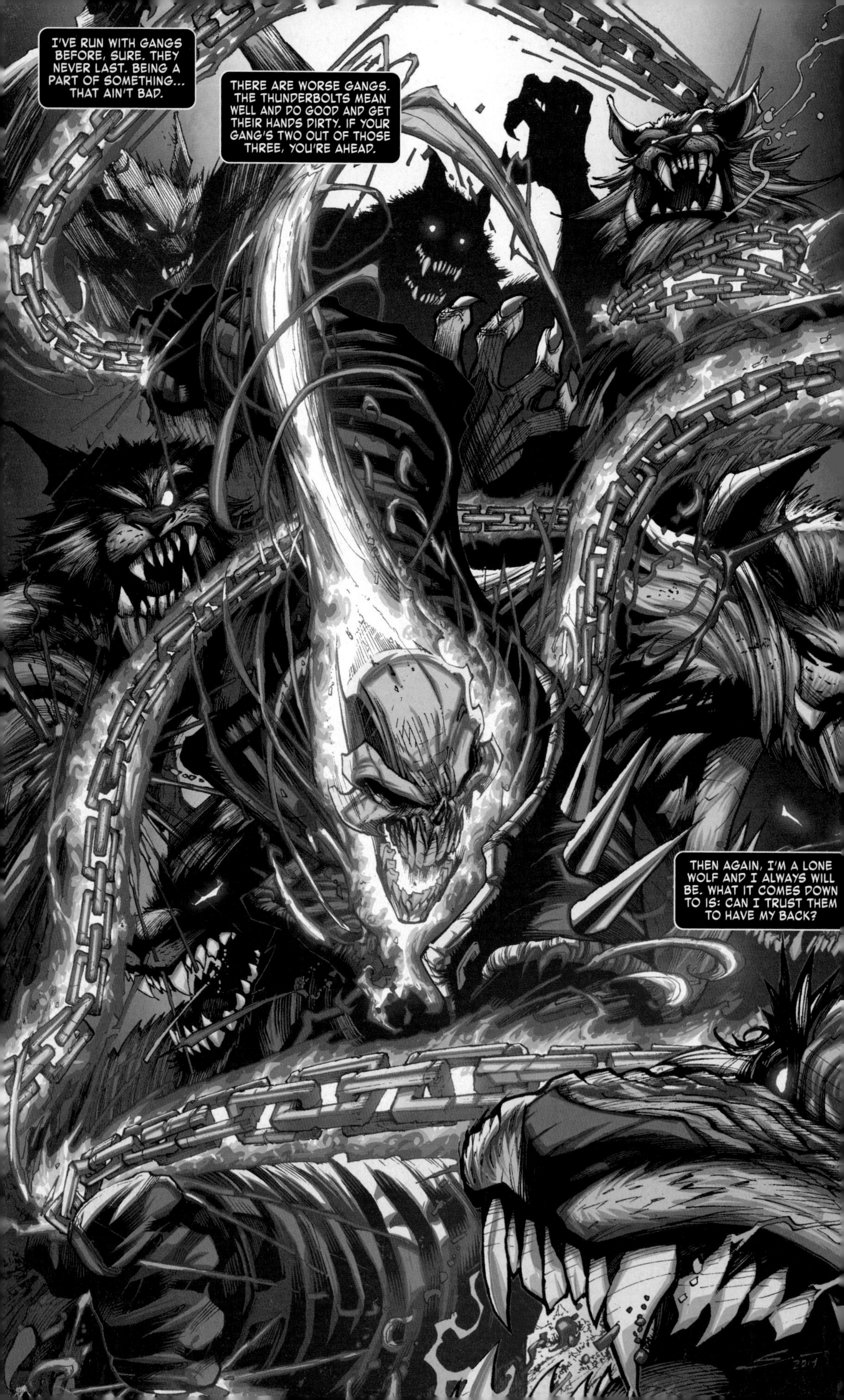
I'VE RUN WITH GANGS BEFORE, SURE. THEY NEVER LAST. BEING A PART OF SOMETHING... THAT AIN'T BAD.
THERE ARE WORSE GANGS. THE THUNDERBOLTS MEAN WELL AND DO GOOD AND GET THEIR HANDS DIRTY. IF YOUR GANG'S TWO OUT OF THOSE THREE, YOU'RE AHEAD.
THEN AGAIN, I'M A LONE WOLF AND I ALWAYS WILL BE. WHAT IT COMES DOWN TO IS: CAN I TRUST THEM TO HAVE MY BACK?

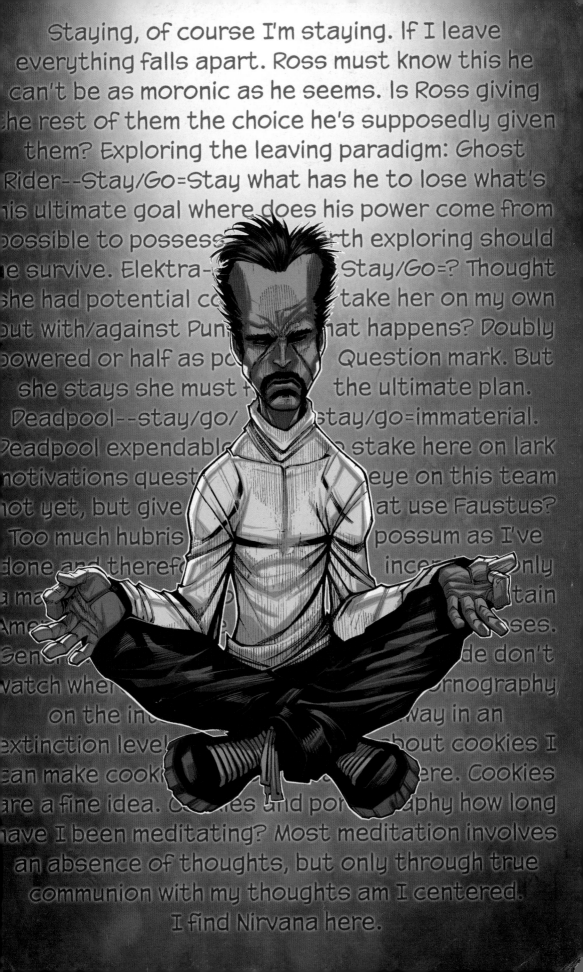

Staying, of course I'm staying. If I leave everything falls apart. Ross must know this he can't be as moronic as he seems. Is Ross giving the rest of them the choice he's supposedly given them? Exploring the leaving paradigm: Ghost Rider--Stay/Go=Stay what has he to lose what's his ultimate goal where does his power come from possible to possess ___ ___rth exploring should ___ survive. Elektra-___ ___ Stay/Go=? Thought she had potential co___ ___ take her on my own ___ut with/against Pun___ ___at happens? Doubly powered or half as p___ ___ Question mark. But she stays she must ___ ___ the ultimate plan. Deadpool--stay/go/___ ___stay/go=immaterial. Deadpool expendabl___ ___o stake here on lark motivations quest___ ___eye on this team ___ot yet, but give ___ ___at use Faustus? Too much hubris ___ ___possum as I've done ___ theref___ ___ ince___ ___nly ___ m___ ___tain Ame___ ___ses. Gen___ ___de don't ___atch whe___ ___rnography on the in___ ___ay in an extinction level ___ ___bout cookies I ___an make cook___ ___ere. Cookies ___re a fine idea. C___ ___ies and por___ ___phy how long ___ave I been meditating? Most meditation involves an absence of thoughts, but only through true communion with my thoughts am I centered. I find Nirvana here.

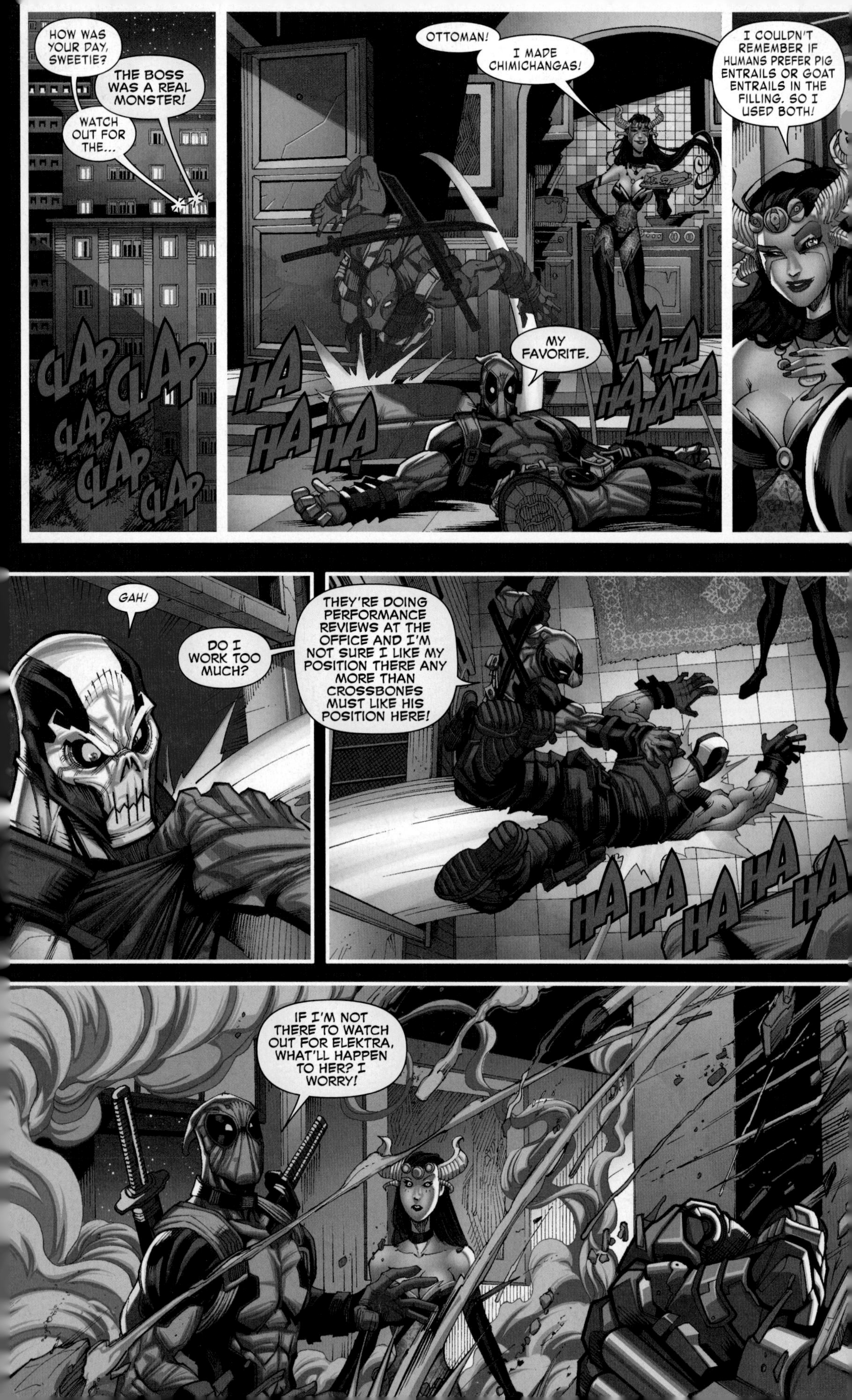
HOW WAS YOUR DAY, SWEETIE?
THE BOSS WAS A REAL MONSTER!
WATCH OUT FOR THE...
CLAP CLAP CLAP CLAP CLAP CLAP
OTTOMAN!
I MADE CHIMICHANGAS!
MY FAVORITE.
HA HA HA
HA HA HA HA HA
I COULDN'T REMEMBER IF HUMANS PREFER PIG ENTRAILS OR GOAT ENTRAILS IN THE FILLING. SO I USED BOTH!
GAH!
DO I WORK TOO MUCH?
THEY'RE DOING PERFORMANCE REVIEWS AT THE OFFICE AND I'M NOT SURE I LIKE MY POSITION THERE ANY MORE THAN CROSSBONES MUST LIKE HIS POSITION HERE!
HA HA HA HA HA HA
IF I'M NOT THERE TO WATCH OUT FOR ELEKTRA, WHAT'LL HAPPEN TO HER? I WORRY!

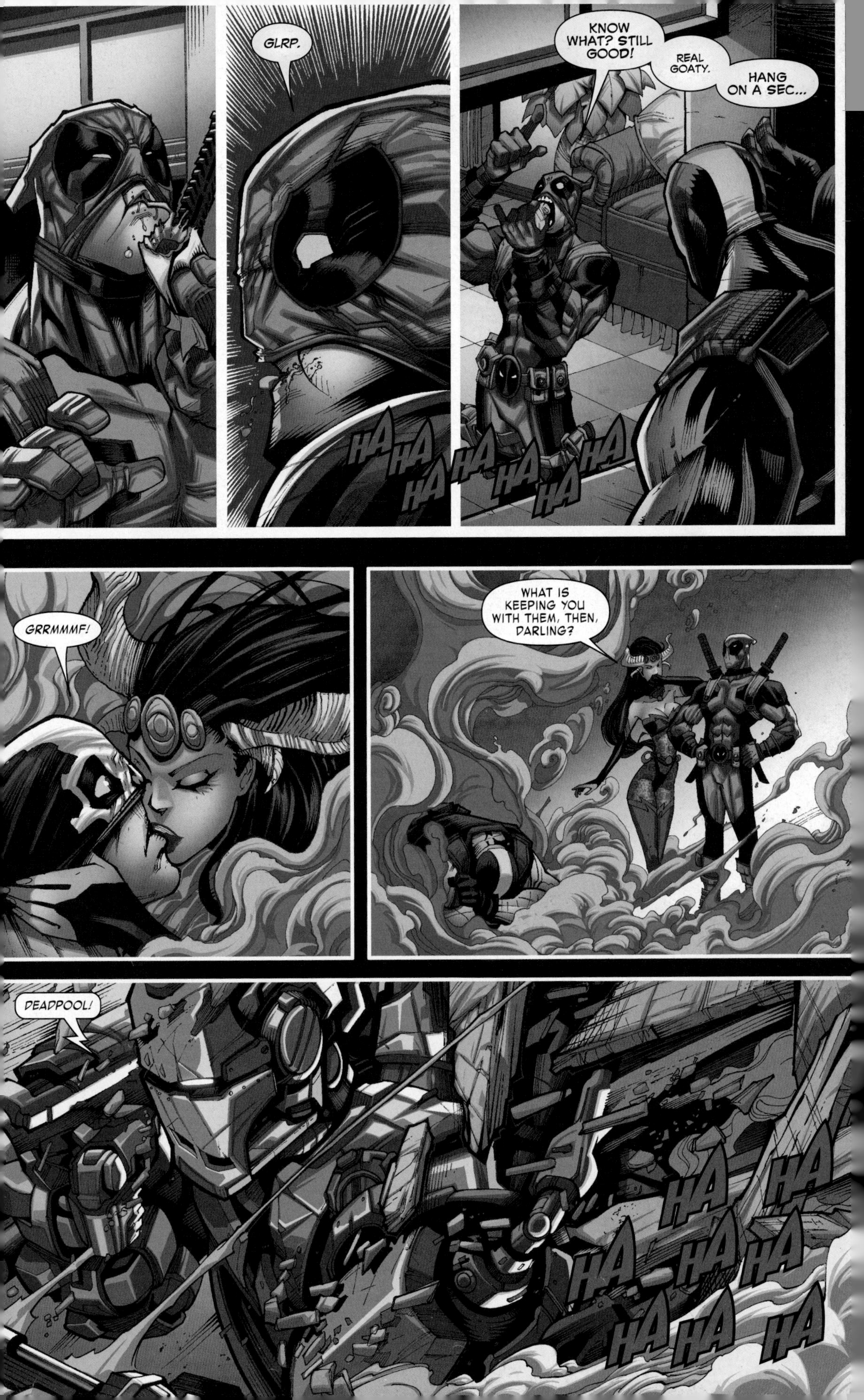
GLRP.
KNOW WHAT? STILL GOOD!
REAL GOATY.
HANG ON A SEC...
HA HA HA HA HA HA HA HA
GRRMMMF!
WHAT IS KEEPING YOU WITH THEM, THEN, DARLING?
DEADPOOL!
HA HA HA HA HA HA HA HA HA

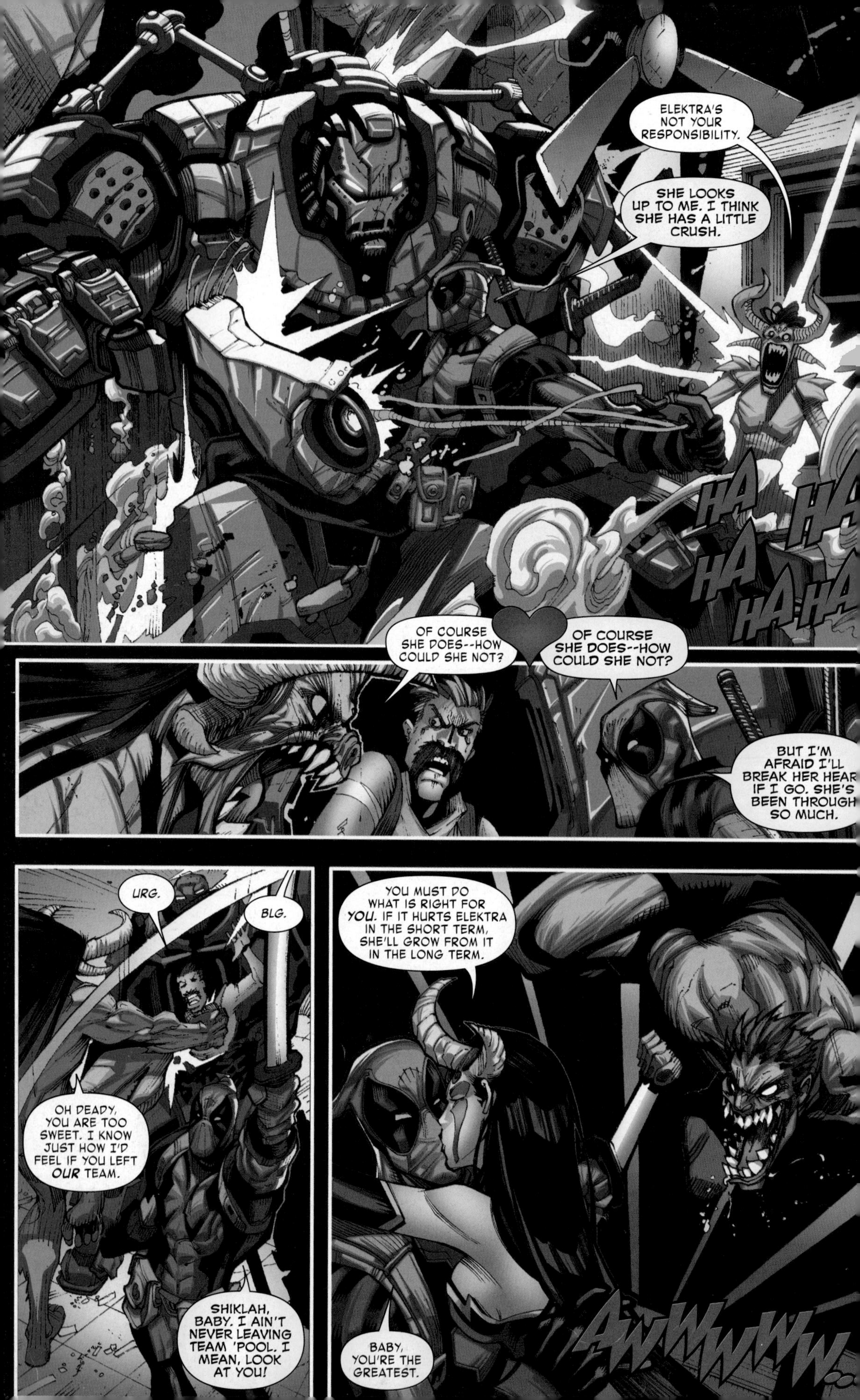
ELEKTRA'S NOT YOUR RESPONSIBILITY.
SHE LOOKS UP TO ME. I THINK SHE HAS A LITTLE CRUSH.
HA HA HA HA HA HA
OF COURSE SHE DOES--HOW COULD SHE NOT?
OF COURSE SHE DOES--HOW COULD SHE NOT?
BUT I'M AFRAID I'LL BREAK HER HEAR IF I GO. SHE'S BEEN THROUGH SO MUCH.
URG.
BLG.
OH DEADY, YOU ARE TOO SWEET. I KNOW JUST HOW I'D FEEL IF YOU LEFT *OUR* TEAM.
SHIKLAH, BABY. I AIN'T NEVER LEAVING TEAM 'POOL. I MEAN, LOOK AT YOU!
YOU MUST DO WHAT IS RIGHT FOR *YOU*. IF IT HURTS ELEKTRA IN THE SHORT TERM, SHE'LL GROW FROM IT IN THE LONG TERM.
BABY, YOU'RE THE GREATEST.
AWWWWW

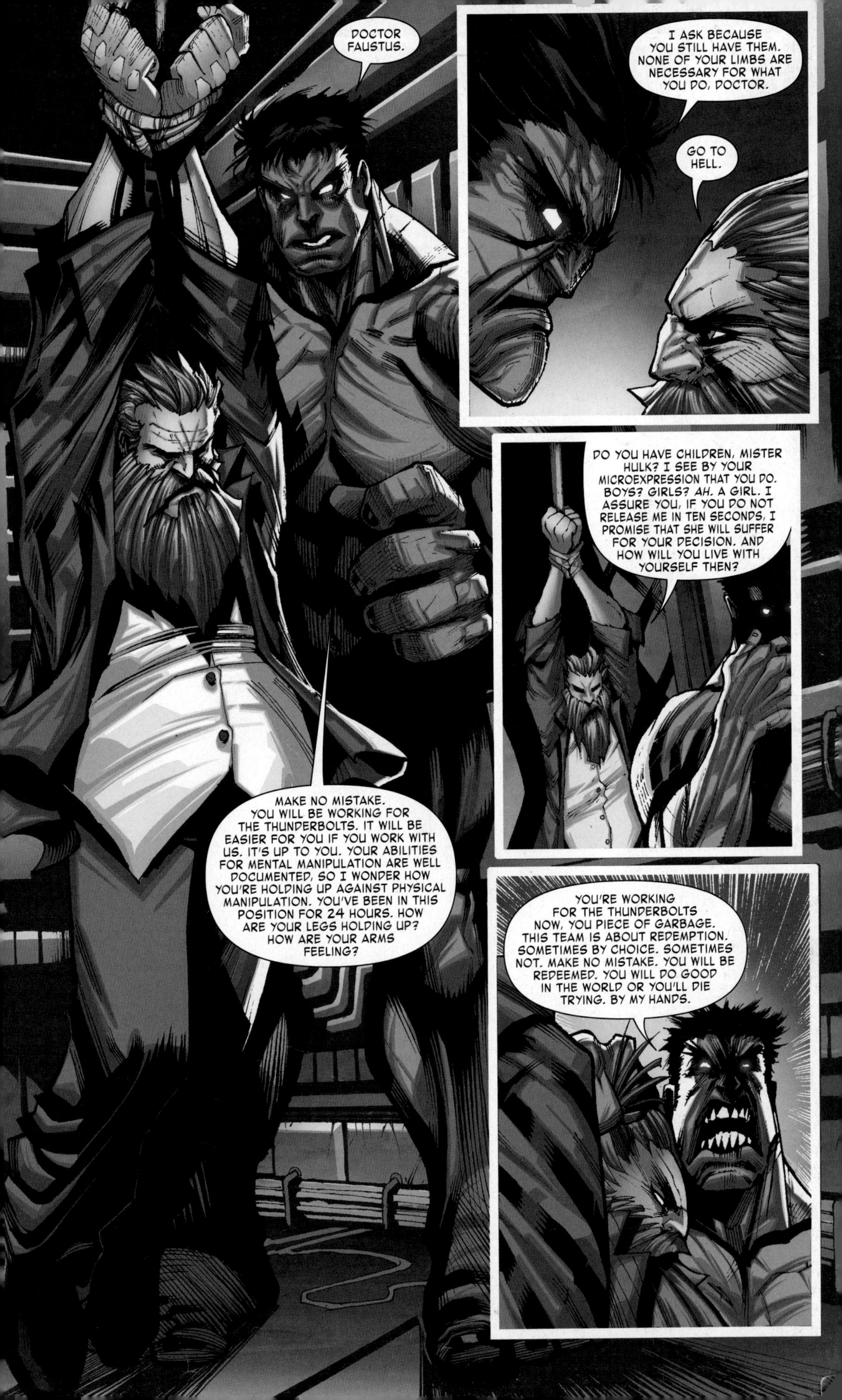
DOCTOR FAUSTUS.
I ASK BECAUSE YOU STILL HAVE THEM. NONE OF YOUR LIMBS ARE NECESSARY FOR WHAT YOU DO, DOCTOR.
GO TO HELL.
MAKE NO MISTAKE. YOU WILL BE WORKING FOR THE THUNDERBOLTS. IT WILL BE EASIER FOR YOU IF YOU WORK WITH US. IT'S UP TO YOU. YOUR ABILITIES FOR MENTAL MANIPULATION ARE WELL DOCUMENTED, SO I WONDER HOW YOU'RE HOLDING UP AGAINST PHYSICAL MANIPULATION. YOU'VE BEEN IN THIS POSITION FOR 24 HOURS. HOW ARE YOUR LEGS HOLDING UP? HOW ARE YOUR ARMS FEELING?
DO YOU HAVE CHILDREN, MISTER HULK? I SEE BY YOUR MICROEXPRESSION THAT YOU DO. BOYS? GIRLS? *AH.* A GIRL. I ASSURE YOU, IF YOU DO NOT RELEASE ME IN TEN SECONDS, I PROMISE THAT SHE WILL SUFFER FOR YOUR DECISION. AND HOW WILL YOU LIVE WITH YOURSELF THEN?
YOU'RE WORKING FOR THE THUNDERBOLTS NOW, YOU PIECE OF GARBAGE. THIS TEAM IS ABOUT REDEMPTION. SOMETIMES BY CHOICE. SOMETIMES NOT. MAKE NO MISTAKE. YOU WILL BE REDEEMED. YOU WILL DO GOOD IN THE WORLD OR YOU'LL DIE TRYING. BY MY HANDS.

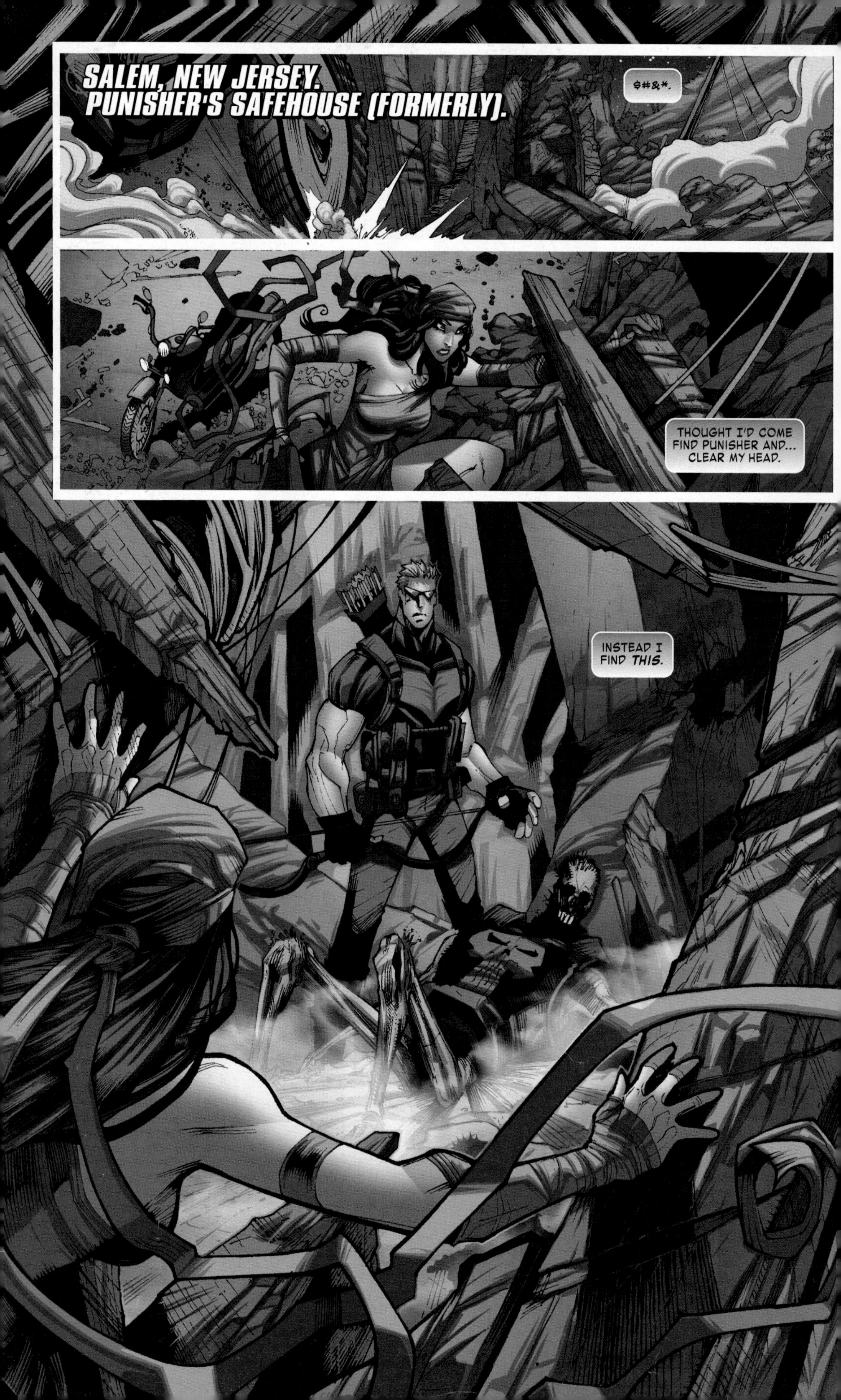
SALEM, NEW JERSEY.
PUNISHER'S SAFEHOUSE (FORMERLY).
$#&*.
THOUGHT I'D COME FIND PUNISHER AND... CLEAR MY HEAD.
INSTEAD I FIND THIS.

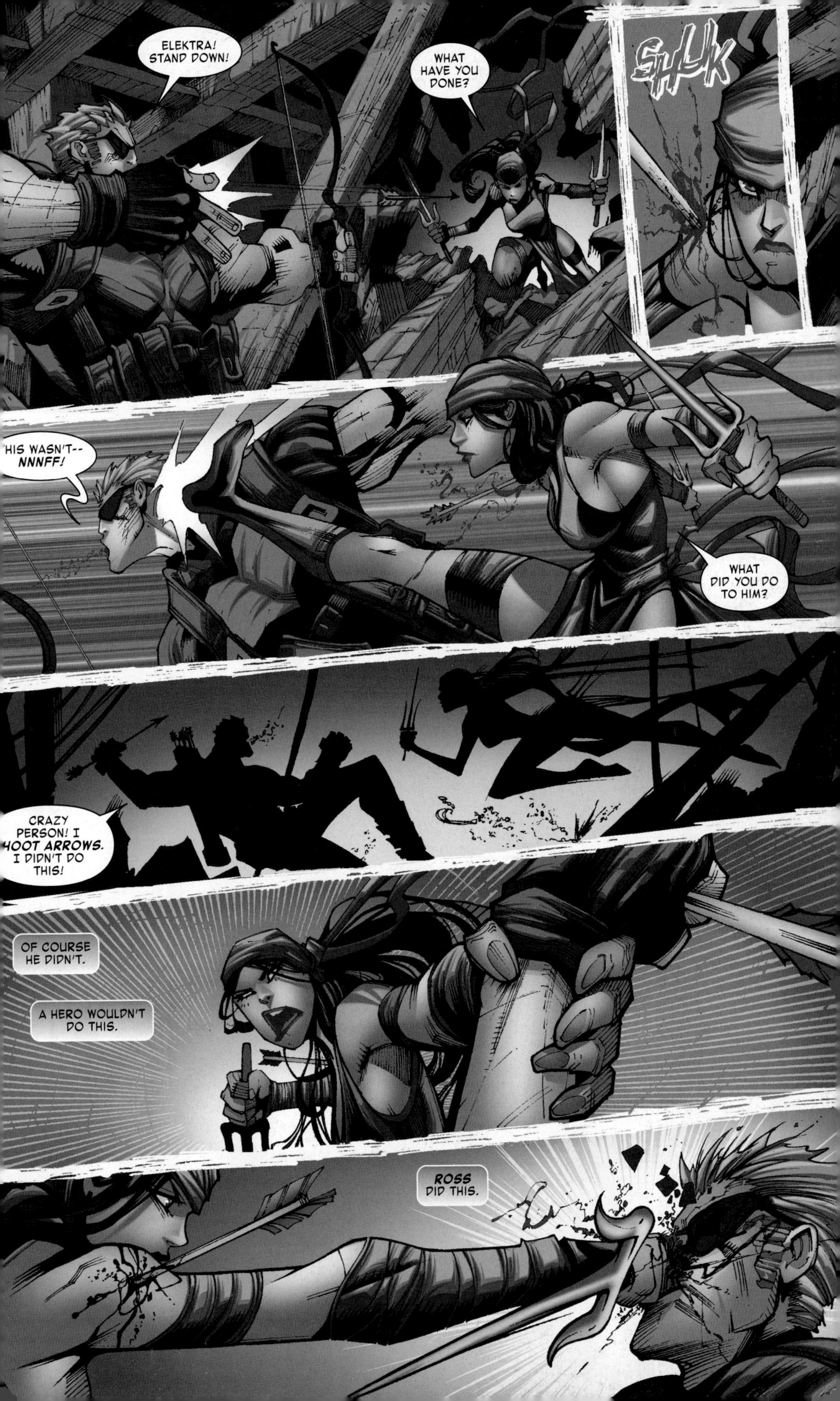

ELEKTRA! STAND DOWN!
WHAT HAVE YOU DONE?
SHUK
THIS WASN'T-- NNNFF!
WHAT DID YOU DO TO HIM?
CRAZY PERSON! I SHOOT ARROWS. I DIDN'T DO THIS!
OF COURSE HE DIDN'T.
A HERO WOULDN'T DO THIS.
ROSS DID THIS.

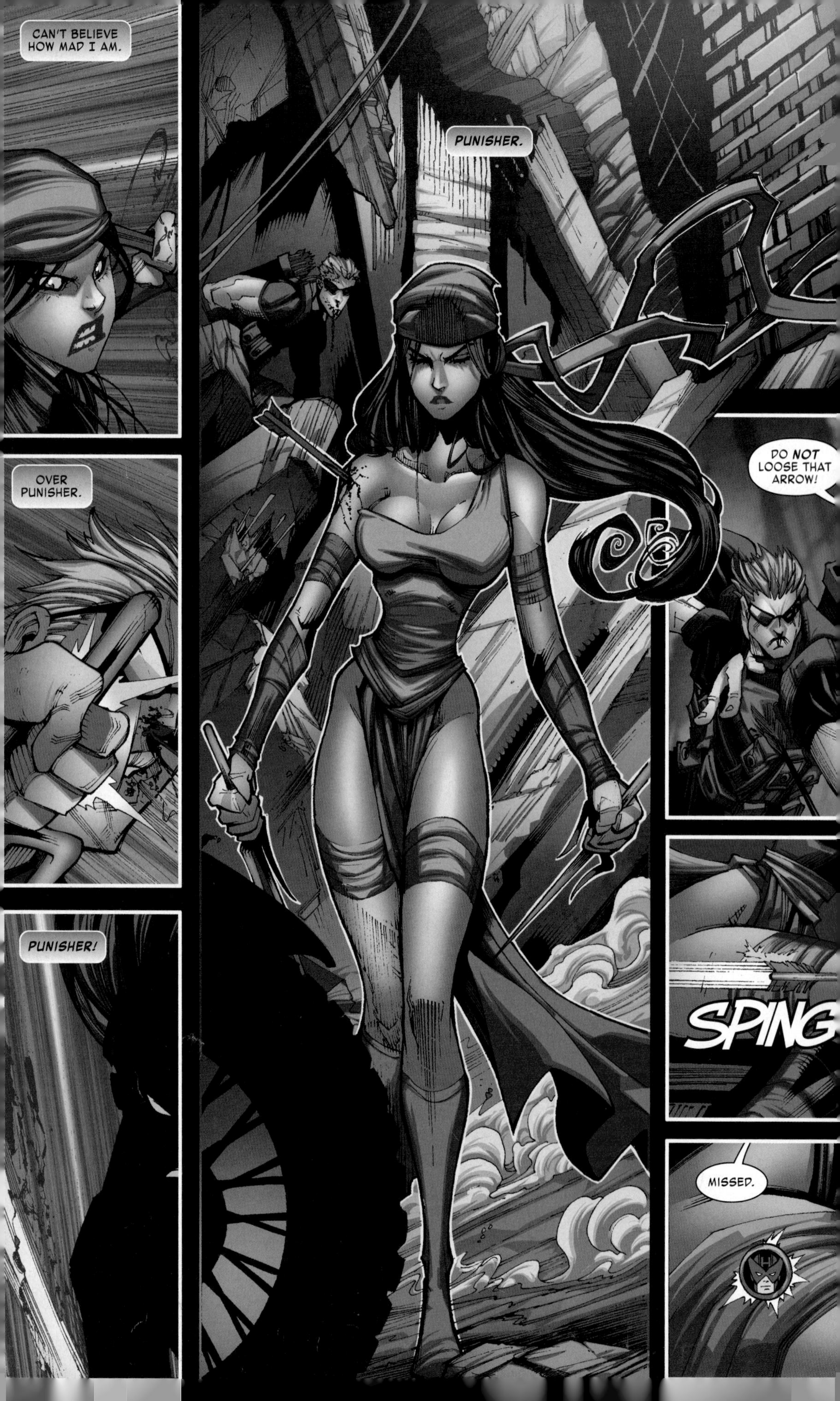
CAN'T BELIEVE HOW MAD I AM.
OVER PUNISHER.
PUNISHER!
PUNISHER.
DO NOT LOOSE THAT ARROW!
SPING
MISSED.

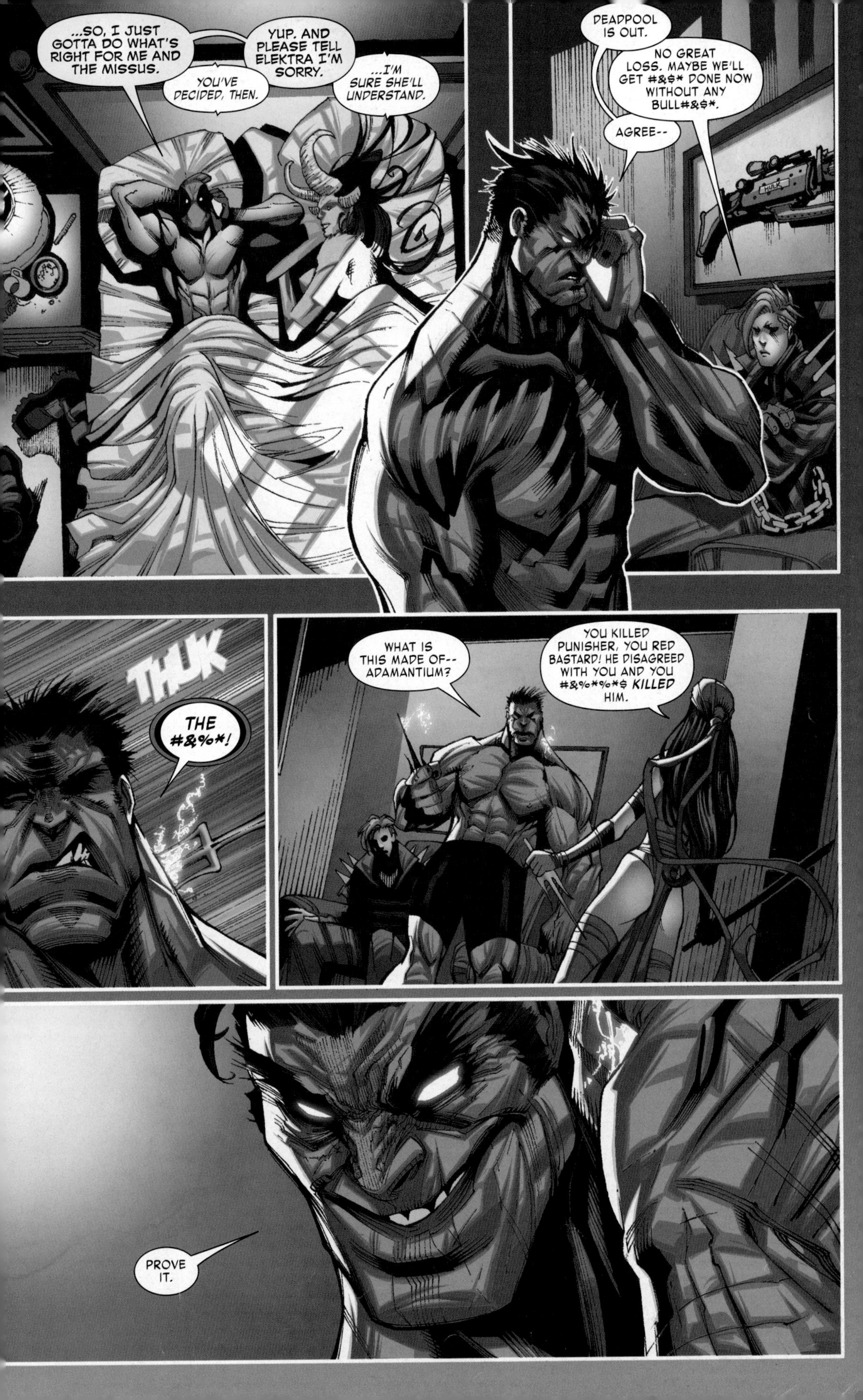
...SO, I JUST GOTTA DO WHAT'S RIGHT FOR ME AND THE MISSUS.
YOU'VE DECIDED, THEN.
YUP. AND PLEASE TELL ELEKTRA I'M SORRY.
...I'M SURE SHE'LL UNDERSTAND.
DEADPOOL IS OUT.
NO GREAT LOSS. MAYBE WE'LL GET #&$* DONE NOW WITHOUT ANY BULL#&$*.
AGREE--
THUK
THE #&%*!
WHAT IS THIS MADE OF-- ADAMANTIUM?
YOU KILLED PUNISHER, YOU RED BASTARD! HE DISAGREED WITH YOU AND YOU #&%*%*$ KILLED HIM.
PROVE IT.

I KNOW IT WAS YOU.

THIS ISN'T A FIGHT YOU CAN WIN.

LEAVE WHILE YOU CAN STILL WALK AWAY FROM THIS. OR STAY. I. DON'T. GIVE A DAMN.

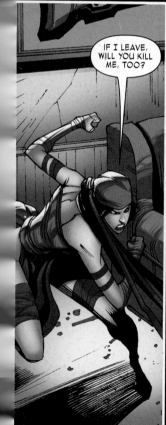

IF I LEAVE, WILL YOU KILL ME, TOO?

IF YOU KEEP THIS UP, I'LL KILL YOU RIGHT NOW.

HULK

BLAM BLAM BLAM

...I KNOW THE SOUND OF THAT GUN.

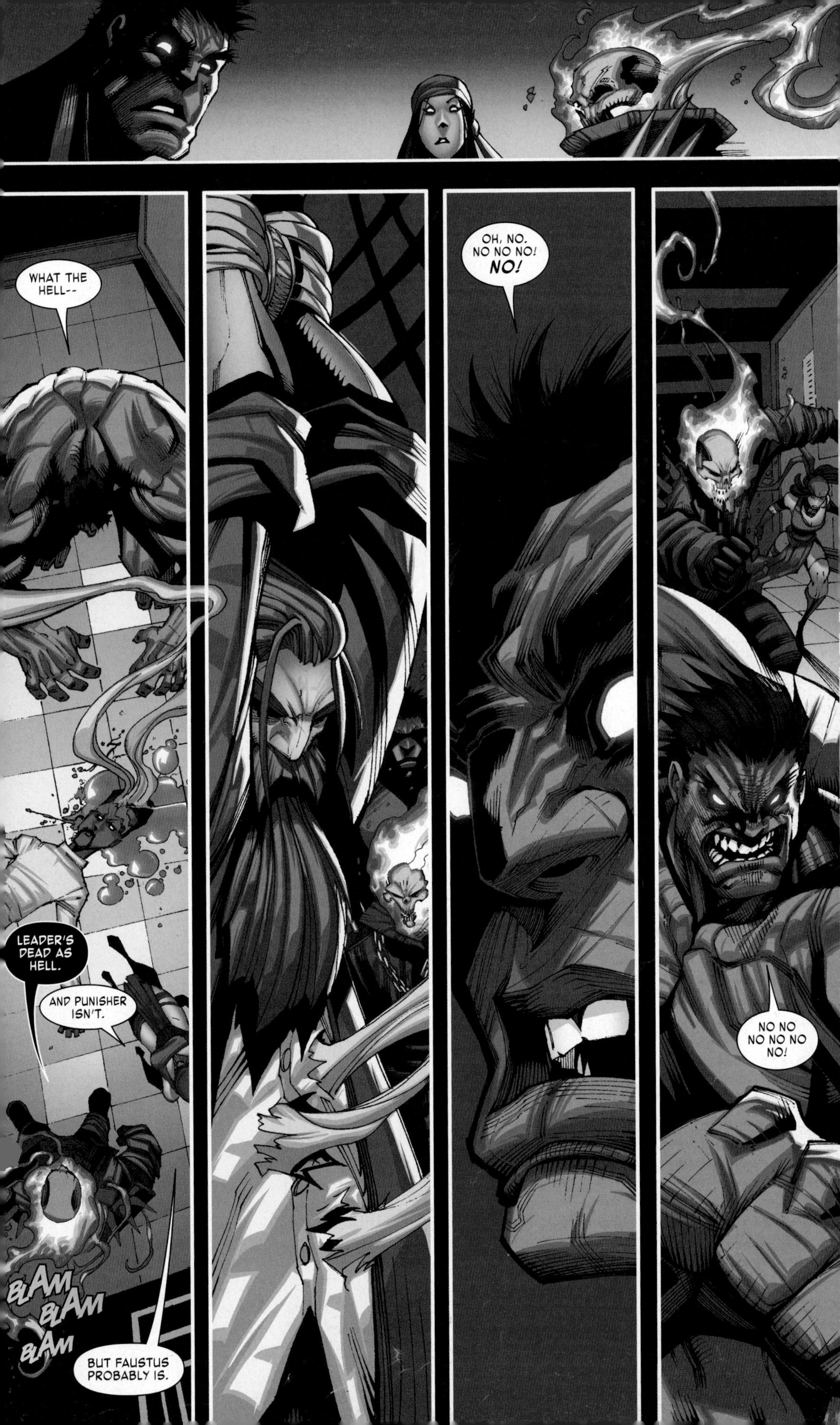
WHAT THE HELL--
OH, NO. NO NO NO! NO!
NO NO NO NO NO NO!
LEADER'S DEAD AS HELL.
AND PUNISHER ISN'T.
BLAM BLAM BLAM
BUT FAUSTUS PROBABLY IS.

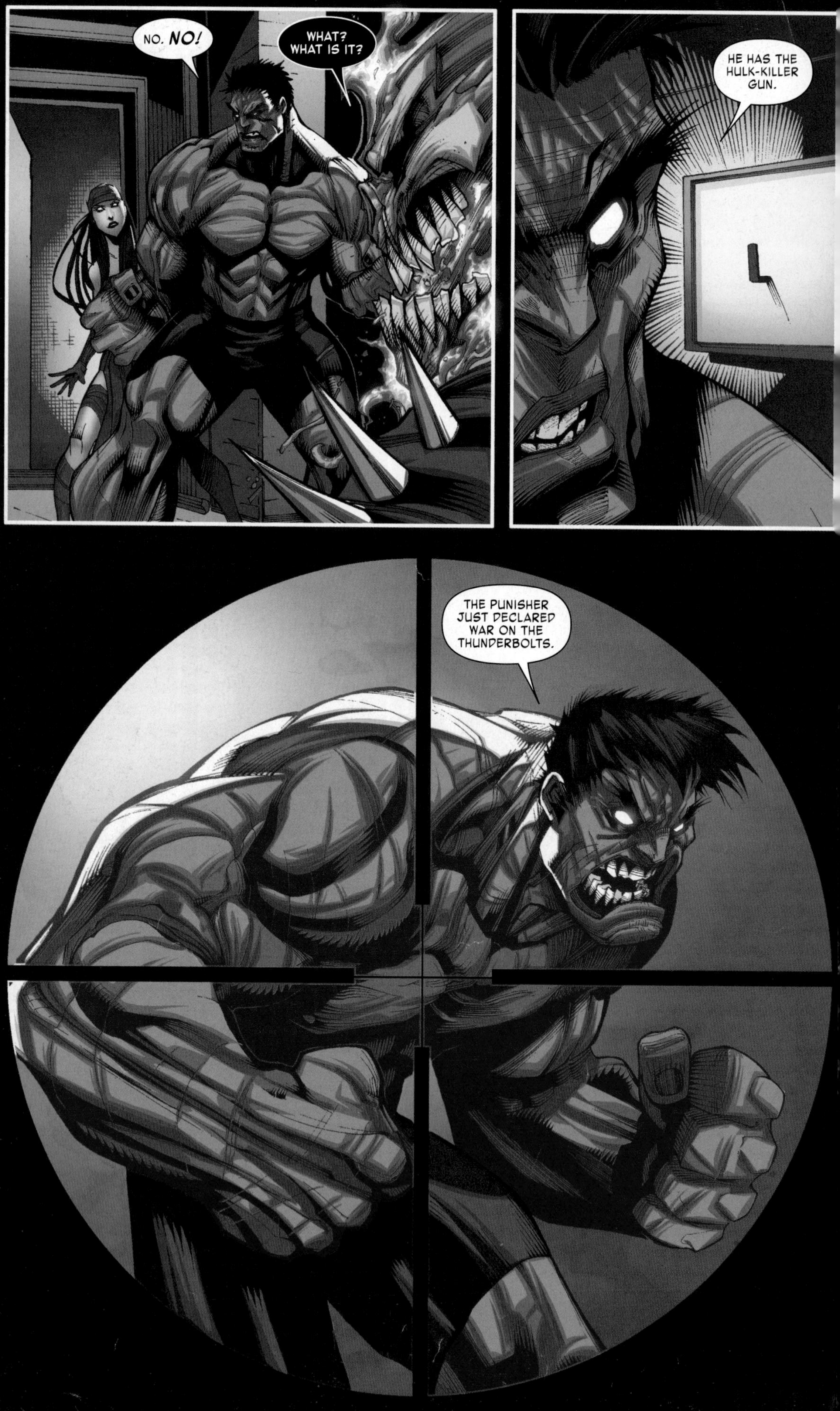
NO. NO!
WHAT? WHAT IS IT?
HE HAS THE HULK-KILLER GUN.
THE PUNISHER JUST DECLARED WAR ON THE THUNDERBOLTS.

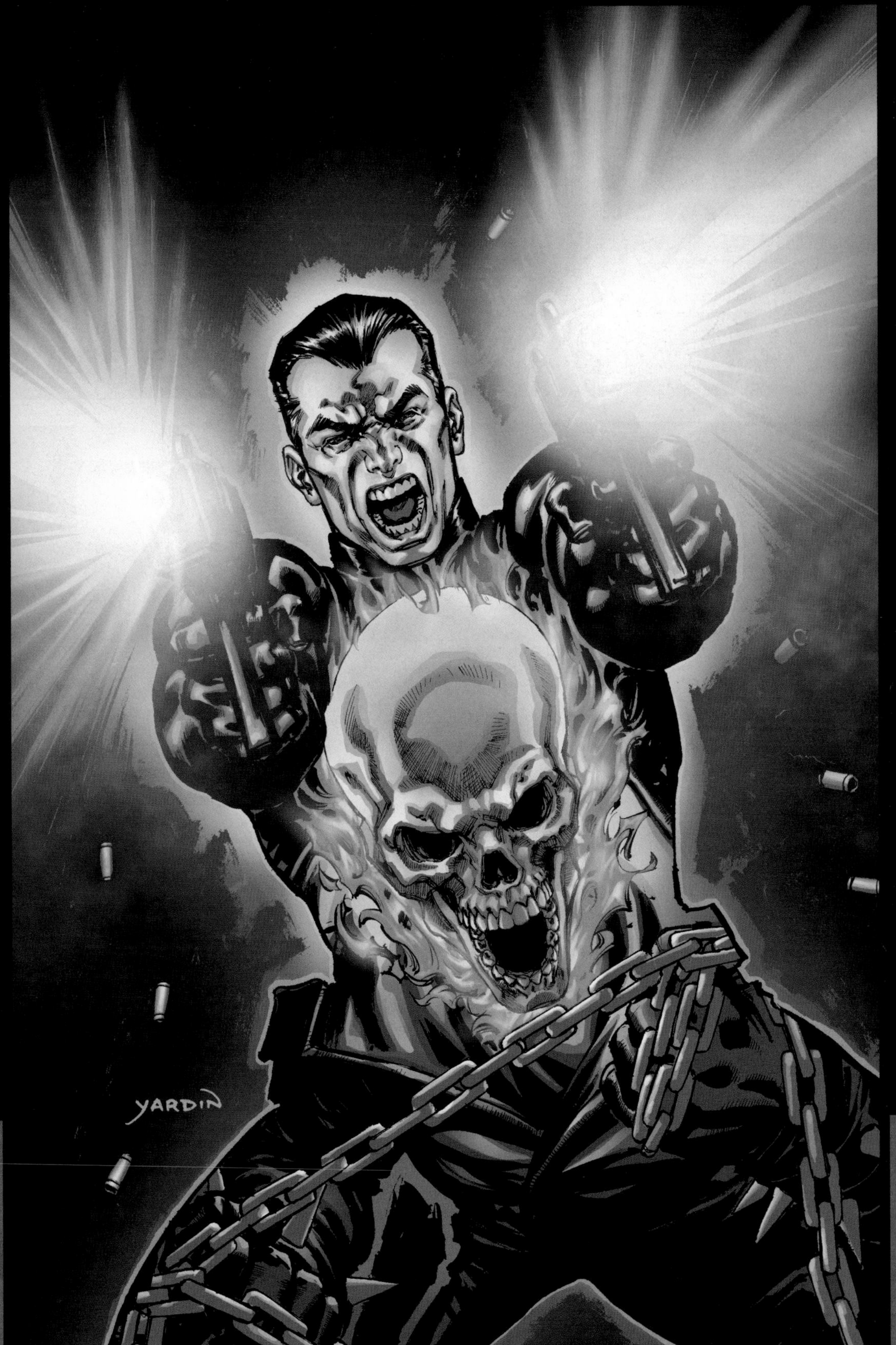
YARDIN

TWENTY-NINE

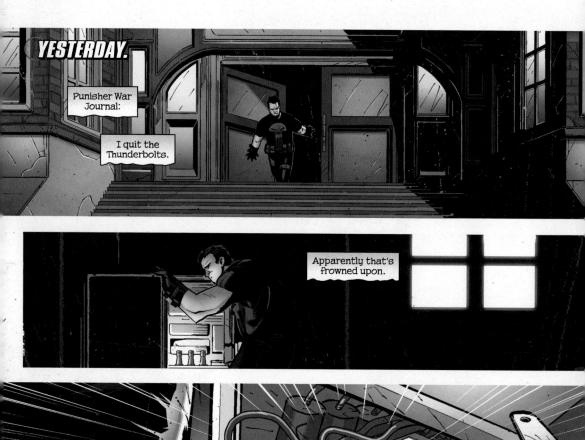

YESTERDAY.

Punisher War Journal:

I quit the Thunderbolts.

Apparently that's frowned upon.

YOU DON'T QUIT US. YOU'RE FIRED

My Proline stainless mini-fridge keeps beers cold, makes ice...

...and like everything else in my life, is reinforced, bulletproofed and bomb-resistant as hell.

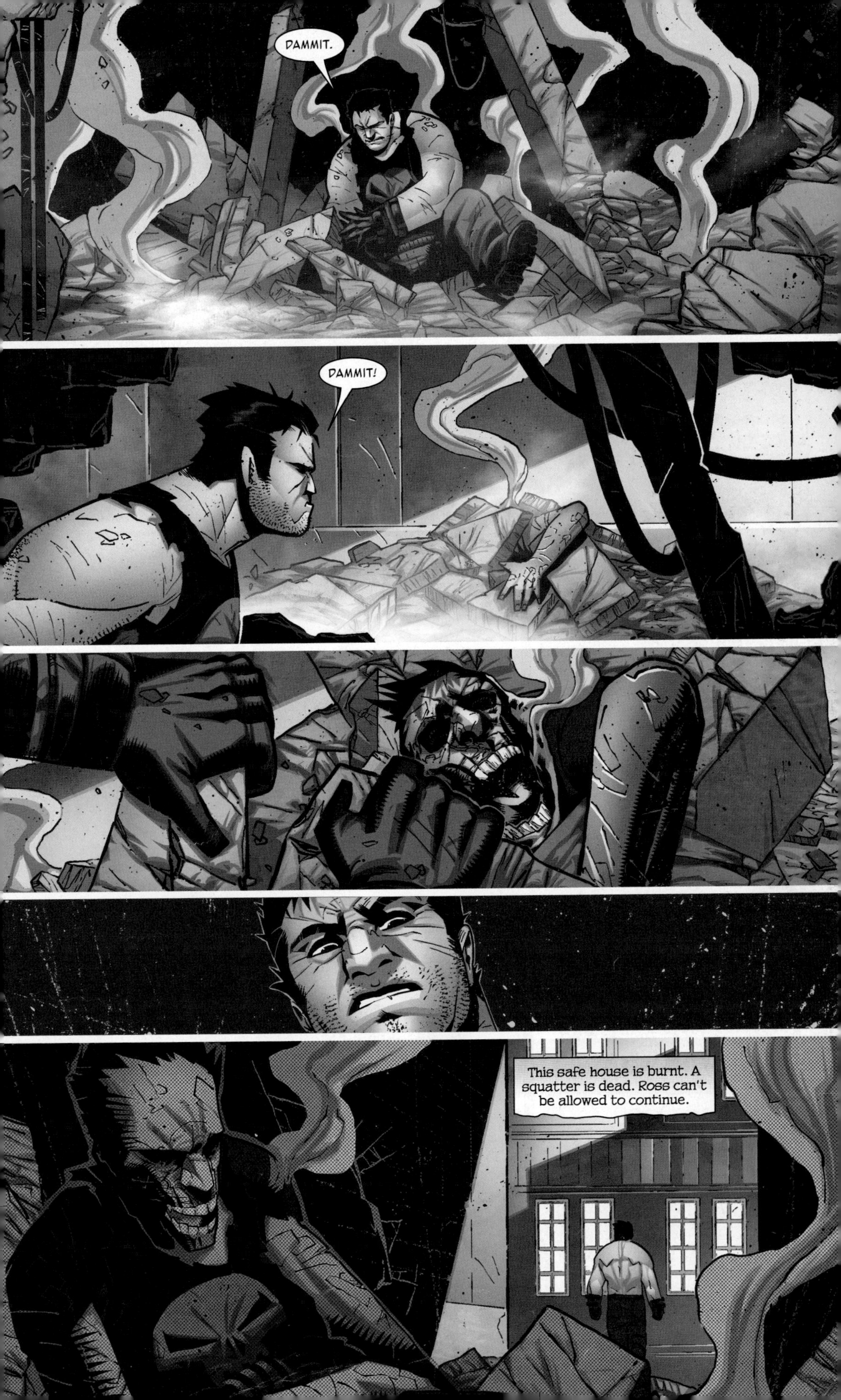
DAMMIT.
DAMMIT!
This safe house is burnt. A squatter is dead. Ross can't be allowed to continue.

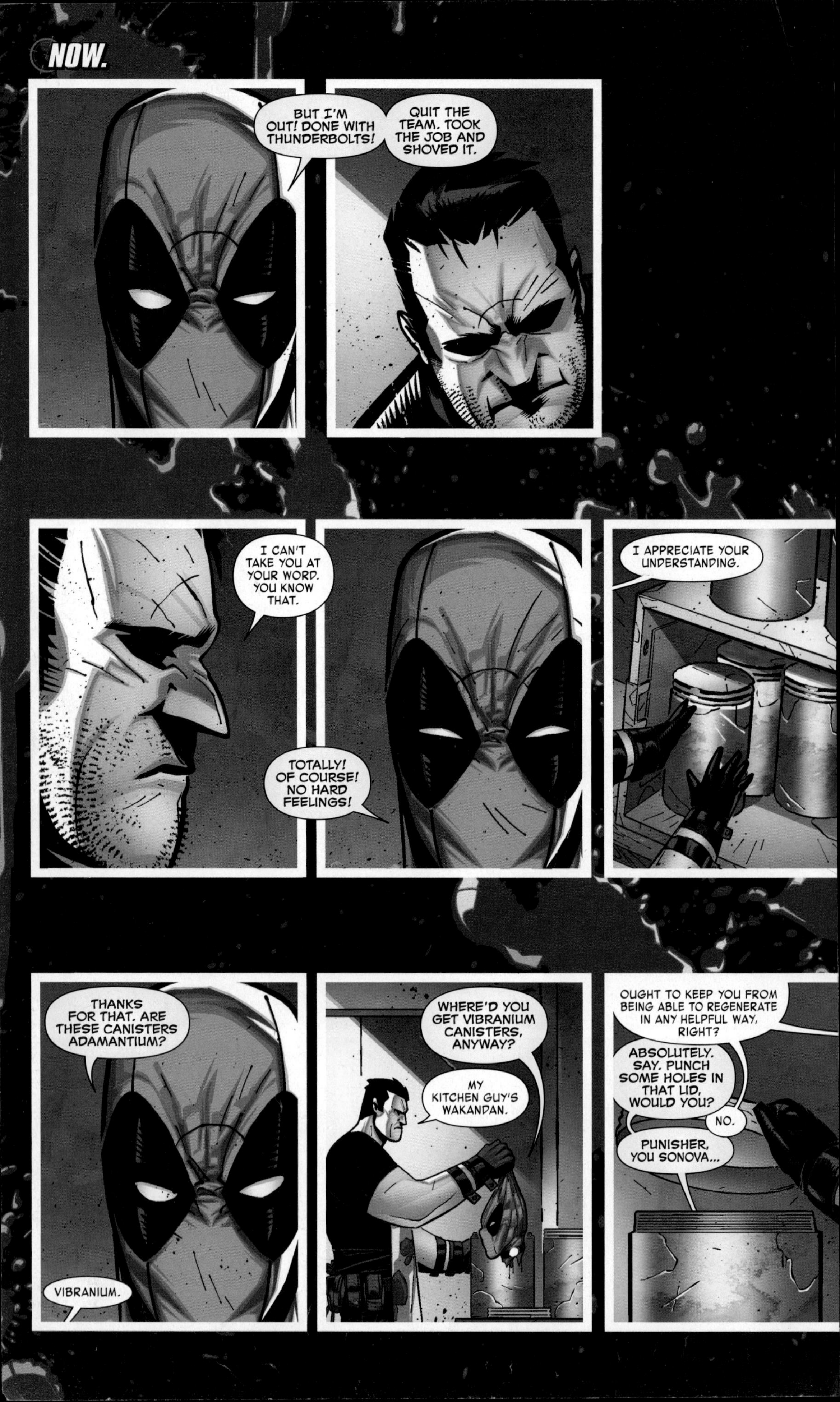
NOW.
BUT I'M OUT! DONE WITH THUNDERBOLTS!
QUIT THE TEAM. TOOK THE JOB AND SHOVED IT.
I CAN'T TAKE YOU AT YOUR WORD. YOU KNOW THAT.
TOTALLY! OF COURSE! NO HARD FEELINGS!
I APPRECIATE YOUR UNDERSTANDING.
THANKS FOR THAT. ARE THESE CANISTERS ADAMANTIUM?
VIBRANIUM.
WHERE'D YOU GET VIBRANIUM CANISTERS, ANYWAY?
MY KITCHEN GUY'S WAKANDAN.
OUGHT TO KEEP YOU FROM BEING ABLE TO REGENERATE IN ANY HELPFUL WAY, RIGHT?
ABSOLUTELY. SAY. PUNCH SOME HOLES IN THAT LID, WOULD YOU?
NO.
PUNISHER, YOU SONOVA...

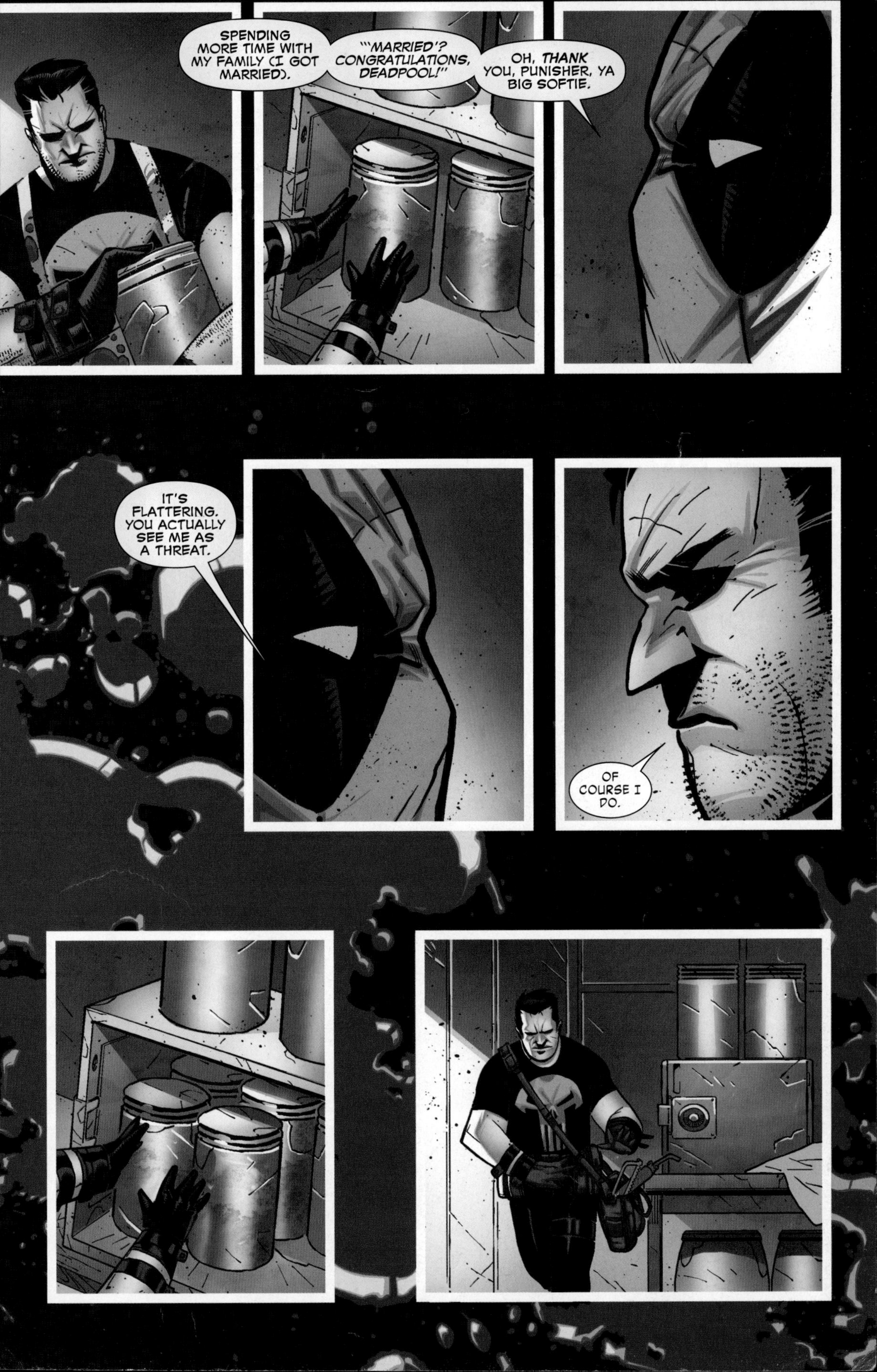
SPENDING MORE TIME WITH MY FAMILY (I GOT MARRIED).
"'MARRIED'? CONGRATULATIONS, DEADPOOL!"
OH, THANK YOU, PUNISHER, YA BIG SOFTIE.
IT'S FLATTERING. YOU ACTUALLY SEE ME AS A THREAT.
OF COURSE I DO.

THIS IS *YOUR* FAULT, ROSS! YOU CAN'T LET HIM QUIT? YOU HAVE TO *MURDER* HIM?

HE DOESN'T SEEM MURDERED TO ME.

NOT HELPING.

I'M NOT HERE TO HELP.

YOU DON'T EVEN HAVE THE DECENCY TO DENY YOU DID IT!

WHEN ROSS MURDERS SOMEONE, THEY STAY DEAD. TELL HER!

SHE'S MADE UP HER MIND.

EVERYTHING WE'VE BEEN THROUGH BUYS ME NOTHING WITH HER!

DOLLARS TO DONUTS YOU'R ON PUNISHER'S LIST, TOO, ELEKTRA!

BECAUSE OF YOU!

DO I NEED TO WORRY ABOUT YOU TOO, ELEK--

--SHE'S GONE.

DAMN NINJAS.

GHOST RIDER. GO GET PUNISHER.

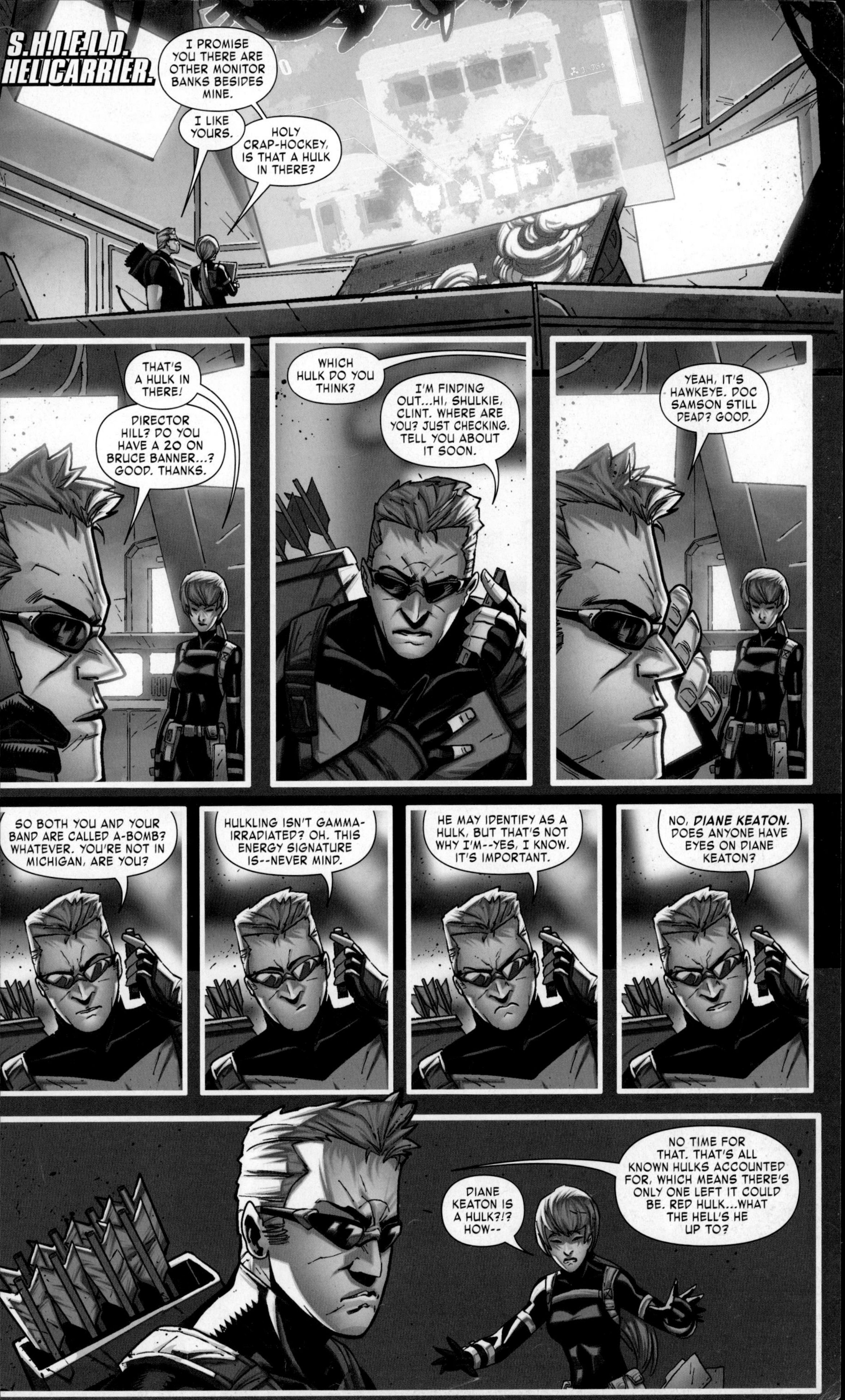
S.H.I.E.L.D. HELICARRIER.
I PROMISE YOU THERE ARE OTHER MONITOR BANKS BESIDES MINE.
I LIKE YOURS.
HOLY CRAP-HOCKEY, IS THAT A HULK IN THERE?
THAT'S A HULK IN THERE!
DIRECTOR HILL? DO YOU HAVE A 20 ON BRUCE BANNER...? GOOD. THANKS.
WHICH HULK DO YOU THINK?
I'M FINDING OUT...HI, SHULKIE, CLINT. WHERE ARE YOU? JUST CHECKING. TELL YOU ABOUT IT SOON.
YEAH, IT'S HAWKEYE. DOC SAMSON STILL DEAD? GOOD.
SO BOTH YOU AND YOUR BAND ARE CALLED A-BOMB? WHATEVER. YOU'RE NOT IN MICHIGAN, ARE YOU?
HULKLING ISN'T GAMMA-IRRADIATED? OH. THIS ENERGY SIGNATURE IS--NEVER MIND.
HE MAY IDENTIFY AS A HULK, BUT THAT'S NOT WHY I'M--YES, I KNOW. IT'S IMPORTANT.
NO, *DIANE KEATON.* DOES ANYONE HAVE EYES ON DIANE KEATON?
DIANE KEATON IS A HULK?!? HOW--
NO TIME FOR THAT. THAT'S ALL KNOWN HULKS ACCOUNTED FOR, WHICH MEANS THERE'S ONLY ONE LEFT IT COULD BE. RED HULK...WHAT THE HELL'S HE UP TO?

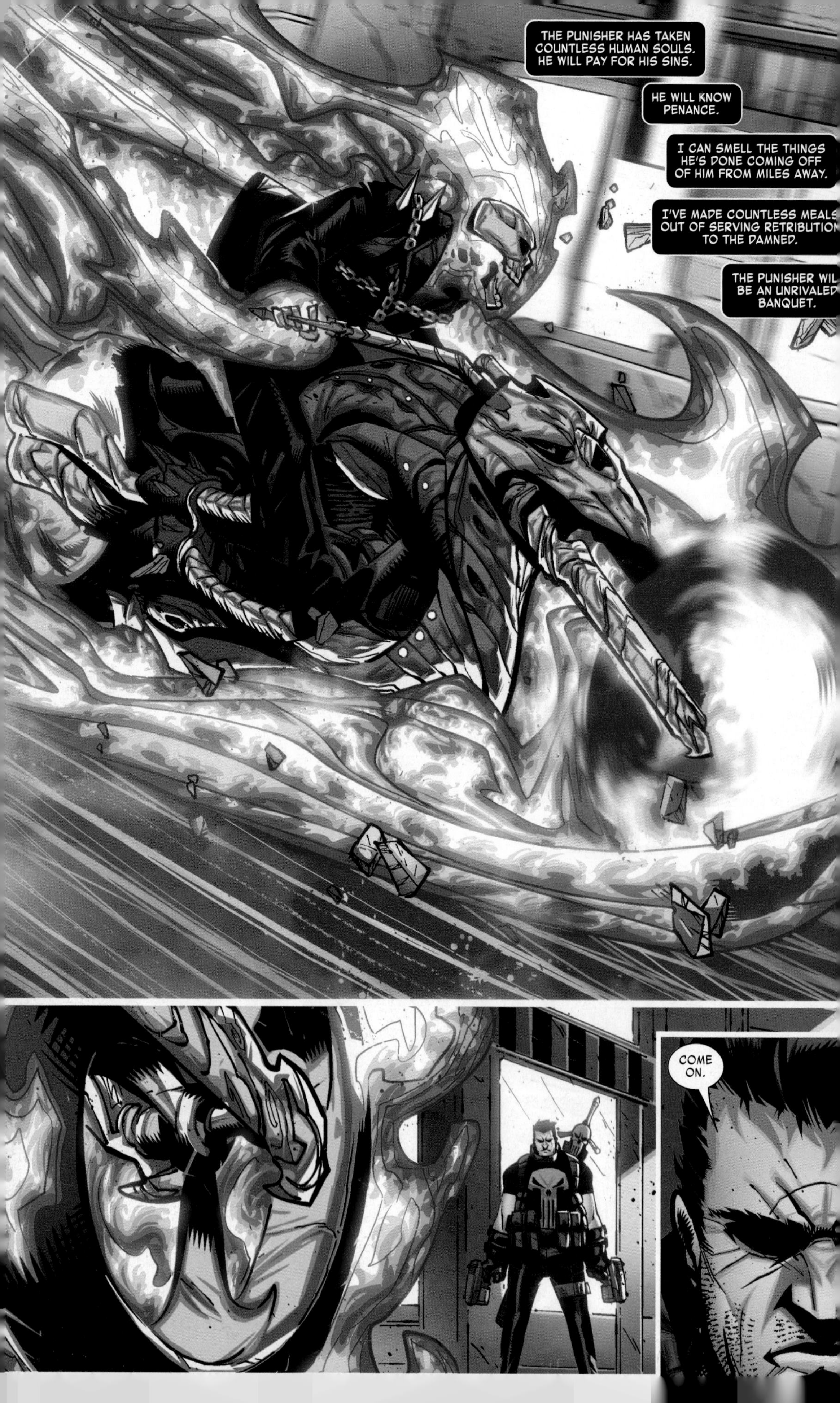
THE PUNISHER HAS TAKEN COUNTLESS HUMAN SOULS. HE WILL PAY FOR HIS SINS.
HE WILL KNOW PENANCE.
I CAN SMELL THE THINGS HE'S DONE COMING OFF OF HIM FROM MILES AWAY.
I'VE MADE COUNTLESS MEALS OUT OF SERVING RETRIBUTION TO THE DAMNED.
THE PUNISHER WILL BE AN UNRIVALED BANQUET.
COME ON.

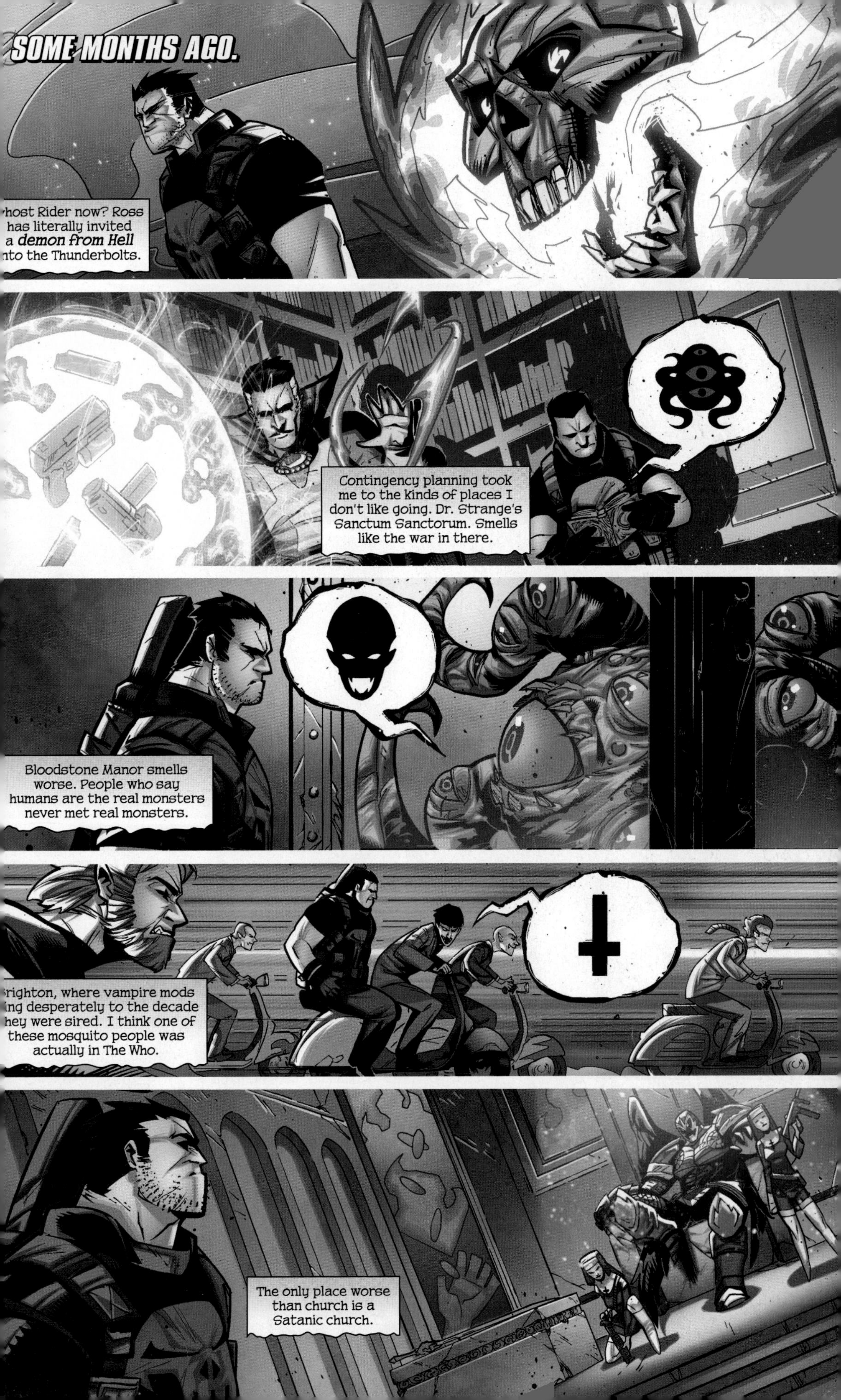
SOME MONTHS AGO.
host Rider now? Ross has literally invited a *demon from Hell* nto the Thunderbolts.
Contingency planning took me to the kinds of places I don't like going. Dr. Strange's Sanctum Sanctorum. Smells like the war in there.
Bloodstone Manor smells worse. People who say humans are the real monsters never met real monsters.
righton, where vampire mods ing desperately to the decade hey were sired. I think one of these mosquito people was actually in The Who.
The only place worse than church is a Satanic church.

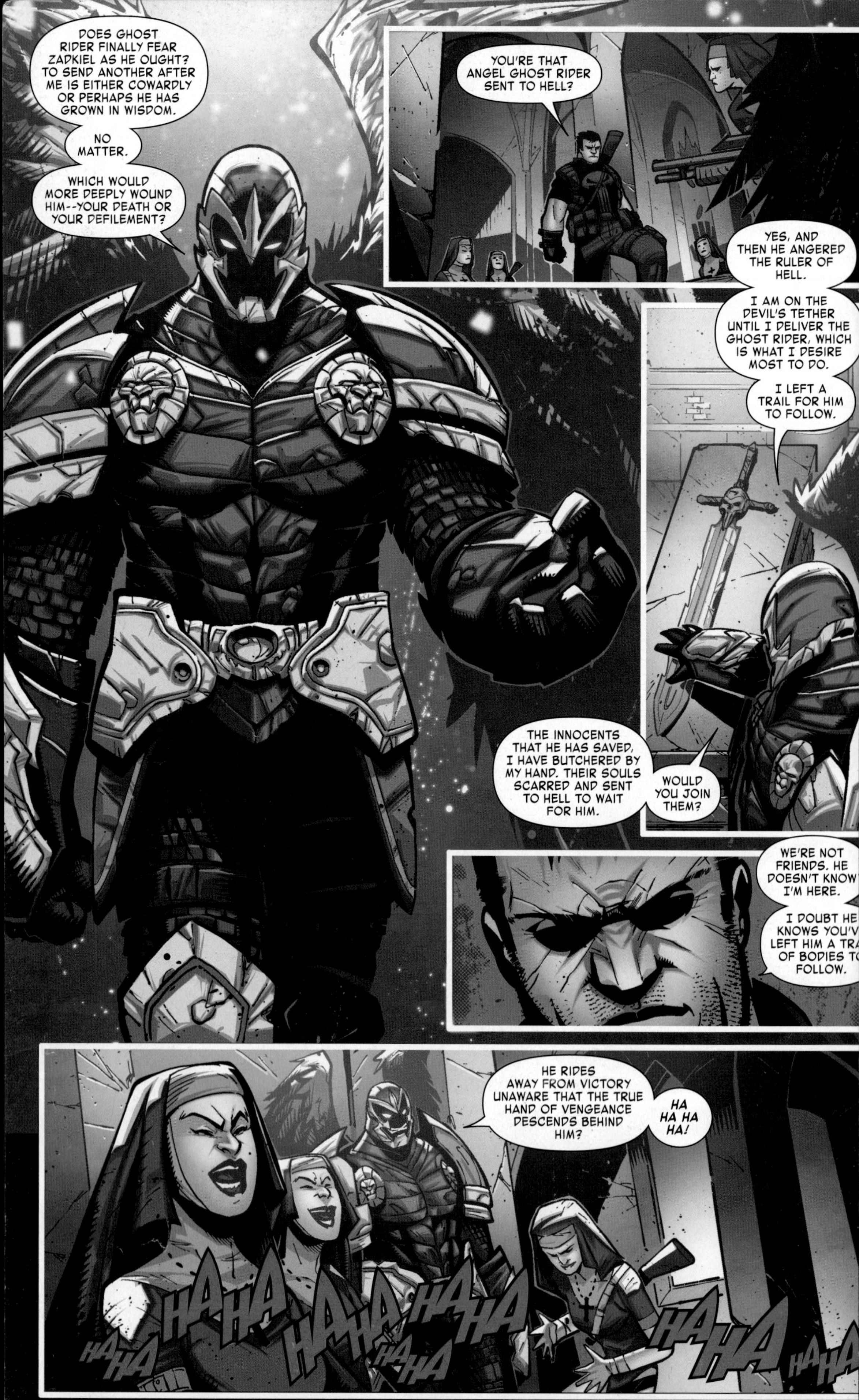

DOES GHOST RIDER FINALLY FEAR ZADKIEL AS HE OUGHT? TO SEND ANOTHER AFTER ME IS EITHER COWARDLY OR PERHAPS HE HAS GROWN IN WISDOM.
NO MATTER.
WHICH WOULD MORE DEEPLY WOUND HIM--YOUR DEATH OR YOUR DEFILEMENT?
YOU'RE THAT ANGEL GHOST RIDER SENT TO HELL?
YES, AND THEN HE ANGERED THE RULER OF HELL.
I AM ON THE DEVIL'S TETHER UNTIL I DELIVER THE GHOST RIDER, WHICH IS WHAT I DESIRE MOST TO DO.
I LEFT A TRAIL FOR HIM TO FOLLOW.
THE INNOCENTS THAT HE HAS SAVED, I HAVE BUTCHERED BY MY HAND. THEIR SOULS SCARRED AND SENT TO HELL TO WAIT FOR HIM.
WOULD YOU JOIN THEM?
WE'RE NOT FRIENDS. HE DOESN'T KNOW I'M HERE.
HE RIDES AWAY FROM VICTORY UNAWARE THAT THE TRUE HAND OF VENGEANCE DESCENDS BEHIND HIM?
HA HA HA HA!
HAHA HAHA HAHA HAHA HAHA HAHA HAHA

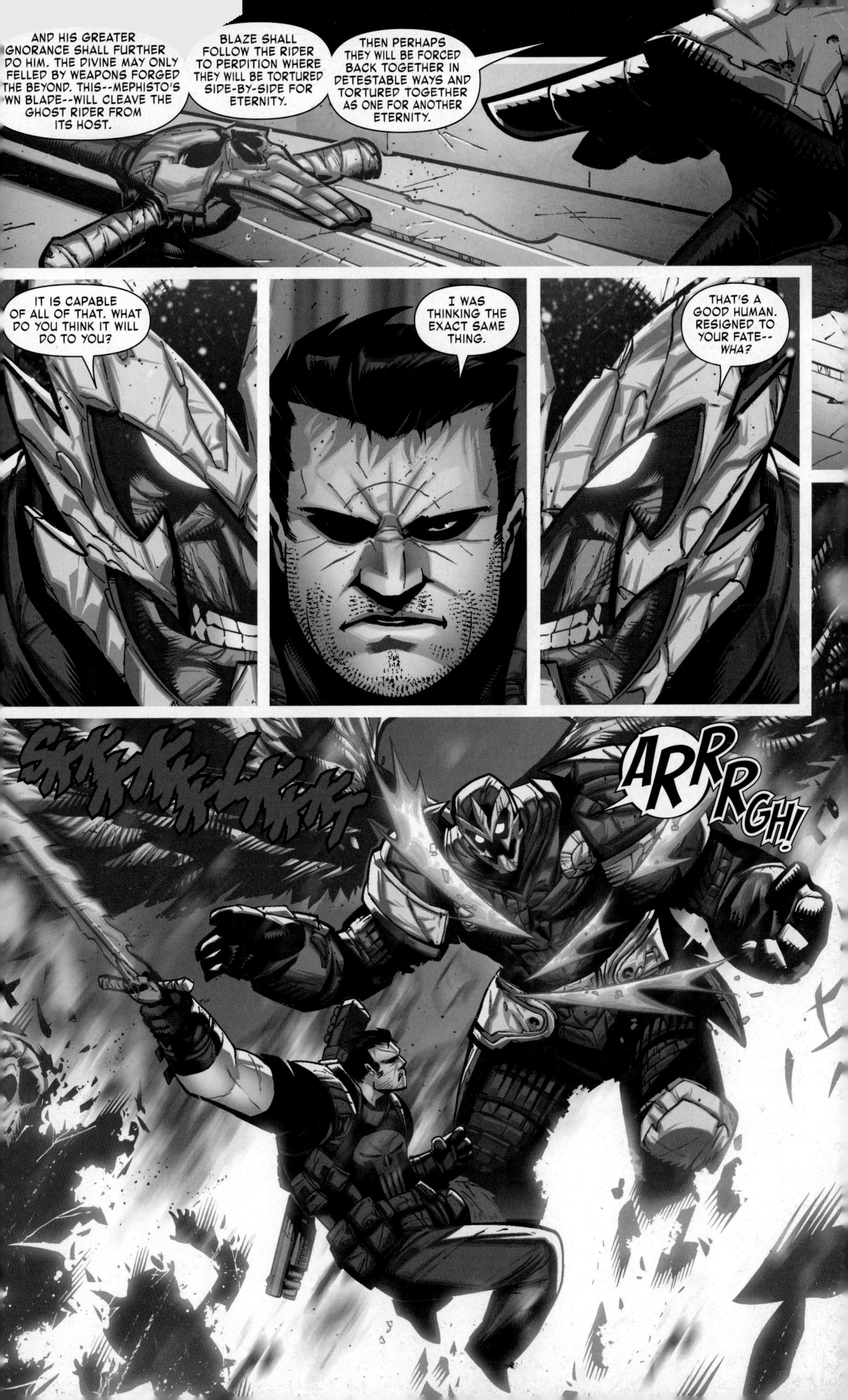
AND HIS GREATER
GNORANCE SHALL FURTHER
DO HIM. THE DIVINE MAY ONLY
FELLED BY WEAPONS FORGED
THE BEYOND. THIS--MEPHISTO'S
WN BLADE--WILL CLEAVE THE
GHOST RIDER FROM
ITS HOST.
BLAZE SHALL FOLLOW THE RIDER TO PERDITION WHERE THEY WILL BE TORTURED SIDE-BY-SIDE FOR ETERNITY.
THEN PERHAPS THEY WILL BE FORCED BACK TOGETHER IN DETESTABLE WAYS AND TORTURED TOGETHER AS ONE FOR ANOTHER ETERNITY.
IT IS CAPABLE OF ALL OF THAT. WHAT DO YOU THINK IT WILL DO TO YOU?
I WAS THINKING THE EXACT SAME THING.
THAT'S A GOOD HUMAN. RESIGNED TO YOUR FATE-- WHA?
SKKKKKLLLLKKK
ARRRRGH!

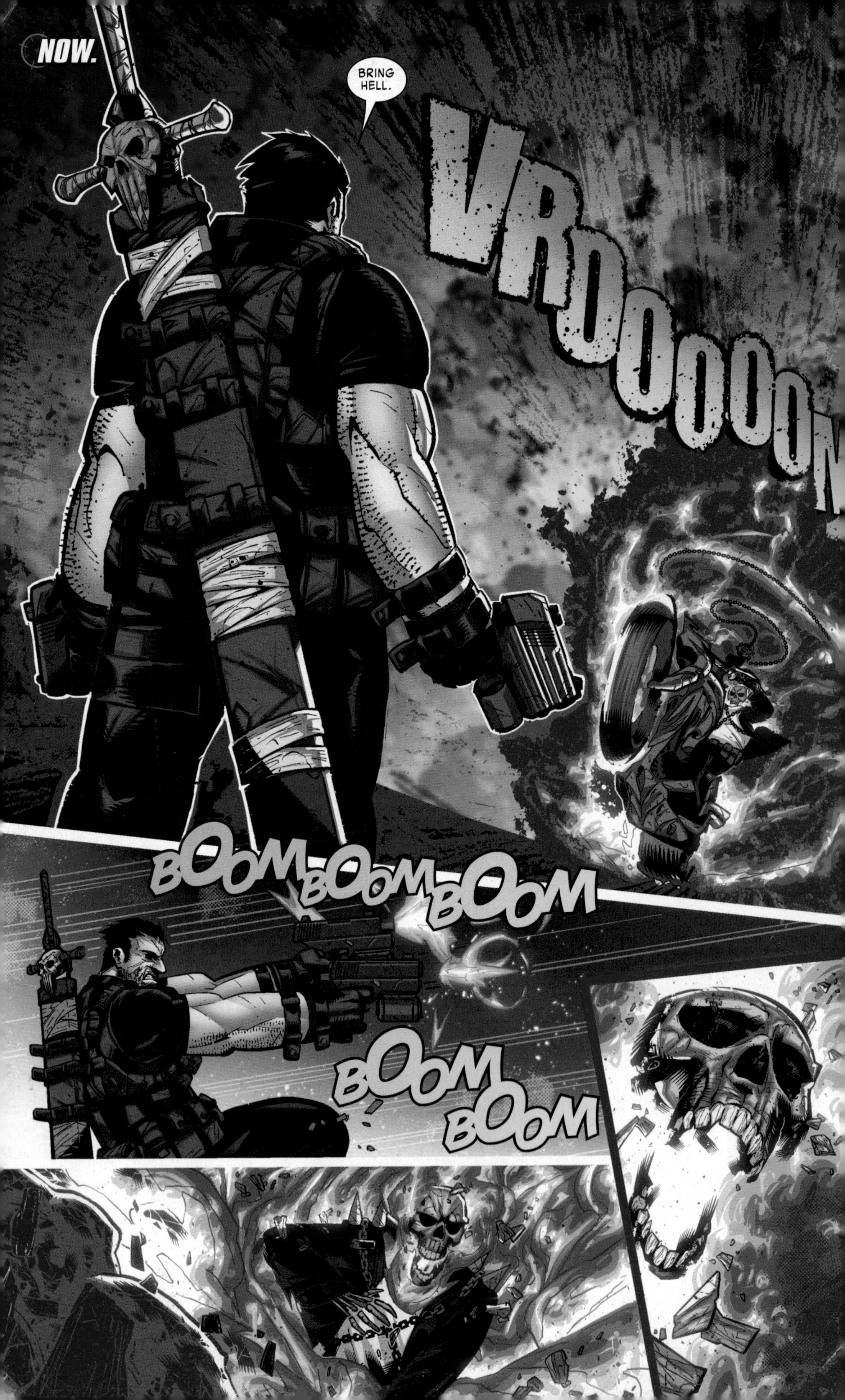
NOW.
BRING HELL.
VROOOOOOON
BOOM BOOM BOOM
BOOM BOOM

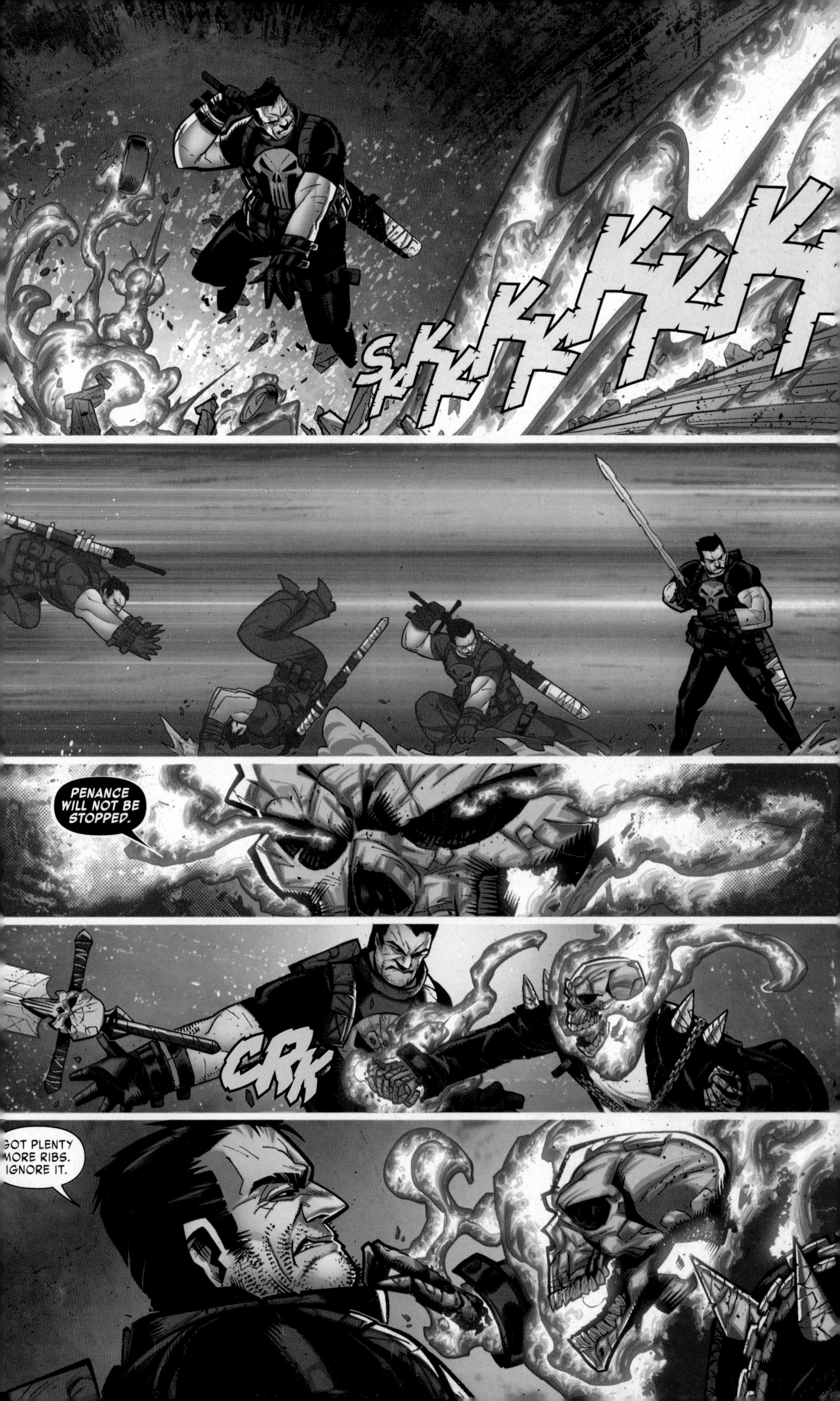

SKAKKKKKKK
PENANCE WILL NOT BE STOPPED.
CRK
GOT PLENTY MORE RIBS. IGNORE IT.

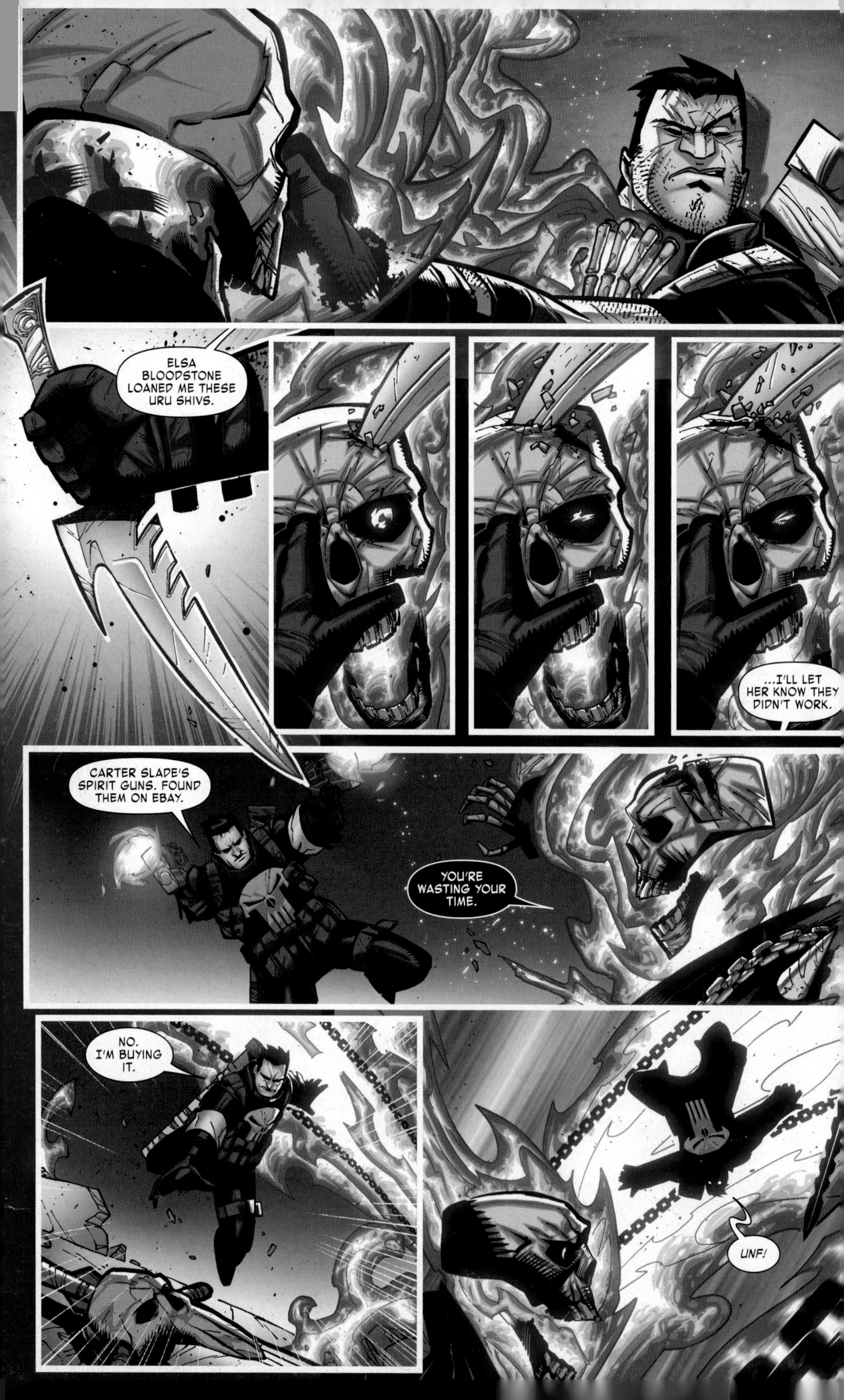
ELSA BLOODSTONE LOANED ME THESE URU SHIVS.
...I'LL LET HER KNOW THEY DIDN'T WORK.
CARTER SLADE'S SPIRIT GUNS. FOUND THEM ON EBAY.
YOU'RE WASTING YOUR TIME.
NO. I'M BUYING IT.
UNF!

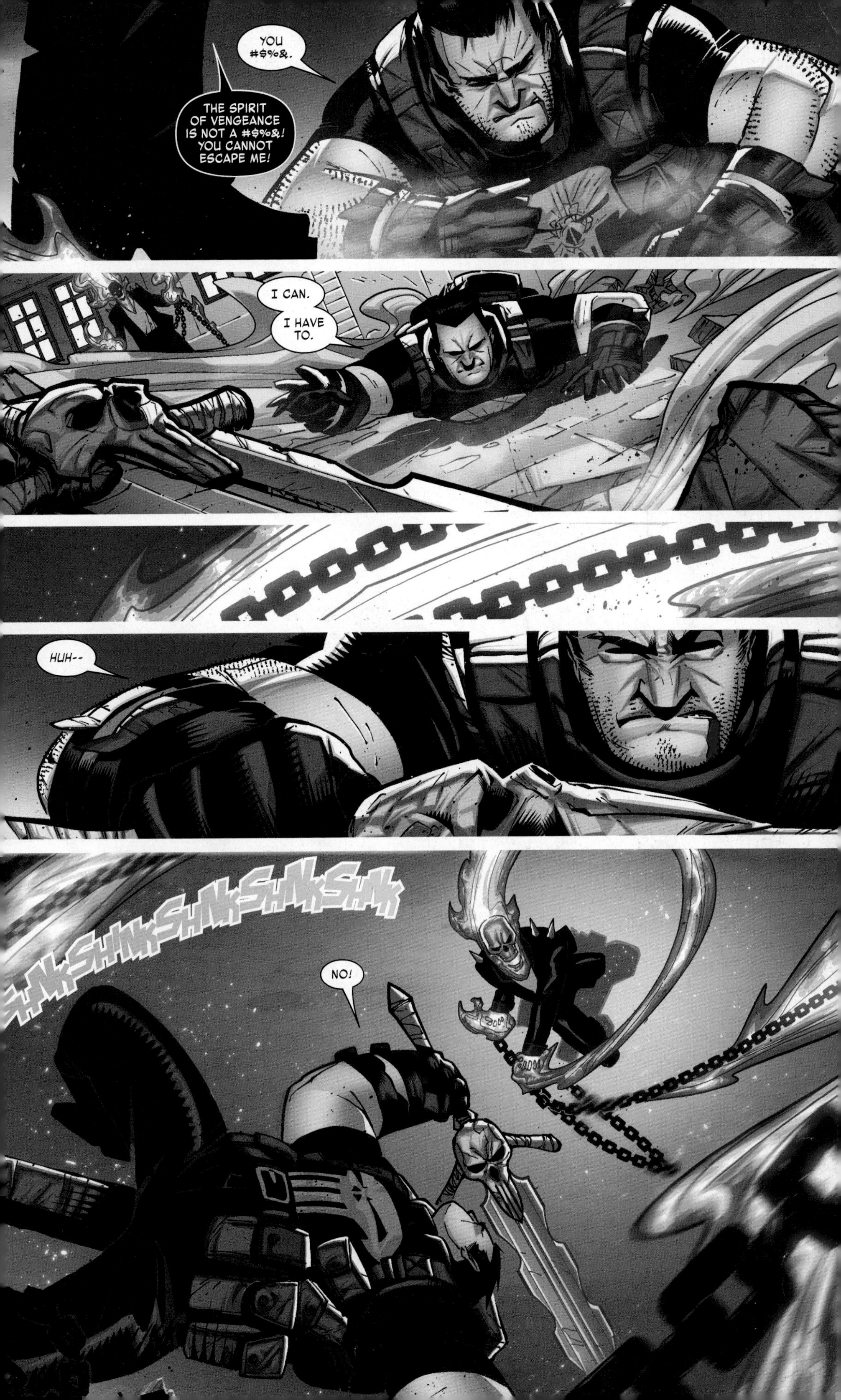
YOU #$%&.
THE SPIRIT OF VENGEANCE IS NOT A #$%&! YOU CANNOT ESCAPE ME!
I CAN.
I HAVE TO.
HUH--
SHNK SHNK SHNK SHNK SHNK
NO!

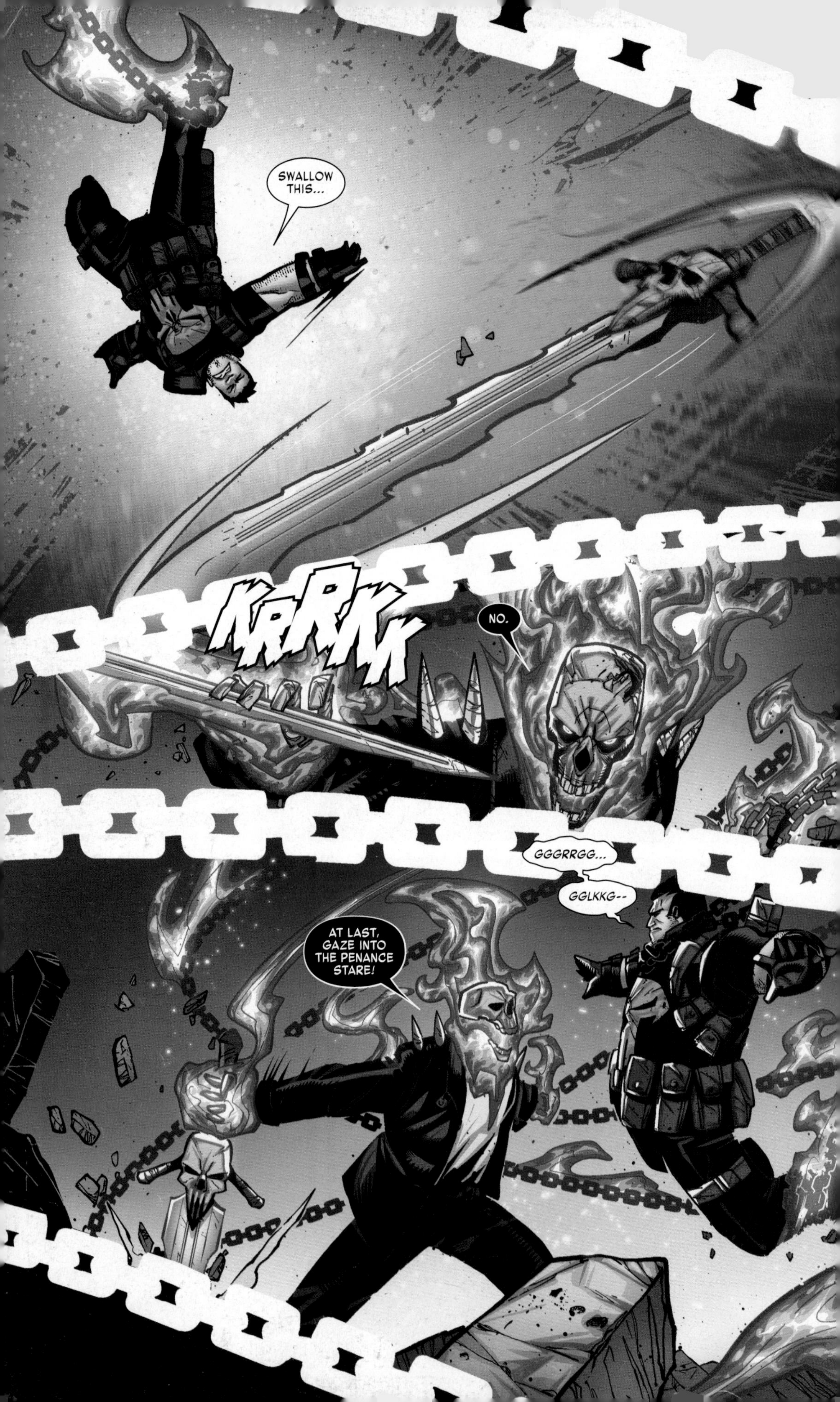
SWALLOW THIS...
KRRKK
NO.
GGGRRGG...
GGLKKG--
AT LAST, GAZE INTO THE PENANCE STARE!

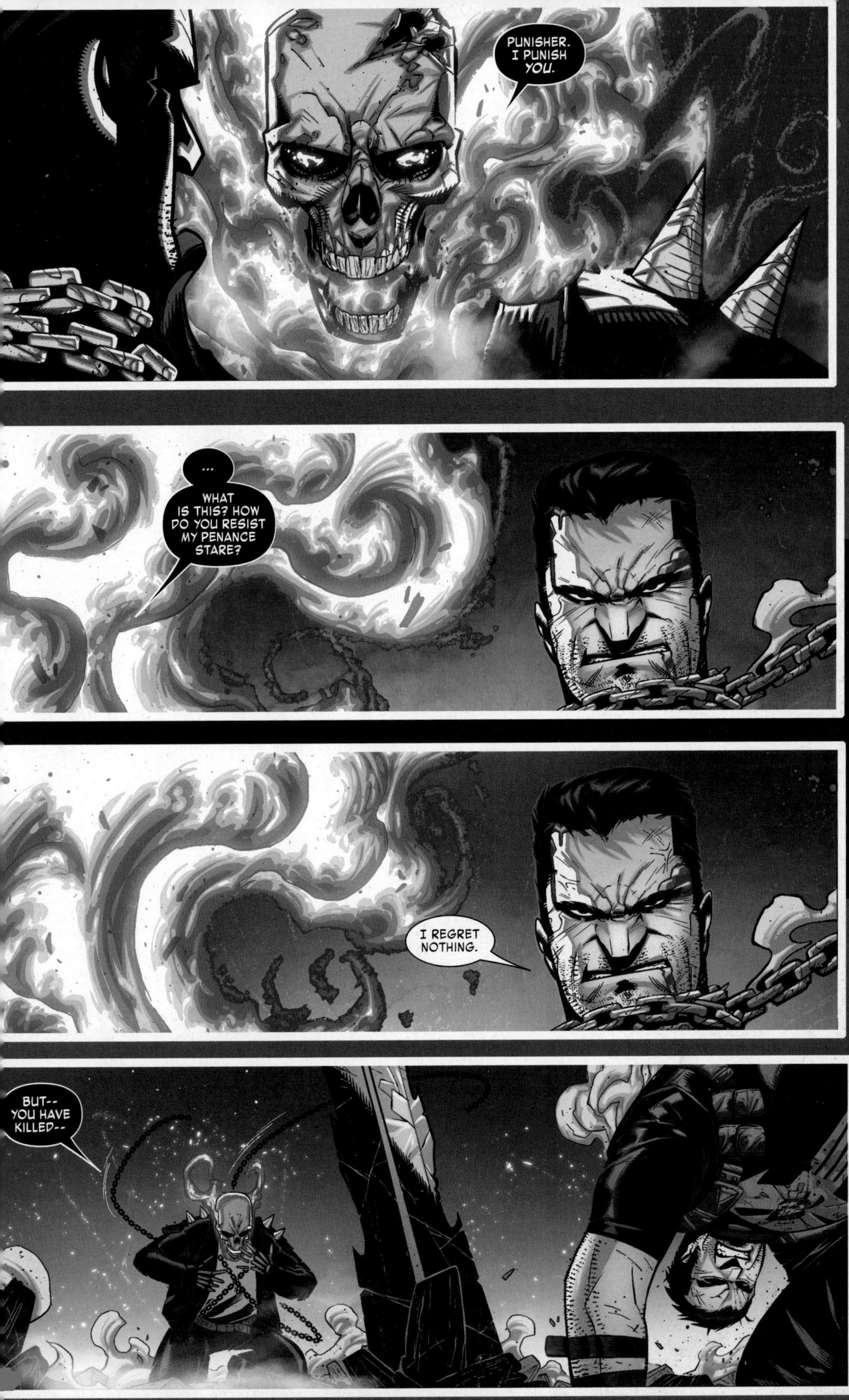
PUNISHER. I PUNISH YOU.
...
WHAT IS THIS? HOW DO YOU RESIST MY PENANCE STARE?
I REGRET NOTHING.
BUT-- YOU HAVE KILLED--

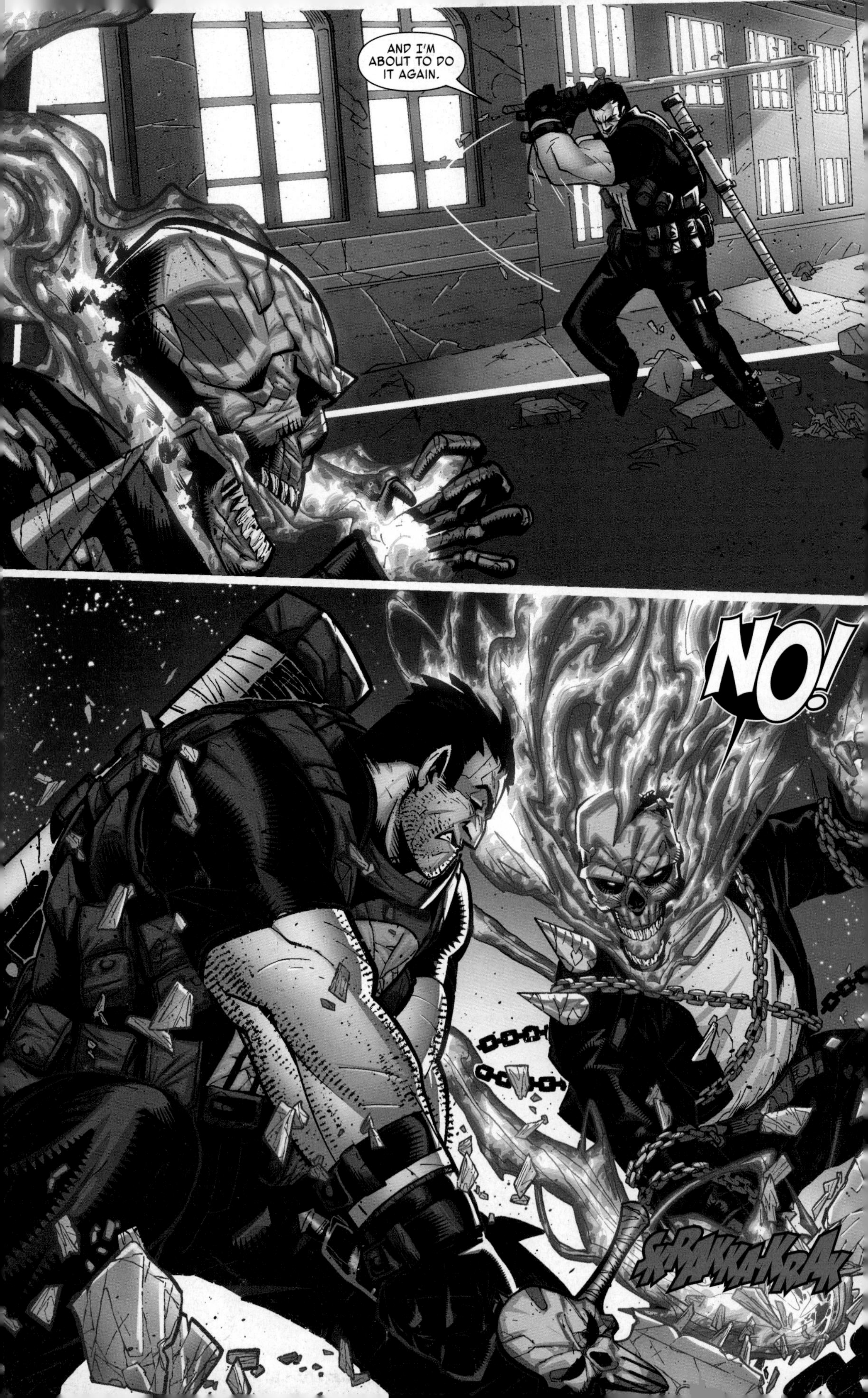
AND I'M ABOUT TO DO IT AGAIN.
NO!
SKRAKKAKKRAK

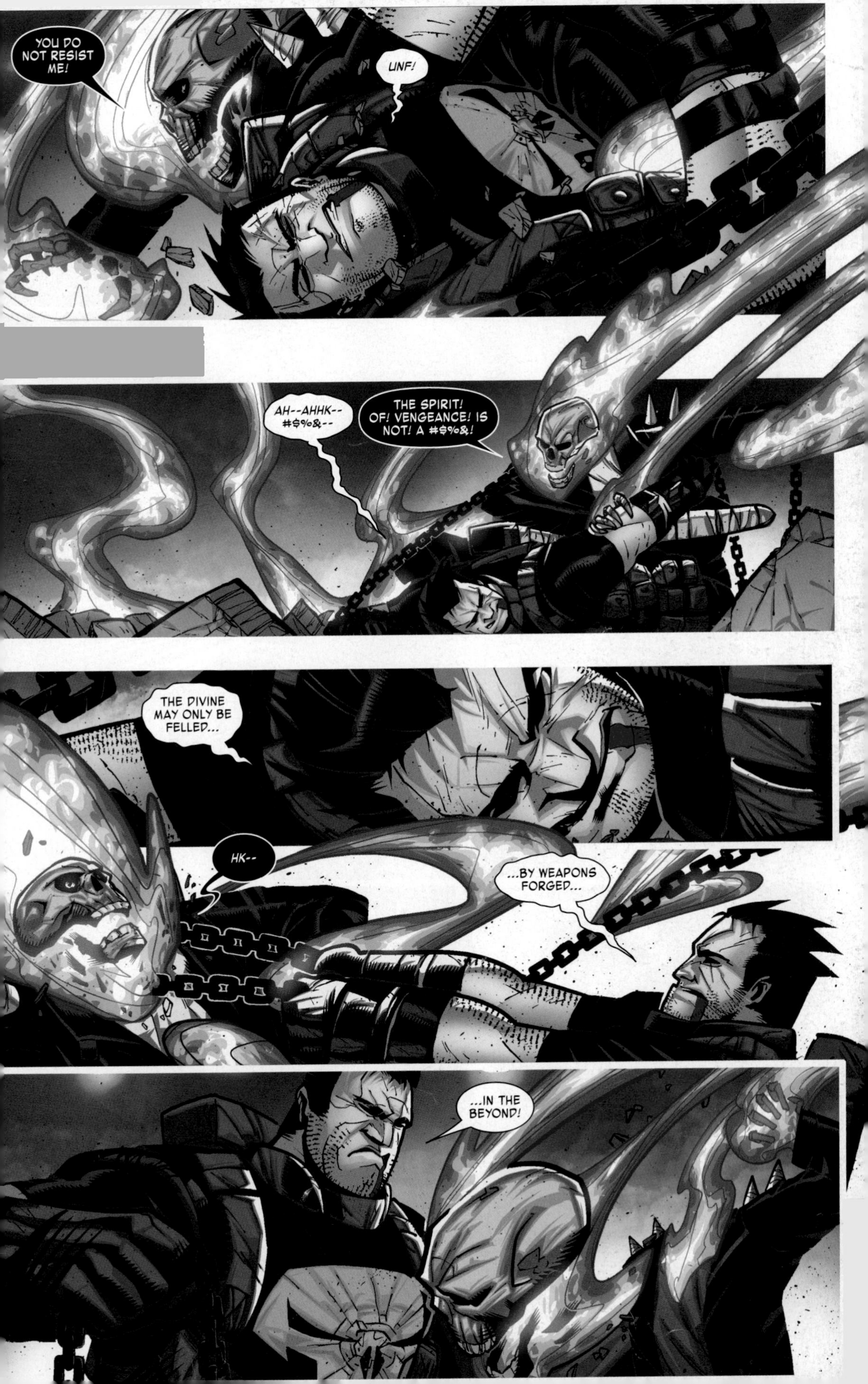
YOU DO NOT RESIST ME!
UNF!
AH--AHHK-- #$%&--
THE SPIRIT! OF! VENGEANCE! IS NOT! A #$%&!
THE DIVINE MAY ONLY BE FELLED...
HK--
...BY WEAPONS FORGED...
...IN THE BEYOND!

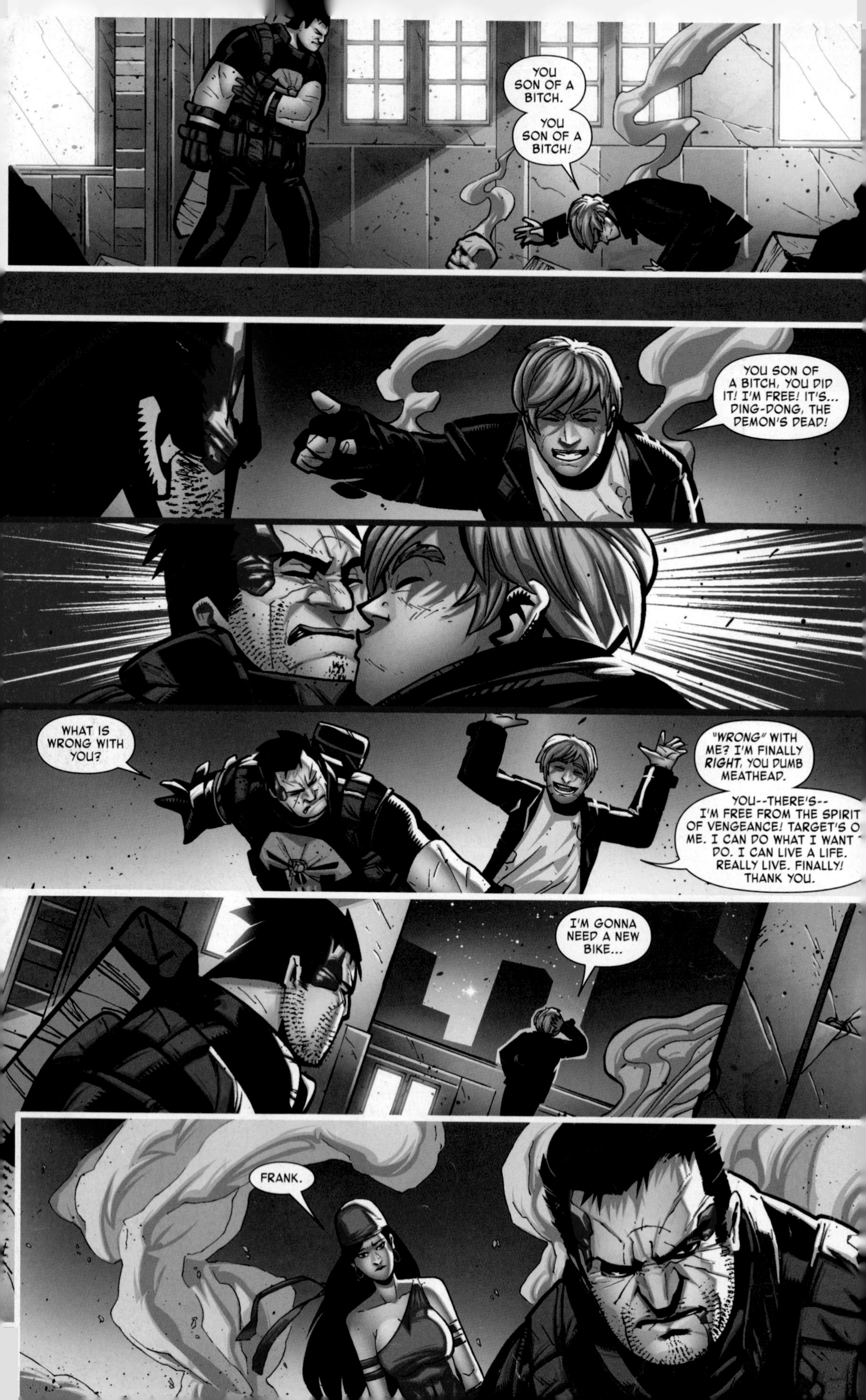
YOU SON OF A BITCH.
YOU SON OF A BITCH!
YOU SON OF A BITCH, YOU DID IT! I'M FREE! IT'S... DING-DONG, THE DEMON'S DEAD!
WHAT IS WRONG WITH YOU?
"WRONG" WITH ME? I'M FINALLY RIGHT, YOU DUMB MEATHEAD.
YOU--THERE'S-- I'M FREE FROM THE SPIRIT OF VENGEANCE! TARGET'S O
ME. I CAN DO WHAT I WANT
DO. I CAN LIVE A LIFE. REALLY LIVE. FINALLY! THANK YOU.
I'M GONNA NEED A NEW BIKE...
FRANK.

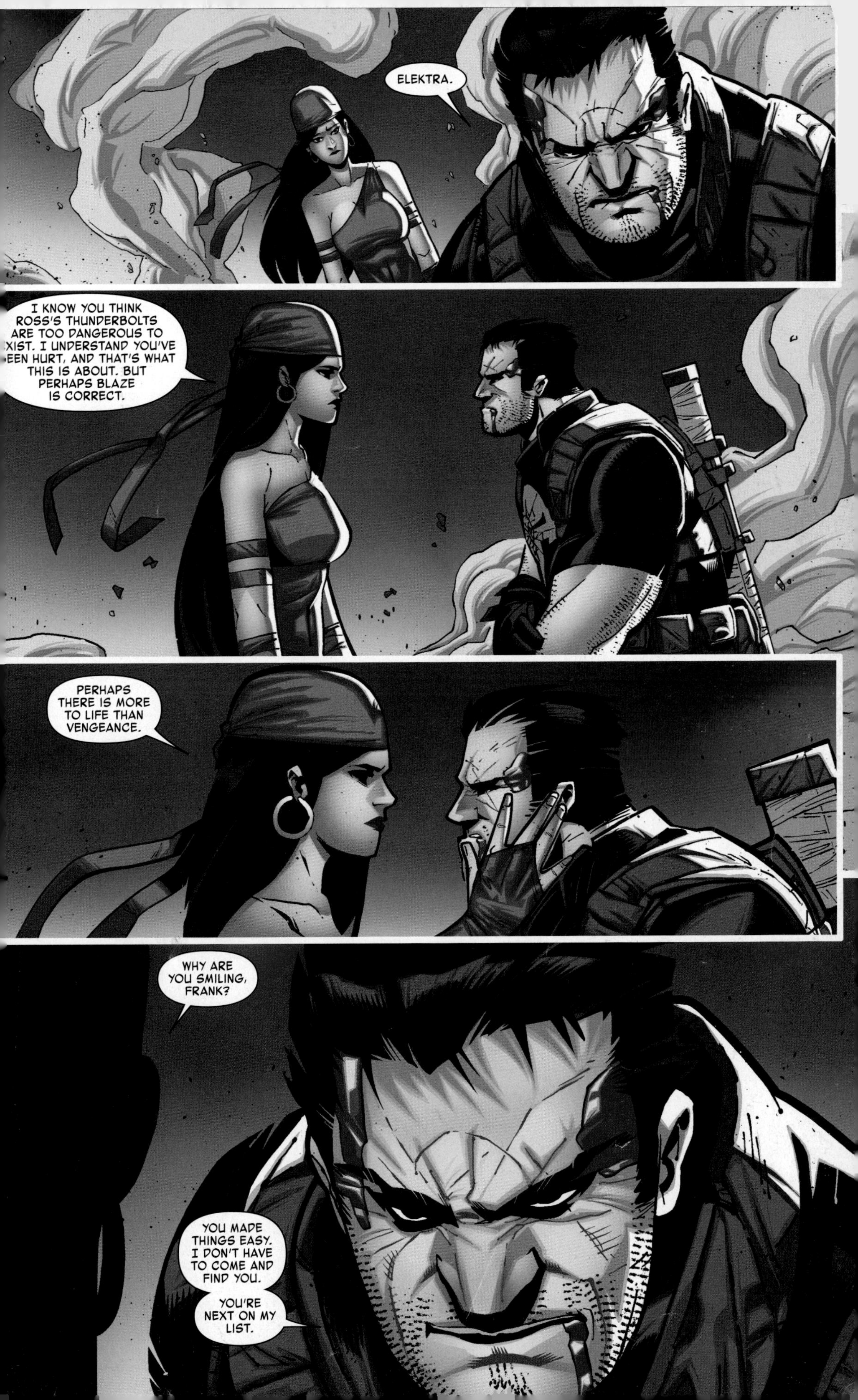
ELEKTRA.
I KNOW YOU THINK ROSS'S THUNDERBOLTS ARE TOO DANGEROUS TO XIST. I UNDERSTAND YOU'VE EEN HURT, AND THAT'S WHAT THIS IS ABOUT. BUT PERHAPS BLAZE IS CORRECT.
PERHAPS THERE IS MORE TO LIFE THAN VENGEANCE.
WHY ARE YOU SMILING, FRANK?
YOU MADE THINGS EASY. I DON'T HAVE TO COME AND FIND YOU.
YOU'RE NEXT ON MY LIST.

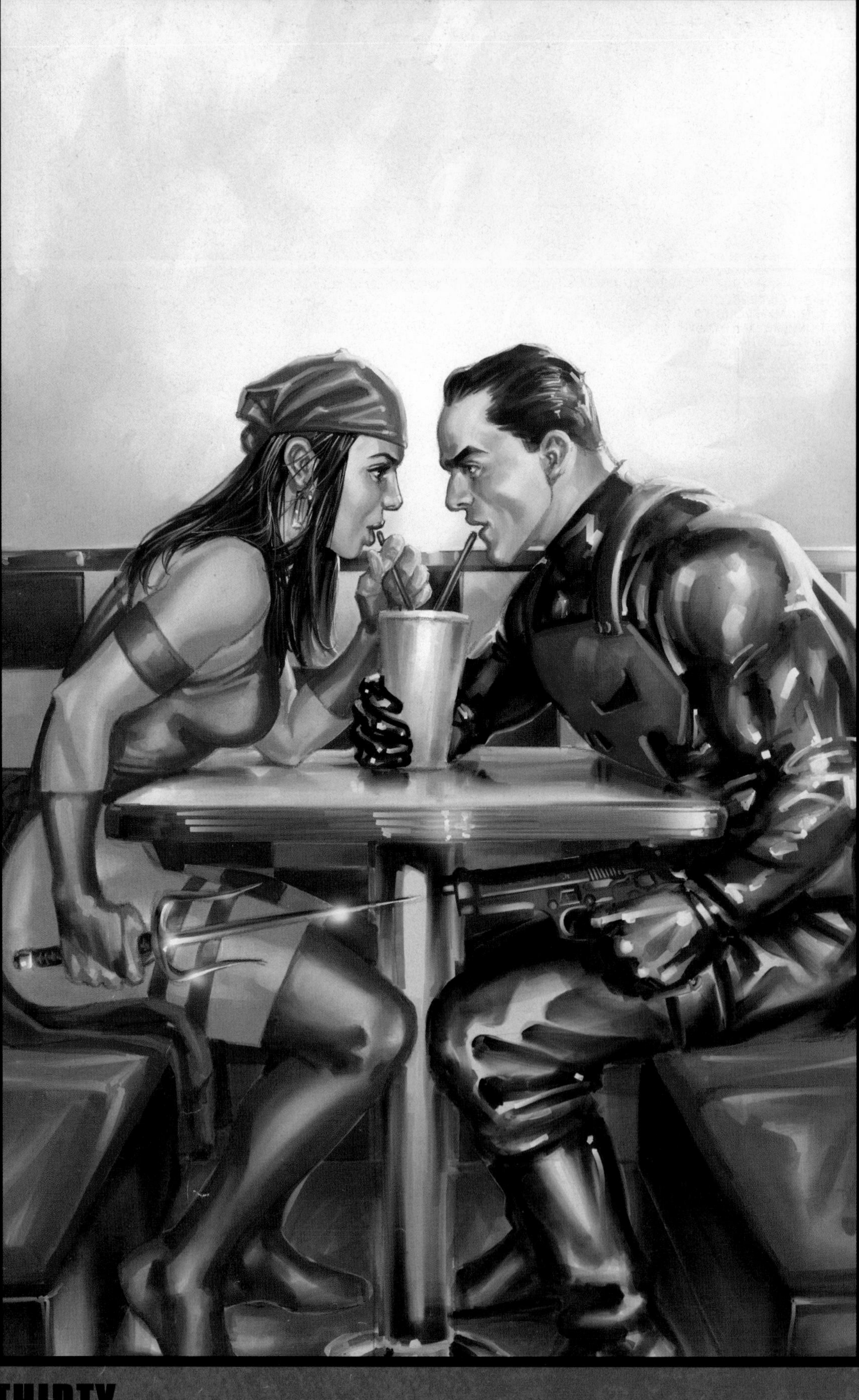

THIRTY

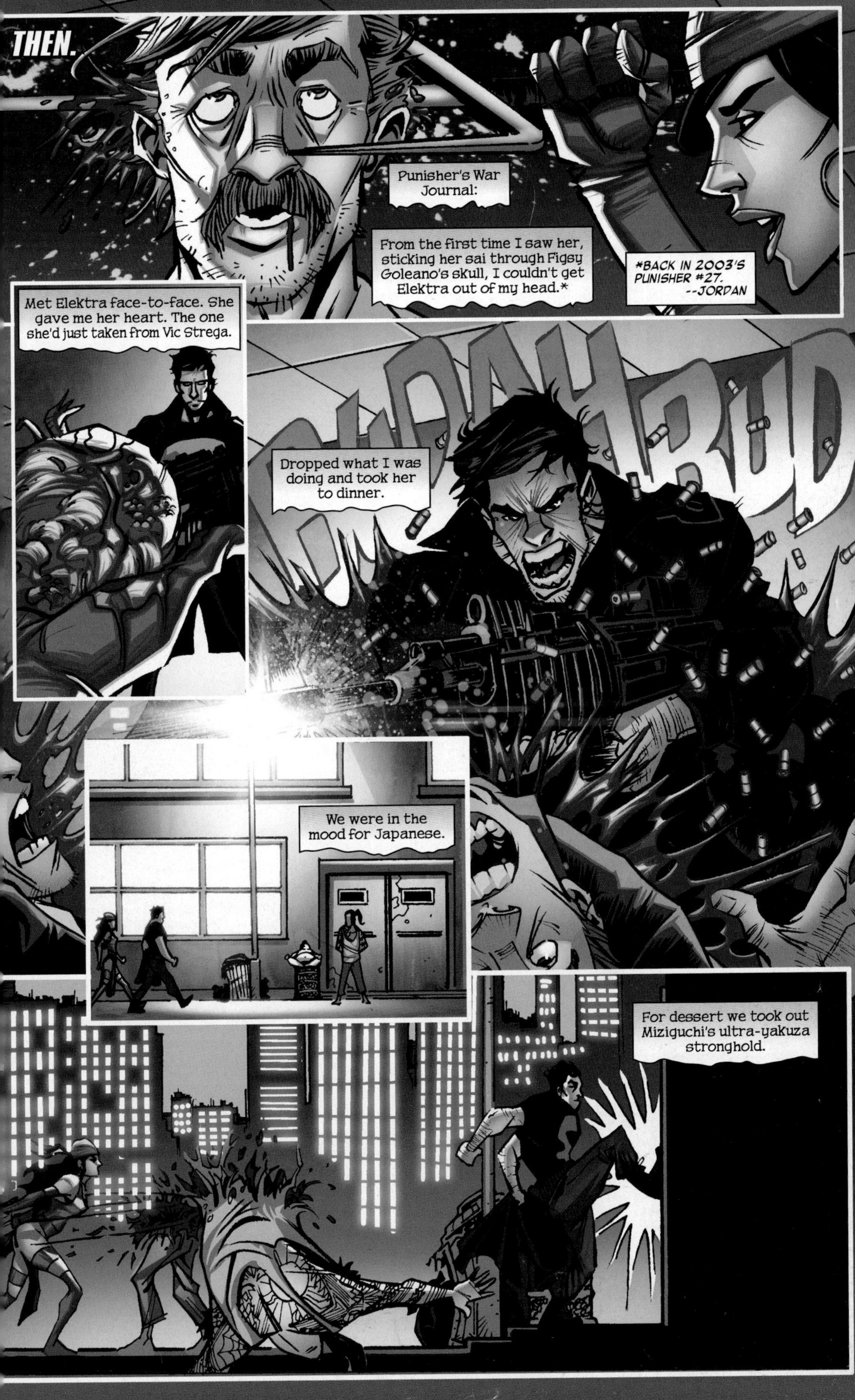
THEN.
Punisher's War Journal:
From the first time I saw her, sticking her sai through Figsy Goleano's skull, I couldn't get Elektra out of my head.*
*BACK IN 2003'S PUNISHER #27. --JORDAN
Met Elektra face-to-face. She gave me her heart. The one she'd just taken from Vic Strega.
Dropped what I was doing and took her to dinner.
We were in the mood for Japanese.
For dessert we took out Miziguchi's ultra-yakuza stronghold.

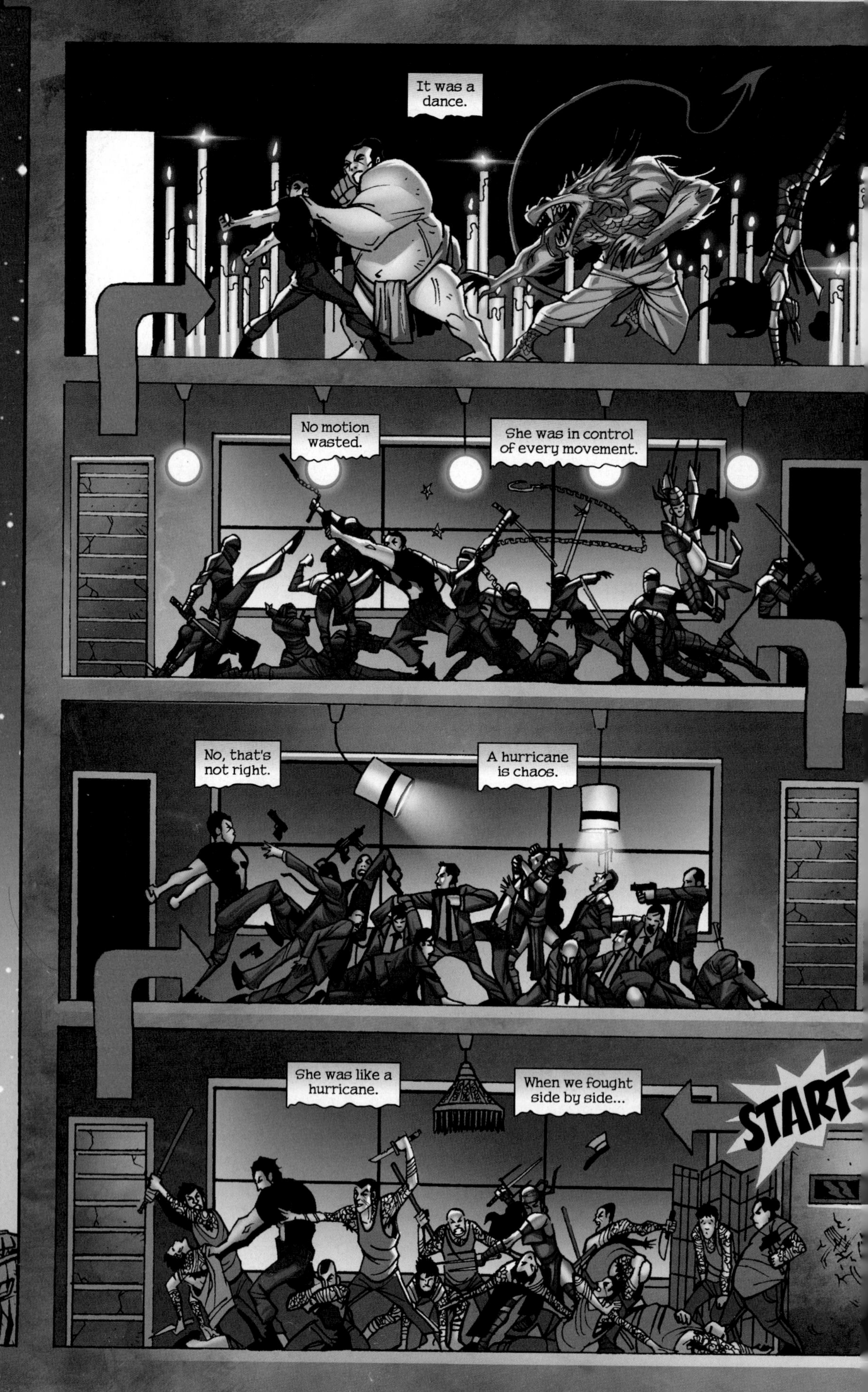
START
When we fought side by side...
She was like a hurricane.
No, that's not right.
A hurricane is chaos.
She was in control of every movement.
No motion wasted.
It was a dance.

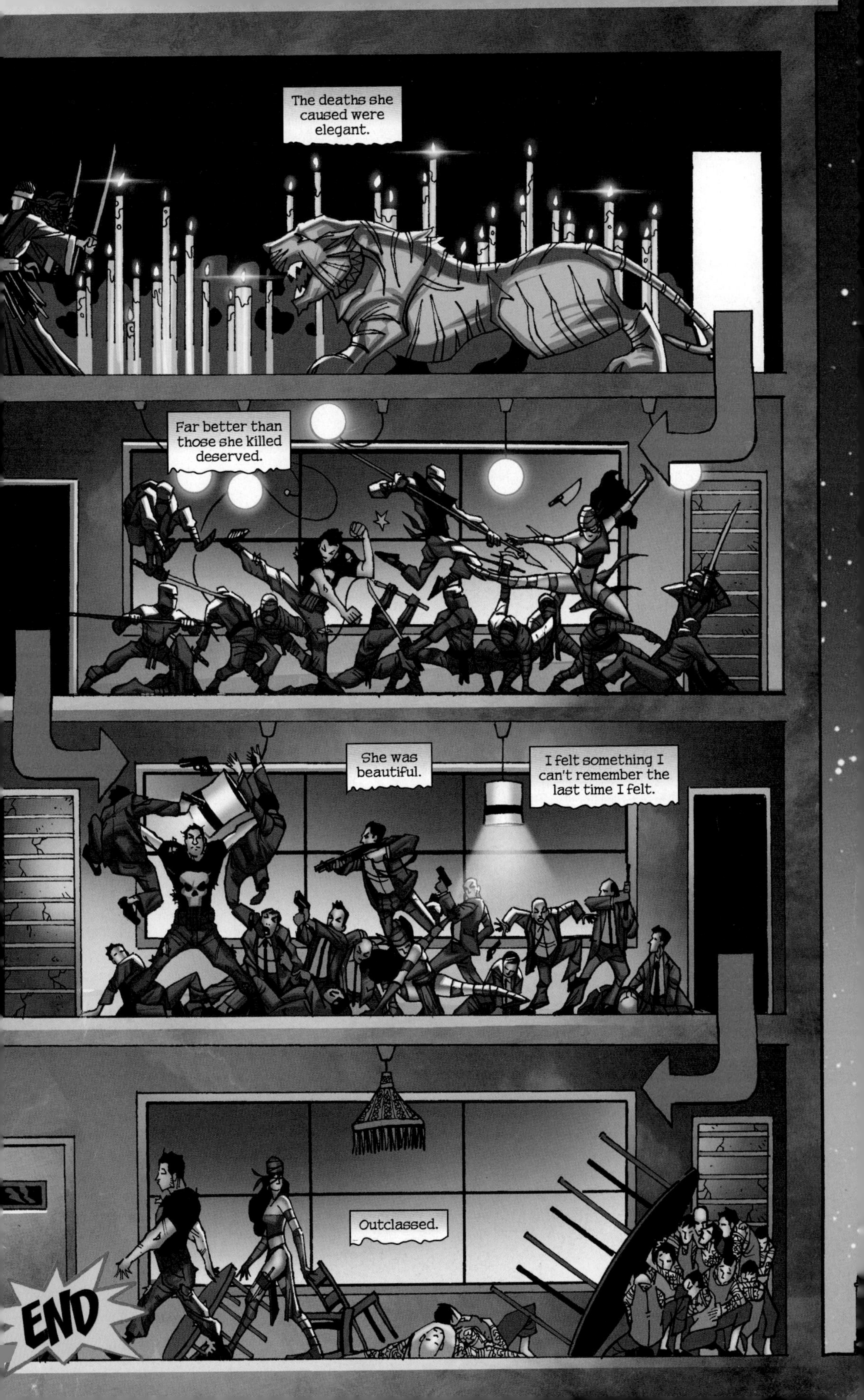
The deaths she caused were elegant.
Far better than those she killed deserved.
She was beautiful.
I felt something I can't remember the last time I felt.
Outclassed.
END

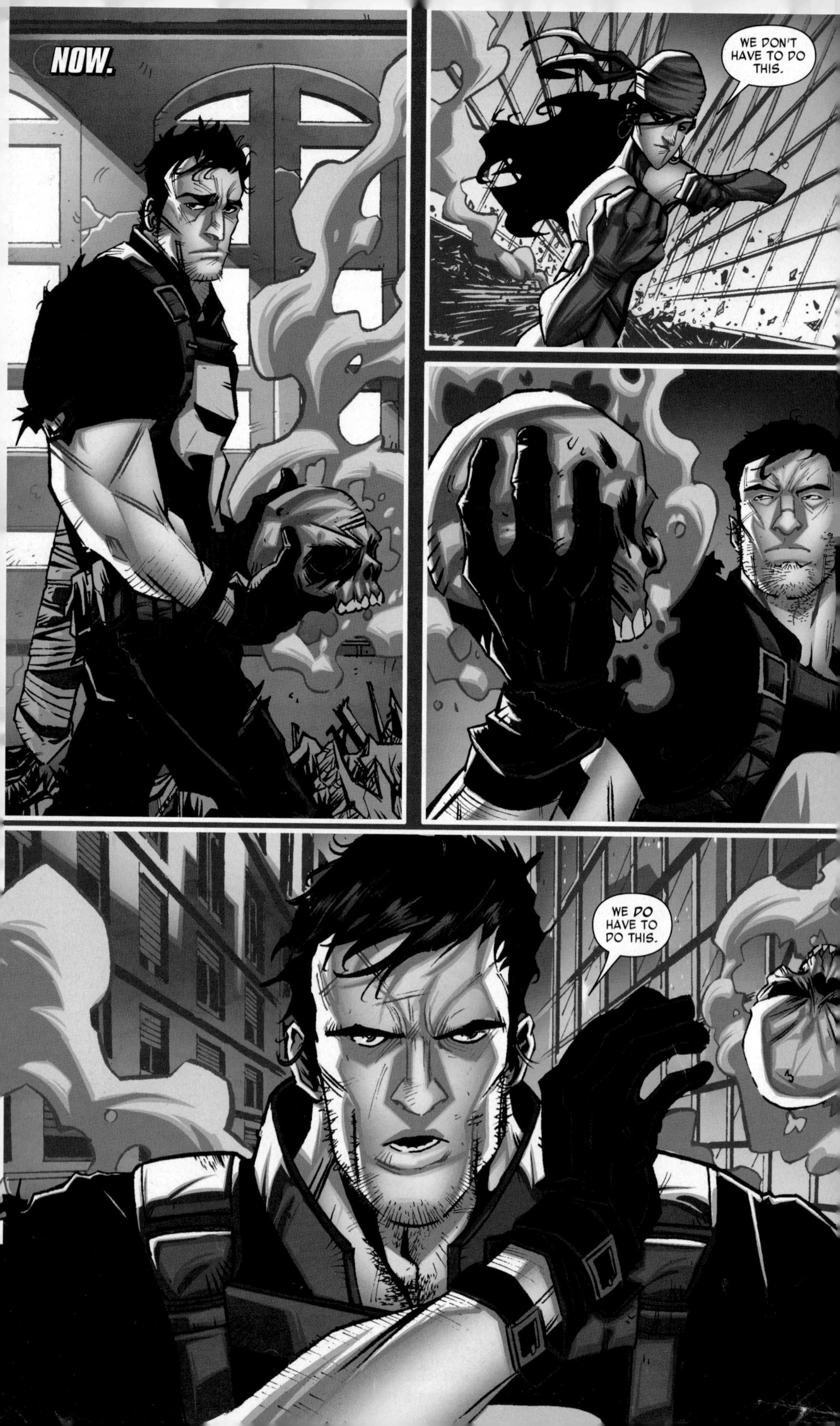
NOW.
WE DON'T HAVE TO DO THIS.
WE DO HAVE TO DO THIS.

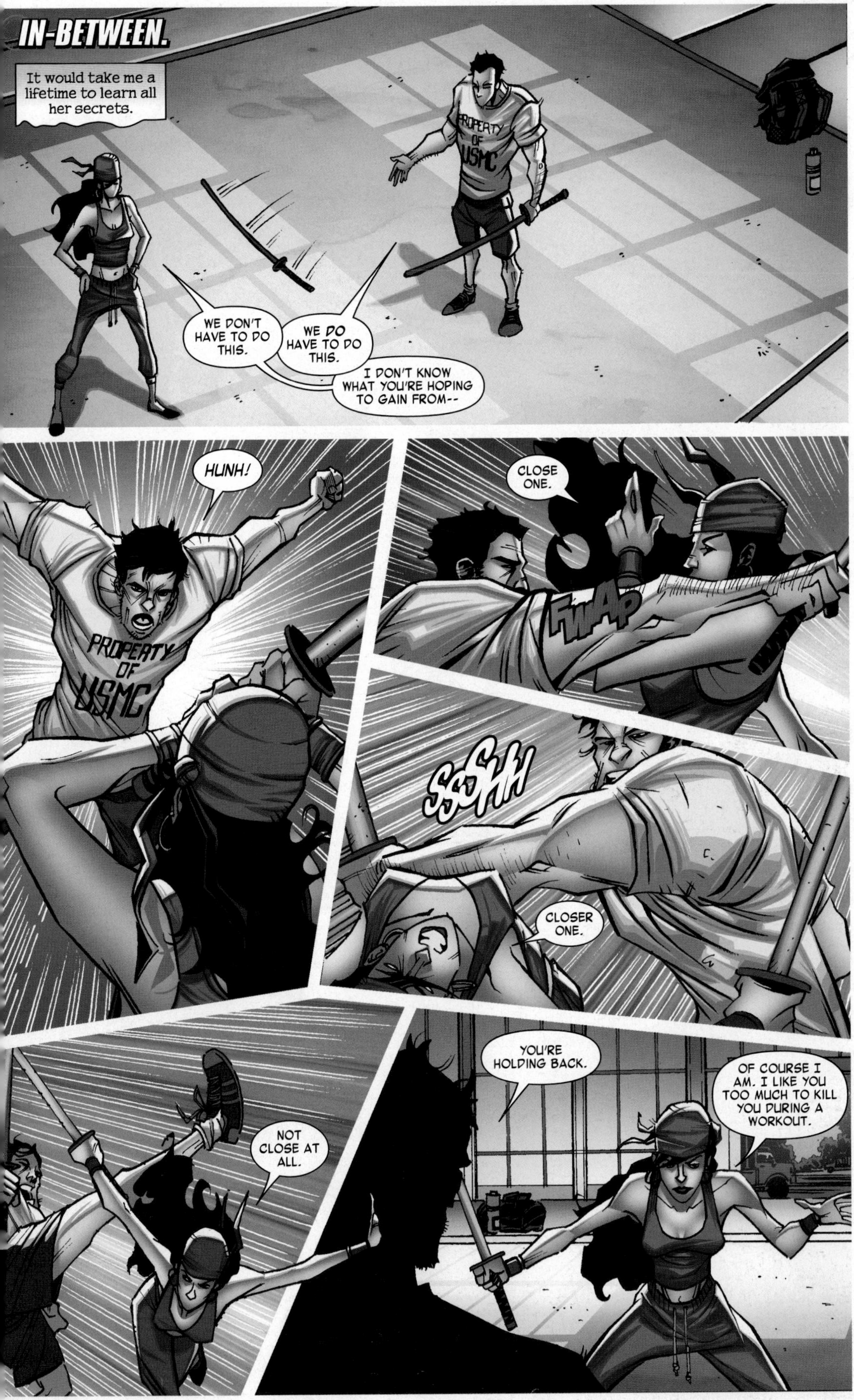
IN-BETWEEN.
It would take me a lifetime to learn all her secrets.
WE DON'T HAVE TO DO THIS.
WE DO HAVE TO DO THIS.
I DON'T KNOW WHAT YOU'RE HOPING TO GAIN FROM--
PROPERTY OF USMC
HUNH!
CLOSE ONE.
FWAP
SSSHH
CLOSER ONE.
NOT CLOSE AT ALL.
YOU'RE HOLDING BACK.
OF COURSE I AM. I LIKE YOU TOO MUCH TO KILL YOU DURING A WORKOUT.

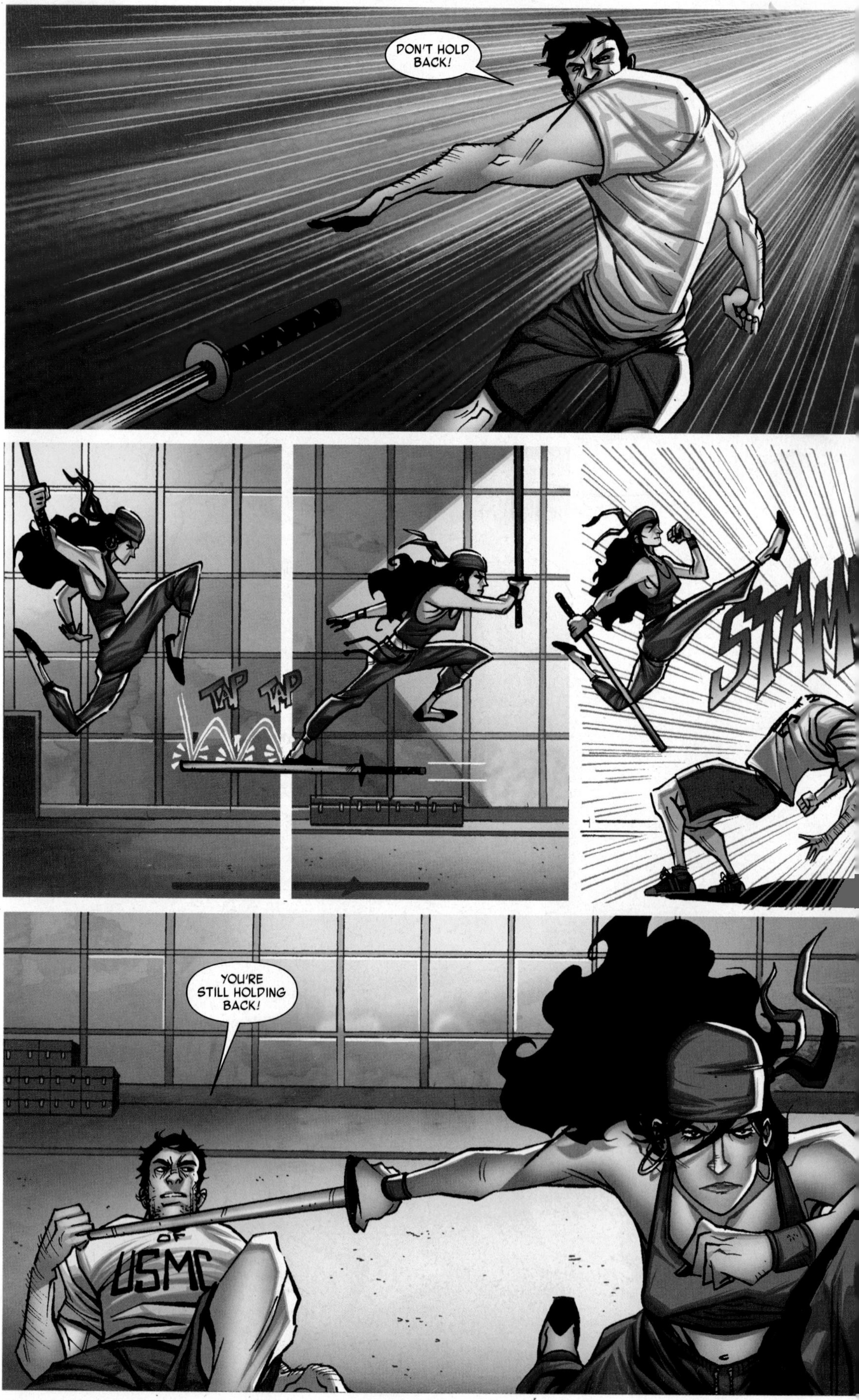
DON'T HOLD BACK!
TAP
TAP
STAM
YOU'RE STILL HOLDING BACK!
OF
USMC

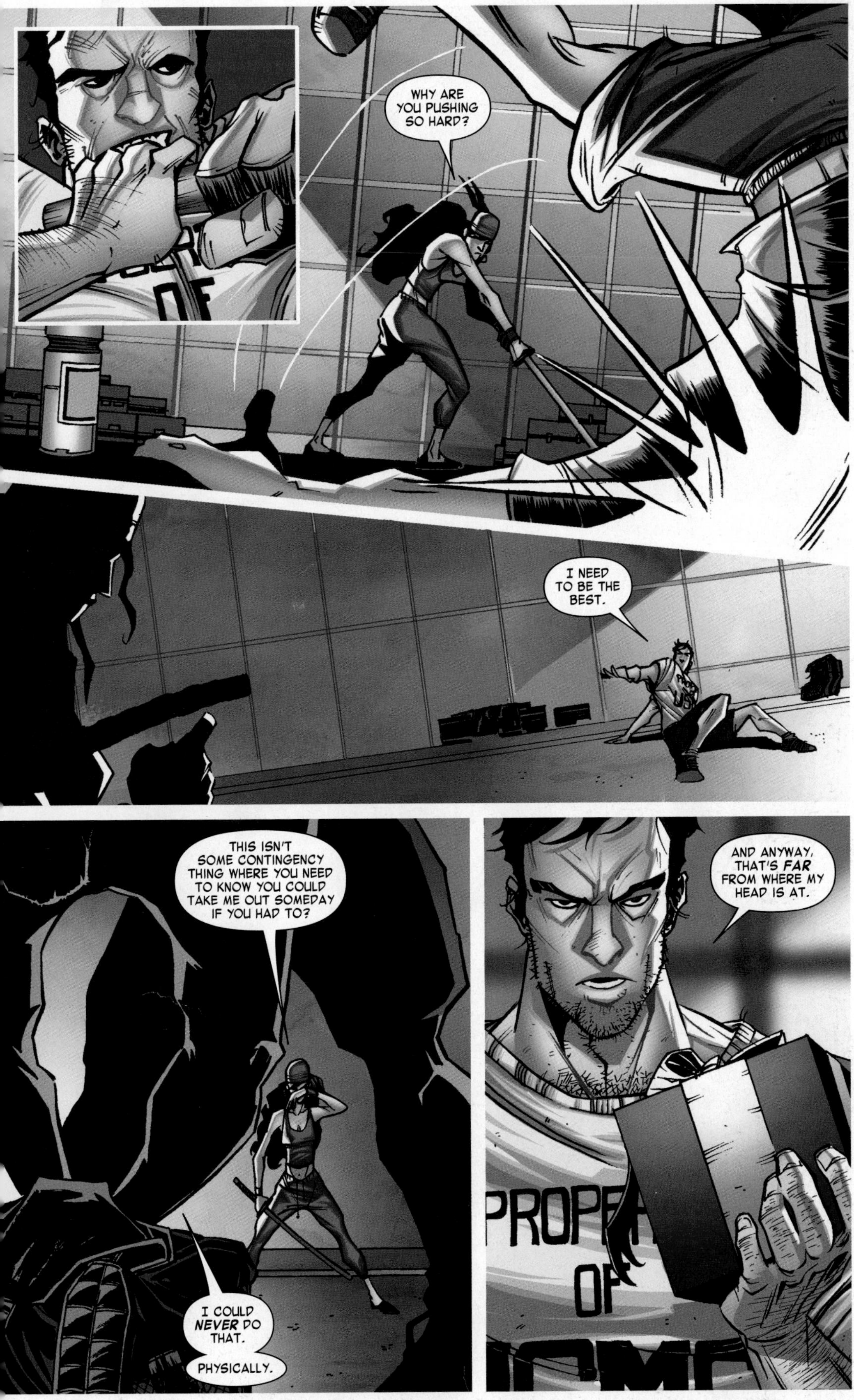

WHY ARE YOU PUSHING SO HARD?
I NEED TO BE THE BEST.
THIS ISN'T SOME CONTINGENCY THING WHERE YOU NEED TO KNOW YOU COULD TAKE ME OUT SOMEDAY IF YOU HAD TO?
I COULD NEVER DO THAT.
PHYSICALLY.
AND ANYWAY, THAT'S FAR FROM WHERE MY HEAD IS AT.

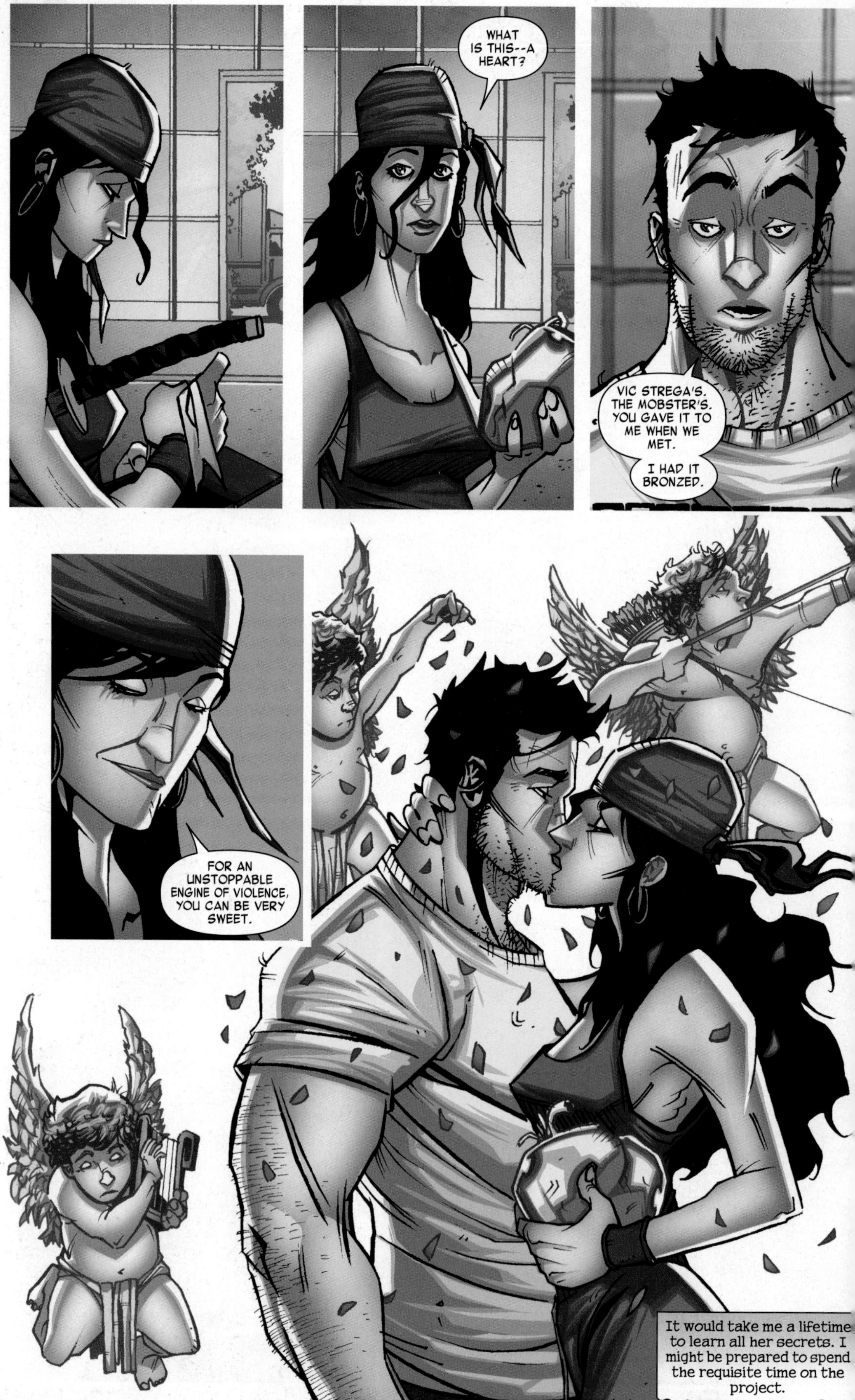
WHAT IS THIS--A HEART?
VIC STREGA'S. THE MOBSTER'S. YOU GAVE IT TO ME WHEN WE MET.
I HAD IT BRONZED.
FOR AN UNSTOPPABLE ENGINE OF VIOLENCE, YOU CAN BE VERY SWEET.
It would take me a lifetime to learn all her secrets. I might be prepared to spend the requisite time on the project.

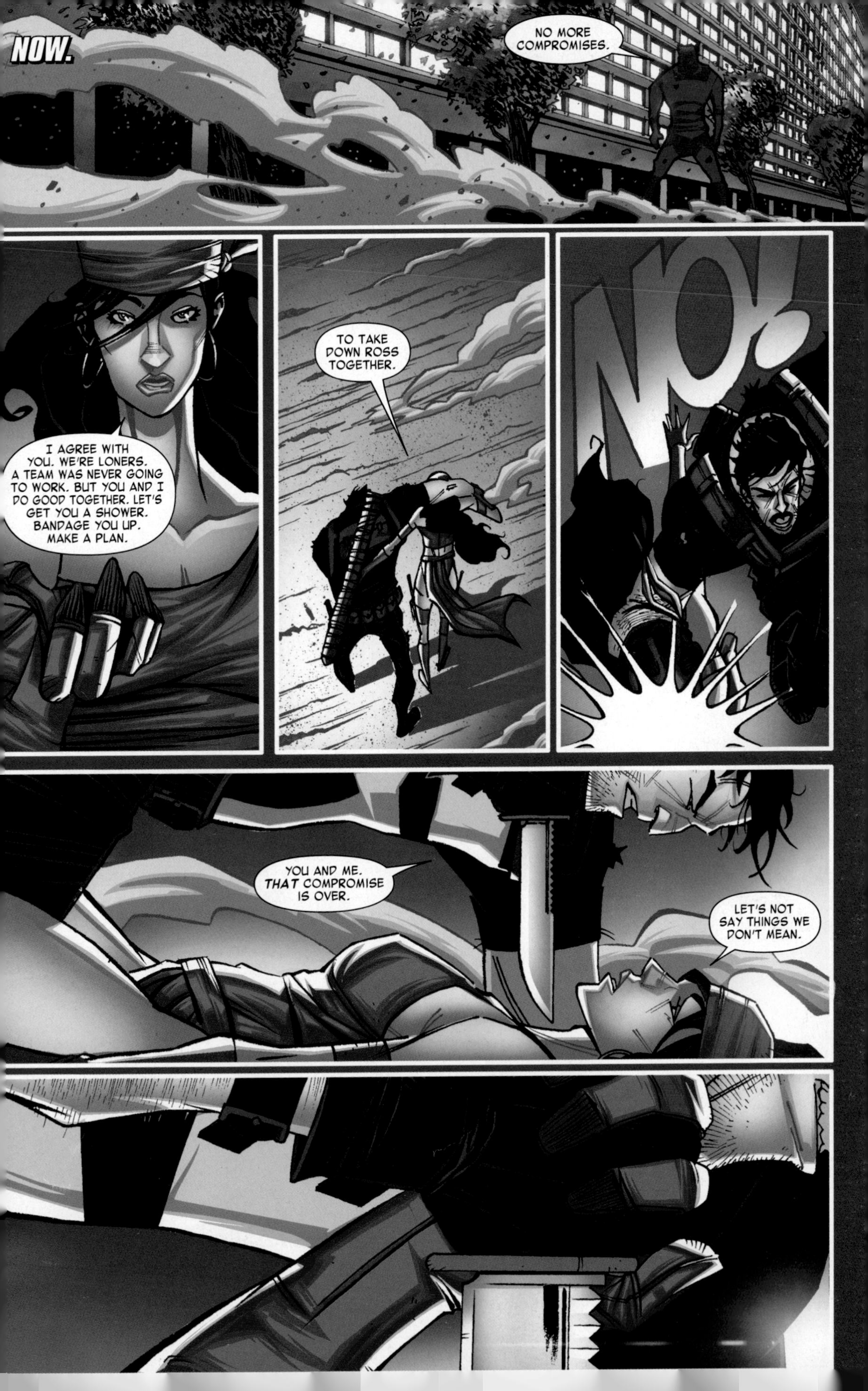
NOW.
NO MORE COMPROMISES.
I AGREE WITH YOU. WE'RE LONERS. A TEAM WAS NEVER GOING TO WORK. BUT YOU AND I DO GOOD TOGETHER. LET'S GET YOU A SHOWER. BANDAGE YOU UP. MAKE A PLAN.
TO TAKE DOWN ROSS TOGETHER.
NO!
YOU AND ME. *THAT* COMPROMISE IS OVER.
LET'S NOT SAY THINGS WE DON'T MEAN.

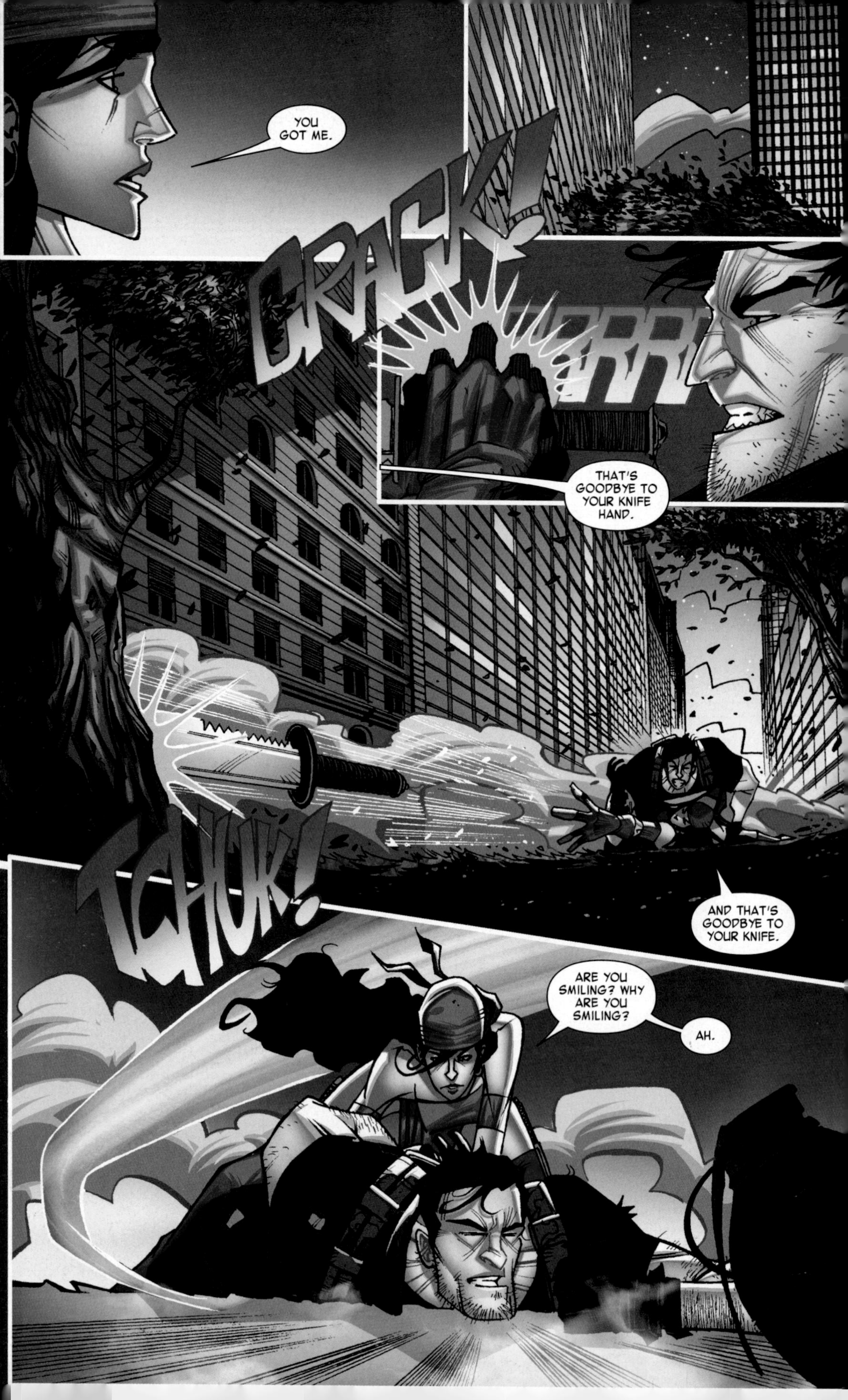
YOU GOT ME.
CRACK!
THAT'S GOODBYE TO YOUR KNIFE HAND.
TCHUK!
AND THAT'S GOODBYE TO YOUR KNIFE.
ARE YOU SMILING? WHY ARE YOU SMILING?
AH.

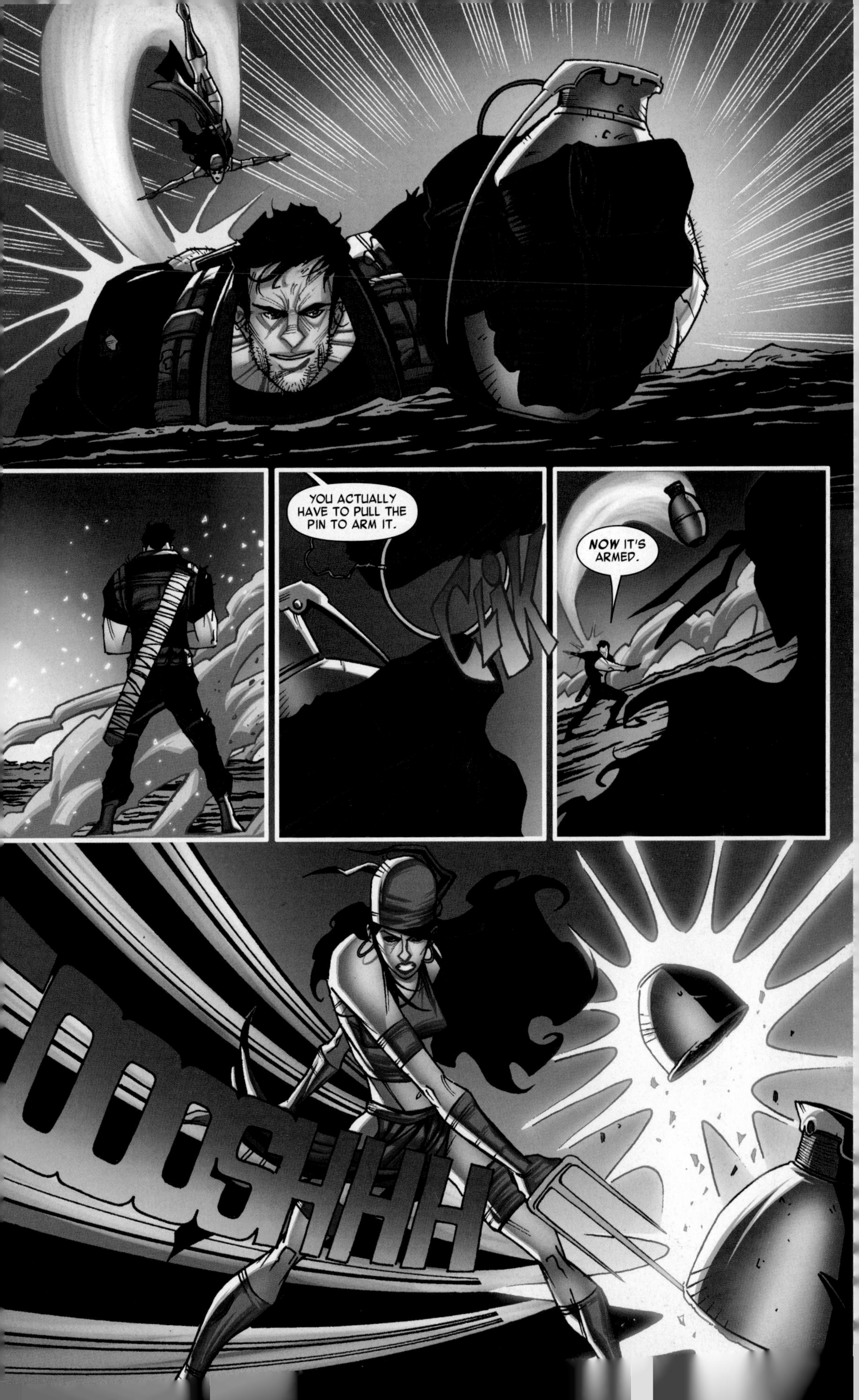
YOU ACTUALLY HAVE TO PULL THE PIN TO ARM IT.
CLIK
NOW IT'S ARMED.
WOOSHHH

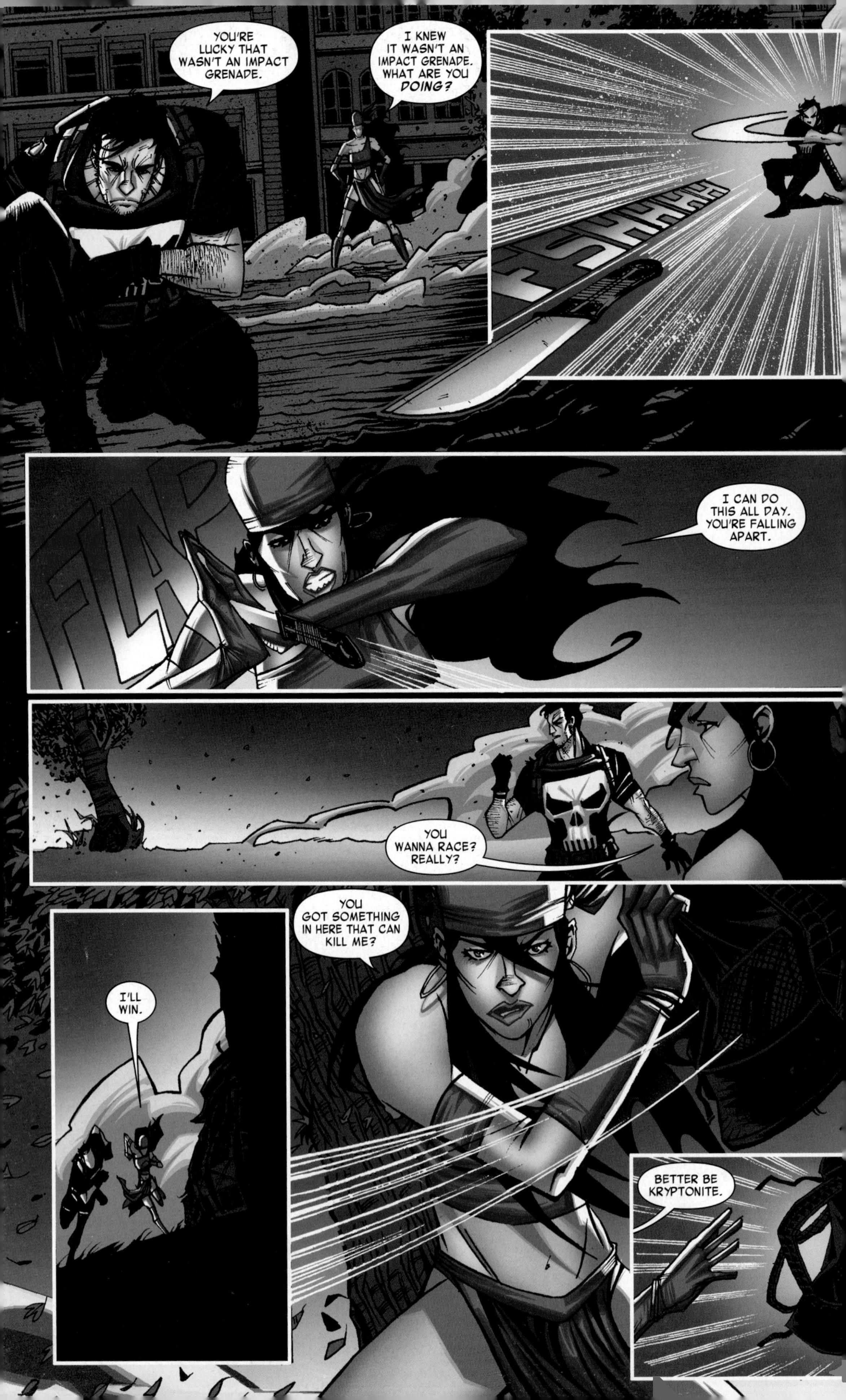
YOU'RE LUCKY THAT WASN'T AN IMPACT GRENADE.
I KNEW IT WASN'T AN IMPACT GRENADE. WHAT ARE YOU DOING?
FSHHHHH
FLAP
I CAN DO THIS ALL DAY. YOU'RE FALLING APART.
YOU WANNA RACE? REALLY?
YOU GOT SOMETHING IN HERE THAT CAN KILL ME?
I'LL WIN.
BETTER BE KRYPTONITE.

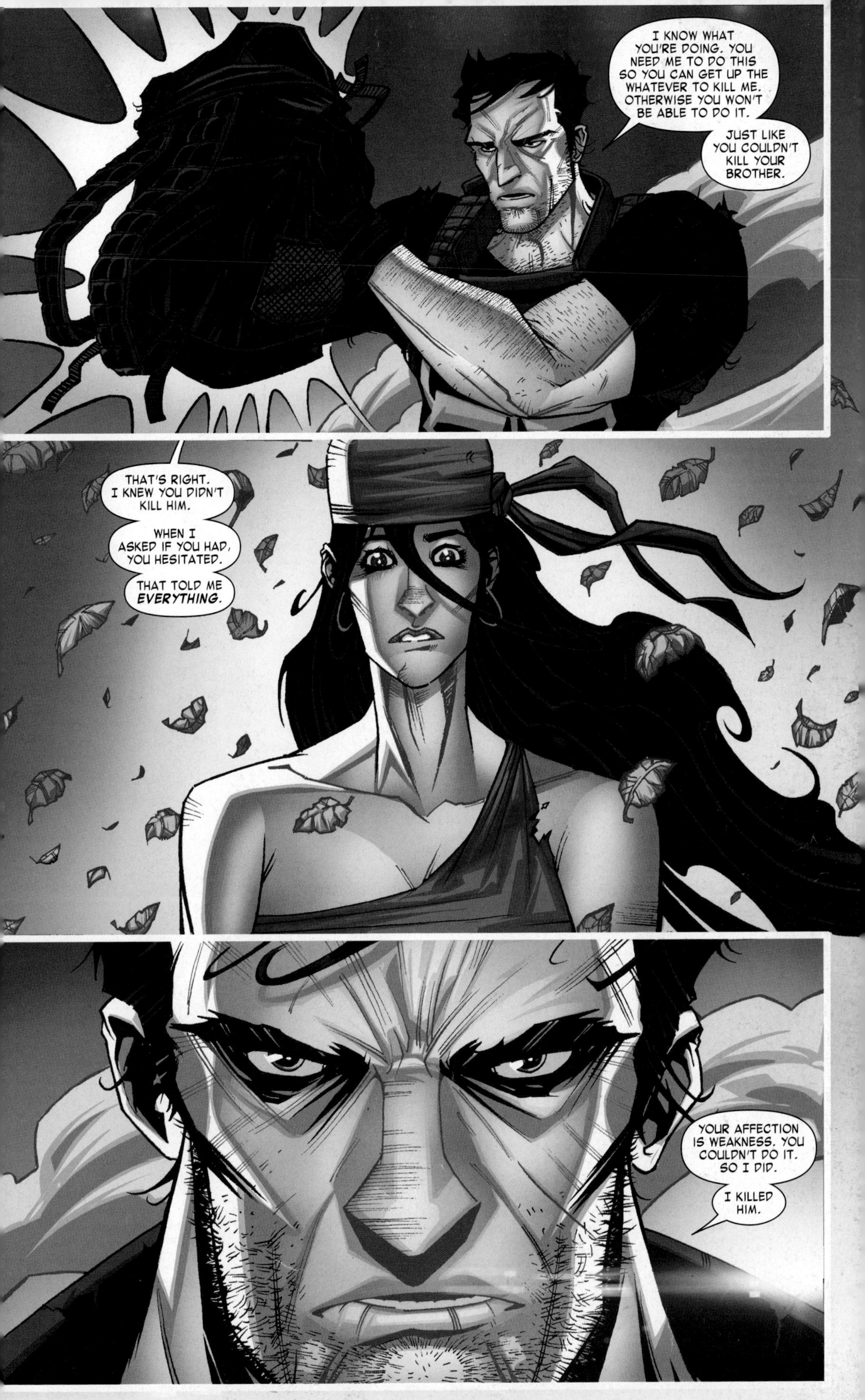
I KNOW WHAT YOU'RE DOING. YOU NEED ME TO DO THIS SO YOU CAN GET UP THE WHATEVER TO KILL ME. OTHERWISE YOU WON'T BE ABLE TO DO IT.
JUST LIKE YOU COULDN'T KILL YOUR BROTHER.
THAT'S RIGHT. I KNEW YOU DIDN'T KILL HIM.
WHEN I ASKED IF YOU HAD, YOU HESITATED.
THAT TOLD ME *EVERYTHING*.
YOUR AFFECTION IS WEAKNESS. YOU COULDN'T DO IT. SO I DID.
I KILLED HIM.

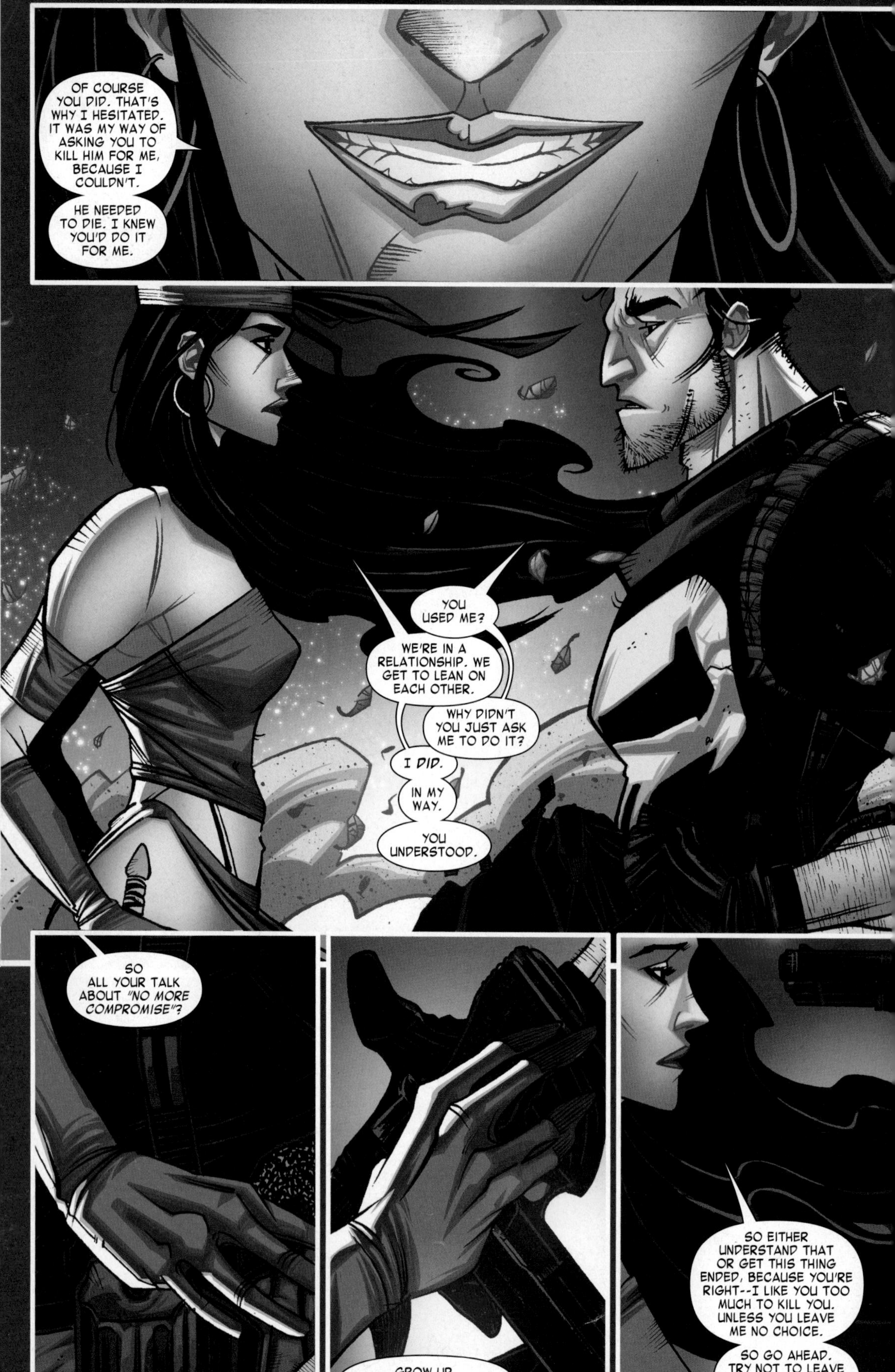
OF COURSE YOU DID. THAT'S WHY I HESITATED. IT WAS MY WAY OF ASKING YOU TO KILL HIM FOR ME, BECAUSE I COULDN'T.
HE NEEDED TO DIE. I KNEW YOU'D DO IT FOR ME.
YOU USED ME?
WE'RE IN A RELATIONSHIP. WE GET TO LEAN ON EACH OTHER.
WHY DIDN'T YOU JUST ASK ME TO DO IT?
I *DID*.
IN MY WAY.
YOU UNDERSTOOD.
SO ALL YOUR TALK ABOUT "NO MORE COMPROMISE"?
GROW UP. BECAUSE RELATIONSHIPS MEAN COMPROMISE.
SO EITHER UNDERSTAND THAT OR GET THIS THING ENDED, BECAUSE YOU'RE RIGHT--I LIKE YOU TOO MUCH TO KILL YOU. UNLESS YOU LEAVE ME NO CHOICE.
SO GO AHEAD. TRY NOT TO LEAVE ME ANY CHOICE. SEE WHAT HAPPENS TO YOU.

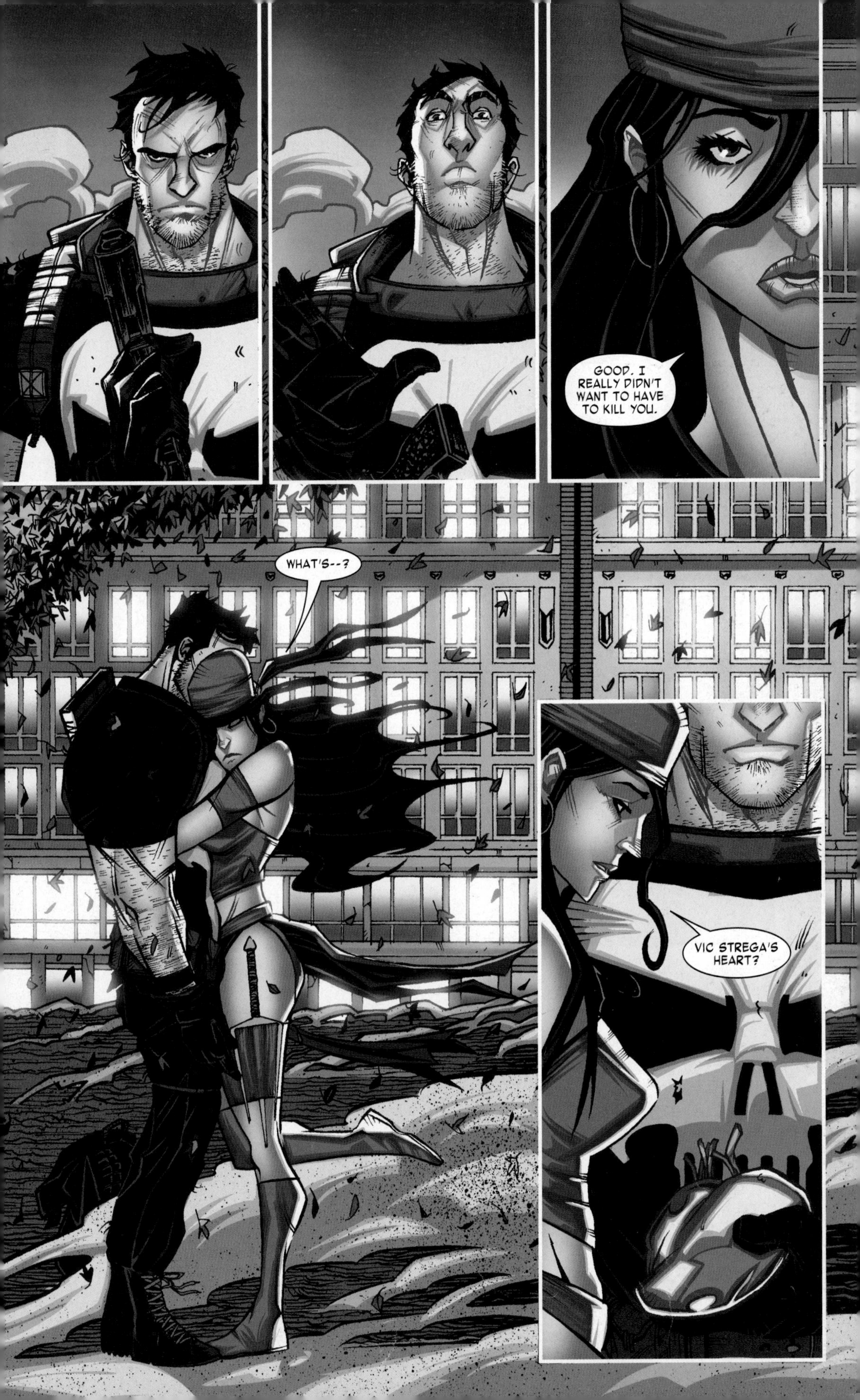
GOOD. I REALLY DIDN'T WANT TO HAVE TO KILL YOU.
WHAT'S--?
VIC STREGA'S HEART?

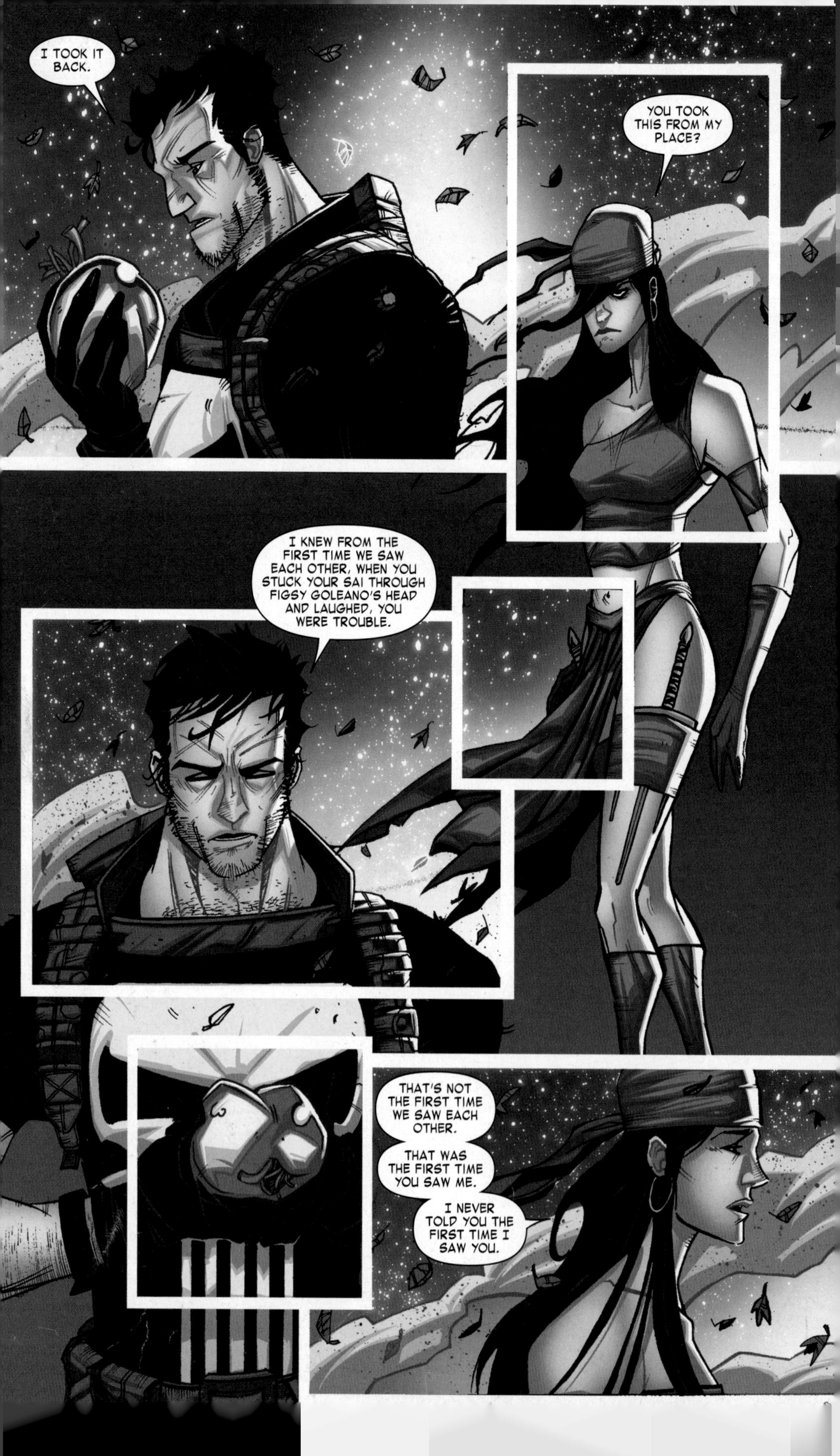
I TOOK IT BACK.
YOU TOOK THIS FROM MY PLACE?
I KNEW FROM THE FIRST TIME WE SAW EACH OTHER, WHEN YOU STUCK YOUR SAI THROUGH FIGSY GOLEANO'S HEAD AND LAUGHED, YOU WERE TROUBLE.
THAT'S NOT THE FIRST TIME WE SAW EACH OTHER.
THAT WAS THE FIRST TIME YOU SAW ME.
I NEVER TOLD YOU THE FIRST TIME I SAW YOU.

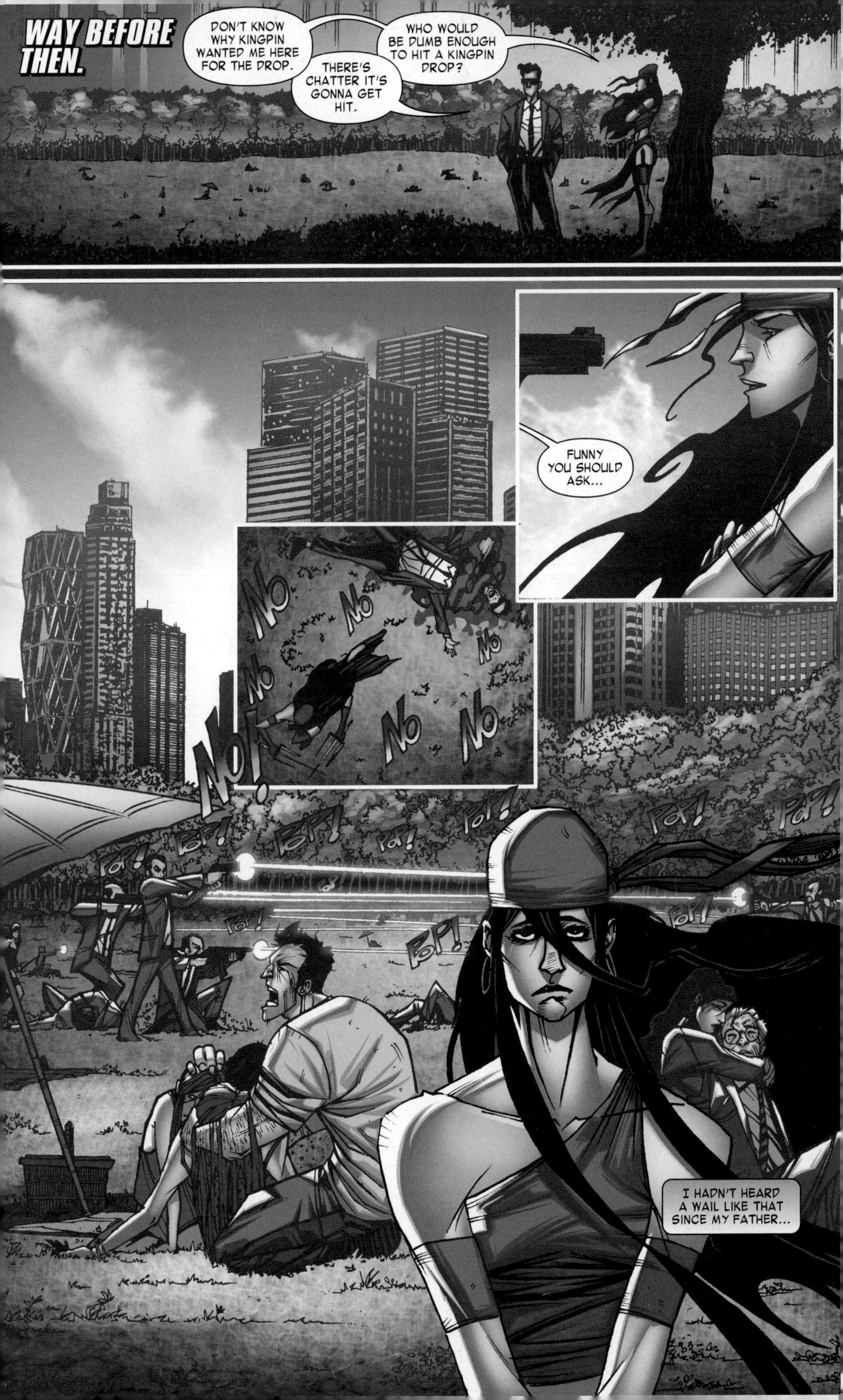
WAY BEFORE THEN.
DON'T KNOW WHY KINGPIN WANTED ME HERE FOR THE DROP.
THERE'S CHATTER IT'S GONNA GET HIT.
WHO WOULD BE DUMB ENOUGH TO HIT A KINGPIN DROP?
FUNNY YOU SHOULD ASK...
NO NO NO NO NO NO
NO!
POP! POP! POP! POP! POP! POP! POP! POP!
I HADN'T HEARD A WAIL LIKE THAT SINCE MY FATHER...

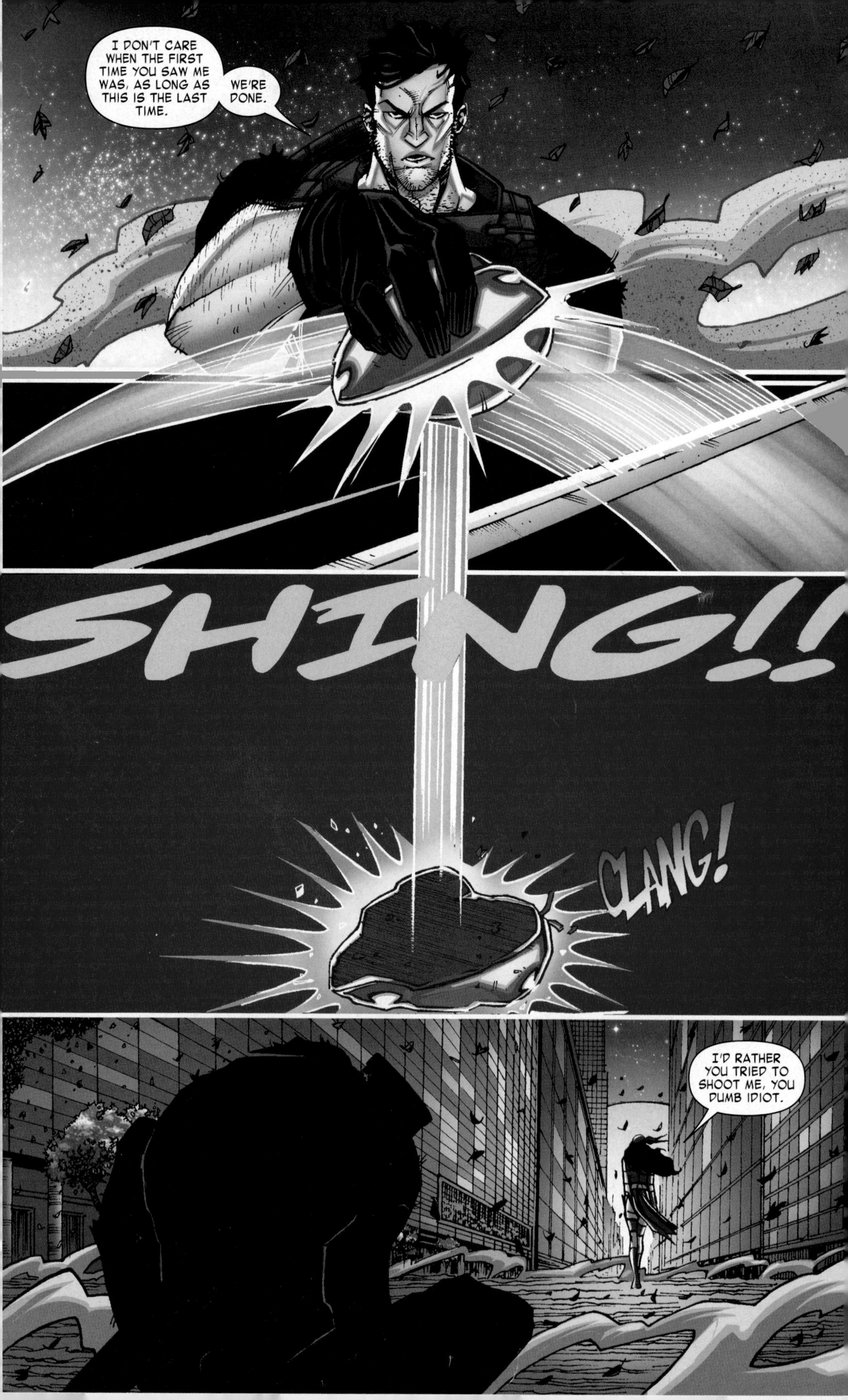
I DON'T CARE WHEN THE FIRST TIME YOU SAW ME WAS, AS LONG AS THIS IS THE LAST TIME.
WE'RE DONE.
SHING!!
CLANG!
I'D RATHER YOU TRIED TO SHOOT ME, YOU DUMB IDIOT.

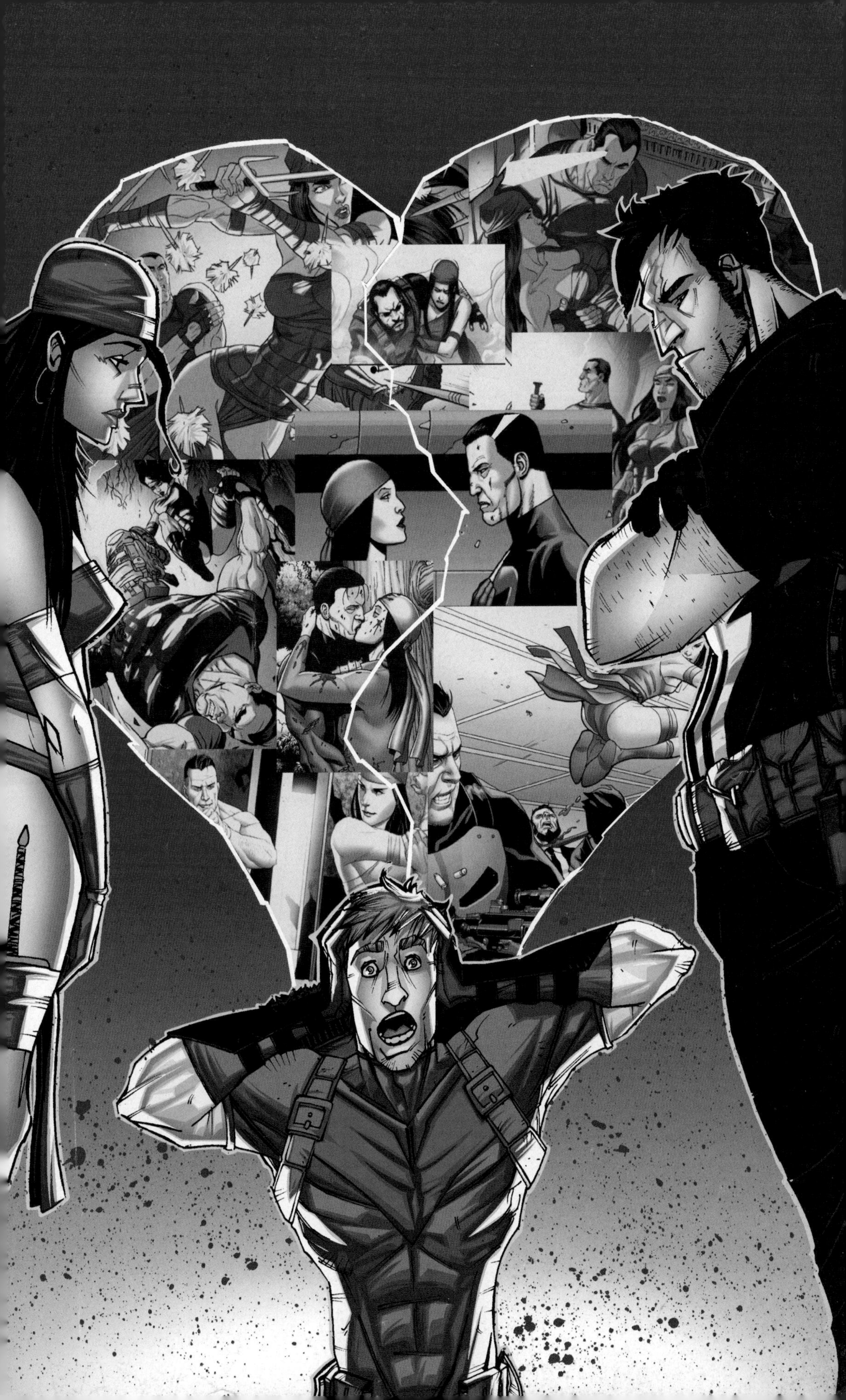

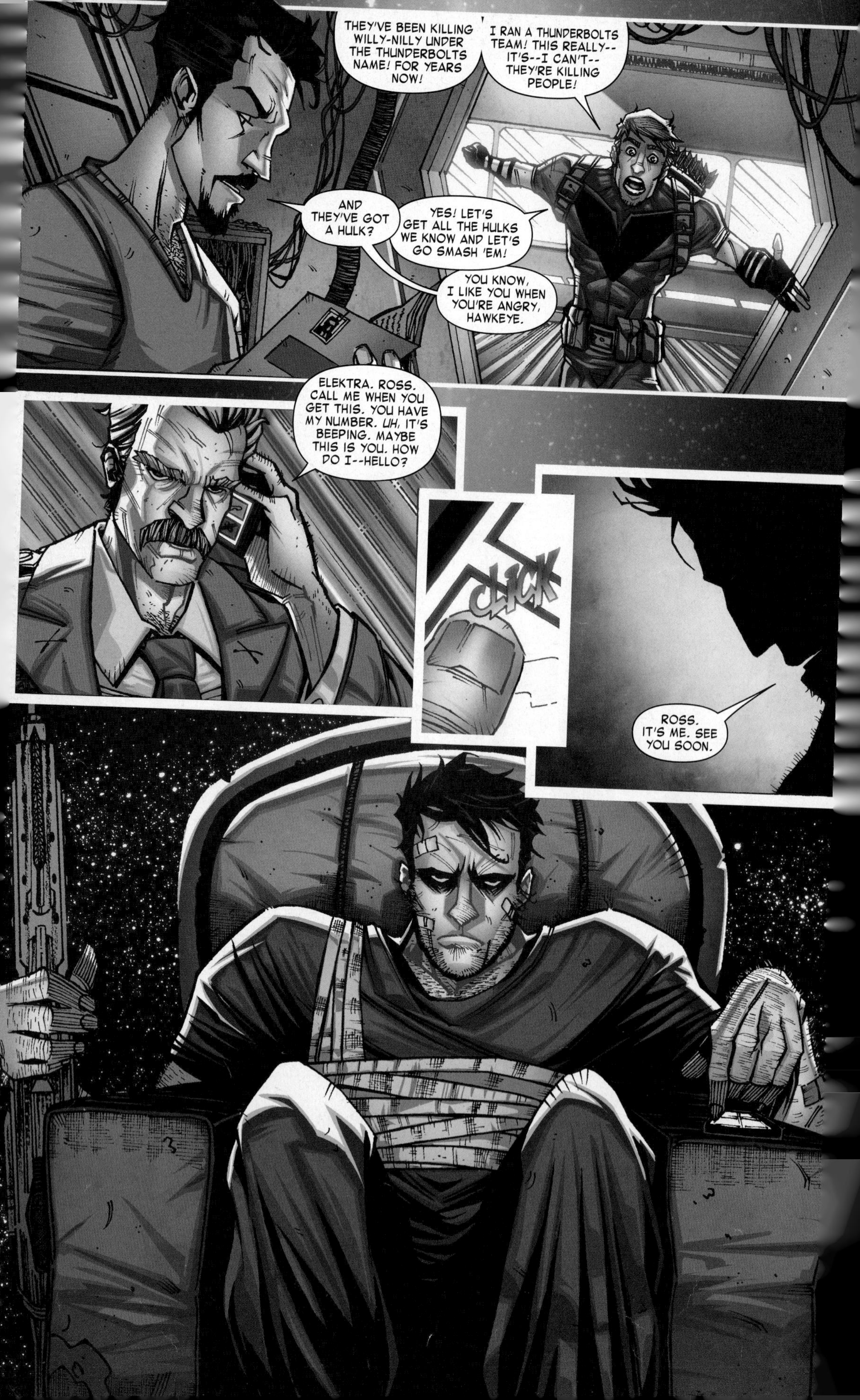
THEY'VE BEEN KILLING WILLY-NILLY UNDER THE THUNDERBOLTS NAME! FOR YEARS NOW!
I RAN A THUNDERBOLTS TEAM! THIS REALLY-- IT'S--I CAN'T-- THEY'RE KILLING PEOPLE!
AND THEY'VE GOT A HULK?
YES! LET'S GET ALL THE HULKS WE KNOW AND LET'S GO SMASH 'EM!
YOU KNOW, I LIKE YOU WHEN YOU'RE ANGRY, HAWKEYE.
ELEKTRA. ROSS. CALL ME WHEN YOU GET THIS. YOU HAVE MY NUMBER. UH, IT'S BEEPING. MAYBE THIS IS YOU. HOW DO I--HELLO?
CLICK
ROSS. IT'S ME. SEE YOU SOON.

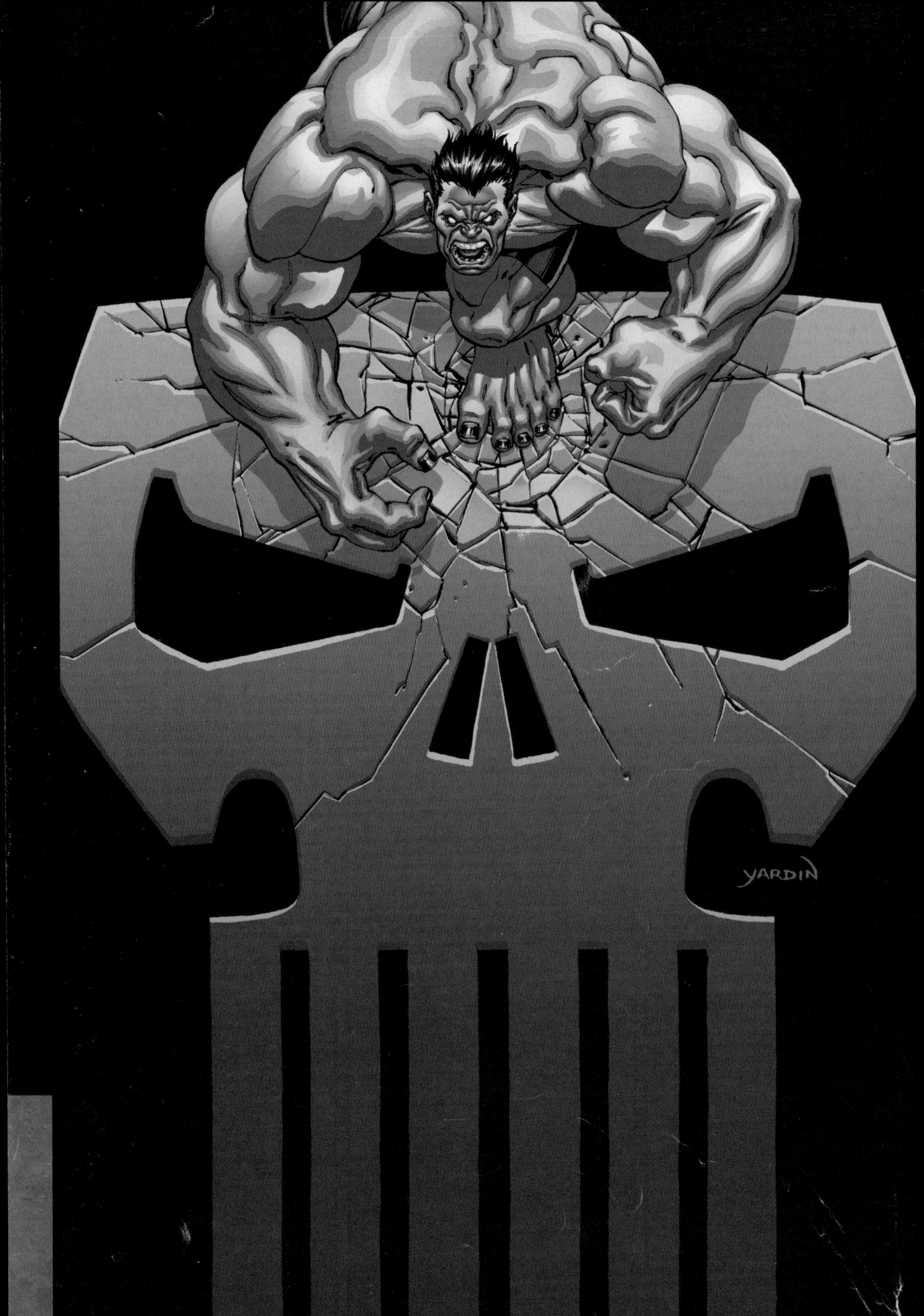
YARDIN

THIRTY-ONE

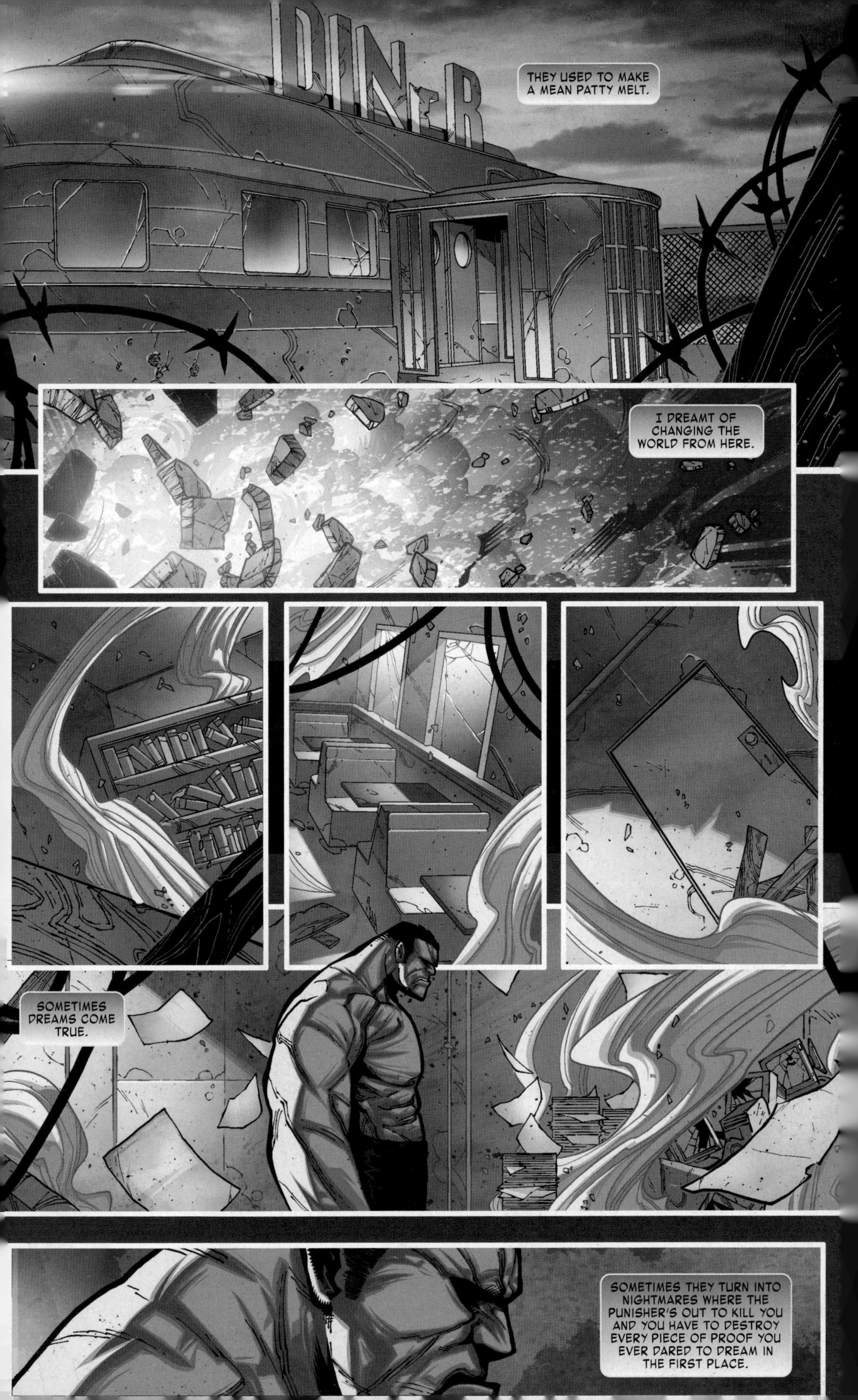
DINER
THEY USED TO MAKE A MEAN PATTY MELT.
I DREAMT OF CHANGING THE WORLD FROM HERE.
SOMETIMES DREAMS COME TRUE.
SOMETIMES THEY TURN INTO NIGHTMARES WHERE THE PUNISHER'S OUT TO KILL YOU AND YOU HAVE TO DESTROY EVERY PIECE OF PROOF YOU EVER DARED TO DREAM IN THE FIRST PLACE.

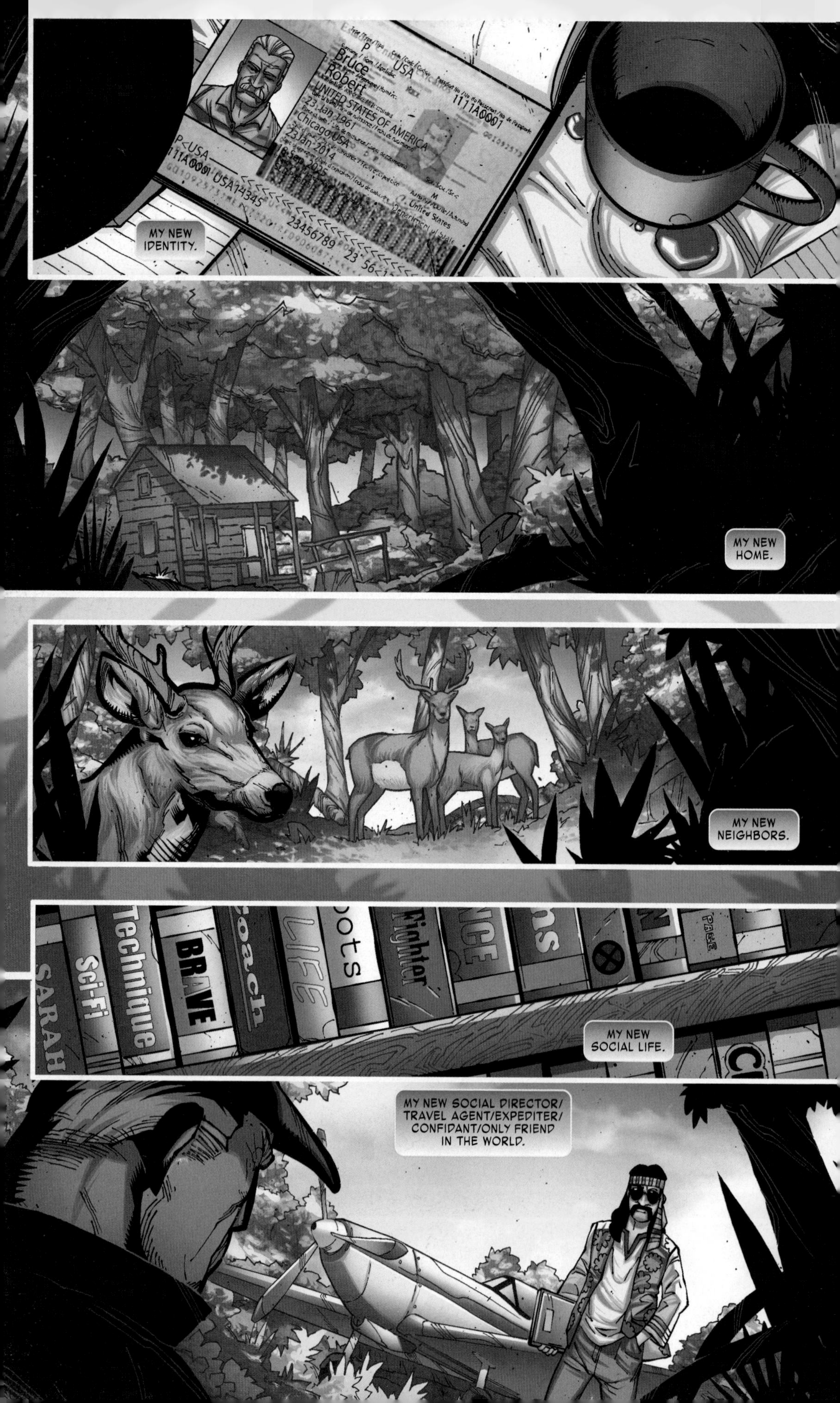
MY NEW IDENTITY.
MY NEW HOME.
MY NEW NEIGHBORS.
MY NEW SOCIAL LIFE.
MY NEW SOCIAL DIRECTOR/ TRAVEL AGENT/EXPEDITER/ CONFIDANT/ONLY FRIEND IN THE WORLD.

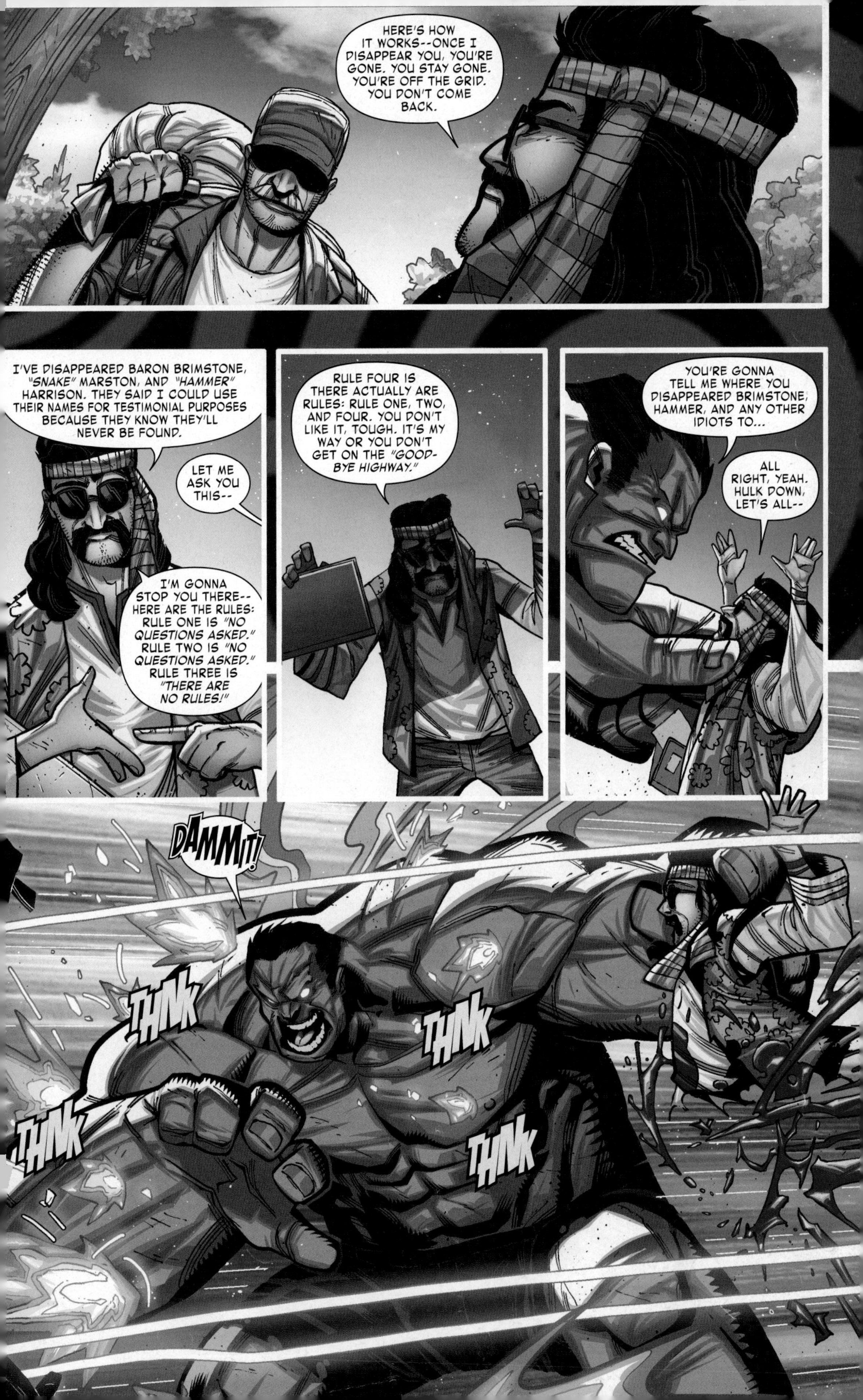
HERE'S HOW IT WORKS--ONCE I DISAPPEAR YOU, YOU'RE GONE. YOU STAY GONE. YOU'RE OFF THE GRID. YOU DON'T COME BACK.
I'VE DISAPPEARED BARON BRIMSTONE, "SNAKE" MARSTON, AND "HAMMER" HARRISON. THEY SAID I COULD USE THEIR NAMES FOR TESTIMONIAL PURPOSES BECAUSE THEY KNOW THEY'LL NEVER BE FOUND.
LET ME ASK YOU THIS--
I'M GONNA STOP YOU THERE--HERE ARE THE RULES: RULE ONE IS "NO QUESTIONS ASKED." RULE TWO IS "NO QUESTIONS ASKED." RULE THREE IS "THERE ARE NO RULES!"
RULE FOUR IS THERE ACTUALLY ARE RULES: RULE ONE, TWO, AND FOUR. YOU DON'T LIKE IT, TOUGH. IT'S MY WAY OR YOU DON'T GET ON THE "GOOD-BYE HIGHWAY."
YOU'RE GONNA TELL ME WHERE YOU DISAPPEARED BRIMSTONE, HAMMER, AND ANY OTHER IDIOTS TO...
ALL RIGHT, YEAH. HULK DOWN, LET'S ALL--
DAMMIT!
THNK
THNK
THNK
THNK

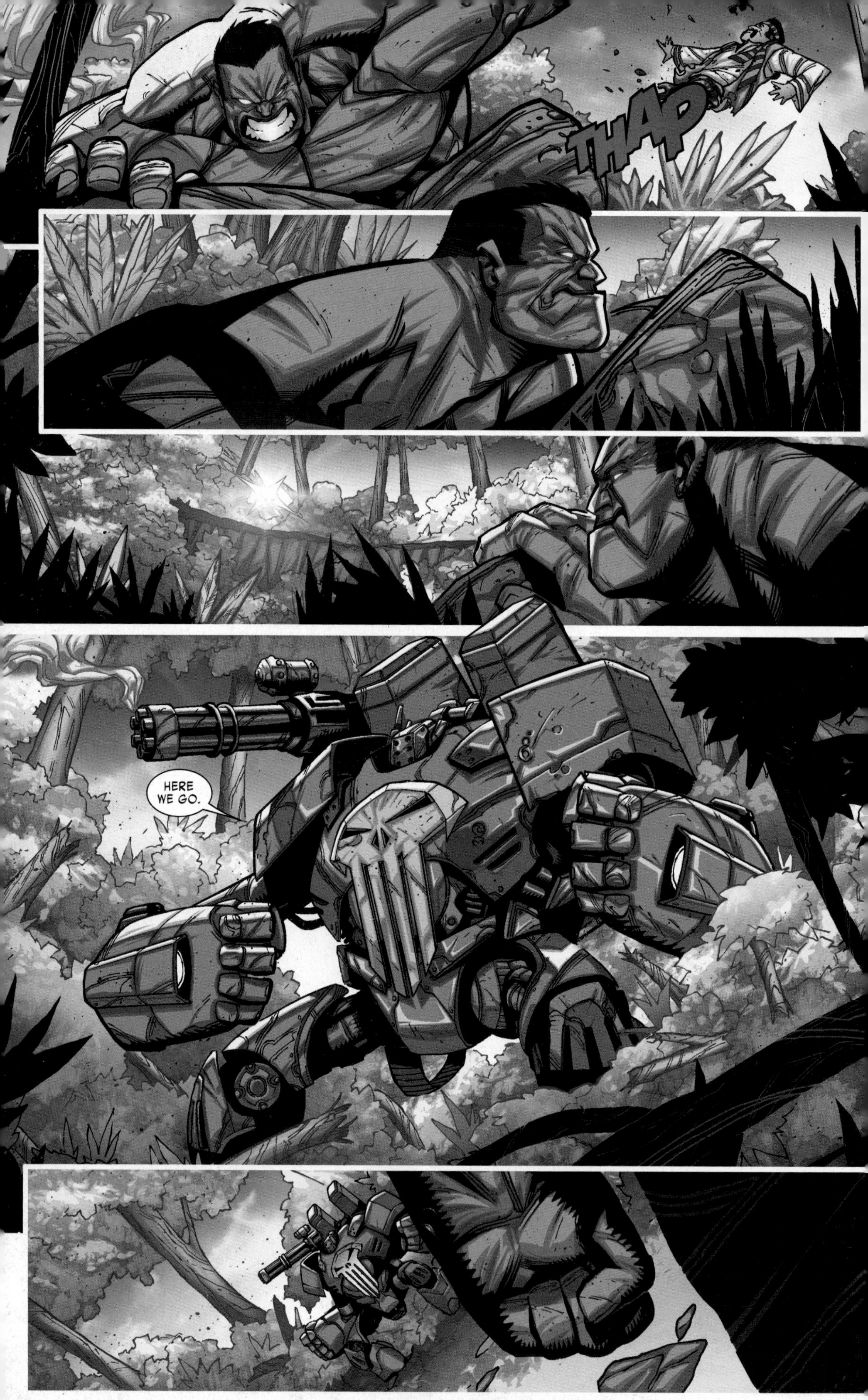
THAP
HERE WE GO.

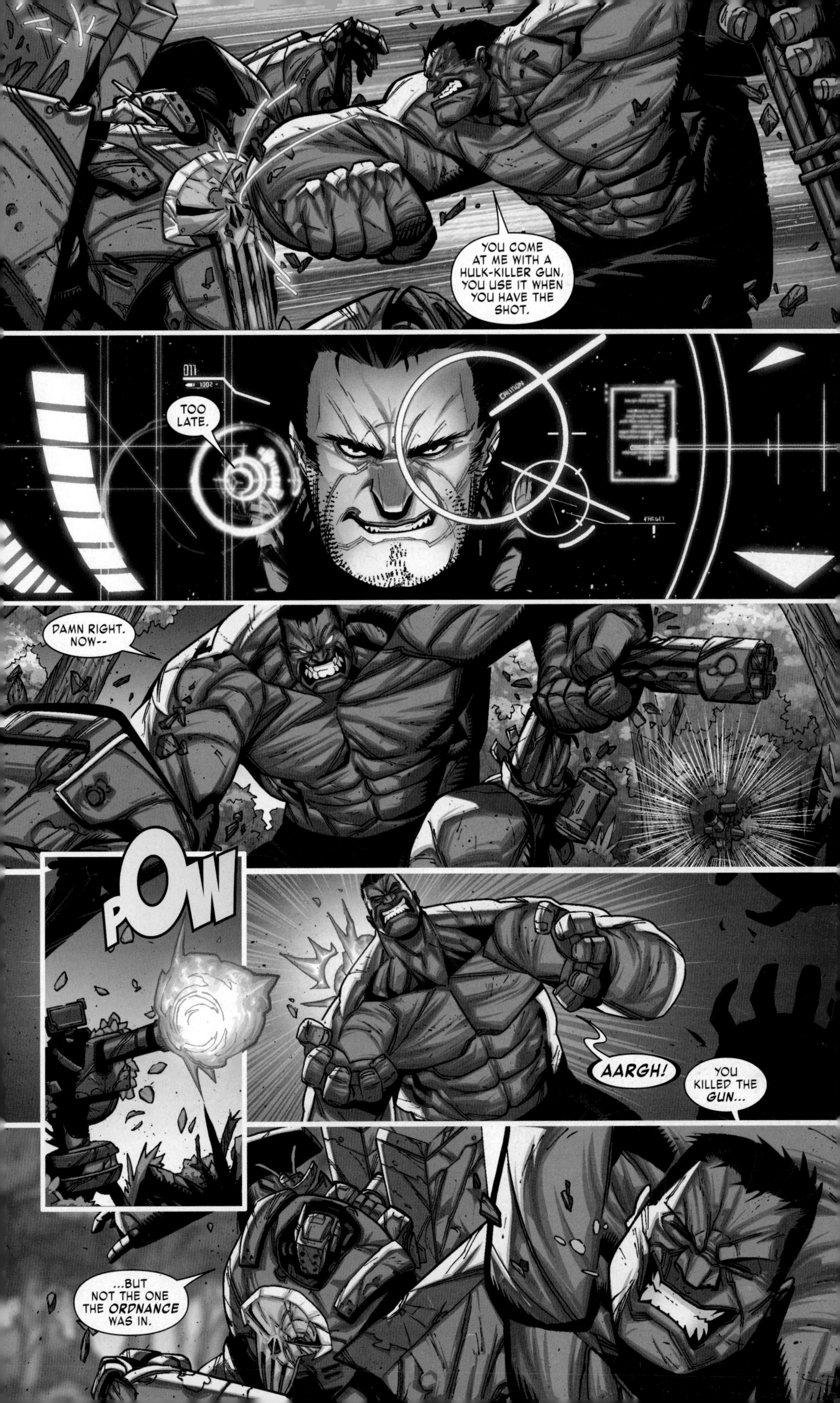
YOU COME AT ME WITH A HULK-KILLER GUN, YOU USE IT WHEN YOU HAVE THE SHOT.
TOO LATE.
DAMN RIGHT. NOW--
POW
AARGH!
YOU KILLED THE *GUN*...
...BUT NOT THE ONE THE *ORDNANCE* WAS IN.

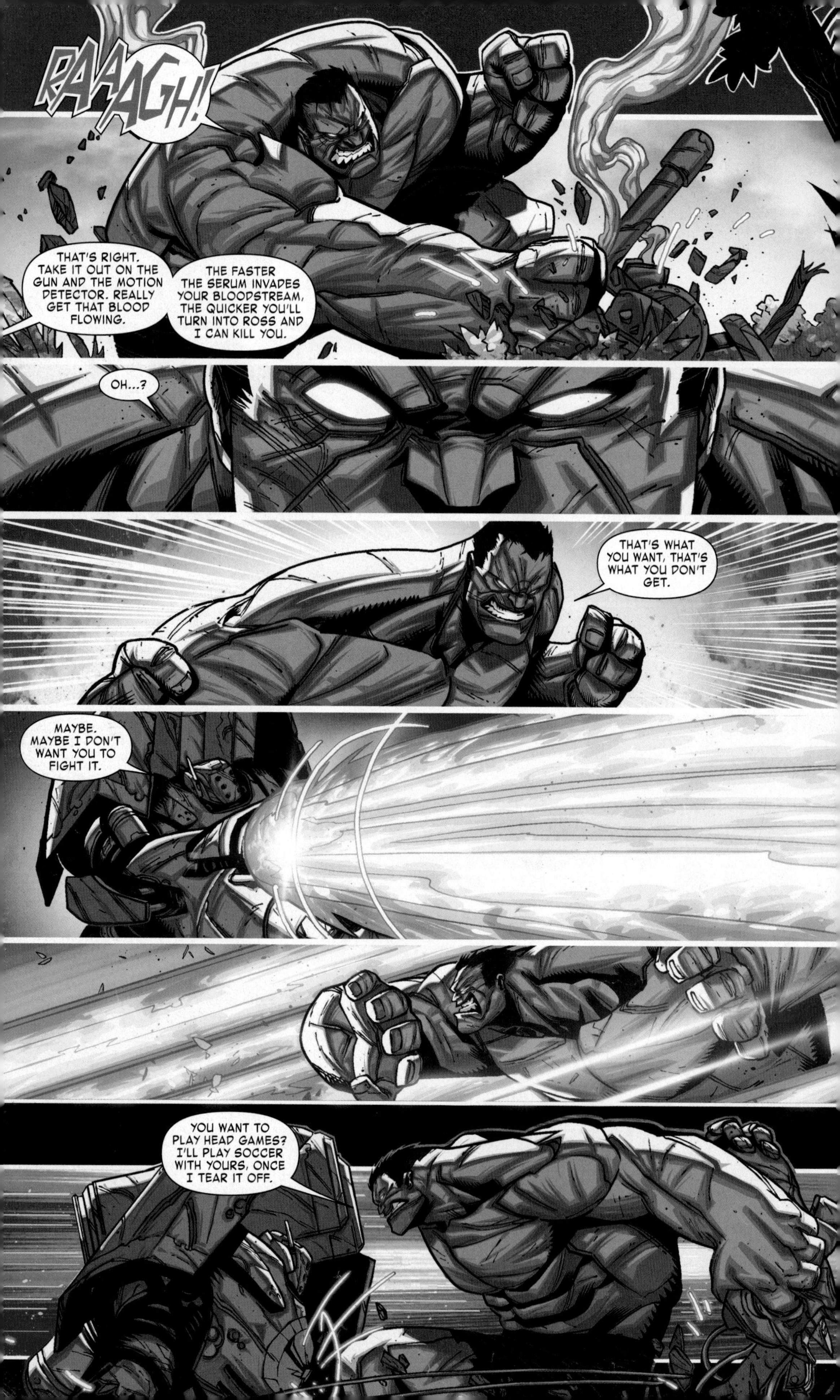
RAAAGH!
THAT'S RIGHT. TAKE IT OUT ON THE GUN AND THE MOTION DETECTOR. REALLY GET THAT BLOOD FLOWING.
THE FASTER THE SERUM INVADES YOUR BLOODSTREAM, THE QUICKER YOU'LL TURN INTO ROSS AND I CAN KILL YOU.
OH...?
THAT'S WHAT YOU WANT, THAT'S WHAT YOU DON'T GET.
MAYBE. MAYBE I DON'T WANT YOU TO FIGHT IT.
YOU WANT TO PLAY HEAD GAMES? I'LL PLAY SOCCER WITH YOURS, ONCE I TEAR IT OFF.

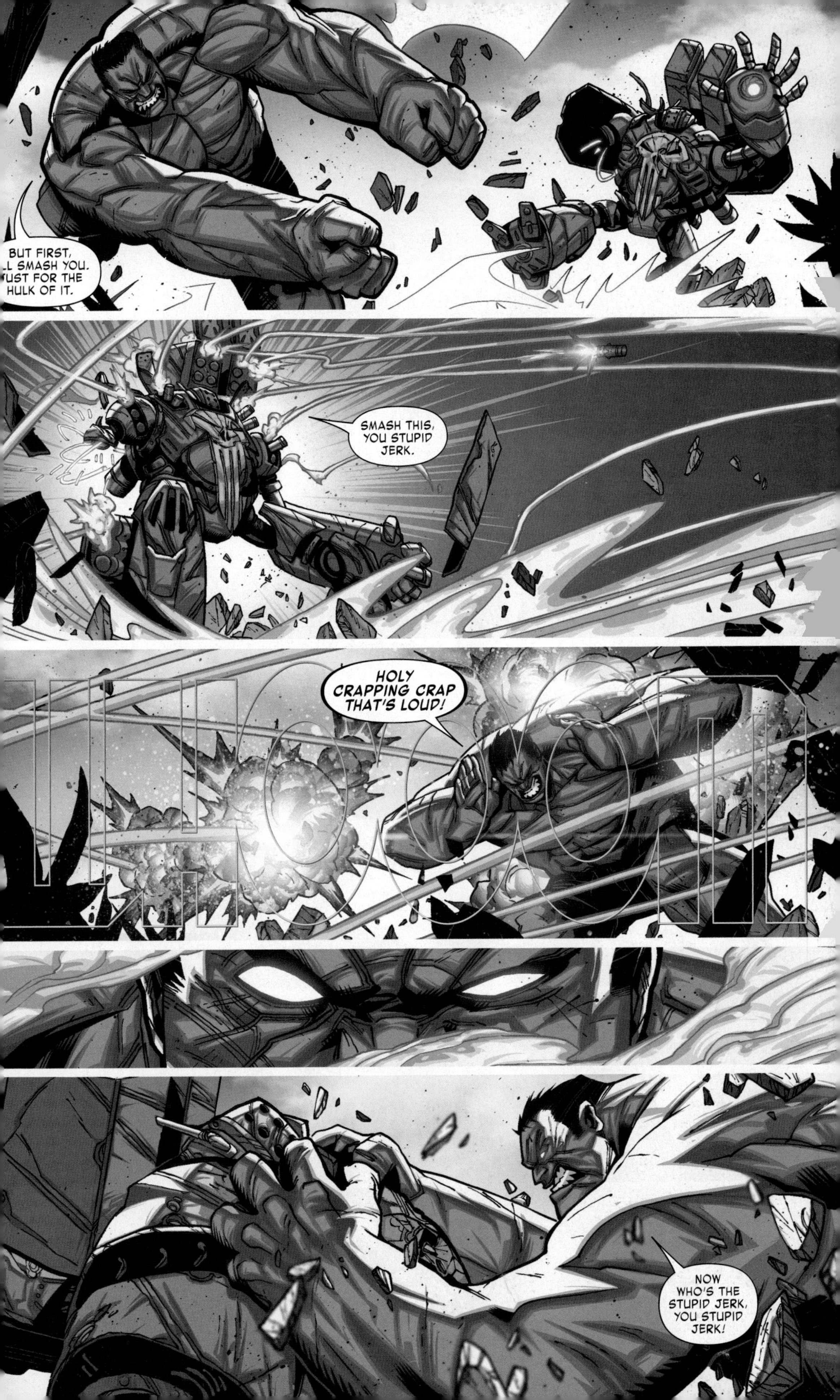
BUT FIRST, L SMASH YOU. UST FOR THE HULK OF IT.
SMASH THIS, YOU STUPID JERK.
HOLY CRAPPING CRAP THAT'S LOUD!
NOW WHO'S THE STUPID JERK, YOU STUPID JERK!

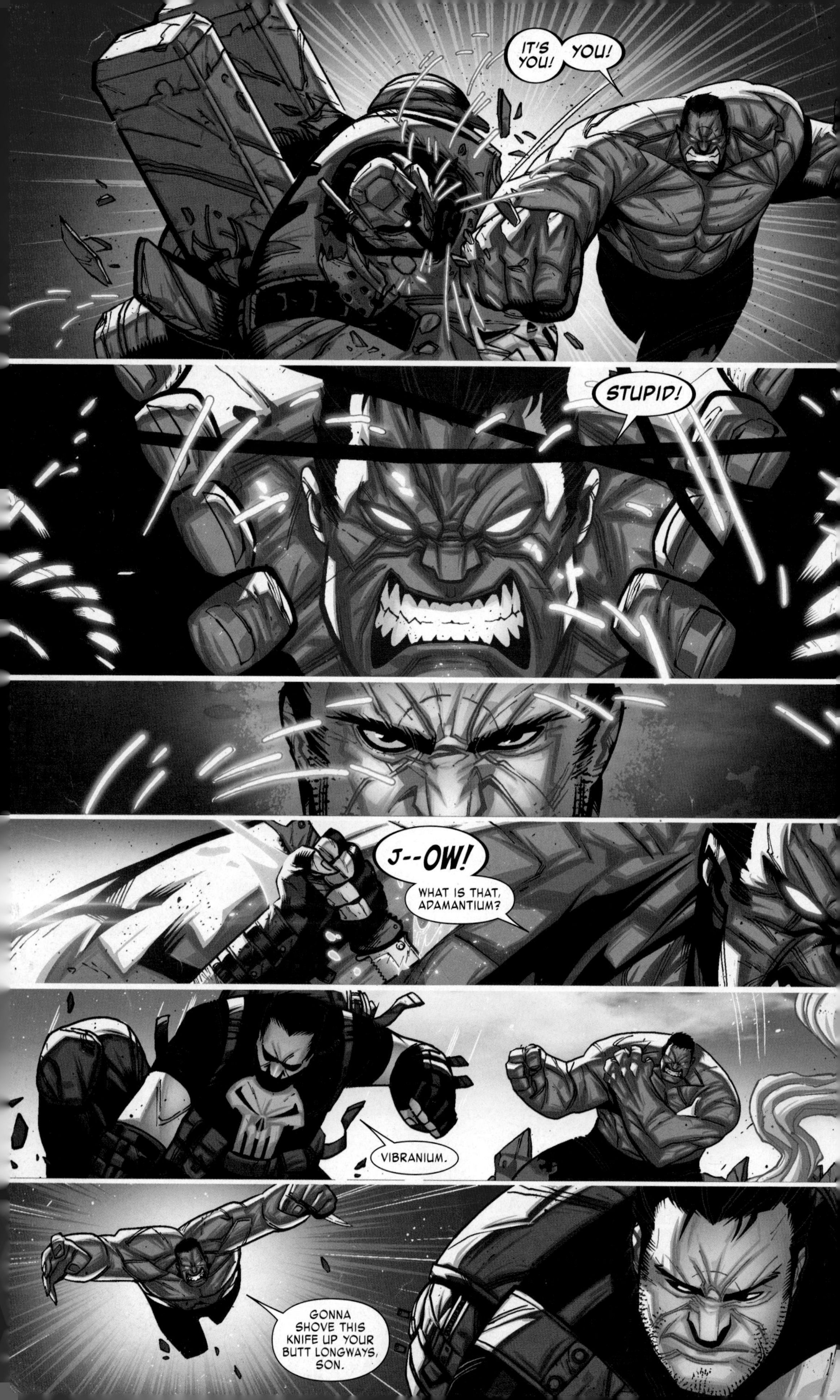
IT'S YOU!
YOU!
STUPID!
J--OW!
WHAT IS THAT, ADAMANTIUM?
VIBRANIUM.
GONNA SHOVE THIS KNIFE UP YOUR BUTT LONGWAYS, SON.

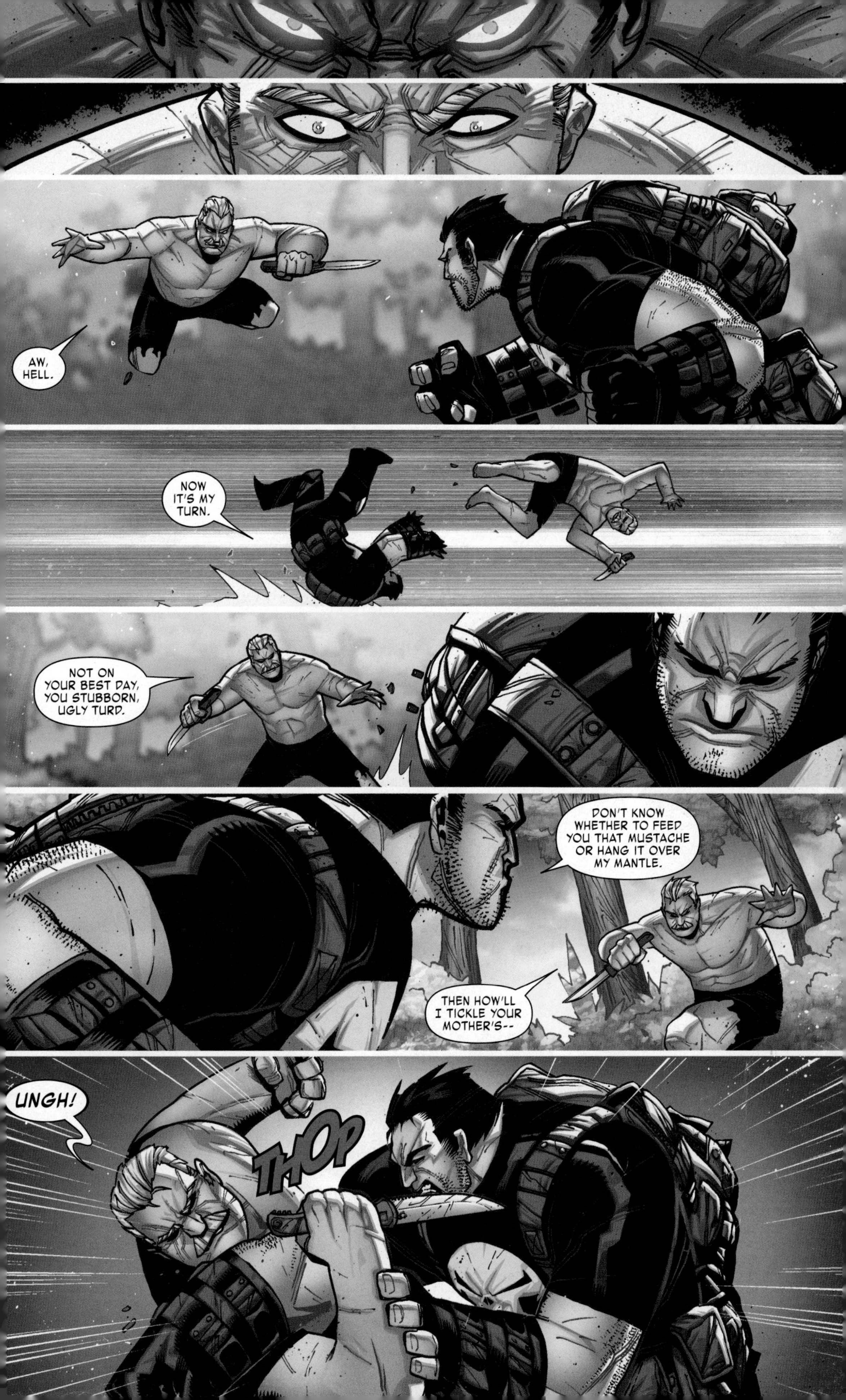
AW, HELL.
NOW IT'S MY TURN.
NOT ON YOUR BEST DAY, YOU STUBBORN, UGLY TURD.
DON'T KNOW WHETHER TO FEED YOU THAT MUSTACHE OR HANG IT OVER MY MANTLE.
THEN HOW'LL I TICKLE YOUR MOTHER'S--
UNGH!
THOP

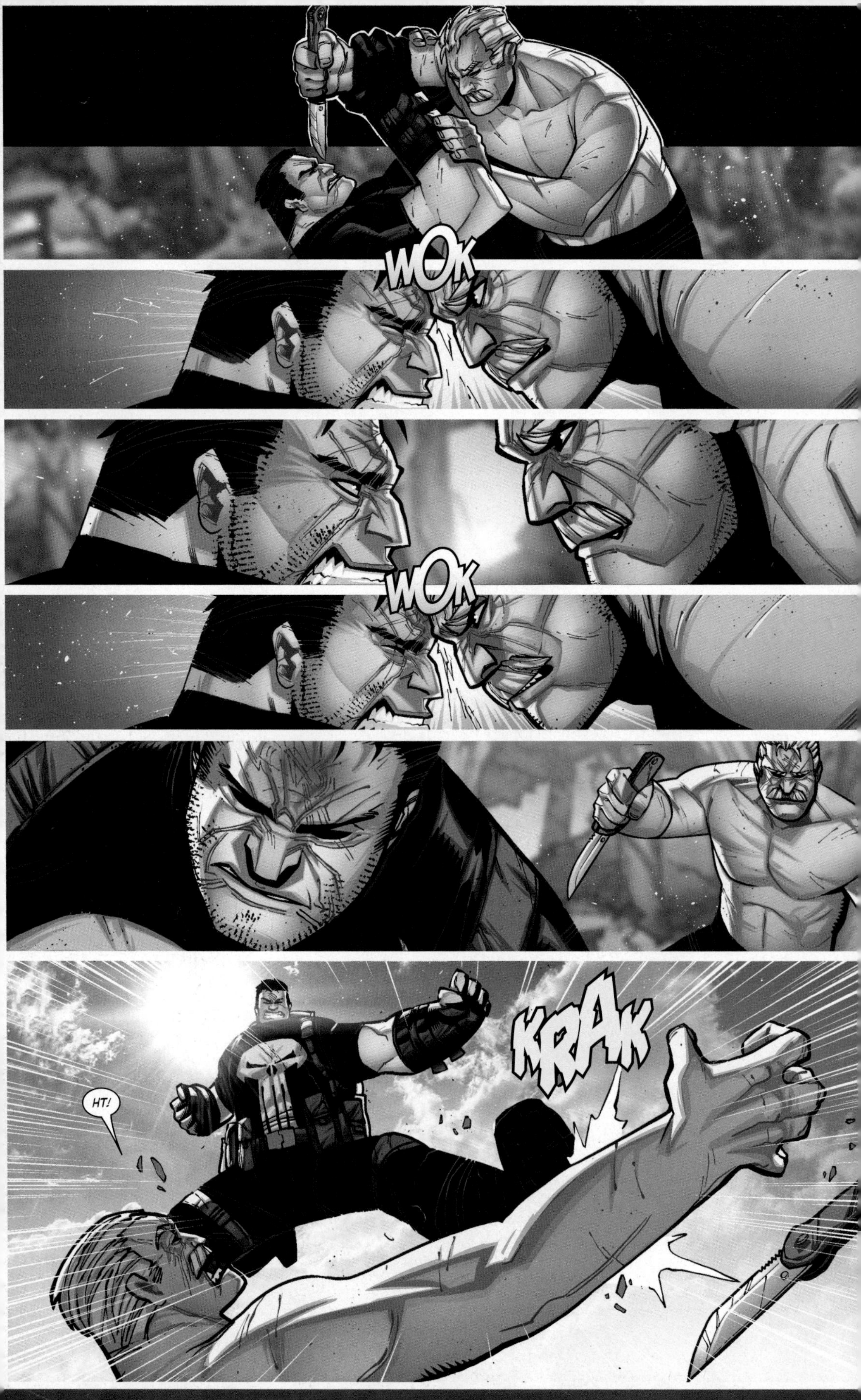
WOK
WOK
HT!
KRAK

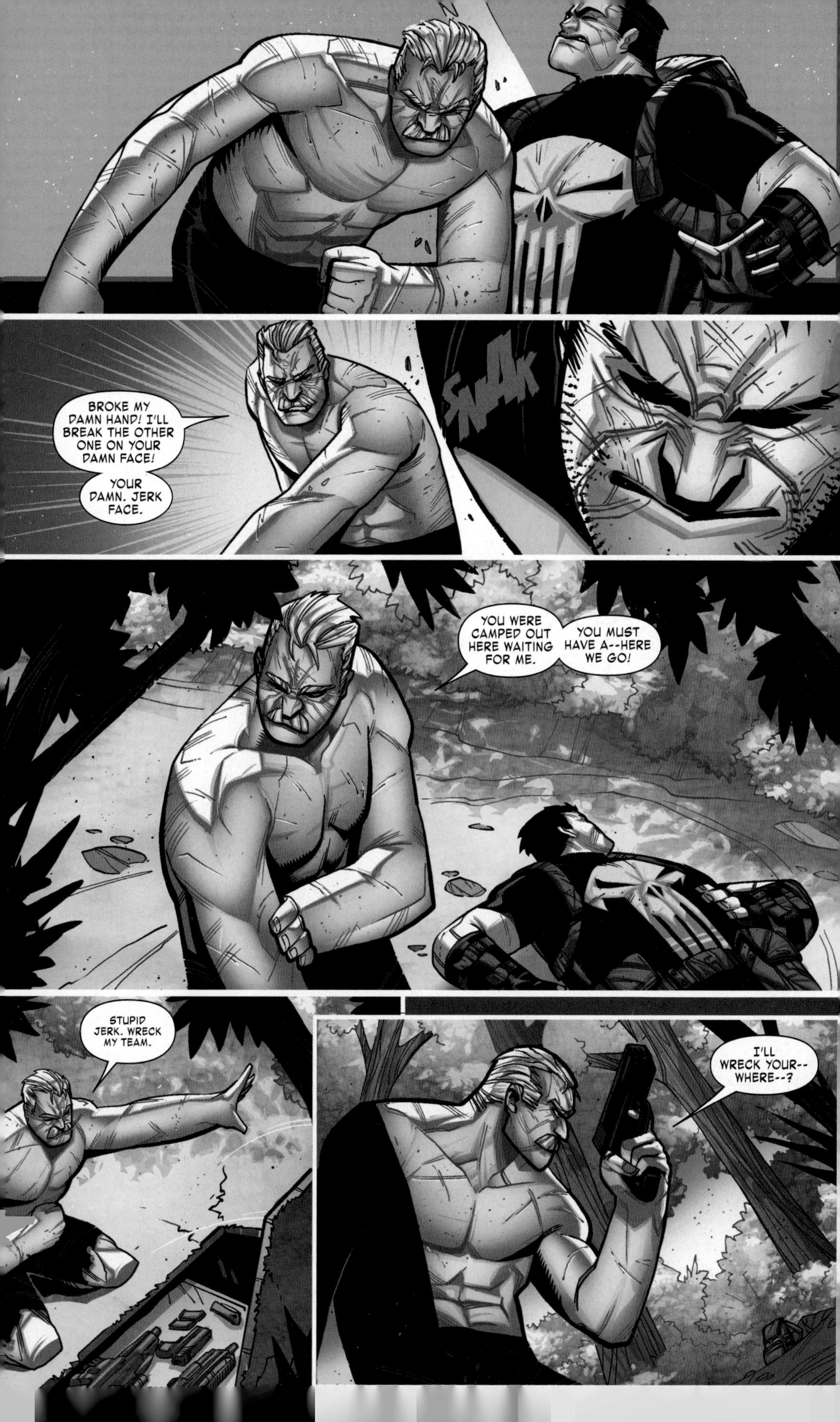

BROKE MY DAMN HAND! I'LL BREAK THE OTHER ONE ON YOUR DAMN FACE!
YOUR DAMN. JERK FACE.
SNAK
YOU WERE CAMPED OUT HERE WAITING FOR ME.
YOU MUST HAVE A--HERE WE GO!
STUPID JERK. WRECK MY TEAM.
I'LL WRECK YOUR-- WHERE--?

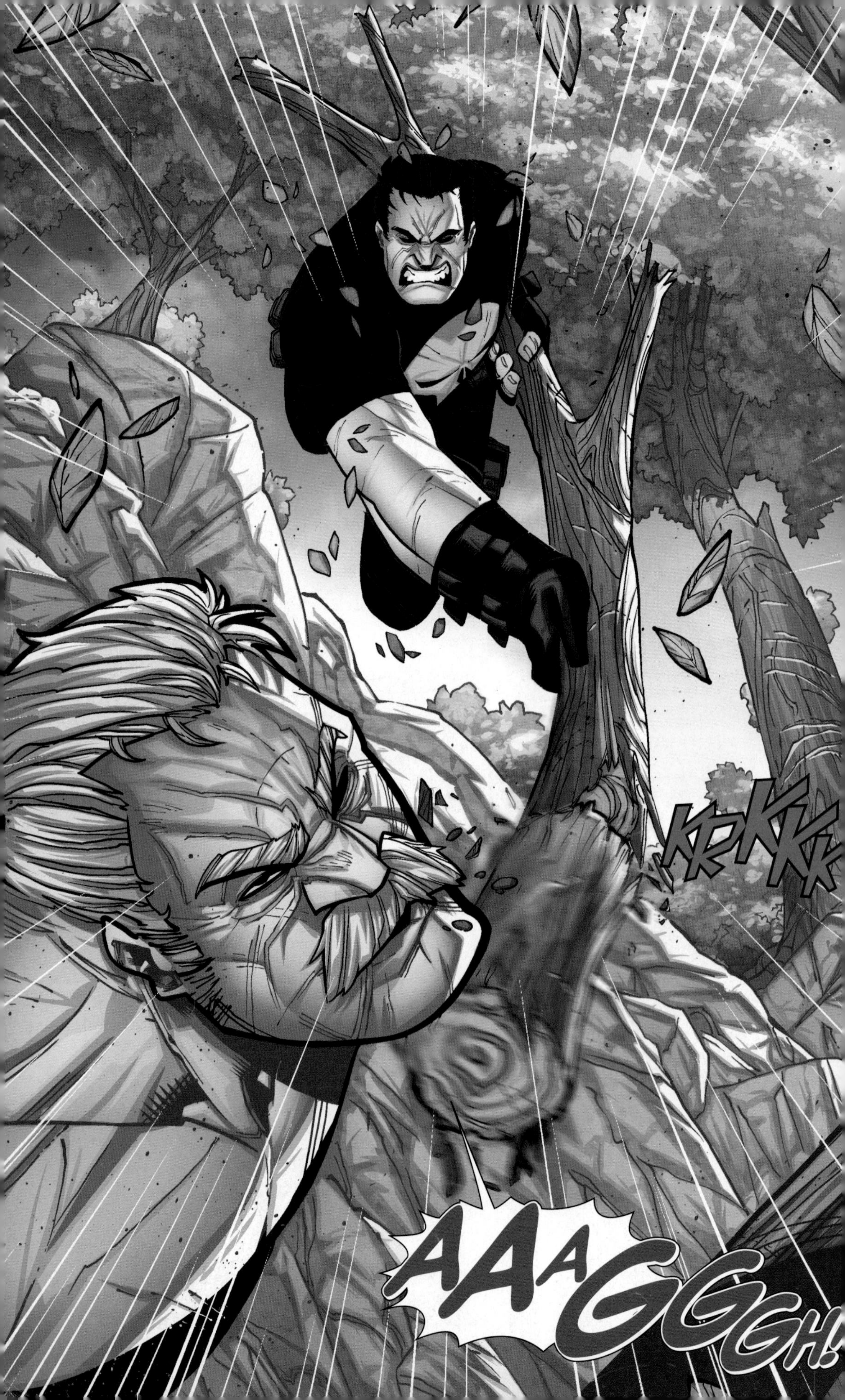
KRKKK
AAAGGGH!

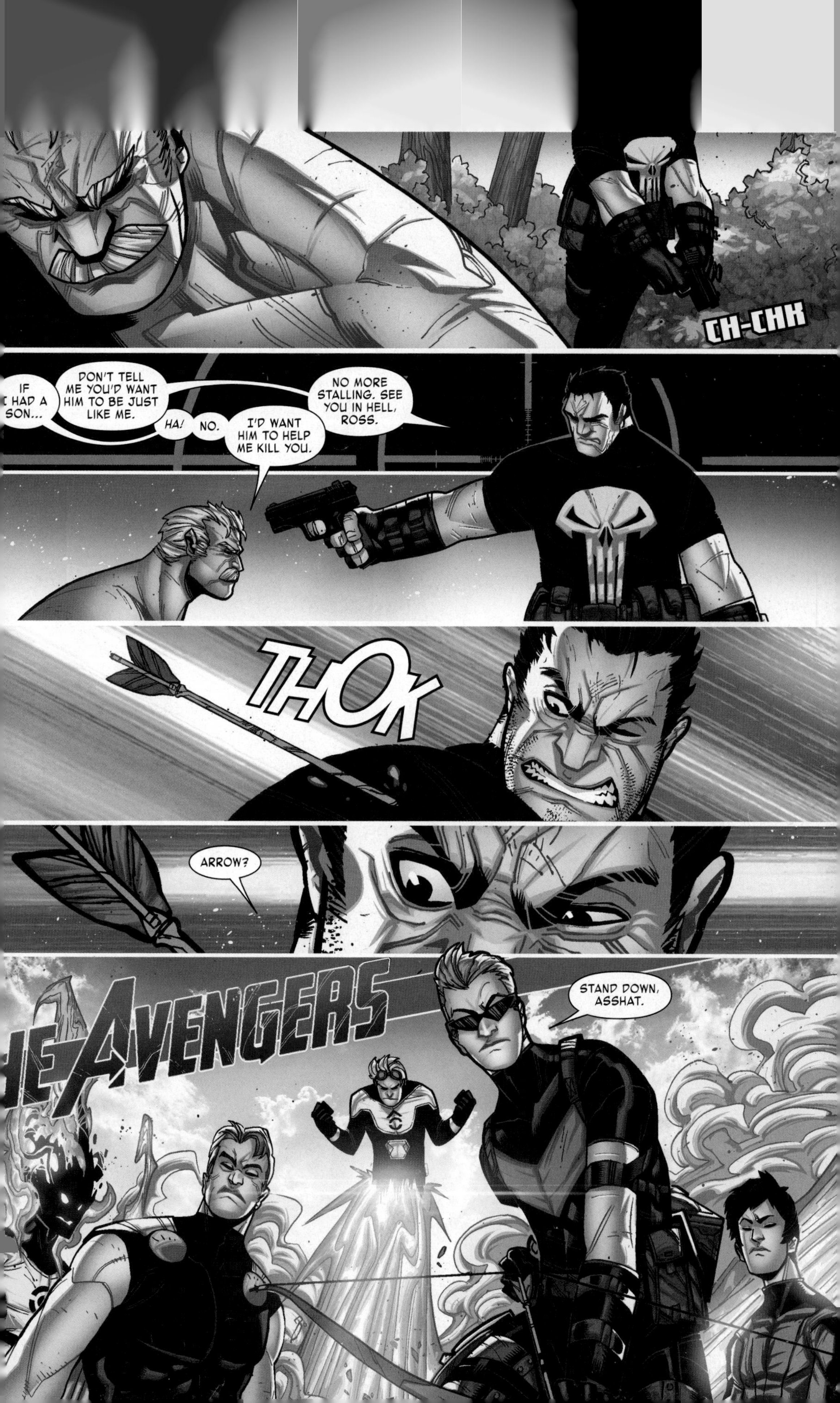
CH-CHK
IF HAD A SON...
DON'T TELL ME YOU'D WANT HIM TO BE JUST LIKE ME.
HA! NO.
I'D WANT HIM TO HELP ME KILL YOU.
NO MORE STALLING. SEE YOU IN HELL, ROSS.
THOK
ARROW?
AVENGERS
STAND DOWN, ASSHAT.

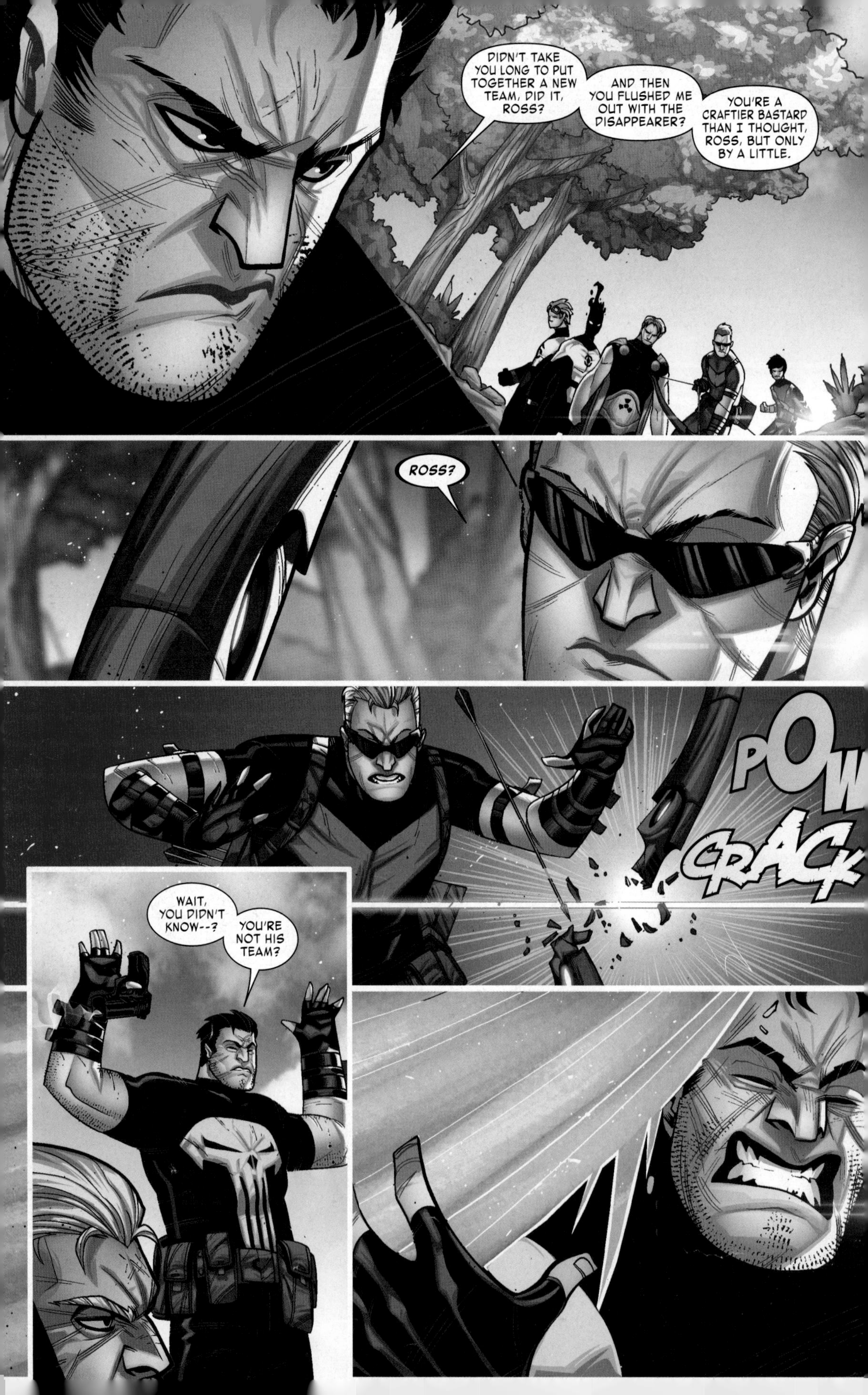
DIDN'T TAKE YOU LONG TO PUT TOGETHER A NEW TEAM, DID IT, ROSS?
AND THEN YOU FLUSHED ME OUT WITH THE DISAPPEARER?
YOU'RE A CRAFTIER BASTARD THAN I THOUGHT, ROSS, BUT ONLY BY A LITTLE.
ROSS?
POW
CRACK
WAIT, YOU DIDN'T KNOW--?
YOU'RE NOT HIS TEAM?

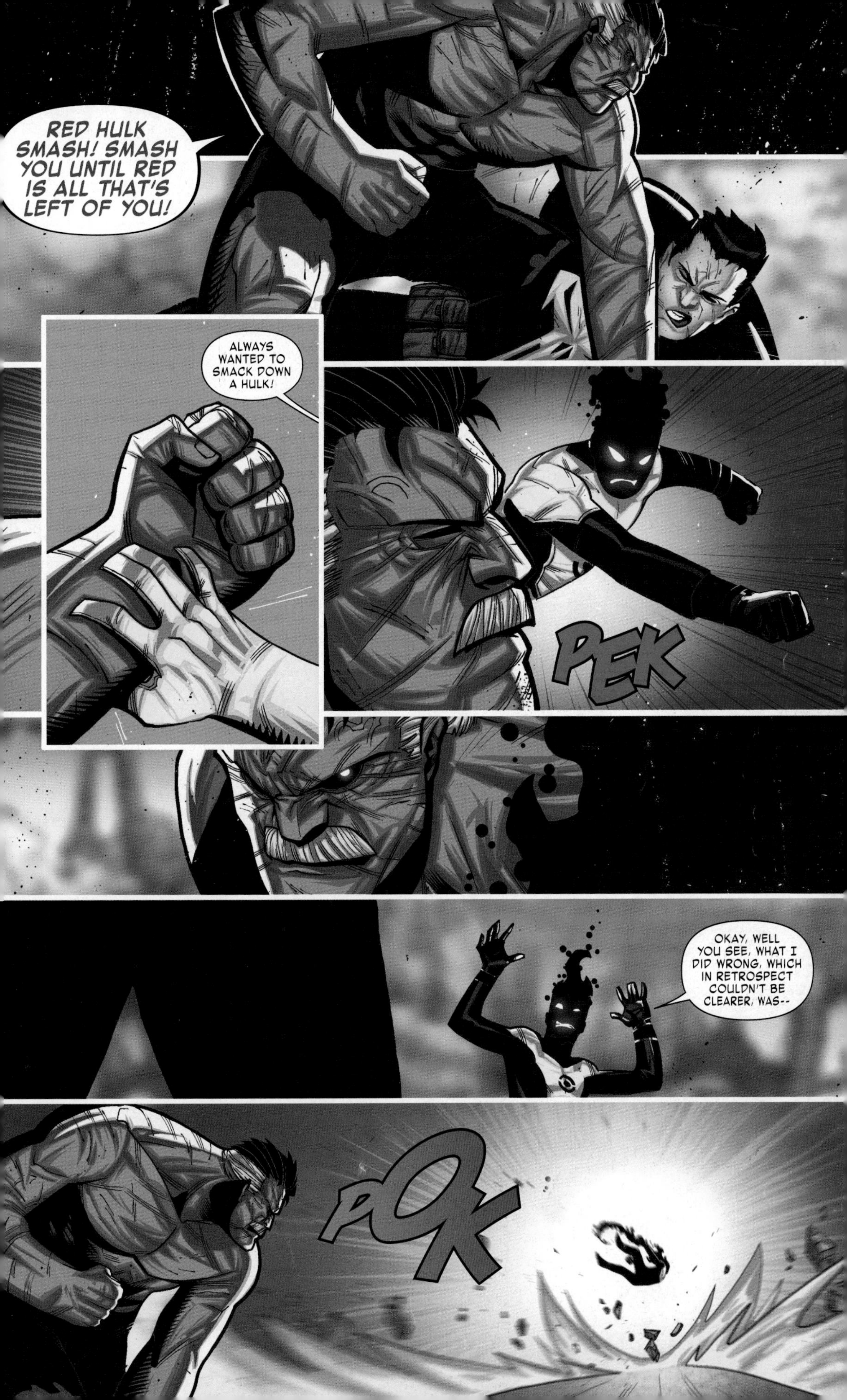
RED HULK SMASH! SMASH YOU UNTIL RED IS ALL THAT'S LEFT OF YOU!
ALWAYS WANTED TO SMACK DOWN A HULK!
PEK
OKAY, WELL YOU SEE, WHAT I DID WRONG, WHICH IN RETROSPECT COULDN'T BE CLEARER, WAS--
POK

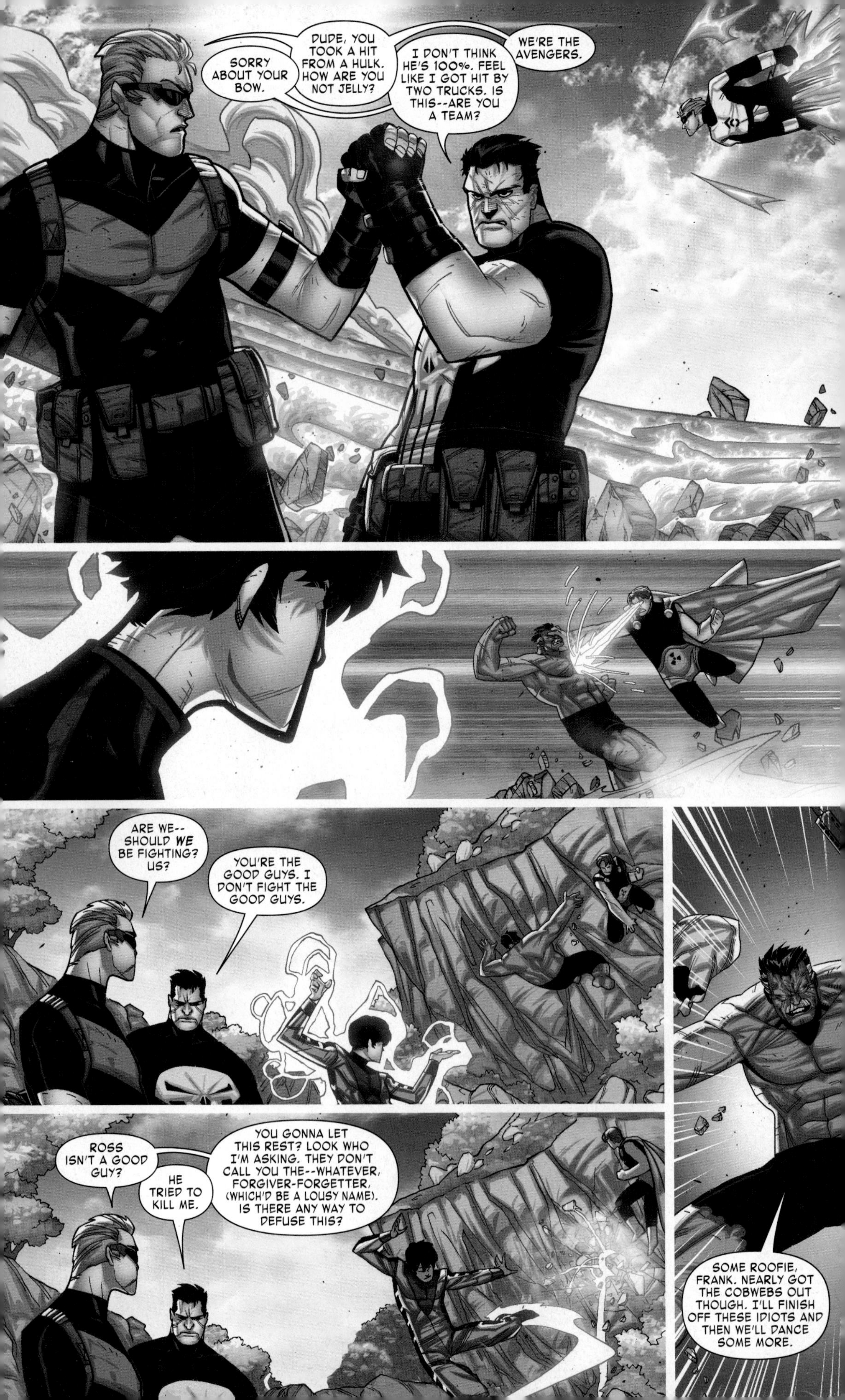
SORRY ABOUT YOUR BOW.
DUDE, YOU TOOK A HIT FROM A HULK. HOW ARE YOU NOT JELLY?
I DON'T THINK HE'S 100%. FEEL LIKE I GOT HIT BY TWO TRUCKS. IS THIS--ARE YOU A TEAM?
WE'RE THE AVENGERS.
ARE WE--SHOULD WE BE FIGHTING? US?
YOU'RE THE GOOD GUYS. I DON'T FIGHT THE GOOD GUYS.
ROSS ISN'T A GOOD GUY?
HE TRIED TO KILL ME.
YOU GONNA LET THIS REST? LOOK WHO I'M ASKING. THEY DON'T CALL YOU THE--WHATEVER, FORGIVER-FORGETTER. (WHICH'D BE A LOUSY NAME). IS THERE ANY WAY TO DEFUSE THIS?
SOME ROOFIE, FRANK. NEARLY GOT THE COBWEBS OUT THOUGH. I'LL FINISH OFF THESE IDIOTS AND THEN WE'LL DANCE SOME MORE.

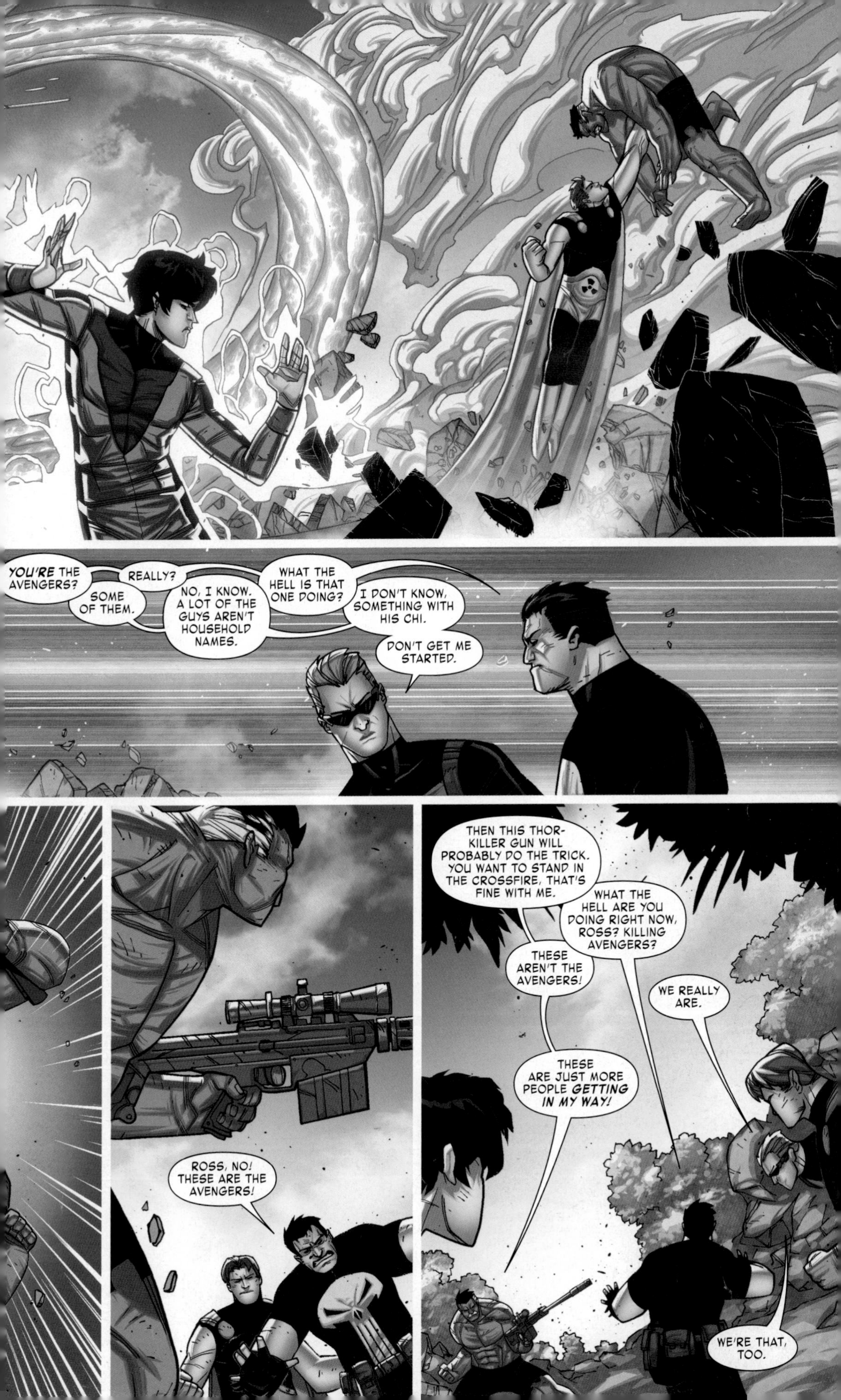
YOU'RE THE AVENGERS?
SOME OF THEM.
REALLY?
NO, I KNOW. A LOT OF THE GUYS AREN'T HOUSEHOLD NAMES.
WHAT THE HELL IS THAT ONE DOING?
I DON'T KNOW, SOMETHING WITH HIS CHI.
DON'T GET ME STARTED.
ROSS, NO! THESE ARE THE AVENGERS!
THEN THIS THOR-KILLER GUN WILL PROBABLY DO THE TRICK. YOU WANT TO STAND IN THE CROSSFIRE, THAT'S FINE WITH ME.
WHAT THE HELL ARE YOU DOING RIGHT NOW, ROSS? KILLING AVENGERS?
THESE AREN'T THE AVENGERS!
THESE ARE JUST MORE PEOPLE GETTING IN MY WAY!
WE REALLY ARE.
WE'RE THAT, TOO.

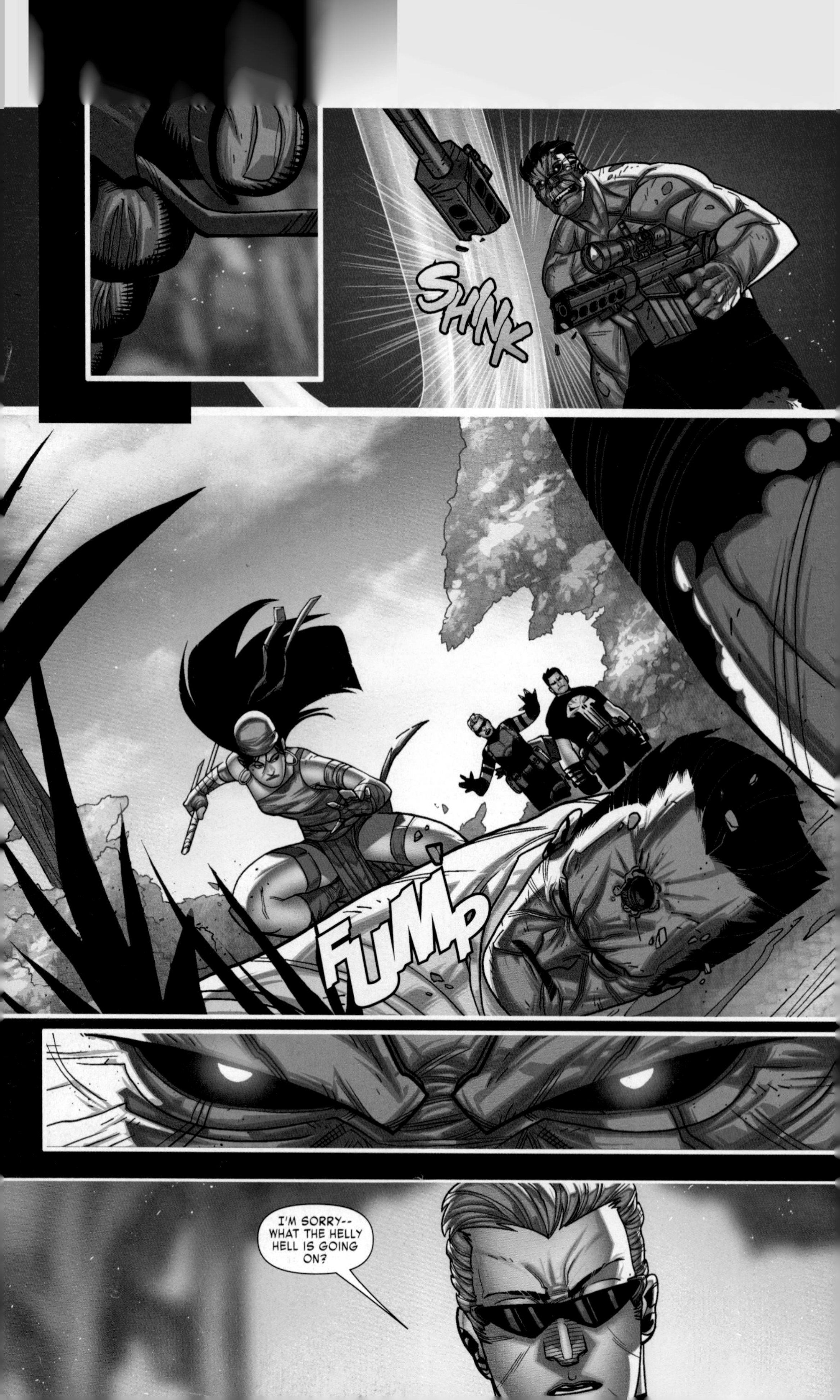
SHINK
FUMP
I'M SORRY--
WHAT THE HELLY
HELL IS GOING
ON?

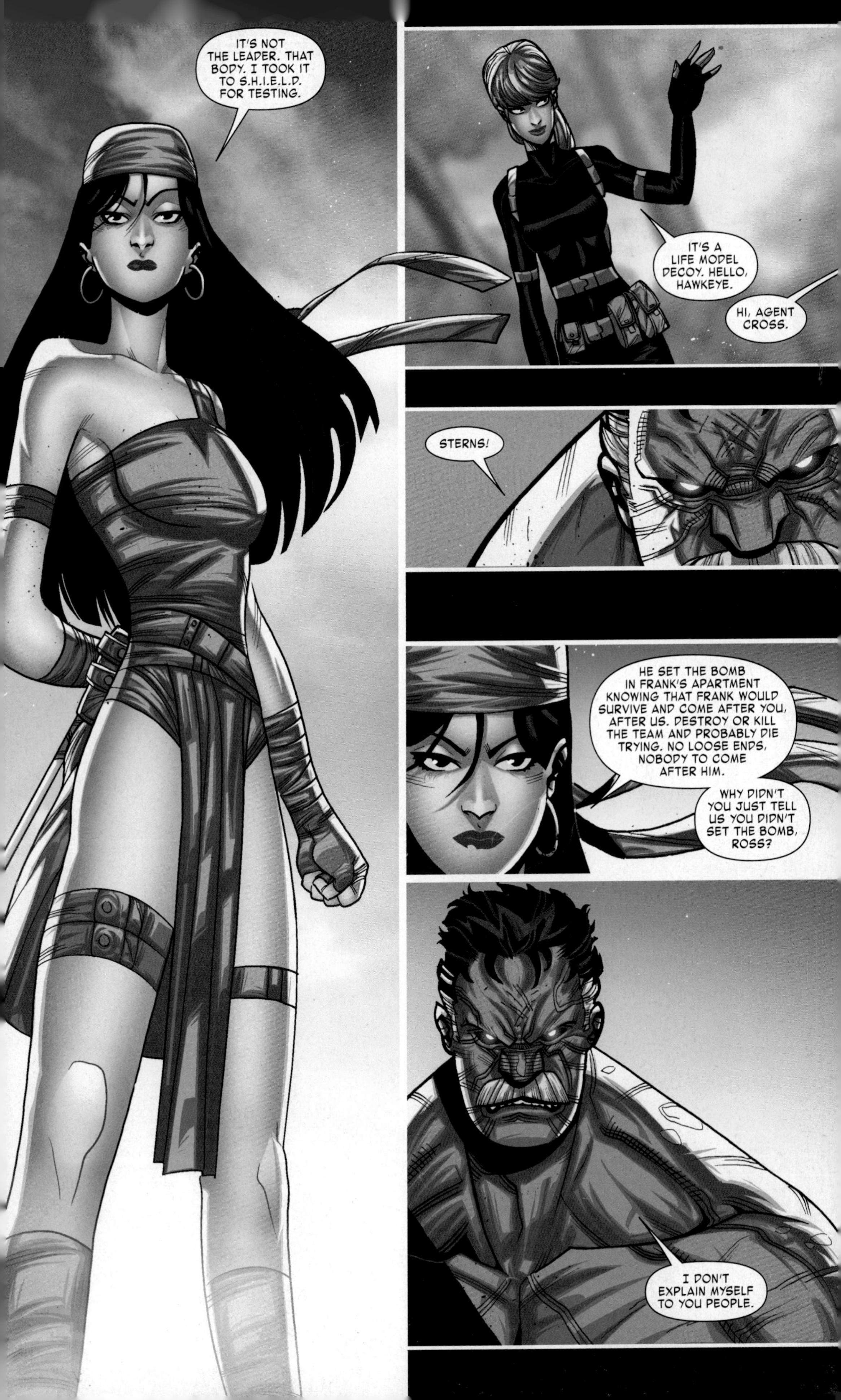
IT'S NOT THE LEADER. THAT BODY. I TOOK IT TO S.H.I.E.L.D. FOR TESTING.
IT'S A LIFE MODEL DECOY. HELLO, HAWKEYE.
HI, AGENT CROSS.
STERNS!
HE SET THE BOMB IN FRANK'S APARTMENT KNOWING THAT FRANK WOULD SURVIVE AND COME AFTER YOU, AFTER US. DESTROY OR KILL THE TEAM AND PROBABLY DIE TRYING. NO LOOSE ENDS, NOBODY TO COME AFTER HIM.
WHY DIDN'T YOU JUST TELL US YOU DIDN'T SET THE BOMB, ROSS?
I DON'T EXPLAIN MYSELF TO YOU PEOPLE.

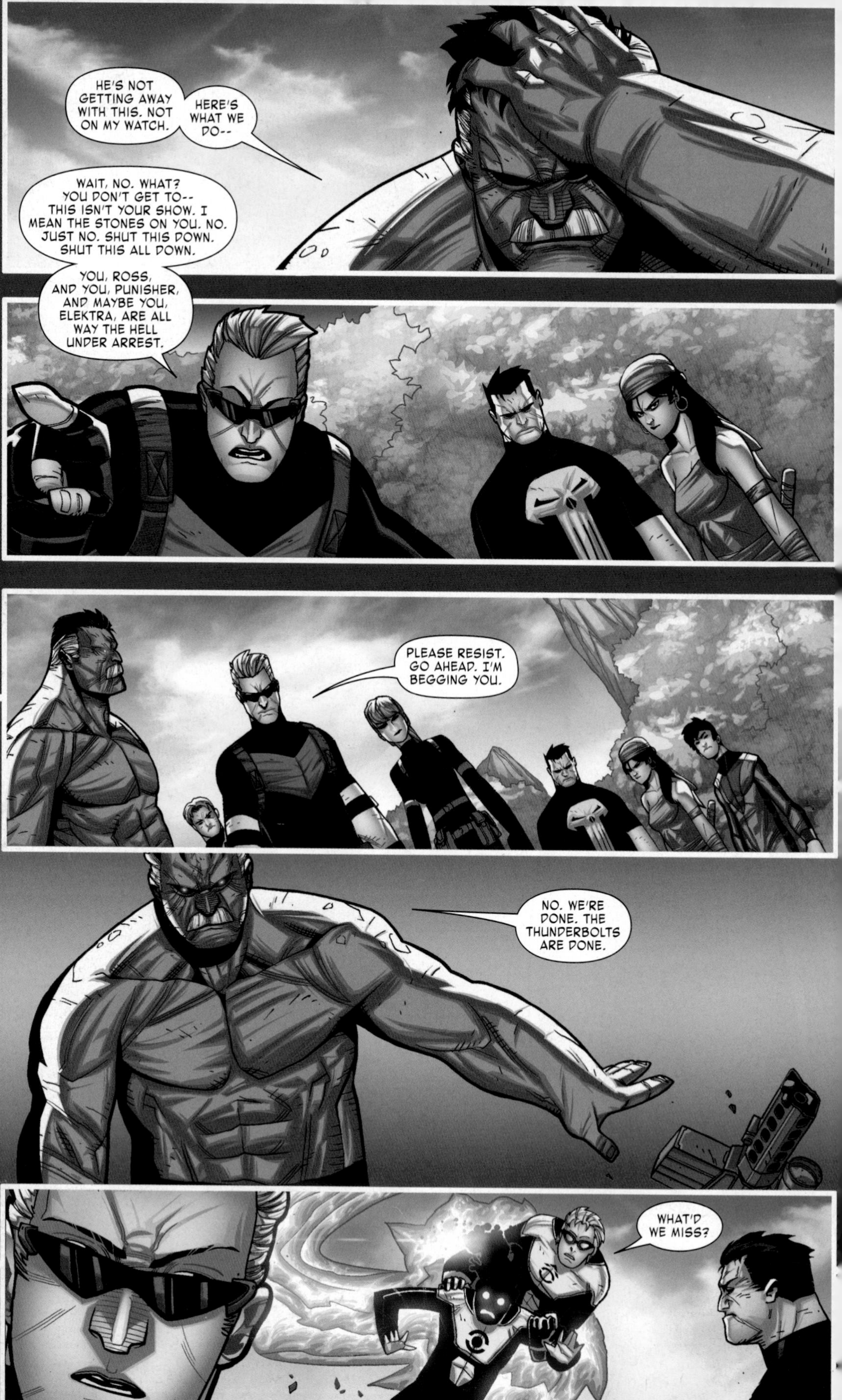
HE'S NOT GETTING AWAY WITH THIS. NOT ON MY WATCH.
HERE'S WHAT WE DO--
WAIT, NO. WHAT? YOU DON'T GET TO-- THIS ISN'T YOUR SHOW. I MEAN THE STONES ON YOU. NO. JUST NO. SHUT THIS DOWN. SHUT THIS ALL DOWN.
YOU, ROSS, AND YOU, PUNISHER, AND MAYBE YOU, ELEKTRA, ARE ALL WAY THE HELL UNDER ARREST.
PLEASE RESIST. GO AHEAD. I'M BEGGING YOU.
NO. WE'RE DONE. THE THUNDERBOLTS ARE DONE.
WHAT'D WE MISS?

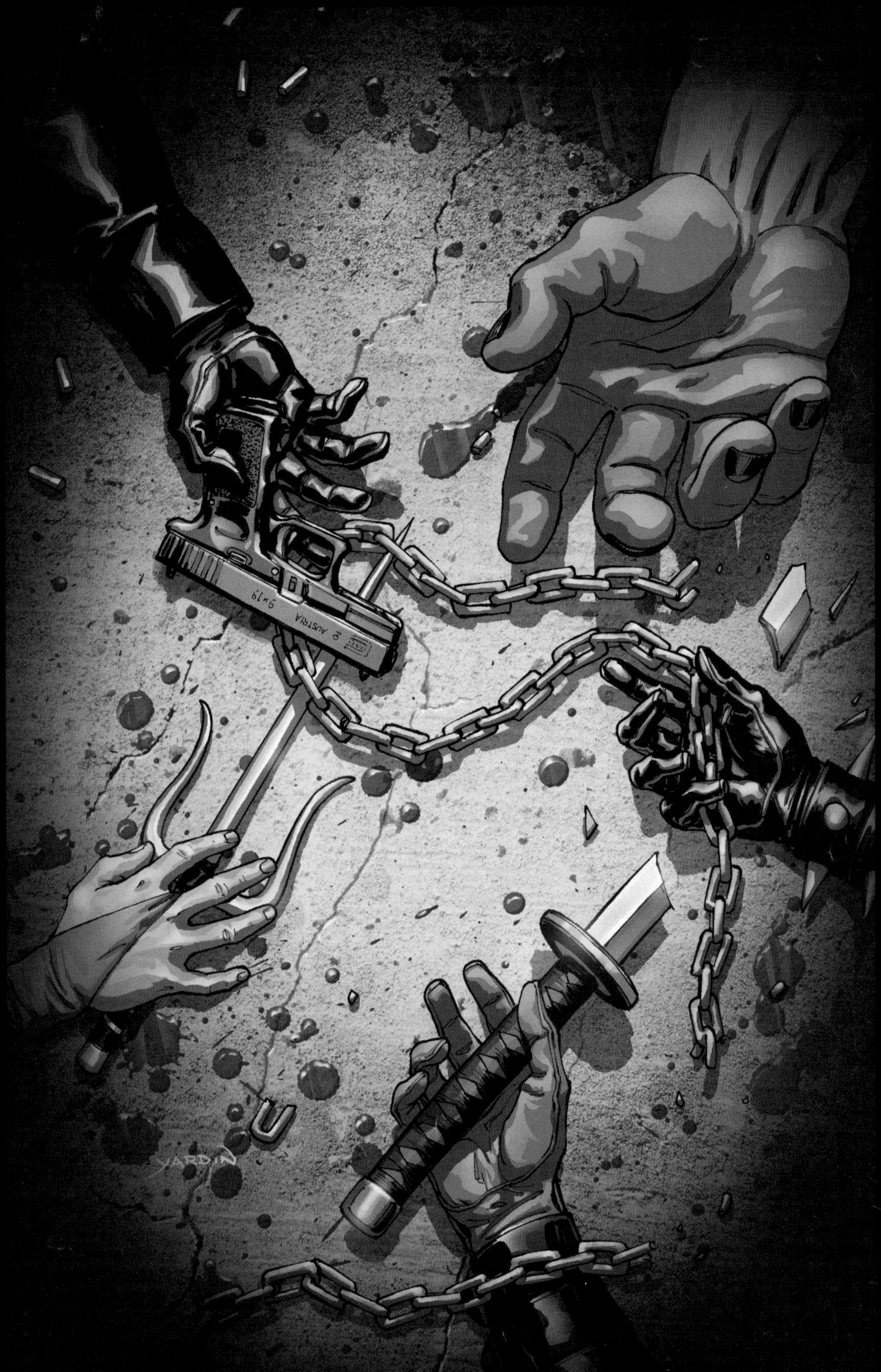
YARDIN

THIRTY-TWO

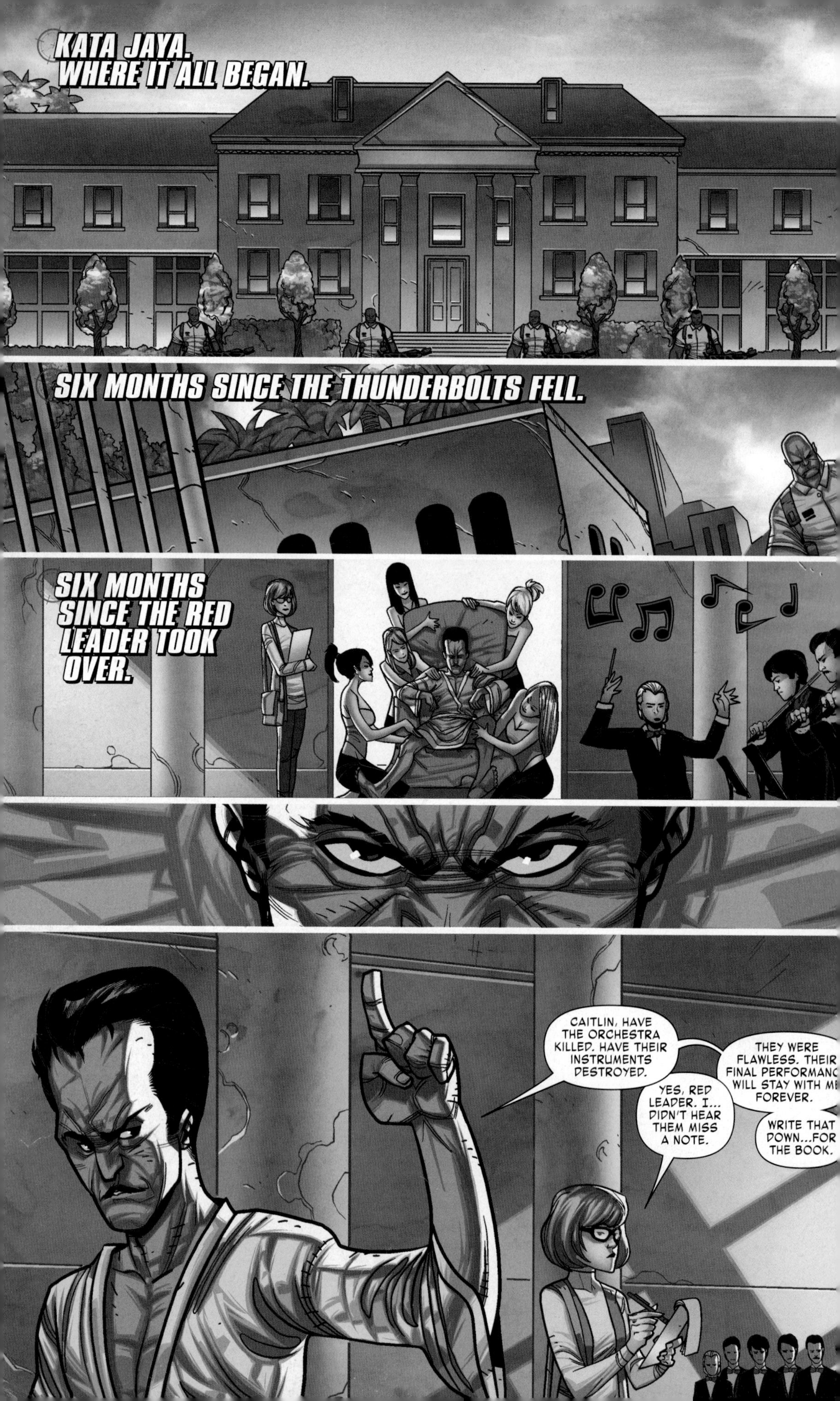

KATA JAYA. WHERE IT ALL BEGAN.
SIX MONTHS SINCE THE THUNDERBOLTS FELL.
SIX MONTHS SINCE THE RED LEADER TOOK OVER.
CAITLIN, HAVE THE ORCHESTRA KILLED. HAVE THEIR INSTRUMENTS DESTROYED.
YES, RED LEADER. I... DIDN'T HEAR THEM MISS A NOTE.
THEY WERE FLAWLESS. THEIR FINAL PERFORMANC WILL STAY WITH M FOREVER.
WRITE THAT DOWN...FOR THE BOOK.

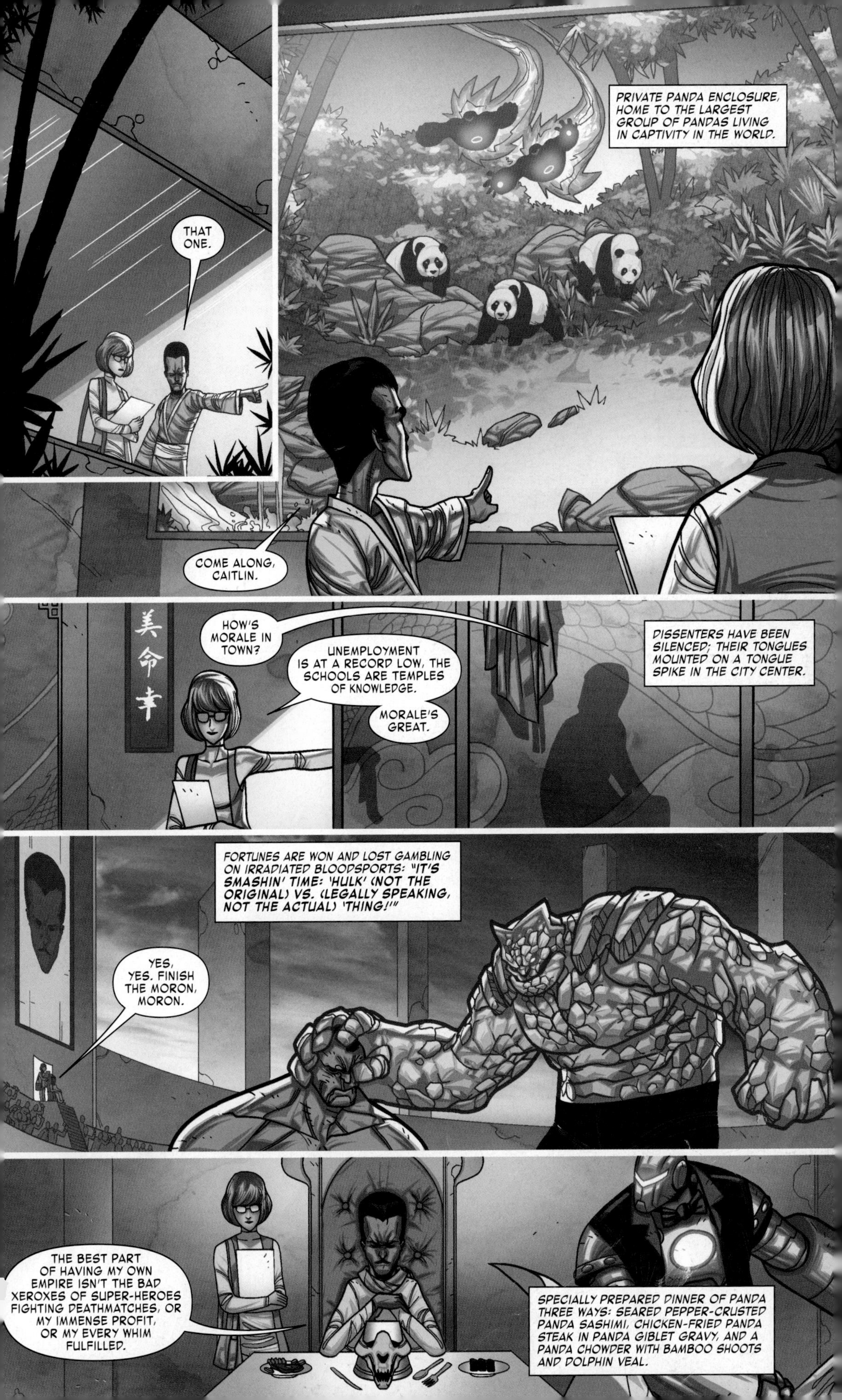
PRIVATE PANDA ENCLOSURE, HOME TO THE LARGEST GROUP OF PANDAS LIVING IN CAPTIVITY IN THE WORLD.
THAT ONE.
COME ALONG, CAITLIN.
HOW'S MORALE IN TOWN?
UNEMPLOYMENT IS AT A RECORD LOW, THE SCHOOLS ARE TEMPLES OF KNOWLEDGE.
MORALE'S GREAT.
DISSENTERS HAVE BEEN SILENCED; THEIR TONGUES MOUNTED ON A TONGUE SPIKE IN THE CITY CENTER.
FORTUNES ARE WON AND LOST GAMBLING ON IRRADIATED BLOODSPORTS: "IT'S SMASHIN' TIME: 'HULK' (NOT THE ORIGINAL) VS. (LEGALLY SPEAKING, NOT THE ACTUAL) 'THING!'"
YES, YES. FINISH THE MORON, MORON.
THE BEST PART OF HAVING MY OWN EMPIRE ISN'T THE BAD XEROXES OF SUPER-HEROES FIGHTING DEATHMATCHES, OR MY IMMENSE PROFIT, OR MY EVERY WHIM FULFILLED.
SPECIALLY PREPARED DINNER OF PANDA THREE WAYS: SEARED PEPPER-CRUSTED PANDA SASHIMI, CHICKEN-FRIED PANDA STEAK IN PANDA GIBLET GRAVY, AND A PANDA CHOWDER WITH BAMBOO SHOOTS AND DOLPHIN VEAL.

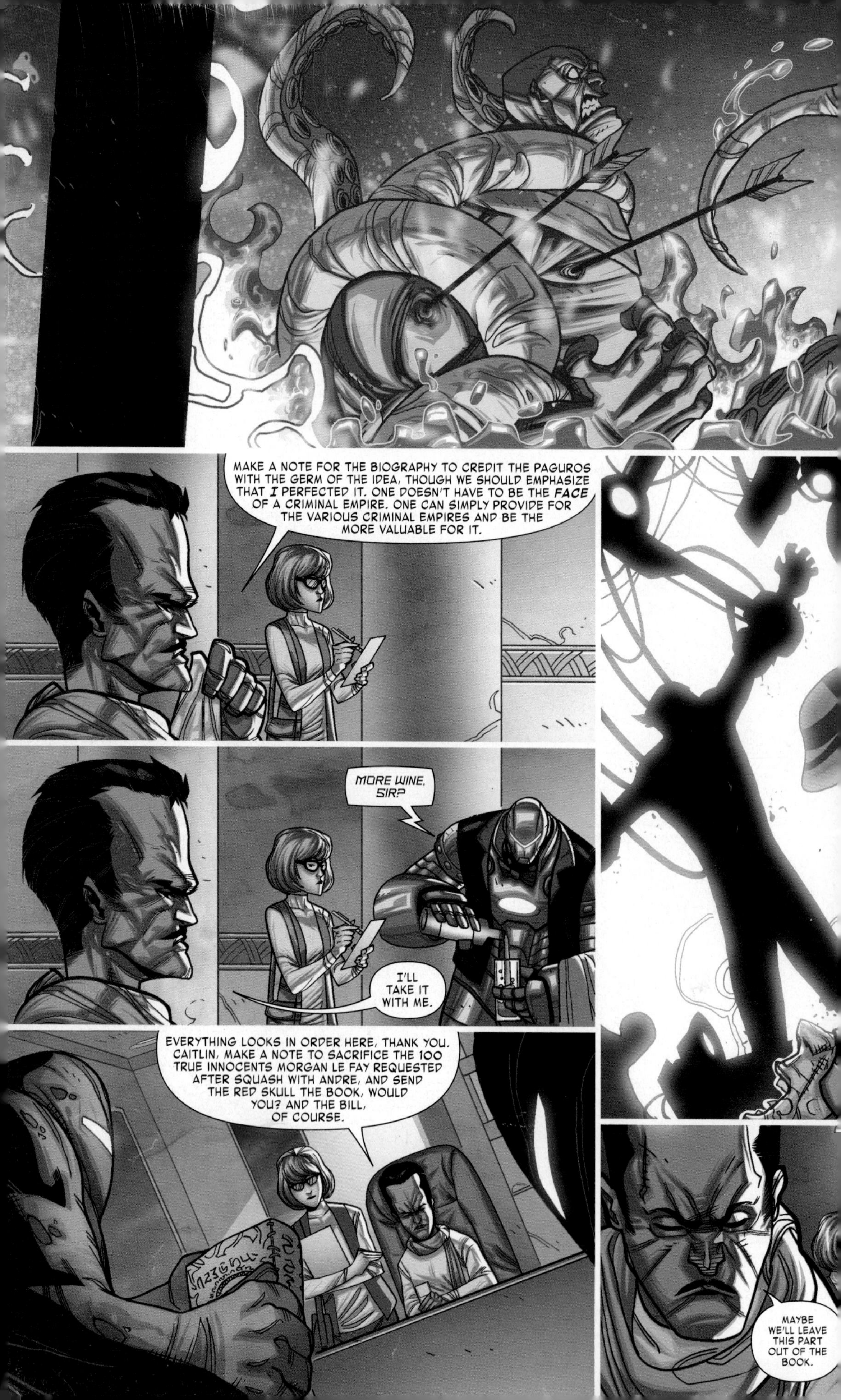
MAKE A NOTE FOR THE BIOGRAPHY TO CREDIT THE PAGUROS WITH THE GERM OF THE IDEA, THOUGH WE SHOULD EMPHASIZE THAT *I* PERFECTED IT. ONE DOESN'T HAVE TO BE THE *FACE* OF A CRIMINAL EMPIRE. ONE CAN SIMPLY PROVIDE FOR THE VARIOUS CRIMINAL EMPIRES AND BE THE MORE VALUABLE FOR IT.
MORE WINE, SIR?
I'LL TAKE IT WITH ME.
EVERYTHING LOOKS IN ORDER HERE, THANK YOU. CAITLIN, MAKE A NOTE TO SACRIFICE THE 100 TRUE INNOCENTS MORGAN LE FAY REQUESTED AFTER SQUASH WITH ANDRE, AND SEND THE RED SKULL THE BOOK, WOULD YOU? AND THE BILL, OF COURSE.
MAYBE WE'LL LEAVE THIS PART OUT OF THE BOOK.

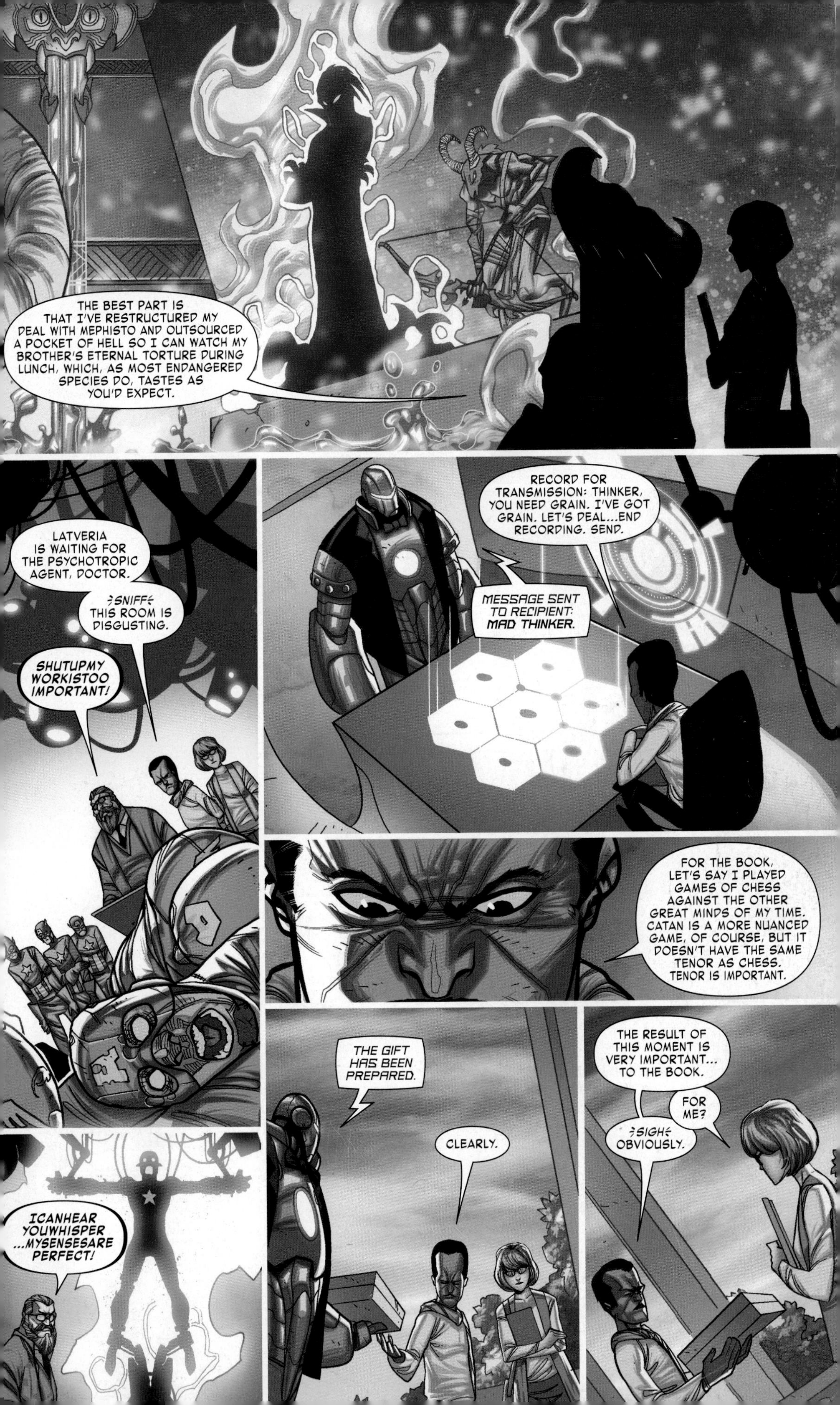
THE BEST PART IS THAT I'VE RESTRUCTURED MY DEAL WITH MEPHISTO AND OUTSOURCED A POCKET OF HELL SO I CAN WATCH MY BROTHER'S ETERNAL TORTURE DURING LUNCH, WHICH, AS MOST ENDANGERED SPECIES DO, TASTES AS YOU'D EXPECT.
LATVERIA IS WAITING FOR THE PSYCHOTROPIC AGENT, DOCTOR.
SNIFF THIS ROOM IS DISGUSTING.
SHUTUPMY WORKISTOO IMPORTANT!
RECORD FOR TRANSMISSION: THINKER, YOU NEED GRAIN. I'VE GOT GRAIN. LET'S DEAL...END RECORDING. SEND.
MESSAGE SENT TO RECIPIENT: MAD THINKER.
FOR THE BOOK, LET'S SAY I PLAYED GAMES OF CHESS AGAINST THE OTHER GREAT MINDS OF MY TIME. CATAN IS A MORE NUANCED GAME, OF COURSE, BUT IT DOESN'T HAVE THE SAME TENOR AS CHESS. TENOR IS IMPORTANT.
ICANHEAR YOUWHISPER ...MYSENSESARE PERFECT!
THE GIFT HAS BEEN PREPARED.
CLEARLY.
THE RESULT OF THIS MOMENT IS VERY IMPORTANT... TO THE BOOK.
FOR ME?
SIGH OBVIOUSLY.

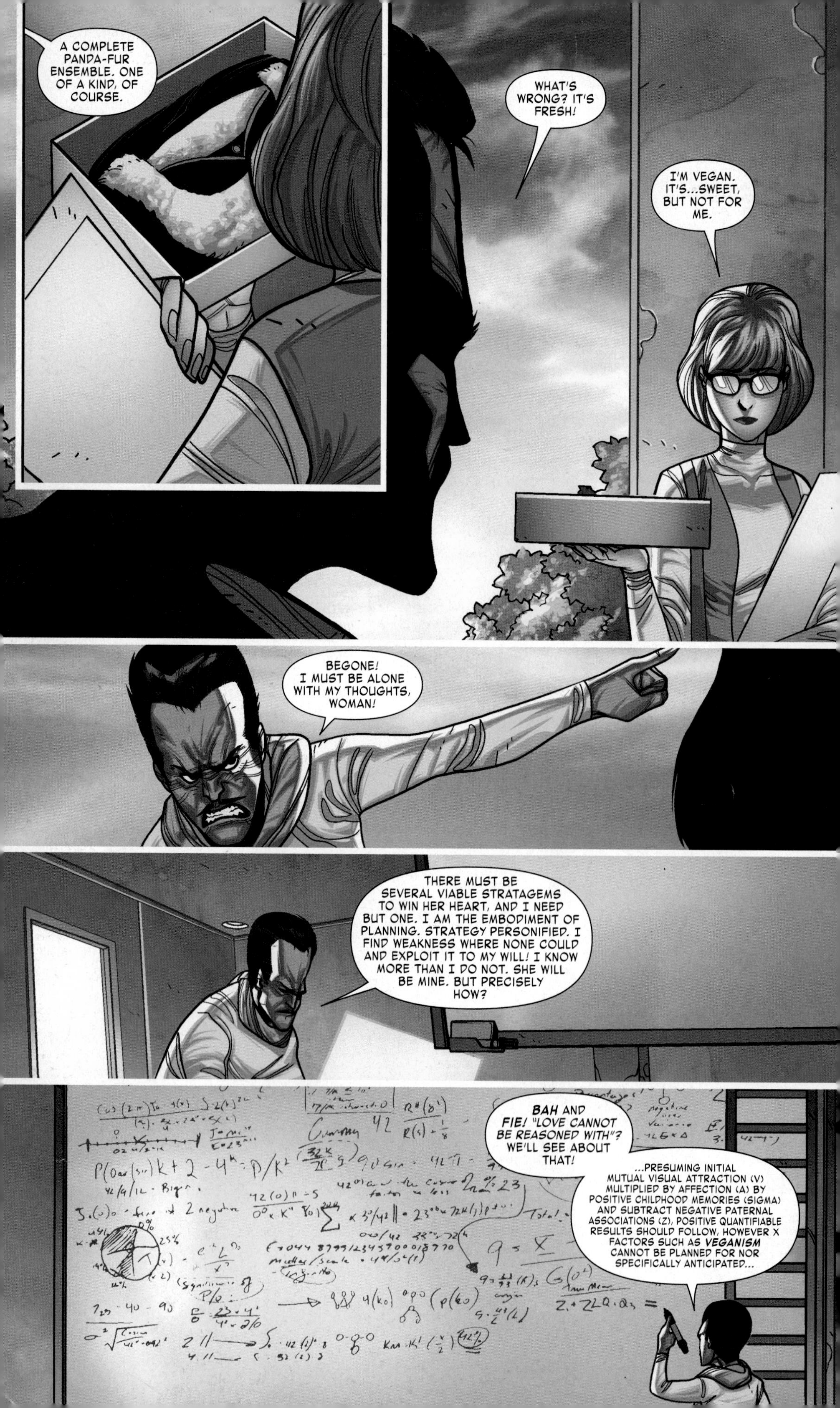
A COMPLETE PANDA-FUR ENSEMBLE. ONE OF A KIND, OF COURSE.
WHAT'S WRONG? IT'S FRESH!
I'M VEGAN. IT'S...SWEET, BUT NOT FOR ME.
BEGONE! I MUST BE ALONE WITH MY THOUGHTS, WOMAN!
THERE MUST BE SEVERAL VIABLE STRATAGEMS TO WIN HER HEART, AND I NEED BUT ONE. I AM THE EMBODIMENT OF PLANNING. STRATEGY PERSONIFIED. I FIND WEAKNESS WHERE NONE COULD AND EXPLOIT IT TO MY WILL! I KNOW MORE THAN I DO NOT. SHE WILL BE MINE. BUT PRECISELY HOW?
BAH AND FIE! "LOVE CANNOT BE REASONED WITH"? WE'LL SEE ABOUT THAT!
...PRESUMING INITIAL MUTUAL VISUAL ATTRACTION (V) MULTIPLIED BY AFFECTION (A) BY POSITIVE CHILDHOOD MEMORIES (SIGMA) AND SUBTRACT NEGATIVE PATERNAL ASSOCIATIONS (Z), POSITIVE QUANTIFIABLE RESULTS SHOULD FOLLOW, HOWEVER X FACTORS SUCH AS VEGANISM CANNOT BE PLANNED FOR NOR SPECIFICALLY ANTICIPATED...

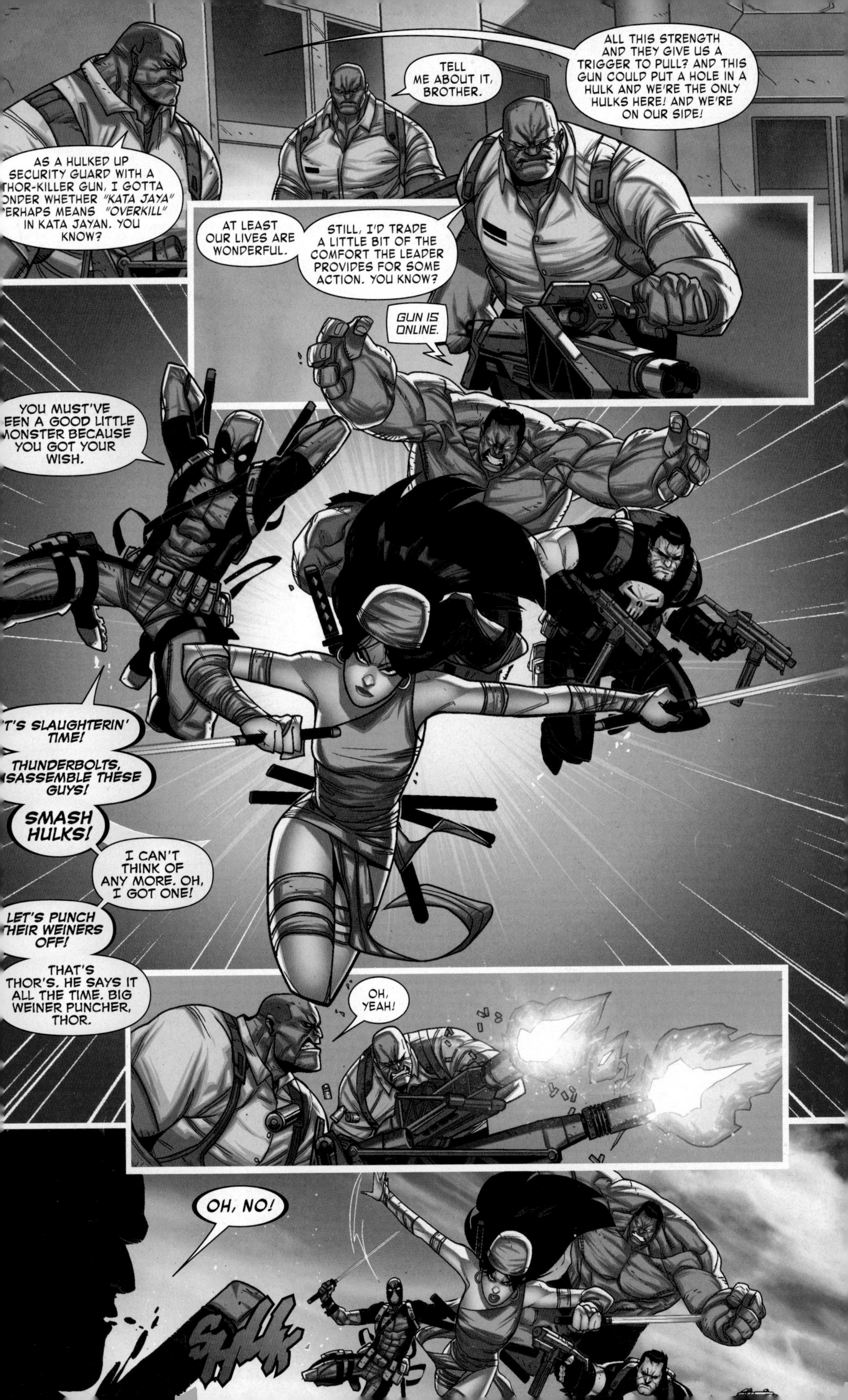
AS A HULKED UP SECURITY GUARD WITH A THOR-KILLER GUN, I GOTTA ONDER WHETHER "KATA JAYA" ERHAPS MEANS "OVERKILL" IN KATA JAYAN. YOU KNOW?
TELL ME ABOUT IT, BROTHER.
ALL THIS STRENGTH AND THEY GIVE US A TRIGGER TO PULL? AND THIS GUN COULD PUT A HOLE IN A HULK AND WE'RE THE ONLY HULKS HERE! AND WE'RE ON OUR SIDE!
AT LEAST OUR LIVES ARE WONDERFUL.
STILL, I'D TRADE A LITTLE BIT OF THE COMFORT THE LEADER PROVIDES FOR SOME ACTION. YOU KNOW?
GUN IS ONLINE.
YOU MUST'VE EEN A GOOD LITTLE MONSTER BECAUSE YOU GOT YOUR WISH.
'T'S SLAUGHTERIN' TIME!
THUNDERBOLTS, ISASSEMBLE THESE GUYS!
SMASH HULKS!
I CAN'T THINK OF ANY MORE. OH, I GOT ONE!
LET'S PUNCH HEIR WEINERS OFF!
THAT'S THOR'S. HE SAYS IT ALL THE TIME. BIG WEINER PUNCHER, THOR.
OH, YEAH!
OH, NO!

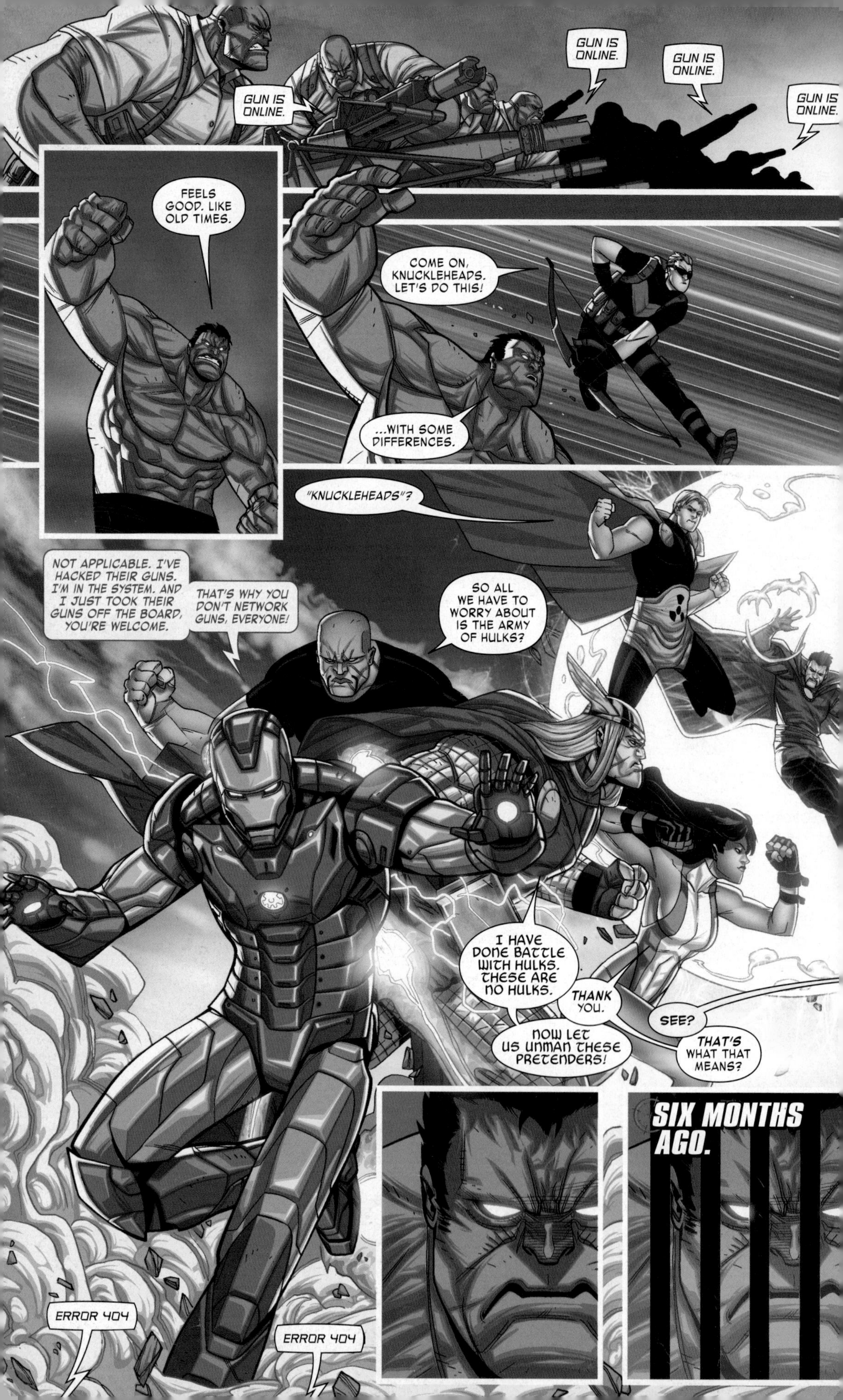
GUN IS ONLINE.
GUN IS ONLINE.
GUN IS ONLINE.
GUN IS ONLINE.
FEELS GOOD. LIKE OLD TIMES.
COME ON, KNUCKLEHEADS. LET'S DO THIS!
...WITH SOME DIFFERENCES.
"KNUCKLEHEADS"?
NOT APPLICABLE. I'VE HACKED THEIR GUNS. I'M IN THE SYSTEM. AND I JUST TOOK THEIR GUNS OFF THE BOARD, YOU'RE WELCOME.
THAT'S WHY YOU DON'T NETWORK GUNS, EVERYONE!
SO ALL WE HAVE TO WORRY ABOUT IS THE ARMY OF HULKS?
I HAVE DONE BATTLE WITH HULKS. THESE ARE NO HULKS.
THANK YOU.
NOW LET US UNMAN THESE PRETENDERS!
SEE?
THAT'S WHAT THAT MEANS?
ERROR 404
ERROR 404
SIX MONTHS AGO.

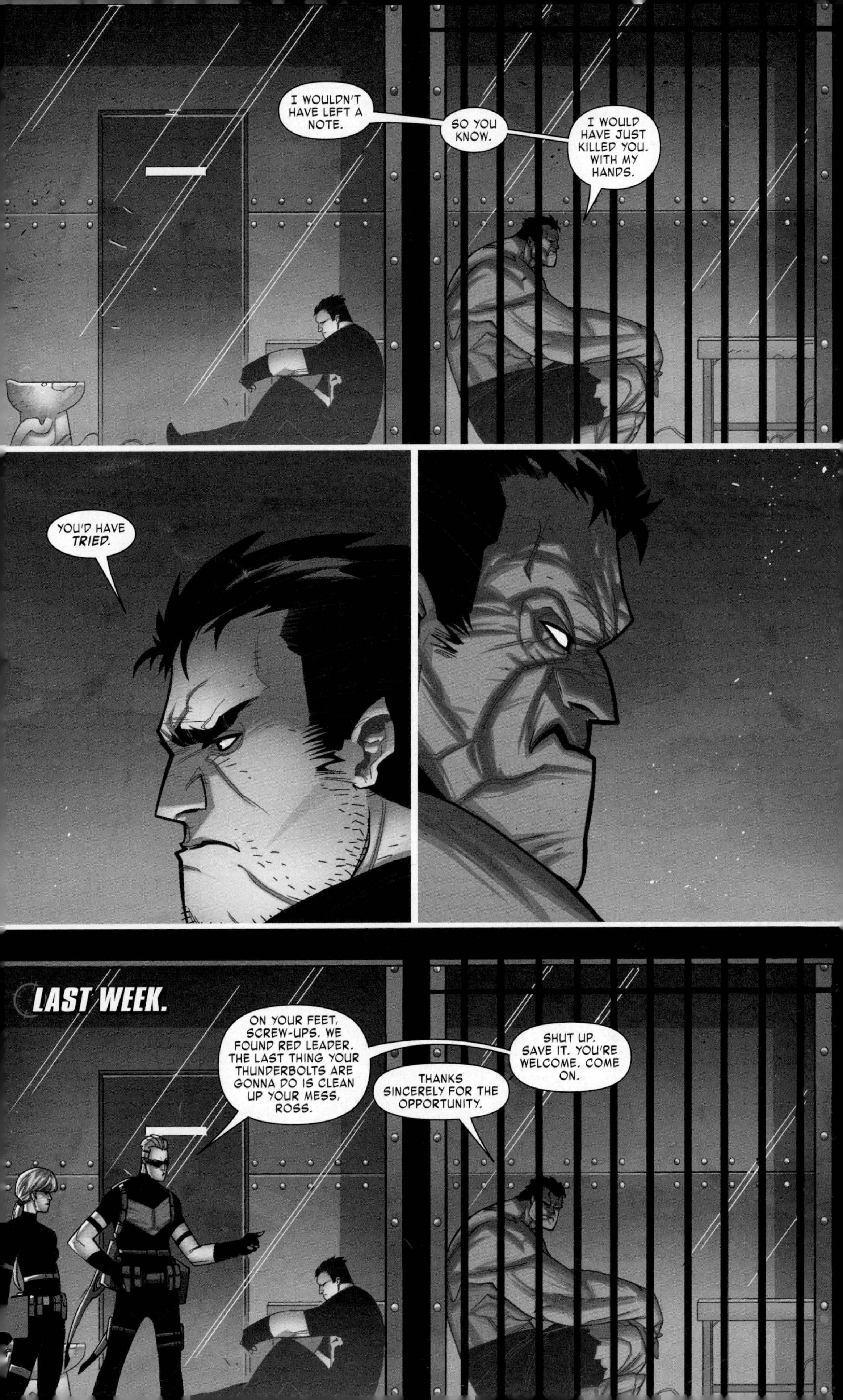
I WOULDN'T HAVE LEFT A NOTE.
SO YOU KNOW.
I WOULD HAVE JUST KILLED YOU. WITH MY HANDS.
YOU'D HAVE *TRIED*.
LAST WEEK.
ON YOUR FEET, SCREW-UPS. WE FOUND RED LEADER. THE LAST THING YOUR THUNDERBOLTS ARE GONNA DO IS CLEAN UP YOUR MESS, ROSS.
THANKS SINCERELY FOR THE OPPORTUNITY.
SHUT UP. SAVE IT. YOU'RE WELCOME. COME ON.

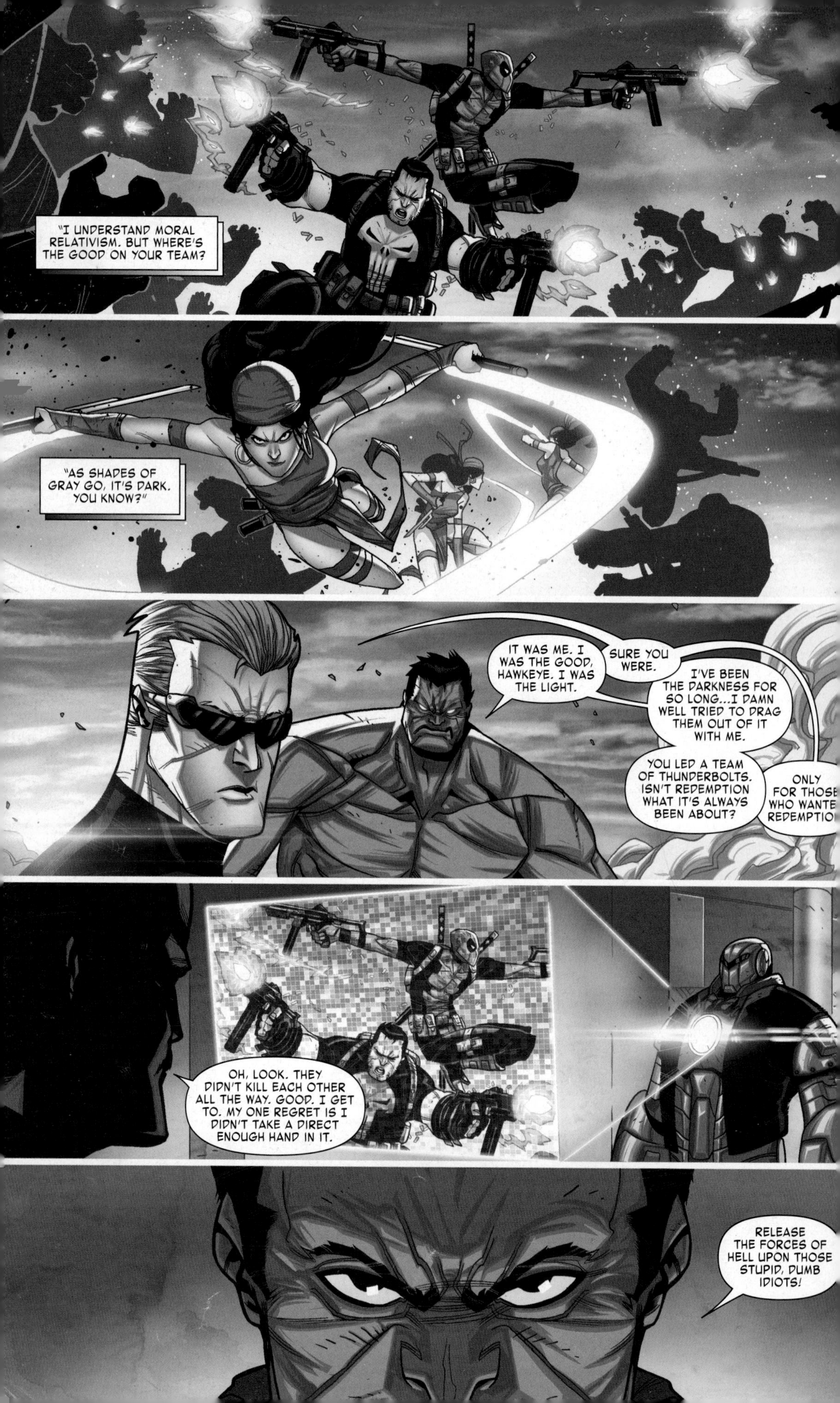
"I UNDERSTAND MORAL RELATIVISM. BUT WHERE'S THE GOOD ON YOUR TEAM?
"AS SHADES OF GRAY GO, IT'S DARK. YOU KNOW?"
IT WAS ME. I WAS THE GOOD, HAWKEYE. I WAS THE LIGHT.
SURE YOU WERE.
I'VE BEEN THE DARKNESS FOR SO LONG...I DAMN WELL TRIED TO DRAG THEM OUT OF IT WITH ME.
YOU LED A TEAM OF THUNDERBOLTS. ISN'T REDEMPTION WHAT IT'S ALWAYS BEEN ABOUT?
ONLY FOR THOSE WHO WANTE REDEMPTIO
OH, LOOK. THEY DIDN'T KILL EACH OTHER ALL THE WAY. GOOD. I GET TO. MY ONE REGRET IS I DIDN'T TAKE A DIRECT ENOUGH HAND IN IT.
RELEASE THE FORCES OF HELL UPON THOSE STUPID, DUMB IDIOTS!

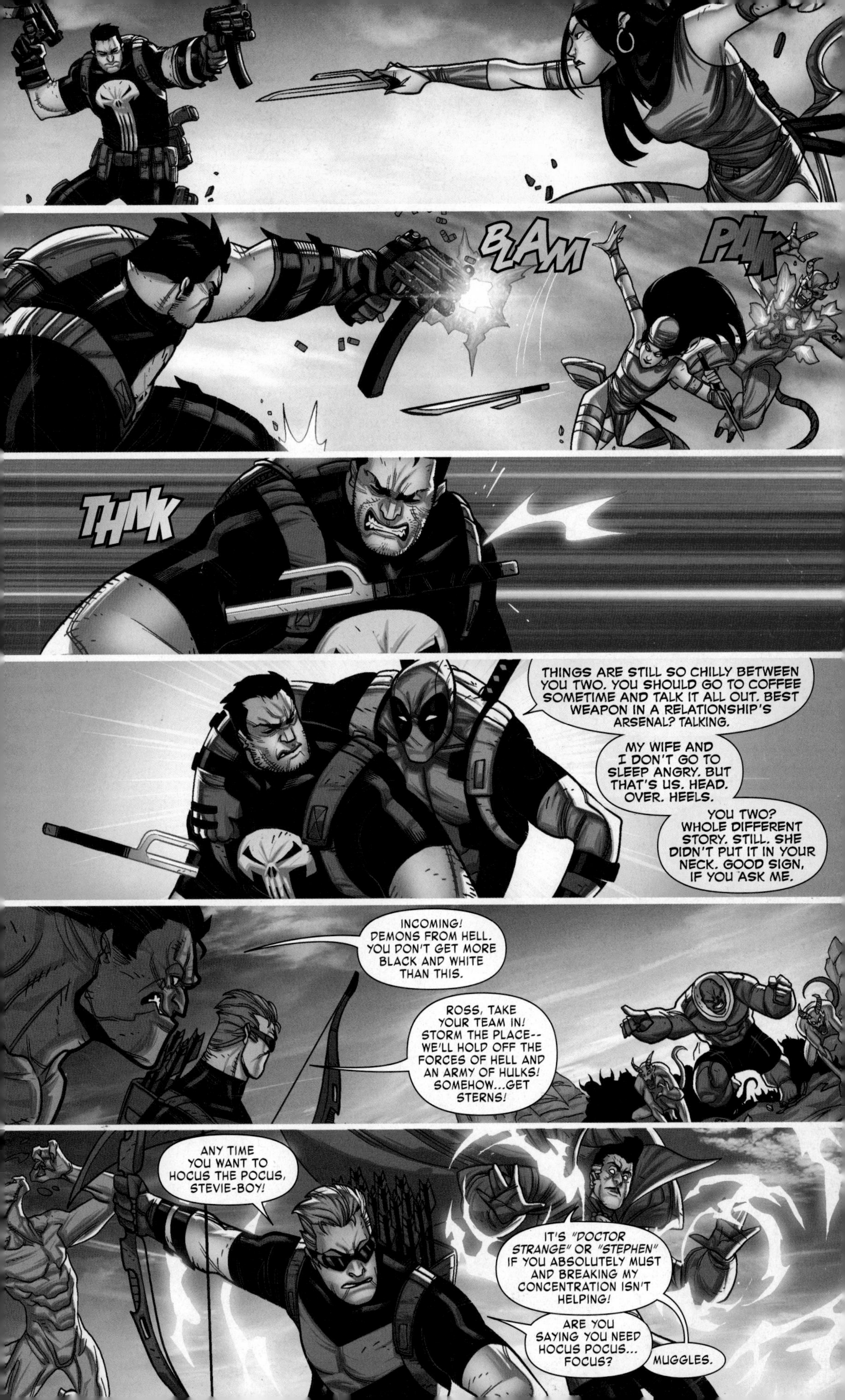
BLAM
PAK
THNK
THINGS ARE STILL SO CHILLY BETWEEN YOU TWO. YOU SHOULD GO TO COFFEE SOMETIME AND TALK IT ALL OUT. BEST WEAPON IN A RELATIONSHIP'S ARSENAL? TALKING.
MY WIFE AND I DON'T GO TO SLEEP ANGRY. BUT THAT'S US. HEAD. OVER. HEELS.
YOU TWO? WHOLE DIFFERENT STORY. STILL. SHE DIDN'T PUT IT IN YOUR NECK. GOOD SIGN, IF YOU ASK ME.
INCOMING! DEMONS FROM HELL. YOU DON'T GET MORE BLACK AND WHITE THAN THIS.
ROSS, TAKE YOUR TEAM IN! STORM THE PLACE-- WE'LL HOLD OFF THE FORCES OF HELL AND AN ARMY OF HULKS! SOMEHOW...GET STERNS!
ANY TIME YOU WANT TO HOCUS THE POCUS, STEVIE-BOY!
IT'S "DOCTOR STRANGE" OR "STEPHEN" IF YOU ABSOLUTELY MUST AND BREAKING MY CONCENTRATION ISN'T HELPING!
ARE YOU SAYING YOU NEED HOCUS POCUS... FOCUS?
MUGGLES.

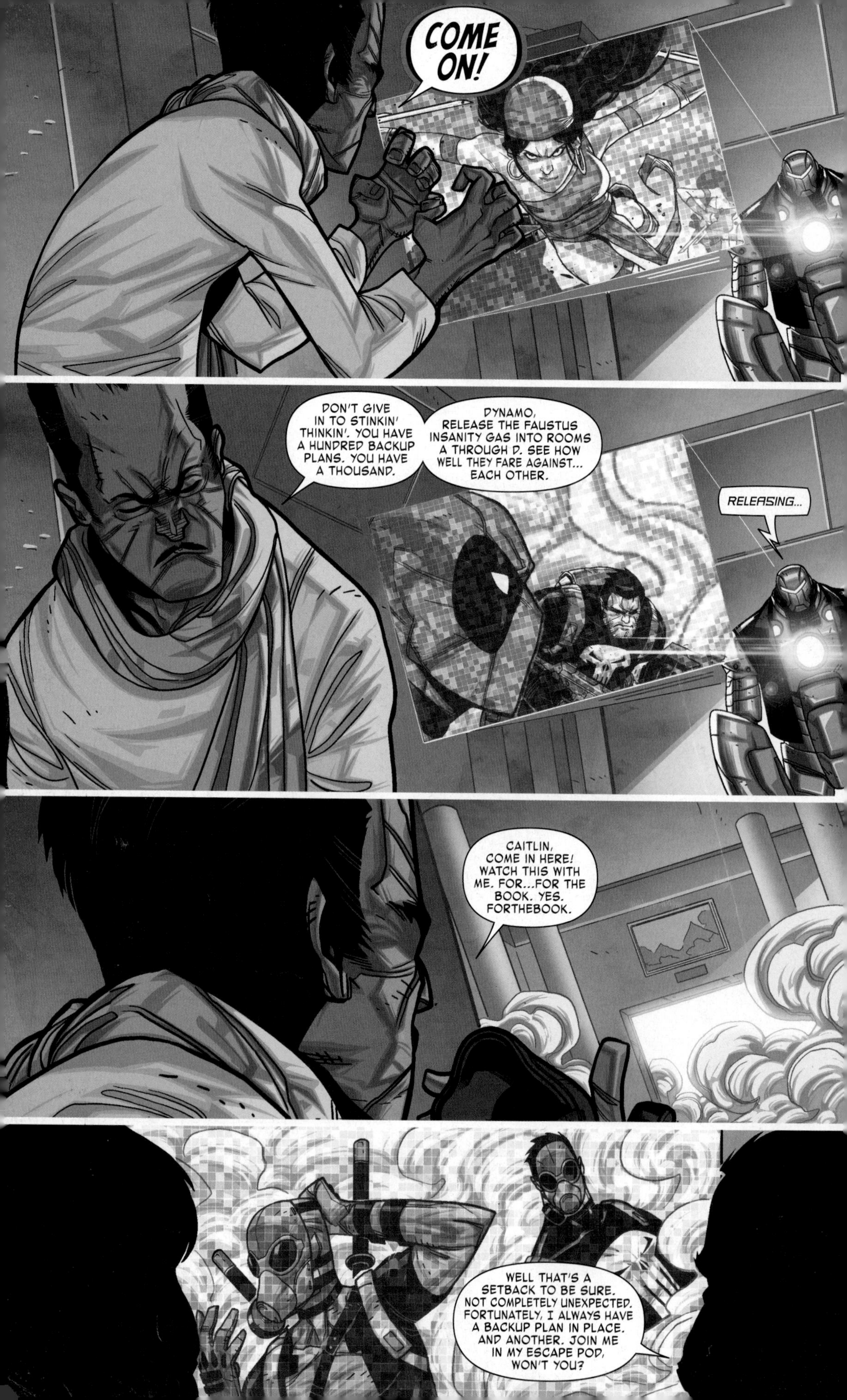
COME ON!
DON'T GIVE IN TO STINKIN' THINKIN'. YOU HAVE A HUNDRED BACKUP PLANS. YOU HAVE A THOUSAND.
DYNAMO, RELEASE THE FAUSTUS INSANITY GAS INTO ROOMS A THROUGH D. SEE HOW WELL THEY FARE AGAINST... EACH OTHER.
RELEASING...
CAITLIN, COME IN HERE! WATCH THIS WITH ME. FOR...FOR THE BOOK. YES. FORTHEBOOK.
WELL THAT'S A SETBACK TO BE SURE. NOT COMPLETELY UNEXPECTED. FORTUNATELY, I ALWAYS HAVE A BACKUP PLAN IN PLACE. AND ANOTHER. JOIN ME IN MY ESCAPE POD, WON'T YOU?

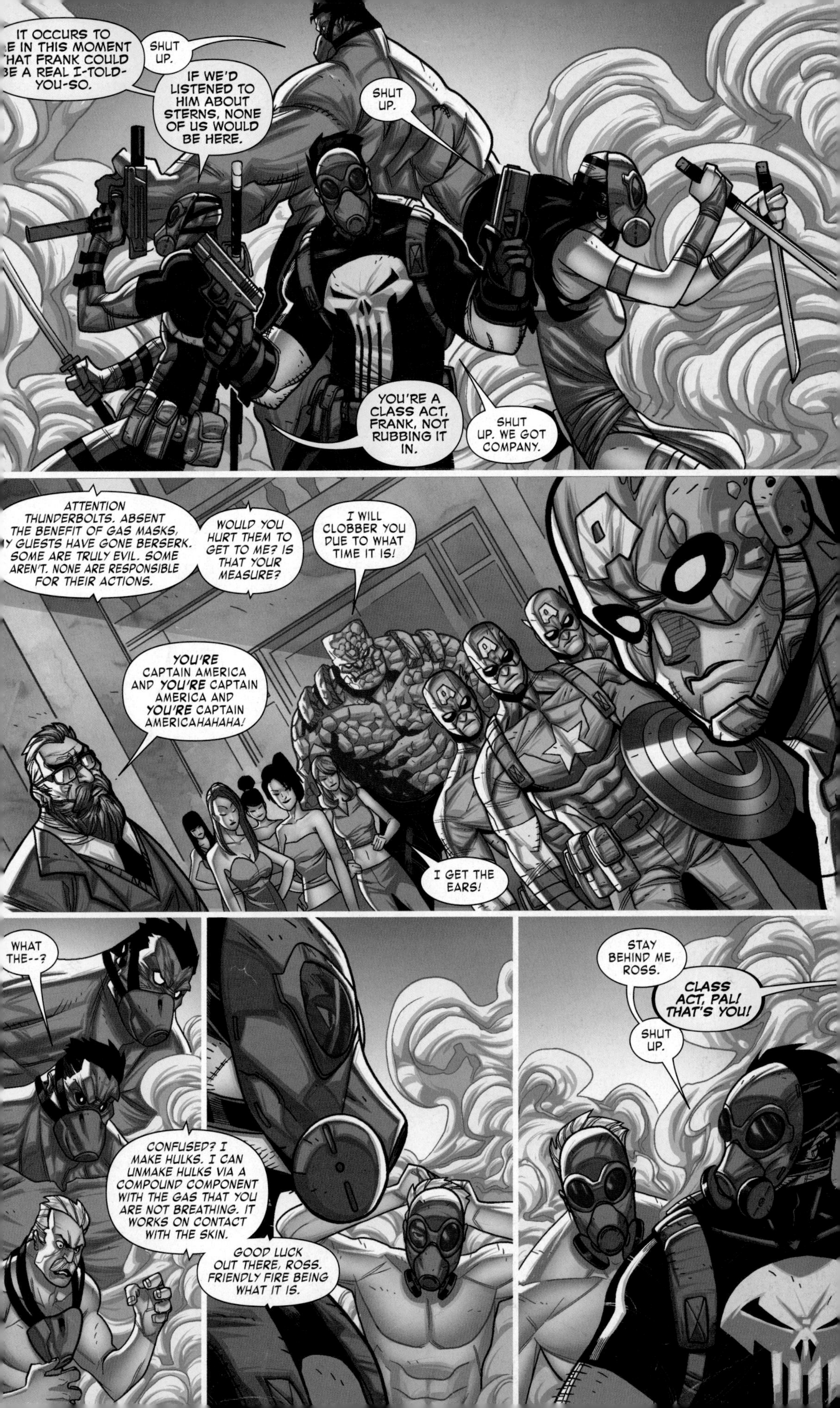
IT OCCURS TO E IN THIS MOMENT HAT FRANK COULD 3E A REAL I-TOLD-YOU-SO.
SHUT UP.
IF WE'D LISTENED TO HIM ABOUT STERNS, NONE OF US WOULD BE HERE.
SHUT UP.
YOU'RE A CLASS ACT, FRANK, NOT RUBBING IT IN.
SHUT UP. WE GOT COMPANY.
ATTENTION THUNDERBOLTS. ABSENT THE BENEFIT OF GAS MASKS, Y GUESTS HAVE GONE BERSERK. SOME ARE TRULY EVIL. SOME AREN'T. NONE ARE RESPONSIBLE FOR THEIR ACTIONS.
WOULD YOU HURT THEM TO GET TO ME? IS THAT YOUR MEASURE?
I WILL CLOBBER YOU DUE TO WHAT TIME IT IS!
YOU'RE CAPTAIN AMERICA AND YOU'RE CAPTAIN AMERICA AND YOU'RE CAPTAIN AMERICAHAHAHA!
I GET THE EARS!
WHAT THE--?
CONFUSED? I MAKE HULKS. I CAN UNMAKE HULKS VIA A COMPOUND COMPONENT WITH THE GAS THAT YOU ARE NOT BREATHING. IT WORKS ON CONTACT WITH THE SKIN.
GOOD LUCK OUT THERE, ROSS. FRIENDLY FIRE BEING WHAT IT IS.
STAY BEHIND ME, ROSS.
CLASS ACT, PAL! THAT'S YOU!
SHUT UP.

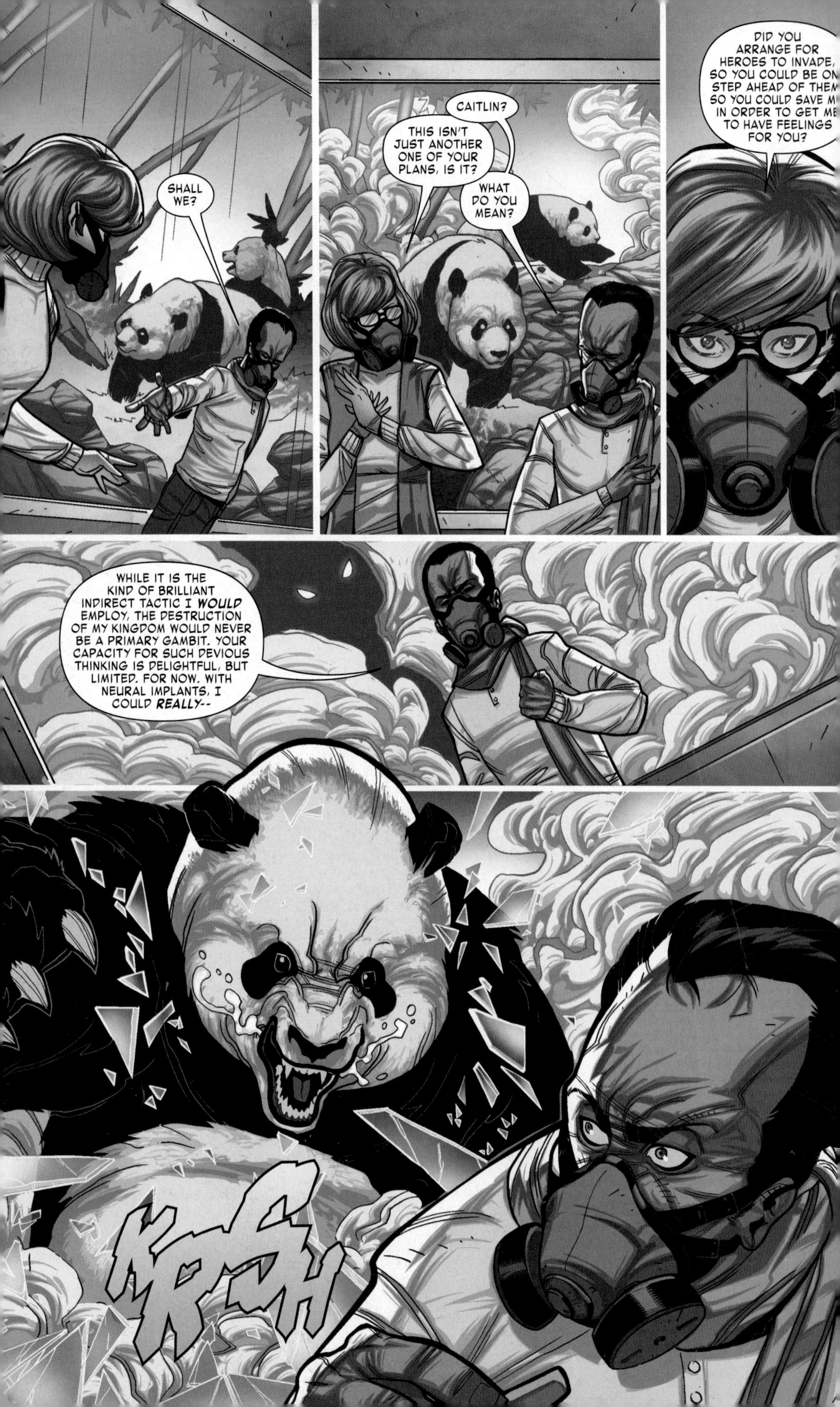
SHALL WE?
CAITLIN?
THIS ISN'T JUST ANOTHER ONE OF YOUR PLANS, IS IT?
WHAT DO YOU MEAN?
DID YOU ARRANGE FOR HEROES TO INVADE, SO YOU COULD BE ON STEP AHEAD OF THEM SO YOU COULD SAVE M IN ORDER TO GET ME TO HAVE FEELINGS FOR YOU?
WHILE IT IS THE KIND OF BRILLIANT INDIRECT TACTIC I WOULD EMPLOY, THE DESTRUCTION OF MY KINGDOM WOULD NEVER BE A PRIMARY GAMBIT. YOUR CAPACITY FOR SUCH DEVIOUS THINKING IS DELIGHTFUL, BUT LIMITED. FOR NOW. WITH NEURAL IMPLANTS, I COULD REALLY--
KRSH

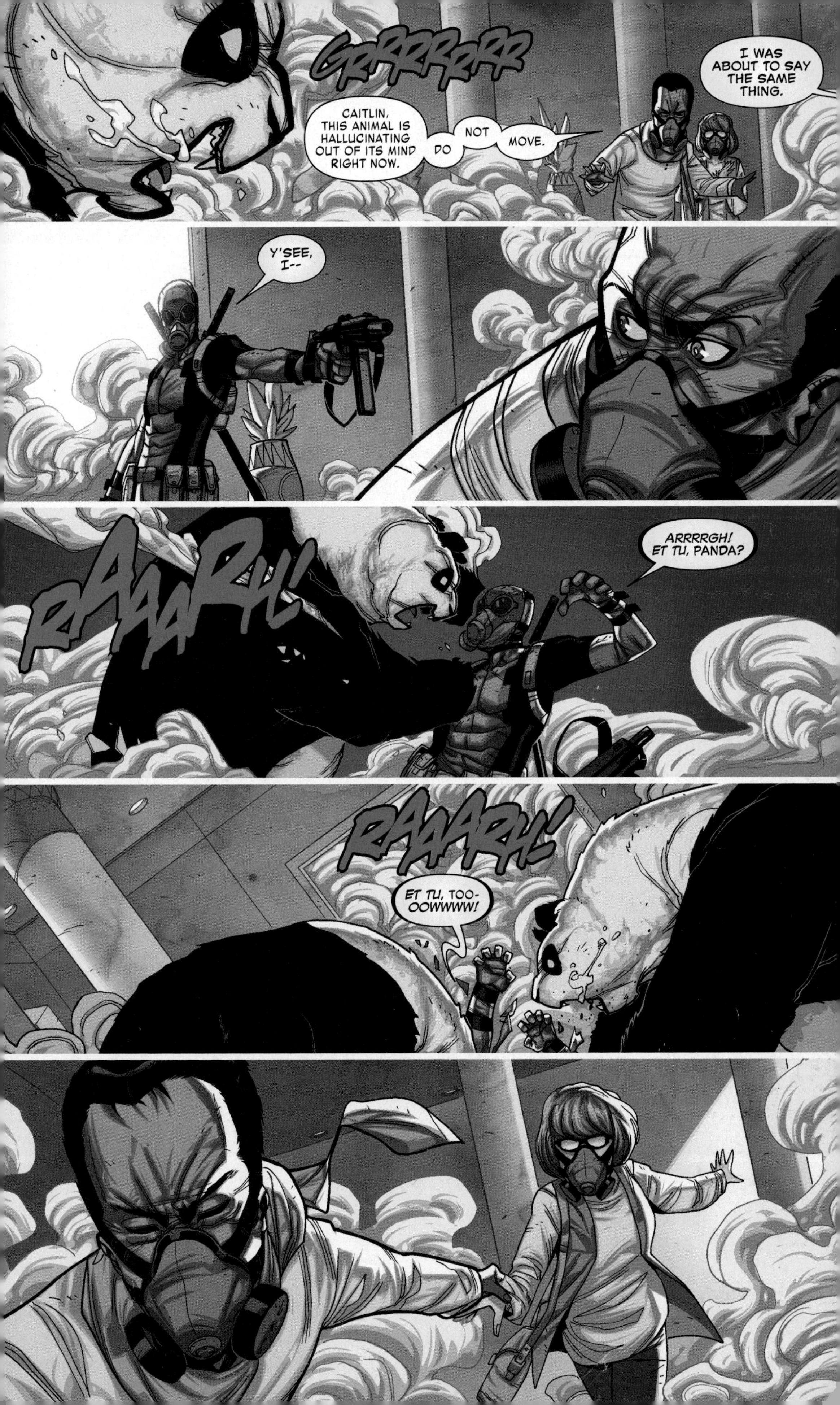
GRRRRRRR
CAITLIN, THIS ANIMAL IS HALLUCINATING OUT OF ITS MIND RIGHT NOW.
DO
NOT
MOVE.
I WAS ABOUT TO SAY THE SAME THING.
Y'SEE, I--
RAAARH!
ARRRRGH! ET TU, PANDA?
RAAARH!
ET TU, TOO-OOWWWW!

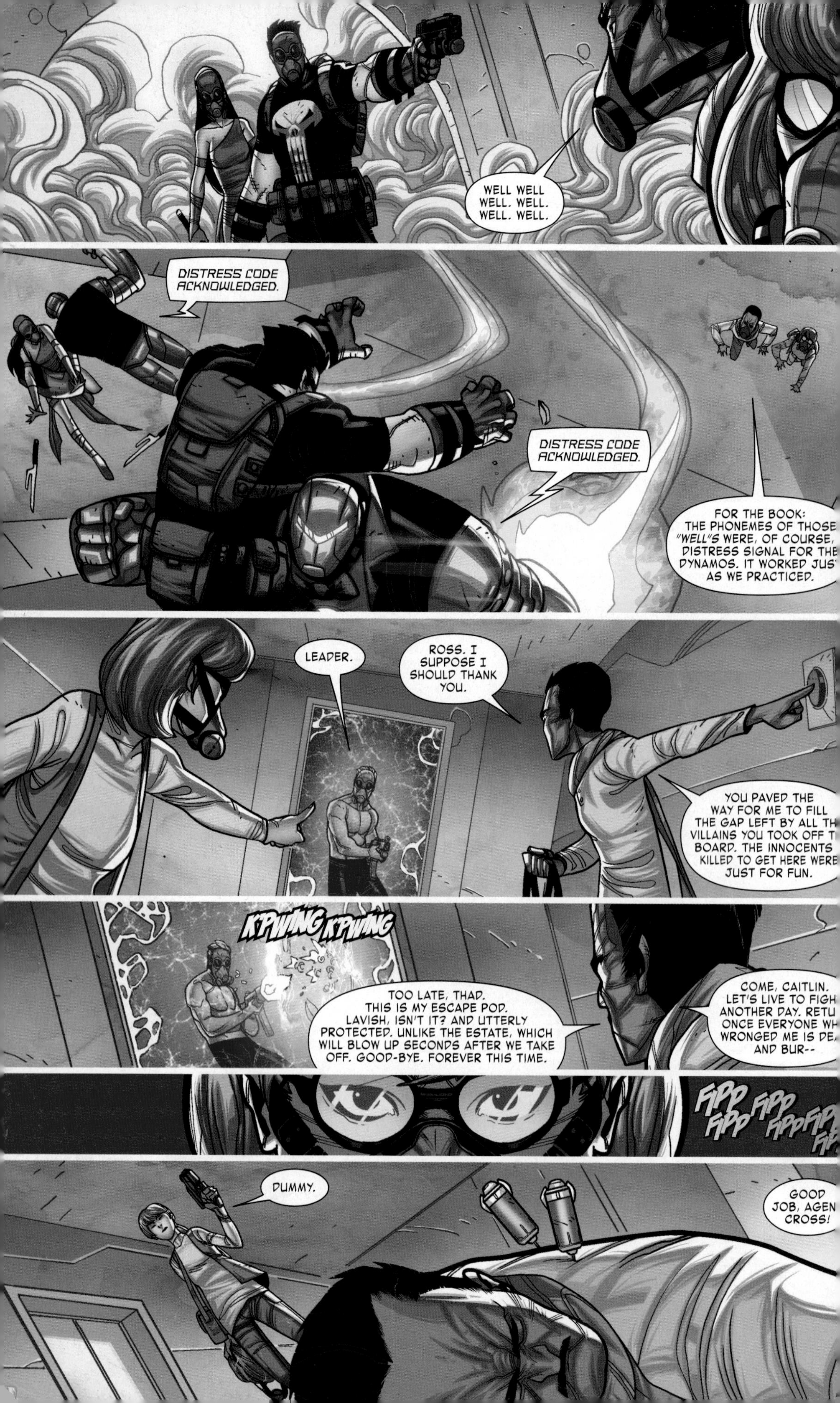
WELL WELL
WELL. WELL.
WELL. WELL.
DISTRESS CODE ACKNOWLEDGED.
DISTRESS CODE ACKNOWLEDGED.
FOR THE BOOK: THE PHONEMES OF THOSE "WELL"S WERE, OF COURSE, DISTRESS SIGNAL FOR THE DYNAMOS. IT WORKED JUST AS WE PRACTICED.
LEADER.
ROSS. I SUPPOSE I SHOULD THANK YOU.
YOU PAVED THE WAY FOR ME TO FILL THE GAP LEFT BY ALL TH VILLAINS YOU TOOK OFF T BOARD. THE INNOCENTS KILLED TO GET HERE WERE JUST FOR FUN.
K'PWING K'PWING
TOO LATE, THAD. THIS IS MY ESCAPE POD. LAVISH, ISN'T IT? AND UTTERLY PROTECTED. UNLIKE THE ESTATE, WHICH WILL BLOW UP SECONDS AFTER WE TAKE OFF. GOOD-BYE. FOREVER THIS TIME.
COME, CAITLIN. LET'S LIVE TO FIGH ANOTHER DAY. RETU ONCE EVERYONE WH WRONGED ME IS DE AND BUR--
FIPP FIPP FIPP FIPP FIPP FIPP FIP
DUMMY.
GOOD JOB, AGEN CROSS!

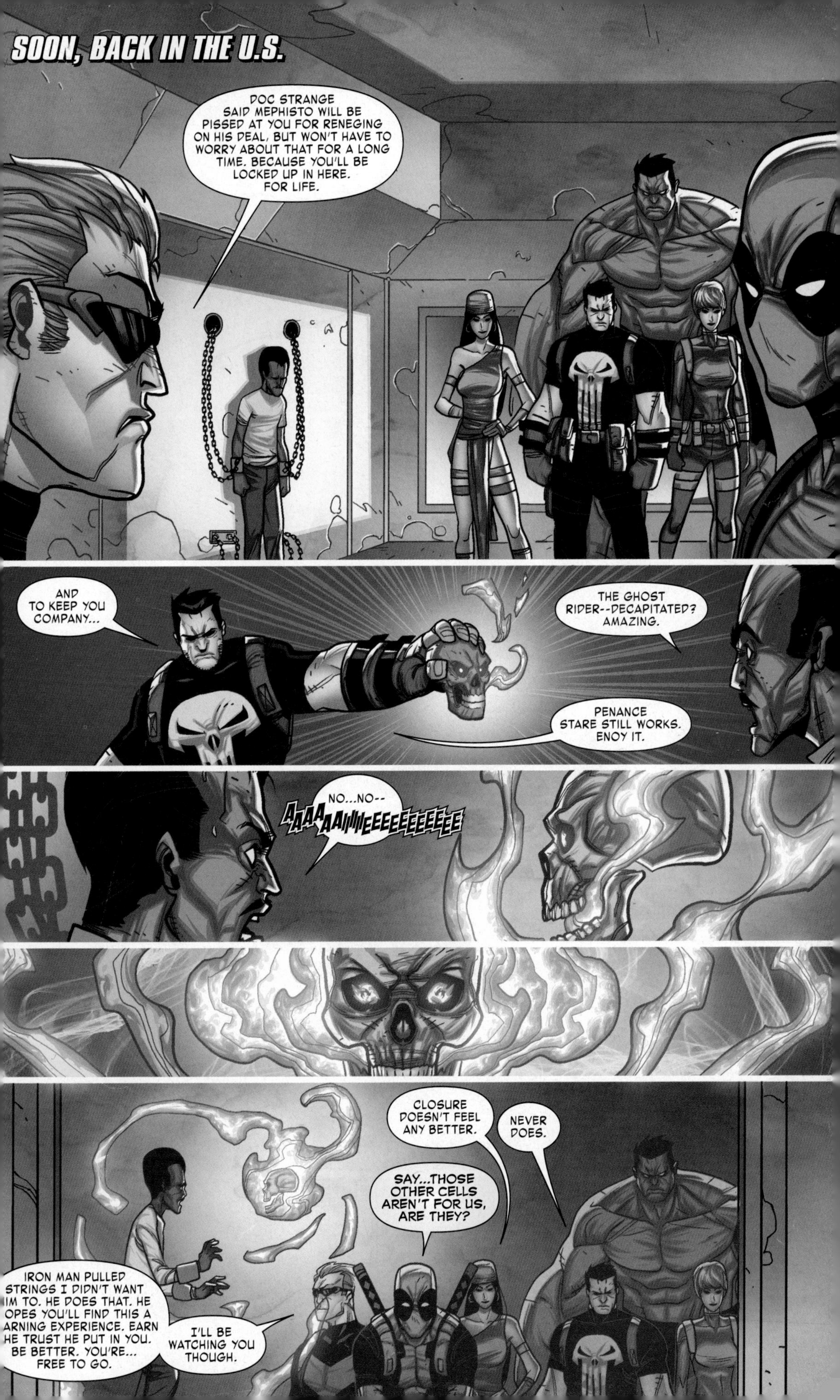
SOON, BACK IN THE U.S.
DOC STRANGE SAID MEPHISTO WILL BE PISSED AT YOU FOR RENEGING ON HIS DEAL, BUT WON'T HAVE TO WORRY ABOUT THAT FOR A LONG TIME. BECAUSE YOU'LL BE LOCKED UP IN HERE. FOR LIFE.
AND TO KEEP YOU COMPANY...
THE GHOST RIDER--DECAPITATED? AMAZING.
PENANCE STARE STILL WORKS. ENOY IT.
NO...NO--
AAAAAIIIIEEEEEEEEEE
CLOSURE DOESN'T FEEL ANY BETTER.
NEVER DOES.
SAY...THOSE OTHER CELLS AREN'T FOR US, ARE THEY?
IRON MAN PULLED STRINGS I DIDN'T WANT IM TO. HE DOES THAT. HE OPES YOU'LL FIND THIS A ARNING EXPERIENCE. EARN HE TRUST HE PUT IN YOU. BE BETTER. YOU'RE... FREE TO GO.
I'LL BE WATCHING YOU THOUGH.

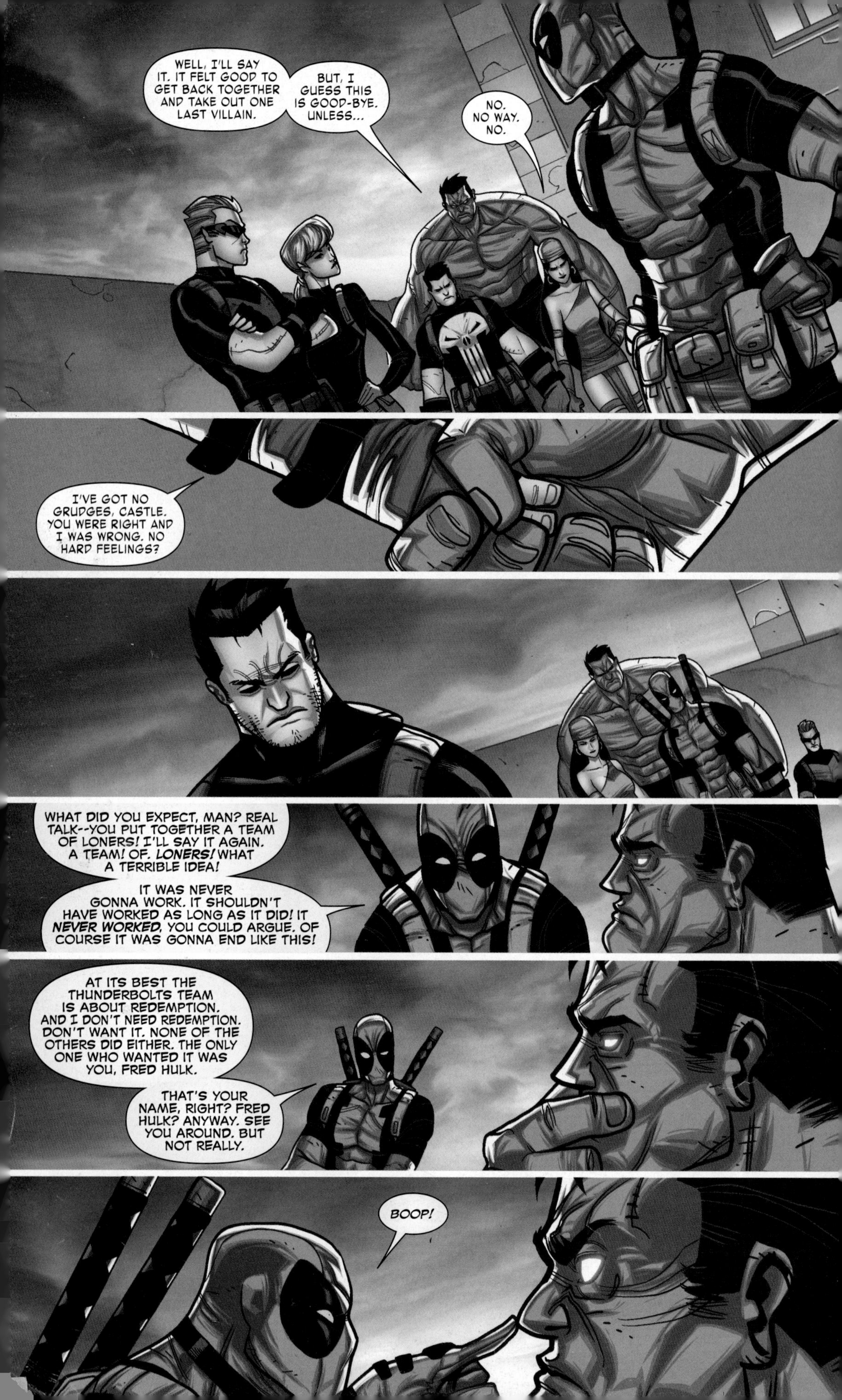
WELL, I'LL SAY IT. IT FELT GOOD TO GET BACK TOGETHER AND TAKE OUT ONE LAST VILLAIN.
BUT, I GUESS THIS IS GOOD-BYE. UNLESS...
NO. NO WAY. NO.
I'VE GOT NO GRUDGES, CASTLE. YOU WERE RIGHT AND I WAS WRONG. NO HARD FEELINGS?
WHAT DID YOU EXPECT, MAN? REAL TALK--YOU PUT TOGETHER A TEAM OF LONERS! I'LL SAY IT AGAIN. A TEAM! OF. LONERS! WHAT A TERRIBLE IDEA!
IT WAS NEVER GONNA WORK. IT SHOULDN'T HAVE WORKED AS LONG AS IT DID! IT NEVER WORKED, YOU COULD ARGUE. OF COURSE IT WAS GONNA END LIKE THIS!
AT ITS BEST THE THUNDERBOLTS TEAM IS ABOUT REDEMPTION. AND I DON'T NEED REDEMPTION. DON'T WANT IT. NONE OF THE OTHERS DID EITHER. THE ONLY ONE WHO WANTED IT WAS YOU, FRED HULK.
THAT'S YOUR NAME, RIGHT? FRED HULK? ANYWAY. SEE YOU AROUND. BUT NOT REALLY.
BOOP!

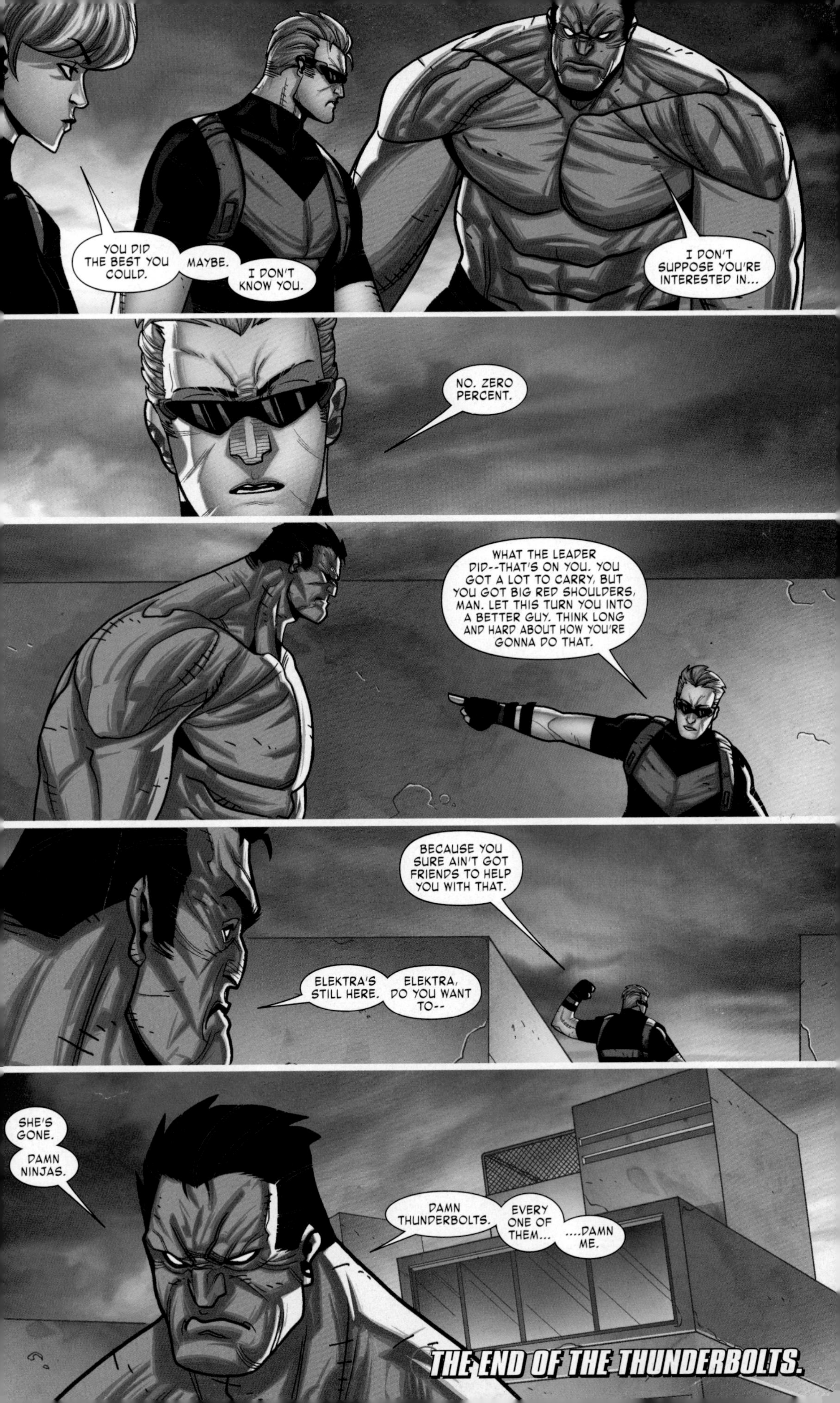
YOU DID THE BEST YOU COULD.
MAYBE.
I DON'T KNOW YOU.
I DON'T SUPPOSE YOU'RE INTERESTED IN...
NO. ZERO PERCENT.
WHAT THE LEADER DID--THAT'S ON YOU. YOU GOT A LOT TO CARRY, BUT YOU GOT BIG RED SHOULDERS, MAN. LET THIS TURN YOU INTO A BETTER GUY. THINK LONG AND HARD ABOUT HOW YOU'RE GONNA DO THAT.
BECAUSE YOU SURE AIN'T GOT FRIENDS TO HELP YOU WITH THAT.
ELEKTRA'S STILL HERE.
ELEKTRA, DO YOU WANT TO--
SHE'S GONE.
DAMN NINJAS.
DAMN THUNDERBOLTS.
EVERY ONE OF THEM...
....DAMN ME.
THE END OF THE THUNDERBOLTS.

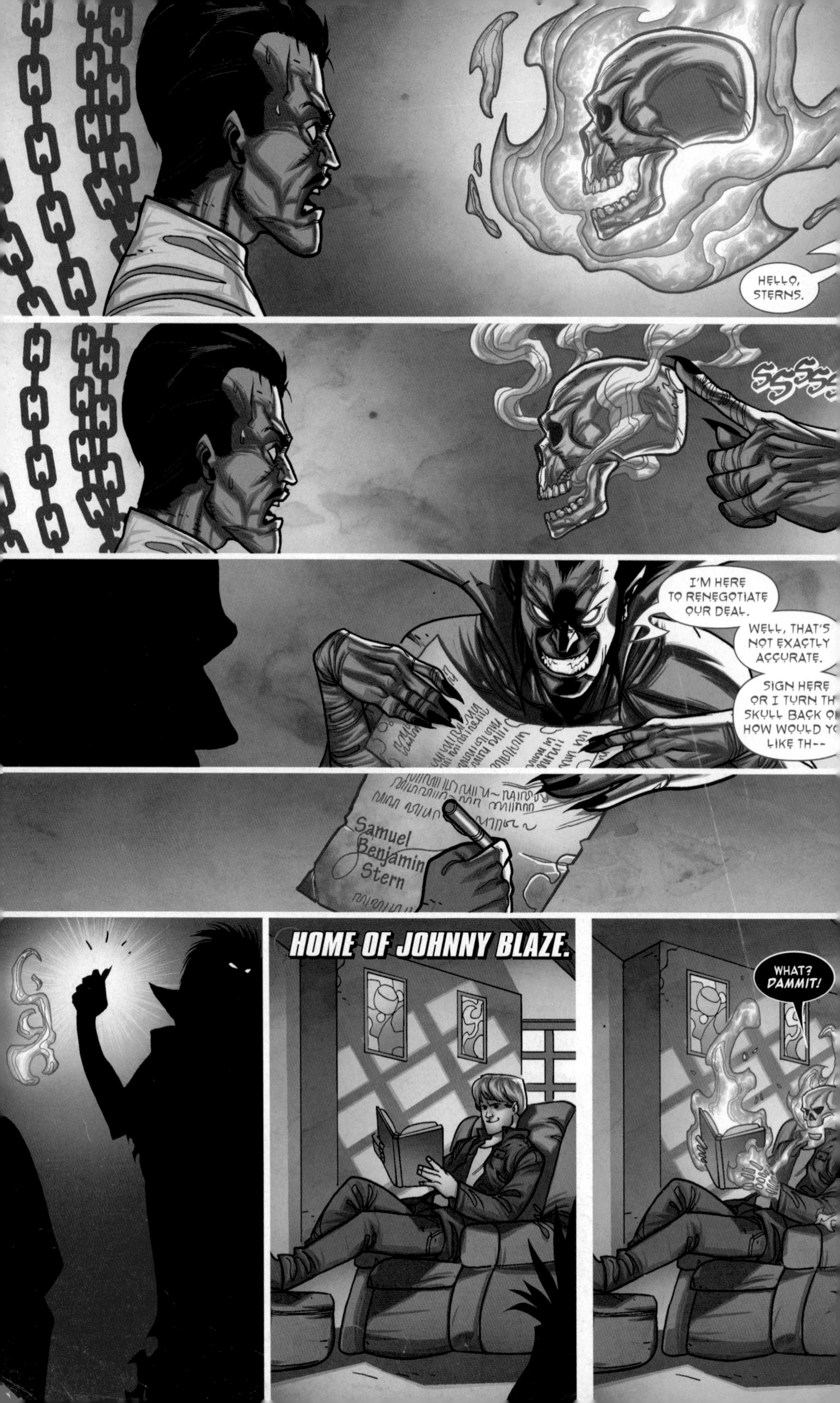
HELLO, STERNS.
SSSSS
I'M HERE TO RENEGOTIATE OUR DEAL.
WELL, THAT'S NOT EXACTLY ACCURATE.
SIGN HERE OR I TURN TH SKULL BACK O HOW WOULD Y LIKE TH--
Samuel Benjamin Stern
HOME OF JOHNNY BLAZE.
WHAT? DAMMIT!

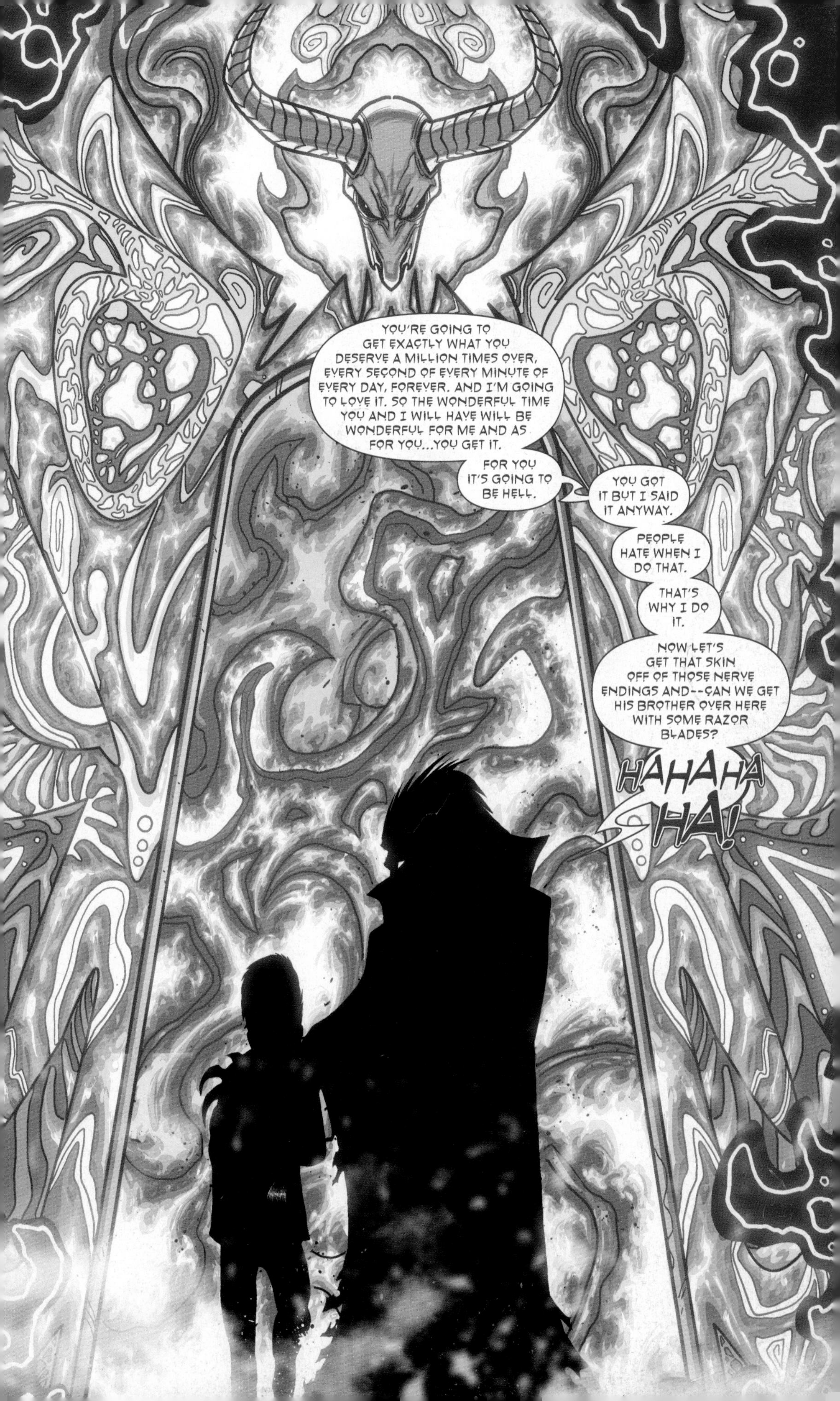
YOU'RE GOING TO GET EXACTLY WHAT YOU DESERVE A MILLION TIMES OVER, EVERY SECOND OF EVERY MINUTE OF EVERY DAY, FOREVER. AND I'M GOING TO LOVE IT. SO THE WONDERFUL TIME YOU AND I WILL HAVE WILL BE WONDERFUL FOR ME AND AS FOR YOU...YOU GET IT.
FOR YOU IT'S GOING TO BE HELL.
YOU GOT IT BUT I SAID IT ANYWAY.
PEOPLE HATE WHEN I DO THAT.
THAT'S WHY I DO IT.
NOW LET'S GET THAT SKIN OFF OF THOSE NERVE ENDINGS AND--CAN WE GET HIS BROTHER OVER HERE WITH SOME RAZOR BLADES?
HAHAHA HA!

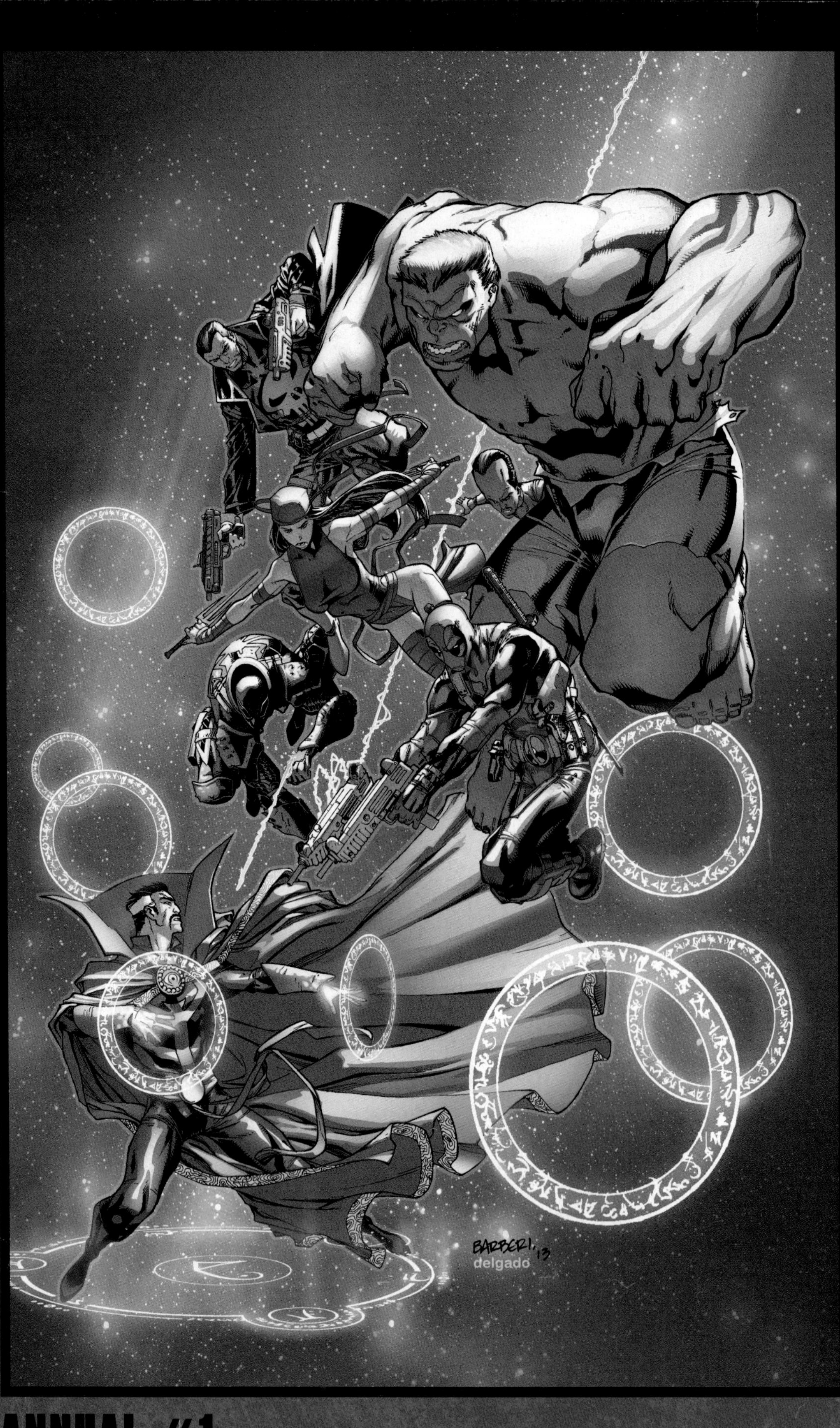
BARBERI '13
delgado

ANNUAL #1

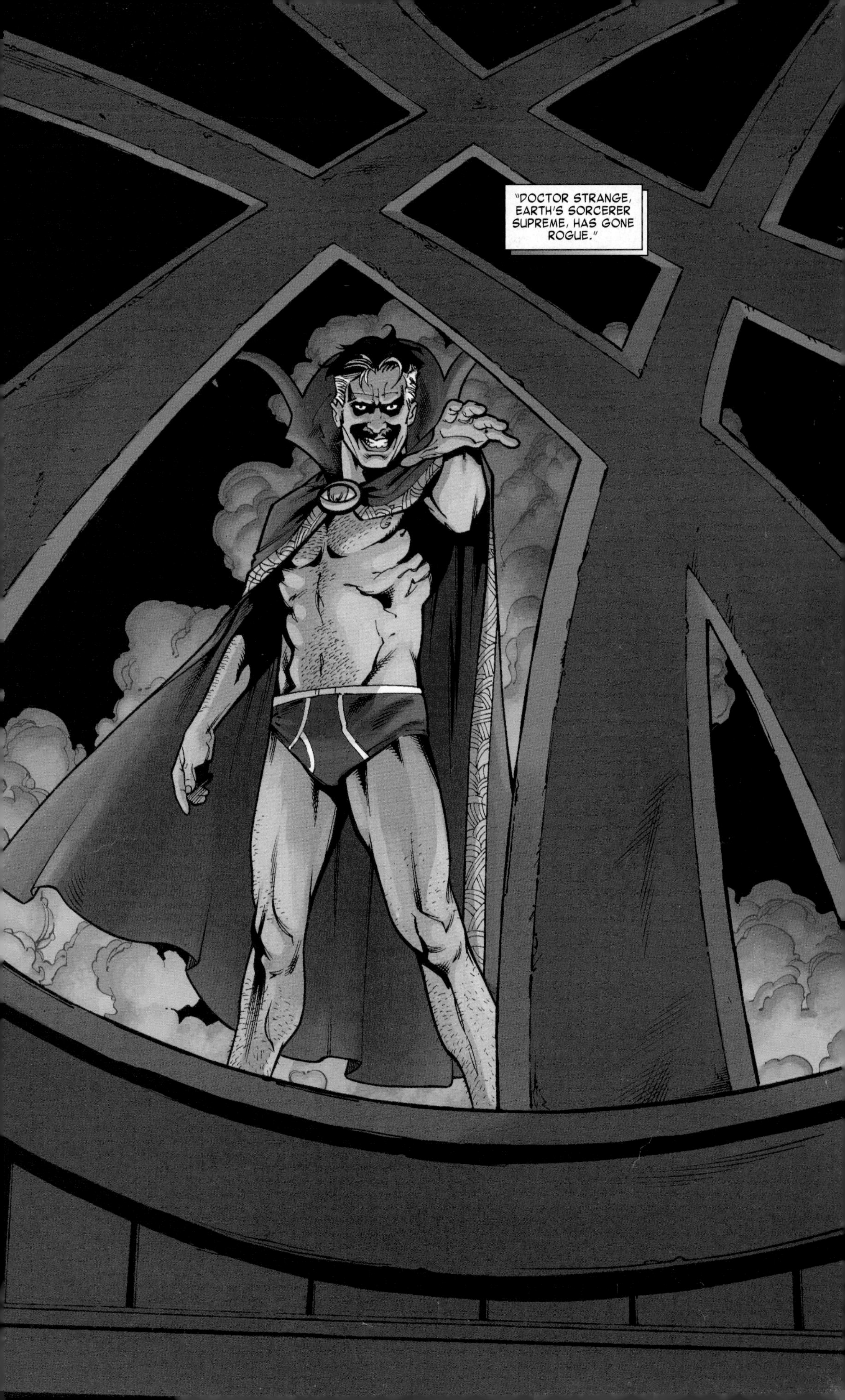
"DOCTOR STRANGE, EARTH'S SORCERER SUPREME, HAS GONE ROGUE."

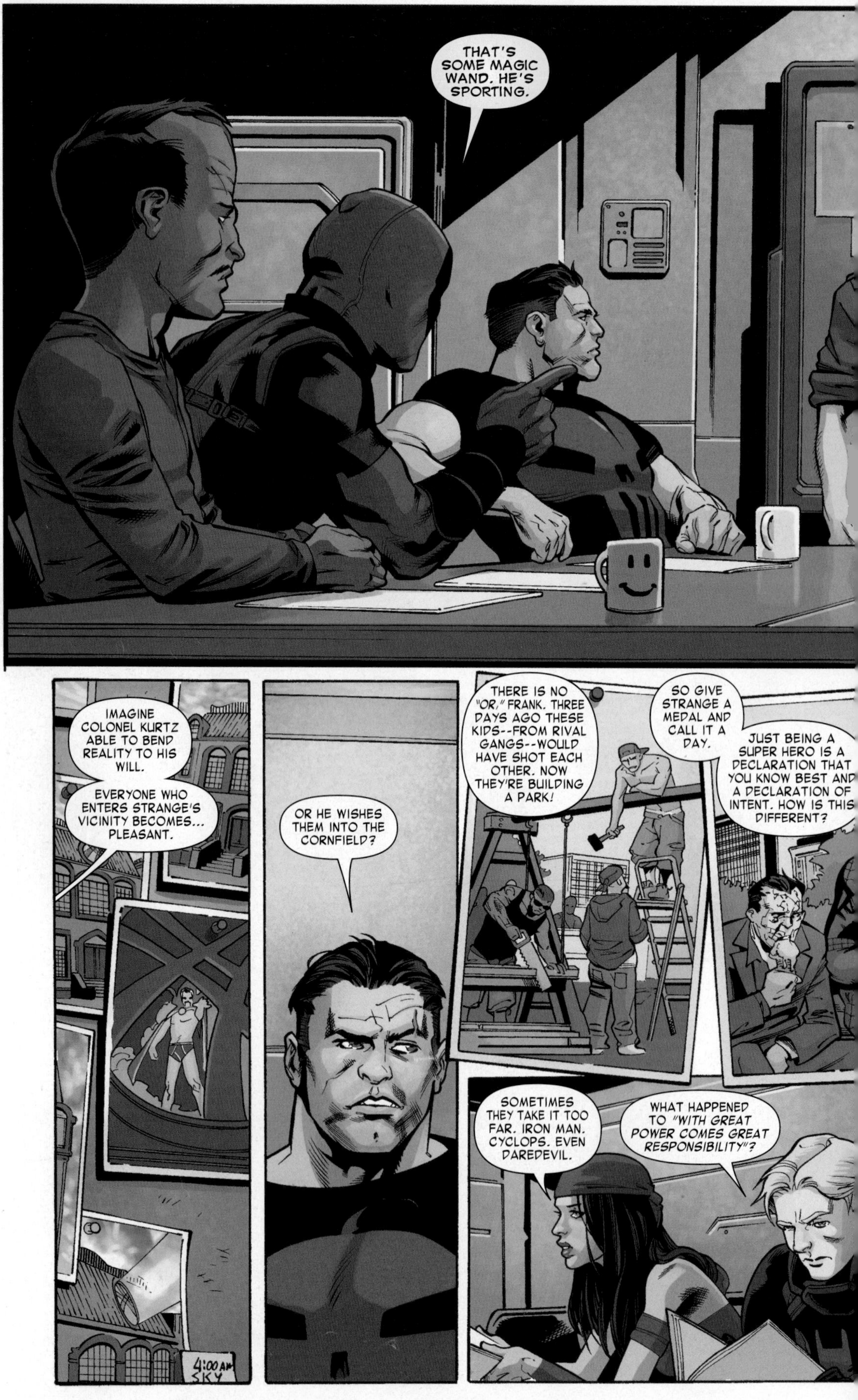

THAT'S SOME MAGIC WAND. HE'S SPORTING.
IMAGINE COLONEL KURTZ ABLE TO BEND REALITY TO HIS WILL.
EVERYONE WHO ENTERS STRANGE'S VICINITY BECOMES... PLEASANT.
OR HE WISHES THEM INTO THE CORNFIELD?
THERE IS NO "OR," FRANK. THREE DAYS AGO THESE KIDS--FROM RIVAL GANGS--WOULD HAVE SHOT EACH OTHER. NOW THEY'RE BUILDING A PARK!
SO GIVE STRANGE A MEDAL AND CALL IT A DAY.
JUST BEING A SUPER HERO IS A DECLARATION THAT YOU KNOW BEST AND A DECLARATION OF INTENT. HOW IS THIS DIFFERENT?
SOMETIMES THEY TAKE IT TOO FAR. IRON MAN. CYCLOPS. EVEN DAREDEVIL.
WHAT HAPPENED TO "WITH GREAT POWER COMES GREAT RESPONSIBILITY"?
4:00 AM SKY

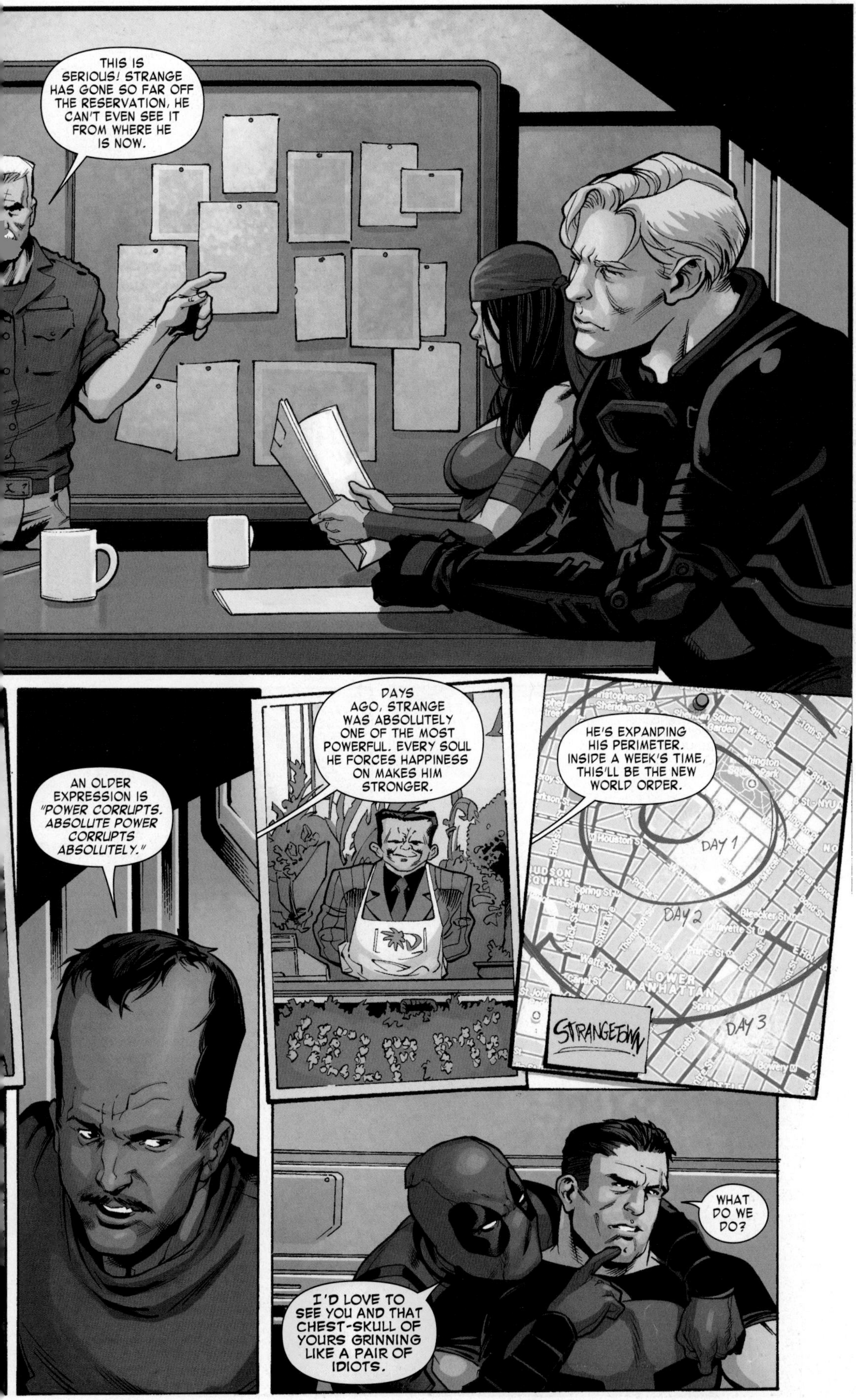
THIS IS SERIOUS! STRANGE HAS GONE SO FAR OFF THE RESERVATION, HE CAN'T EVEN SEE IT FROM WHERE HE IS NOW.
AN OLDER EXPRESSION IS "POWER CORRUPTS. ABSOLUTE POWER CORRUPTS ABSOLUTELY."
DAYS AGO, STRANGE WAS ABSOLUTELY ONE OF THE MOST POWERFUL. EVERY SOUL HE FORCES HAPPINESS ON MAKES HIM STRONGER.
HE'S EXPANDING HIS PERIMETER. INSIDE A WEEK'S TIME, THIS'LL BE THE NEW WORLD ORDER.
DAY 1
DAY 2
DAY 3
STRANGETOWN
LOWER MANHATTAN
WHAT DO WE DO?
I'D LOVE TO SEE YOU AND THAT CHEST-SKULL OF YOURS GRINNING LIKE A PAIR OF IDIOTS.

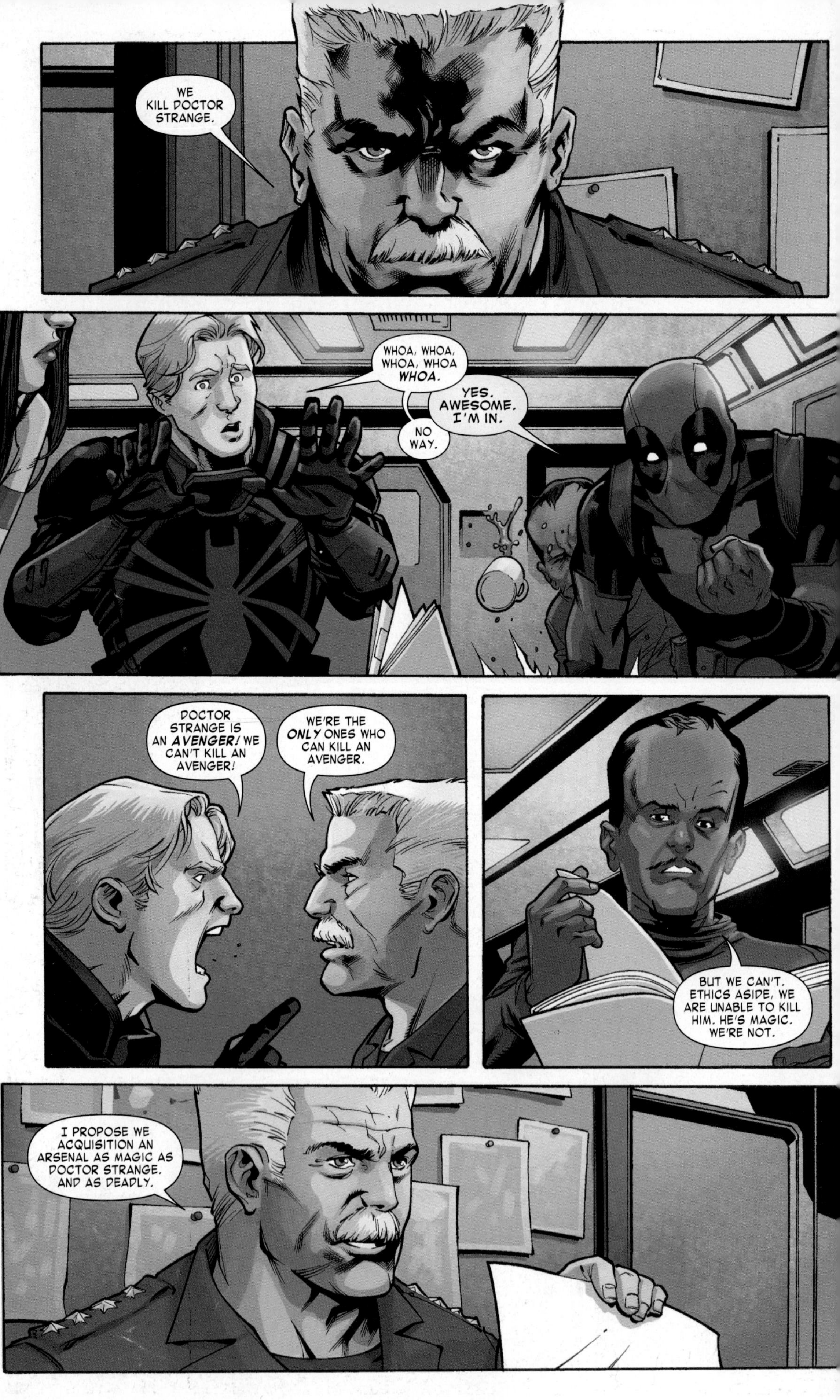
WE KILL DOCTOR STRANGE.
WHOA, WHOA, WHOA, WHOA WHOA.
NO WAY.
YES. AWESOME. I'M IN.
DOCTOR STRANGE IS AN AVENGER! WE CAN'T KILL AN AVENGER!
WE'RE THE ONLY ONES WHO CAN KILL AN AVENGER.
BUT WE CAN'T. ETHICS ASIDE, WE ARE UNABLE TO KILL HIM. HE'S MAGIC. WE'RE NOT.
I PROPOSE WE ACQUISITION AN ARSENAL AS MAGIC AS DOCTOR STRANGE. AND AS DEADLY.

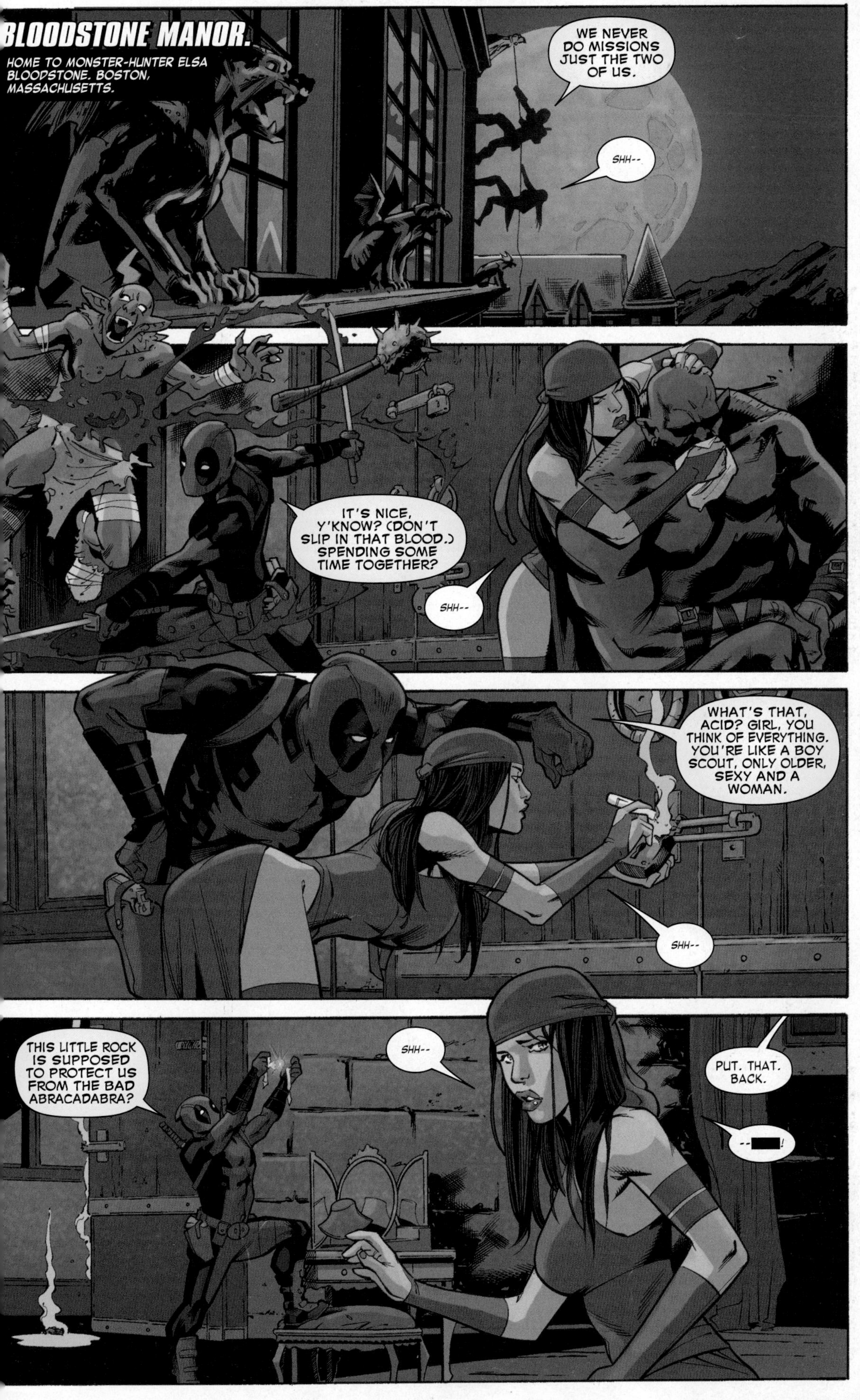
BLOODSTONE MANOR.
HOME TO MONSTER-HUNTER ELSA BLOODSTONE. BOSTON, MASSACHUSETTS.
WE NEVER DO MISSIONS JUST THE TWO OF US.
SHH--
IT'S NICE, Y'KNOW? (DON'T SLIP IN THAT BLOOD.) SPENDING SOME TIME TOGETHER?
SHH--
WHAT'S THAT, ACID? GIRL, YOU THINK OF EVERYTHING. YOU'RE LIKE A BOY SCOUT, ONLY OLDER, SEXY AND A WOMAN.
SHH--
THIS LITTLE ROCK IS SUPPOSED TO PROTECT US FROM THE BAD ABRACADABRA?
SHH--
PUT. THAT. BACK.
--[redacted]!

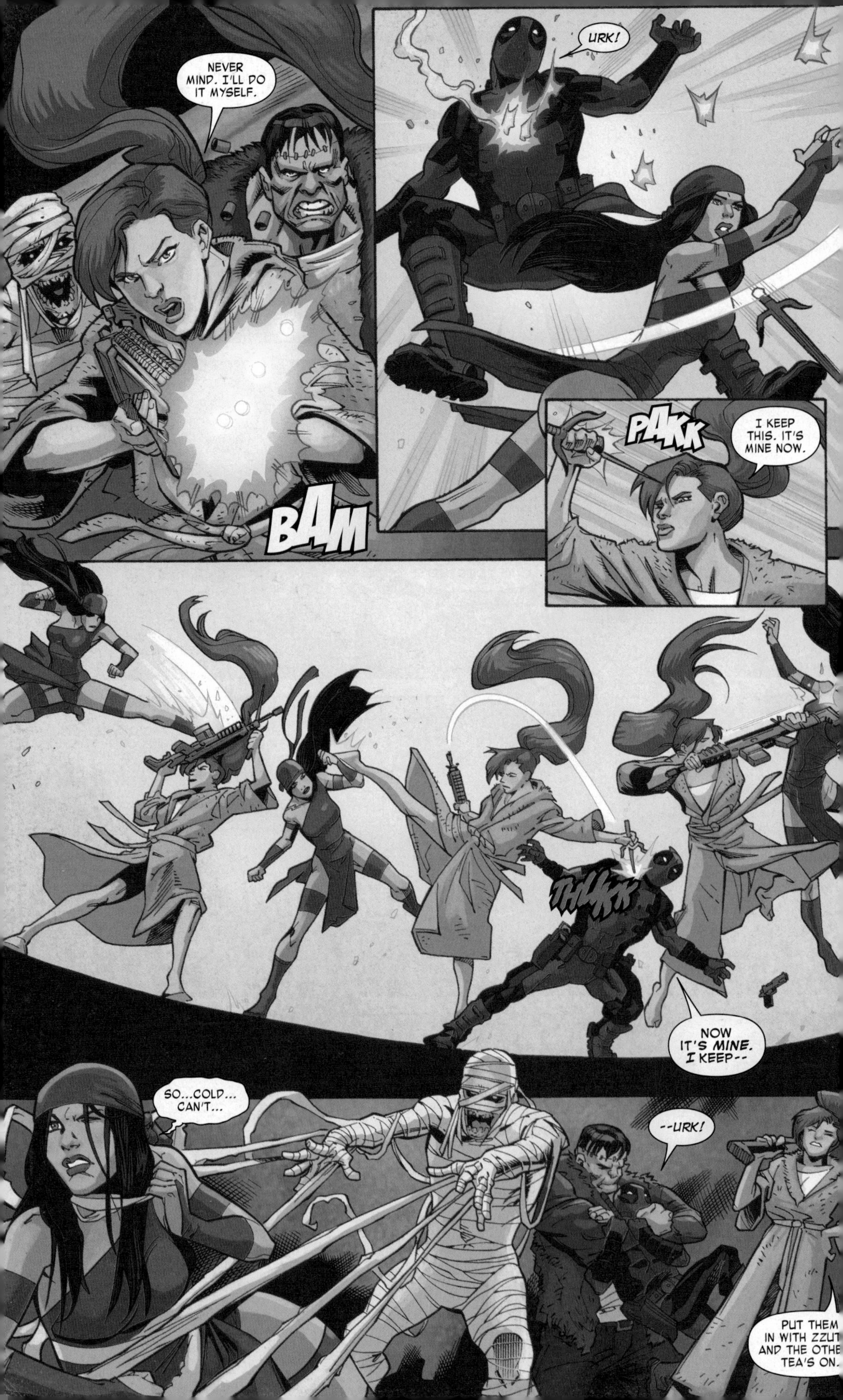
NEVER MIND. I'LL DO IT MYSELF.
BAM
URK!
PAKK
I KEEP THIS. IT'S MINE NOW.
THUKK
NOW IT'S MINE. I KEEP--
SO...COLD... CAN'T...
--URK!
PUT THEM IN WITH ZZUT AND THE OTHE TEA'S ON.

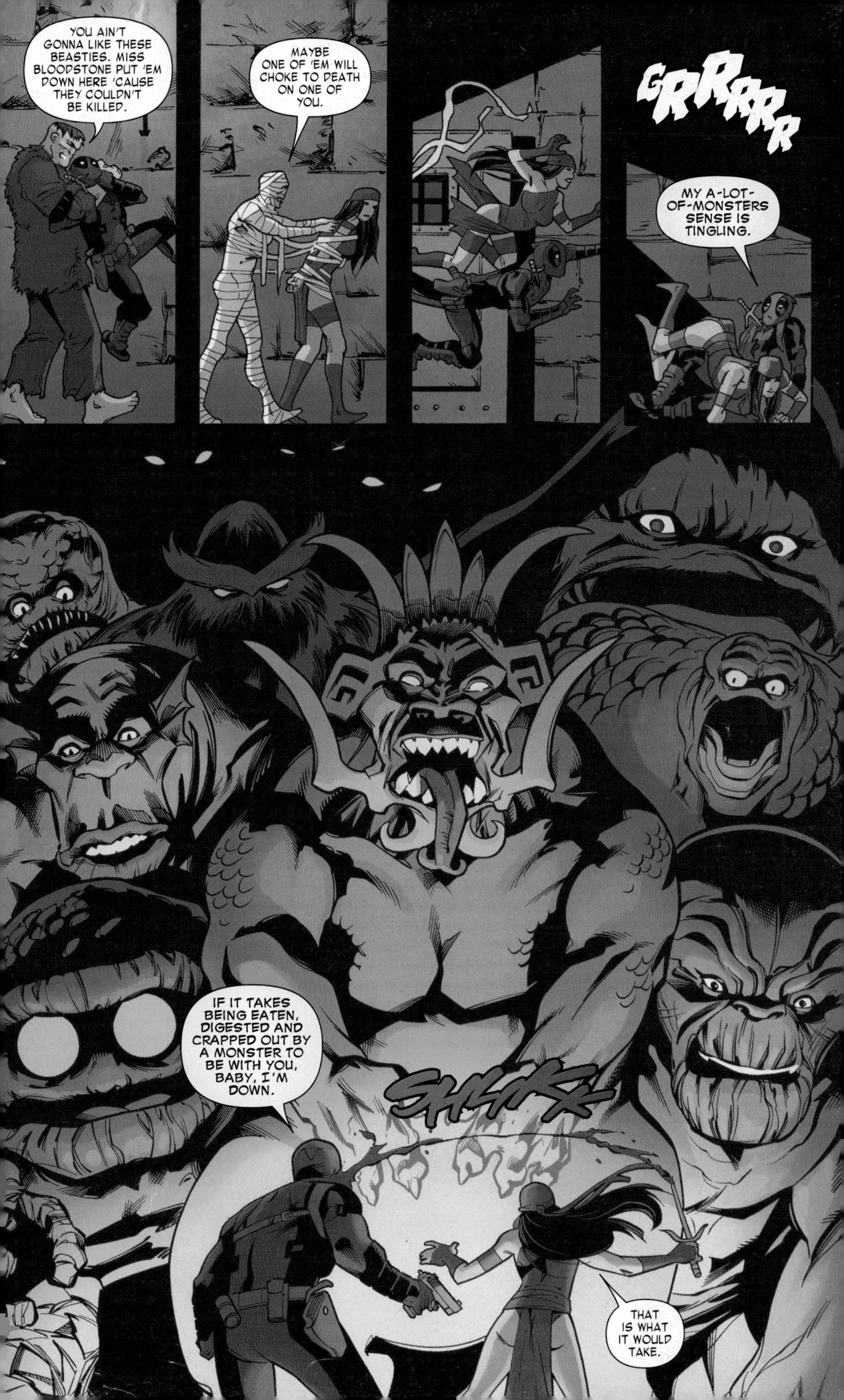
YOU AIN'T GONNA LIKE THESE BEASTIES. MISS BLOODSTONE PUT 'EM DOWN HERE 'CAUSE THEY COULDN'T BE KILLED.
MAYBE ONE OF 'EM WILL CHOKE TO DEATH ON ONE OF YOU.
GRRRRR
MY A-LOT-OF-MONSTERS SENSE IS TINGLING.
IF IT TAKES BEING EATEN, DIGESTED AND CRAPPED OUT BY A MONSTER TO BE WITH YOU, BABY, I'M DOWN.
SHLIKK
THAT IS WHAT IT WOULD TAKE.

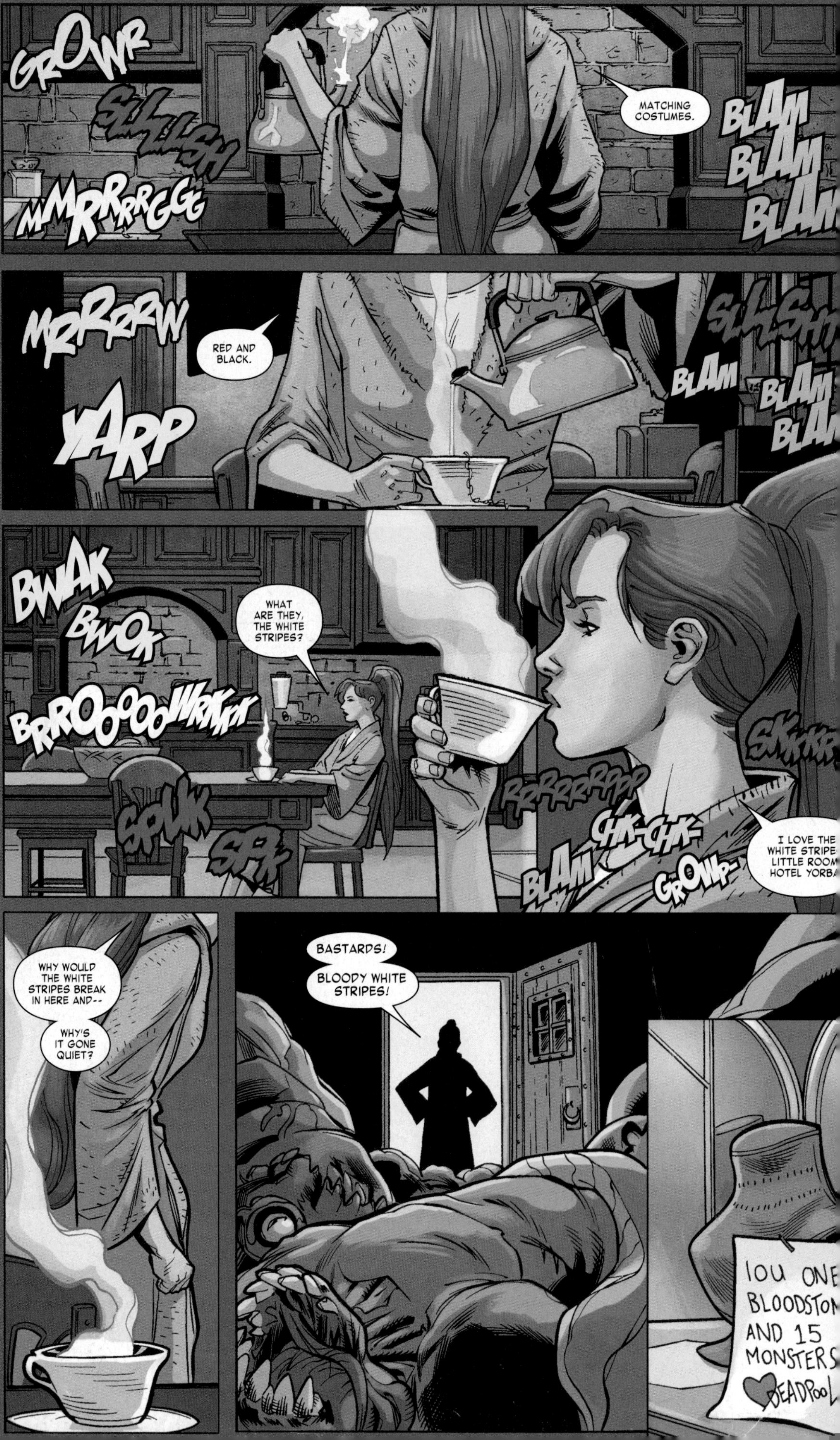
GROWR
MMRRRRGGG
MATCHING COSTUMES.
BLAM
BLAM
MRRRRRW
RED AND BLACK.
YARP
BLAM
BLAM
BLAM
BWAK
BWOK
WHAT ARE THEY, THE WHITE STRIPES?
SPLUK
SPK
BLAM
CHK-CHK-
GROWP-
I LOVE THE
WHITE STRIPE
LITTLE ROOM
HOTEL YORBA
WHY WOULD THE WHITE STRIPES BREAK IN HERE AND--
WHY'S IT GONE QUIET?
BASTARDS!
BLOODY WHITE STRIPES!
IOU ONE
BLOODSTON
AND 15
MONSTERS
DEADPOOL

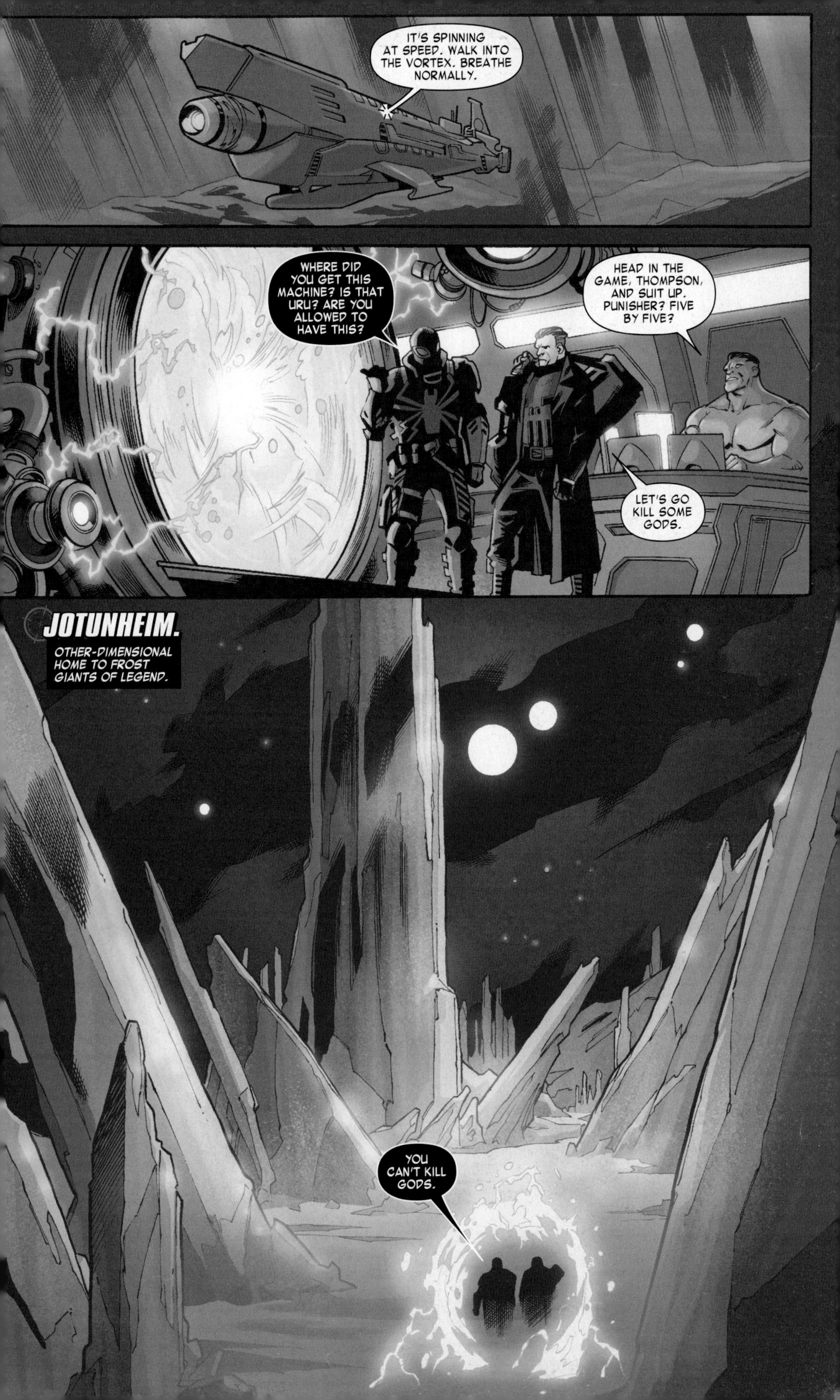
IT'S SPINNING AT SPEED. WALK INTO THE VORTEX. BREATHE NORMALLY.
WHERE DID YOU GET THIS MACHINE? IS THAT URU? ARE YOU ALLOWED TO HAVE THIS?
HEAD IN THE GAME, THOMPSON, AND SUIT UP. PUNISHER? FIVE BY FIVE?
LET'S GO KILL SOME GODS.
JOTUNHEIM.
OTHER-DIMENSIONAL HOME TO FROST GIANTS OF LEGEND.
YOU CAN'T KILL GODS.

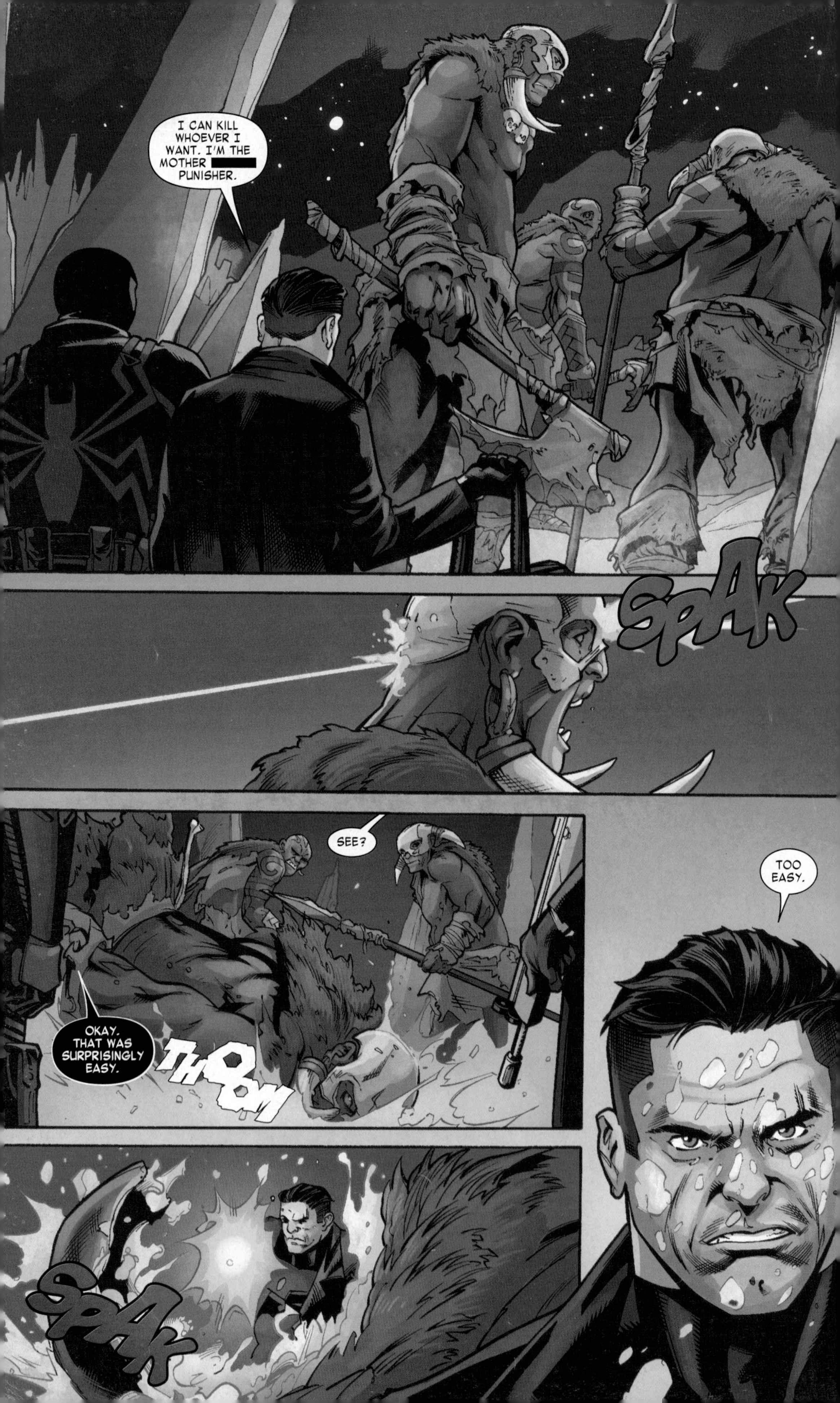

I CAN KILL WHOEVER I WANT. I'M THE MOTHER [redacted] PUNISHER.
SPAK
SEE?
TOO EASY.
OKAY. THAT WAS SURPRISINGLY EASY.
THOOM
SPAK

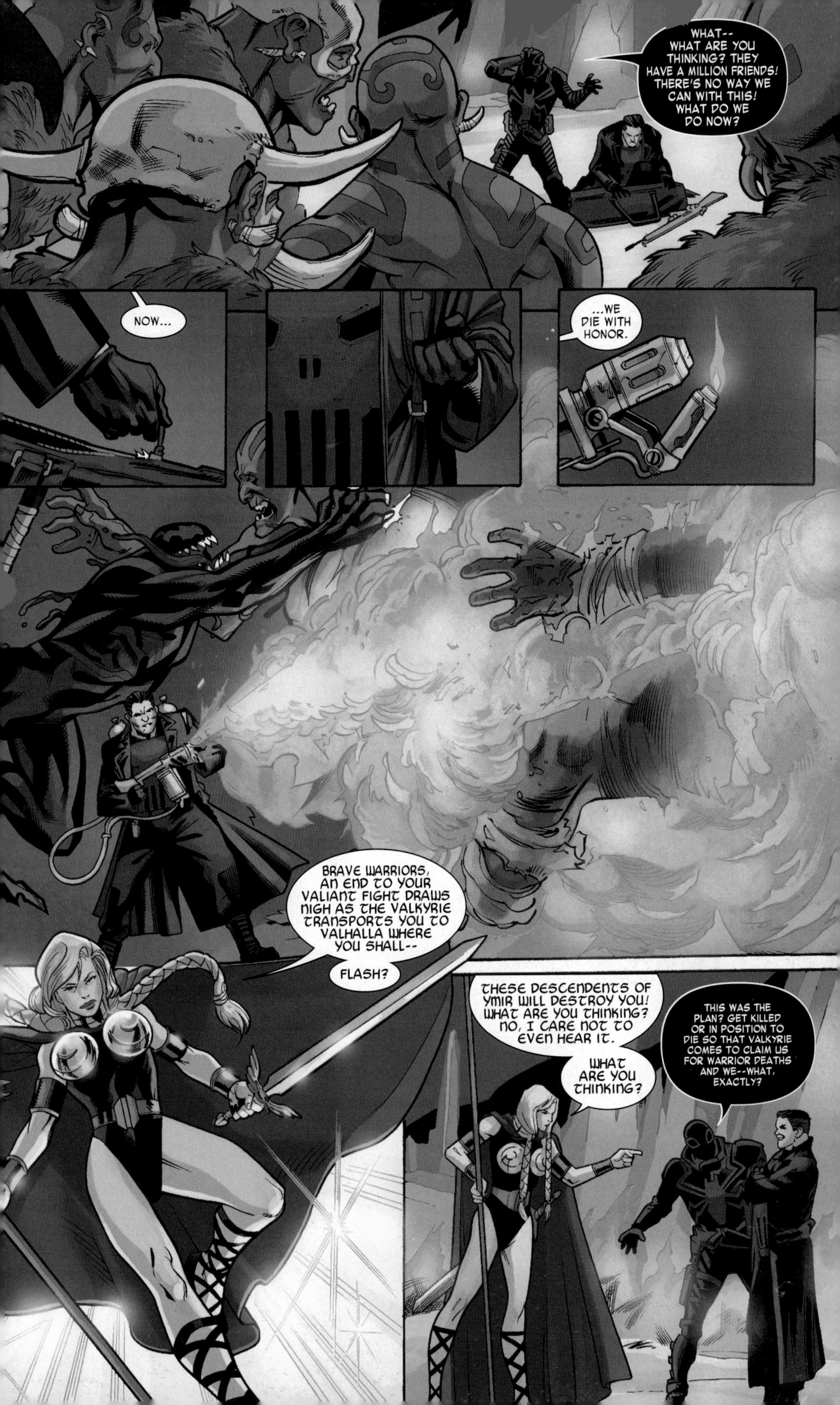
WHAT-- WHAT ARE YOU THINKING? THEY HAVE A MILLION FRIENDS! THERE'S NO WAY WE CAN WITH THIS! WHAT DO WE DO NOW?
NOW...
...WE DIE WITH HONOR.
BRAVE WARRIORS, AN END TO YOUR VALIANT FIGHT DRAWS NIGH AS THE VALKYRIE TRANSPORTS YOU TO VALHALLA WHERE YOU SHALL--
FLASH?
THESE DESCENDENTS OF YMIR WILL DESTROY YOU! WHAT ARE YOU THINKING? NO, I CARE NOT TO EVEN HEAR IT.
WHAT ARE YOU THINKING?
THIS WAS THE PLAN? GET KILLED OR IN POSITION TO DIE SO THAT VALKYRIE COMES TO CLAIM US FOR WARRIOR DEATHS AND WE--WHAT, EXACTLY?

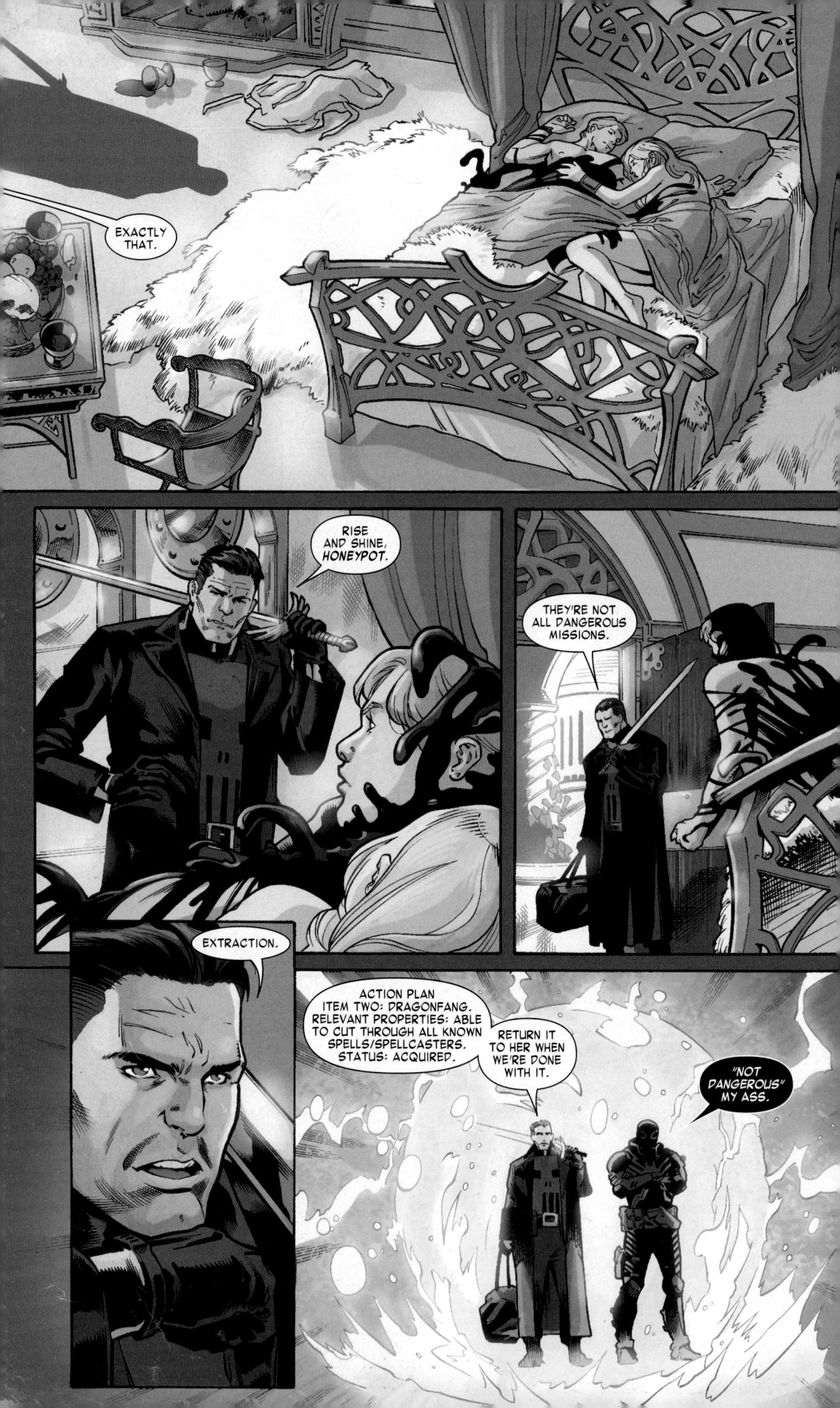
EXACTLY THAT.
RISE AND SHINE, *HONEYPOT.*
THEY'RE NOT ALL DANGEROUS MISSIONS.
EXTRACTION.
ACTION PLAN ITEM TWO: DRAGONFANG. RELEVANT PROPERTIES: ABLE TO CUT THROUGH ALL KNOWN SPELLS/SPELLCASTERS. STATUS: ACQUIRED.
RETURN IT TO HER WHEN WE'RE DONE WITH IT.
"NOT DANGEROUS" MY ASS.

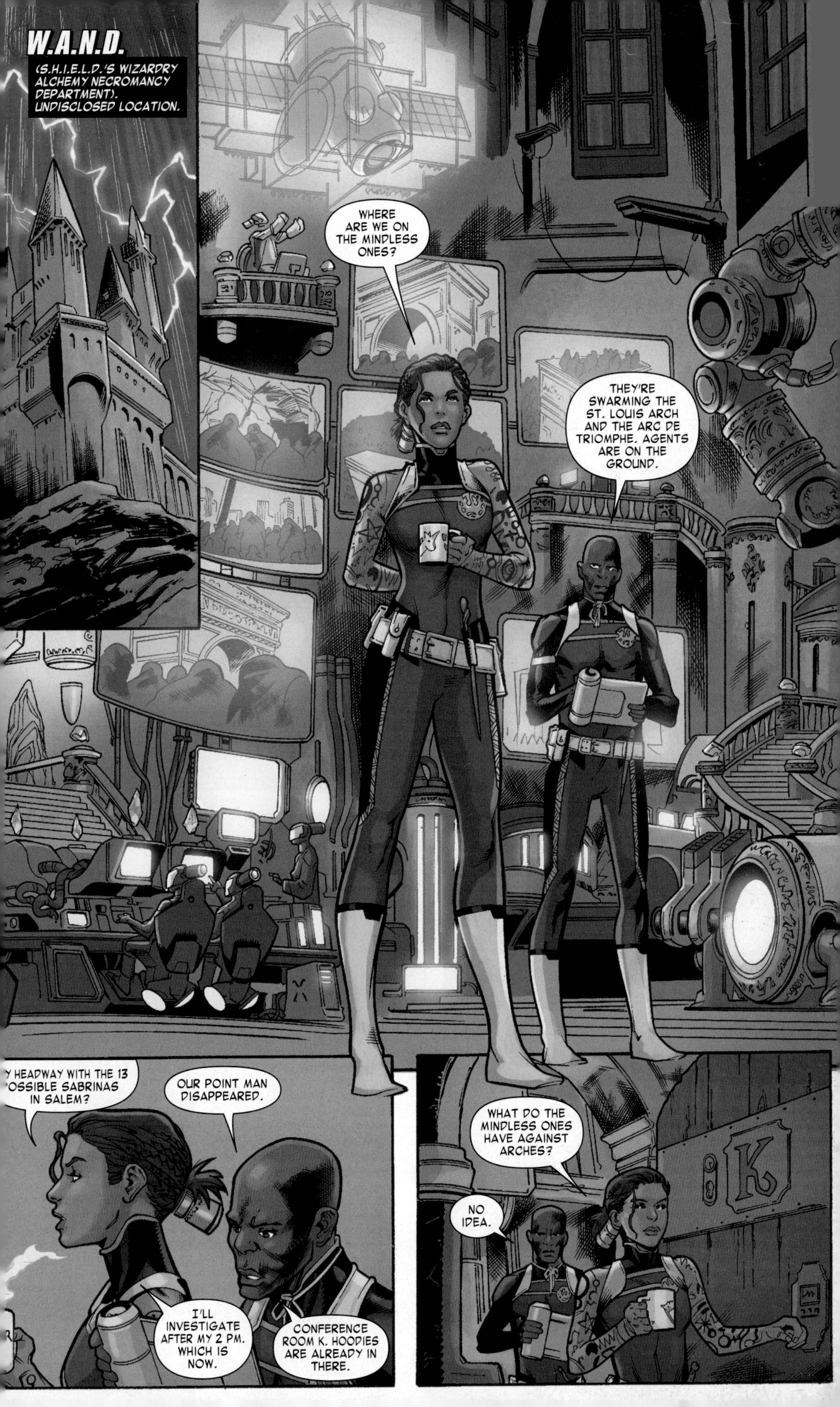
W.A.N.D.
(S.H.I.E.L.D.'S WIZARDRY ALCHEMY NECROMANCY DEPARTMENT). UNDISCLOSED LOCATION.
WHERE ARE WE ON THE MINDLESS ONES?
THEY'RE SWARMING THE ST. LOUIS ARCH AND THE ARC DE TRIOMPHE. AGENTS ARE ON THE GROUND.
Y HEADWAY WITH THE 13 OSSIBLE SABRINAS IN SALEM?
OUR POINT MAN DISAPPEARED.
I'LL INVESTIGATE AFTER MY 2 PM. WHICH IS NOW.
CONFERENCE ROOM K. HOODIES ARE ALREADY IN THERE.
WHAT DO THE MINDLESS ONES HAVE AGAINST ARCHES?
NO IDEA.
K

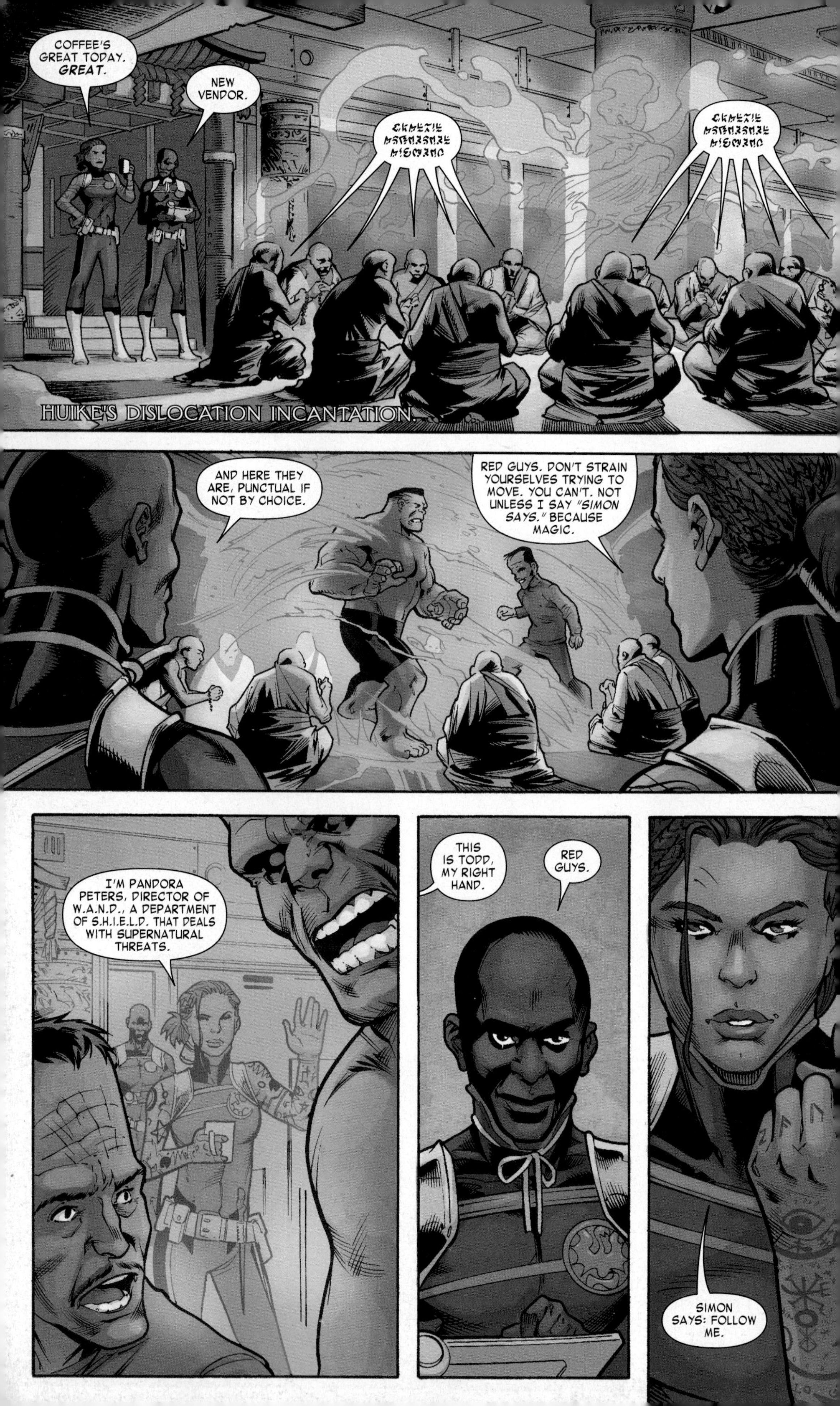

COFFEE'S GREAT TODAY. GREAT.
NEW VENDOR.
HUIKE'S DISLOCATION INCANTATION.
AND HERE THEY ARE, PUNCTUAL IF NOT BY CHOICE.
RED GUYS. DON'T STRAIN YOURSELVES TRYING TO MOVE. YOU CAN'T. NOT UNLESS I SAY "SIMON SAYS." BECAUSE MAGIC.
I'M PANDORA PETERS, DIRECTOR OF W.A.N.D., A DEPARTMENT OF S.H.I.E.L.D. THAT DEALS WITH SUPERNATURAL THREATS.
THIS IS TODD, MY RIGHT HAND.
RED GUYS.
SIMON SAYS: FOLLOW ME.

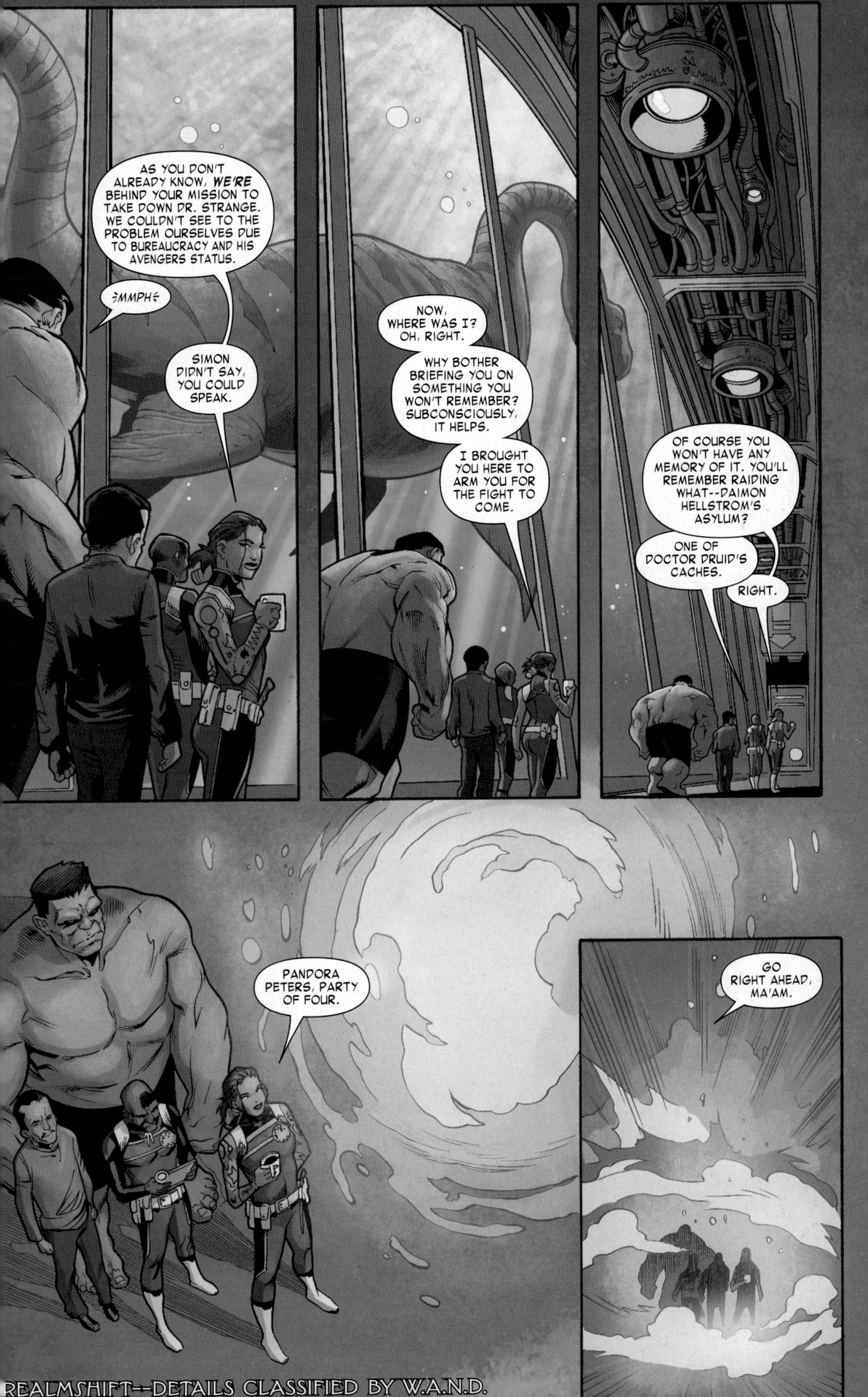
AS YOU DON'T ALREADY KNOW, *WE'RE* BEHIND YOUR MISSION TO TAKE DOWN DR. STRANGE. WE COULDN'T SEE TO THE PROBLEM OURSELVES DUE TO BUREAUCRACY AND HIS AVENGERS STATUS.
MMPH
SIMON DIDN'T SAY, YOU COULD SPEAK.
NOW, WHERE WAS I? OH, RIGHT.
WHY BOTHER BRIEFING YOU ON SOMETHING YOU WON'T REMEMBER? SUBCONSCIOUSLY, IT HELPS.
I BROUGHT YOU HERE TO ARM YOU FOR THE FIGHT TO COME.
OF COURSE YOU WON'T HAVE ANY MEMORY OF IT. YOU'LL REMEMBER RAIDING WHAT--DAIMON HELLSTROM'S ASYLUM?
ONE OF DOCTOR DRUID'S CACHES.
RIGHT.
PANDORA PETERS, PARTY OF FOUR.
GO RIGHT AHEAD, MA'AM.
REALMSHIFT--DETAILS CLASSIFIED BY W.A.N.D.

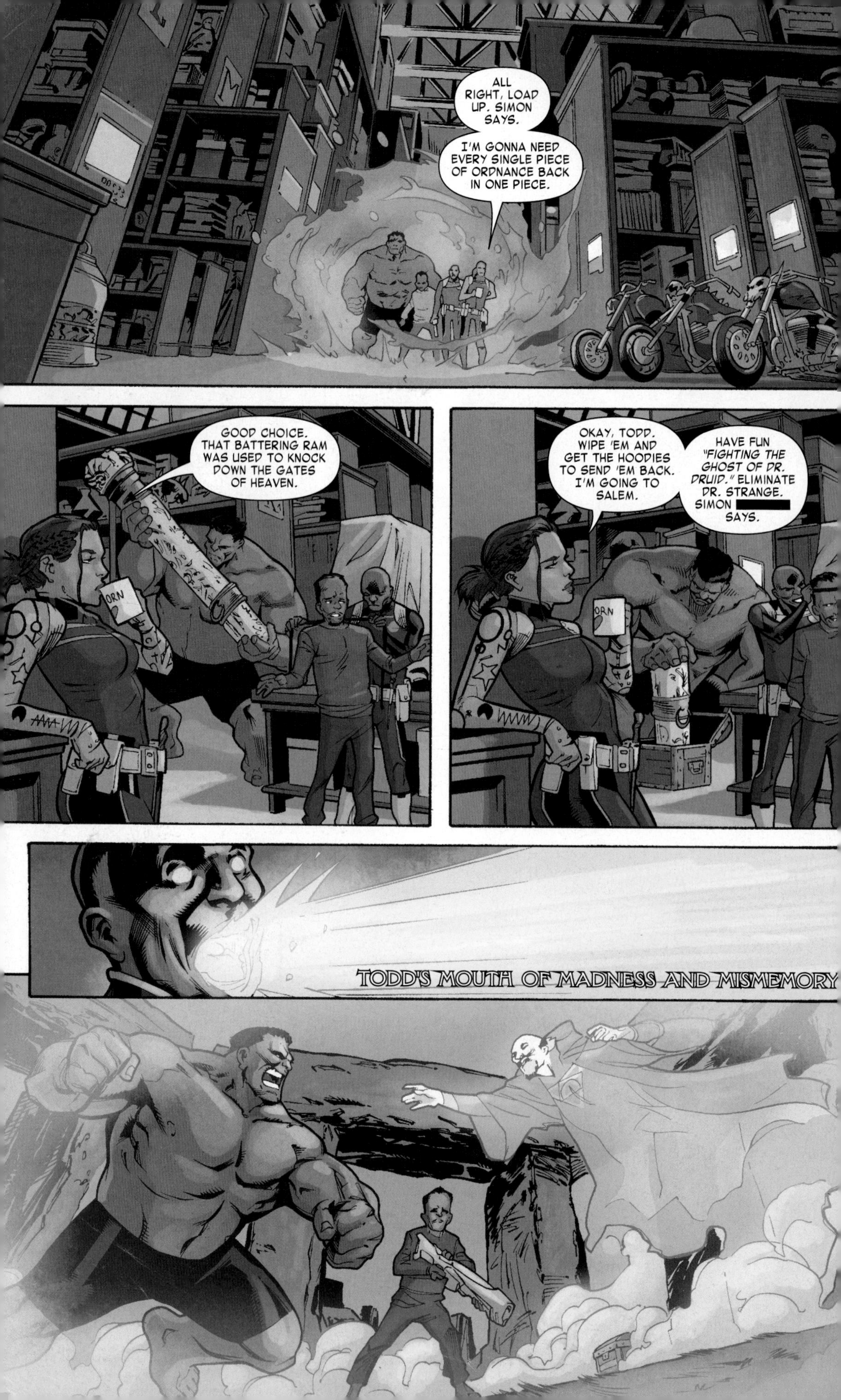
ALL RIGHT, LOAD UP. SIMON SAYS.
I'M GONNA NEED EVERY SINGLE PIECE OF ORDNANCE BACK IN ONE PIECE.
GOOD CHOICE. THAT BATTERING RAM WAS USED TO KNOCK DOWN THE GATES OF HEAVEN.
ORN
OKAY, TODD. WIPE 'EM AND GET THE HOODIES TO SEND 'EM BACK. I'M GOING TO SALEM.
HAVE FUN "FIGHTING THE GHOST OF DR. DRUID." ELIMINATE DR. STRANGE. SIMON [redacted] SAYS.
ORN
TODD'S MOUTH OF MADNESS AND MISMEMORY

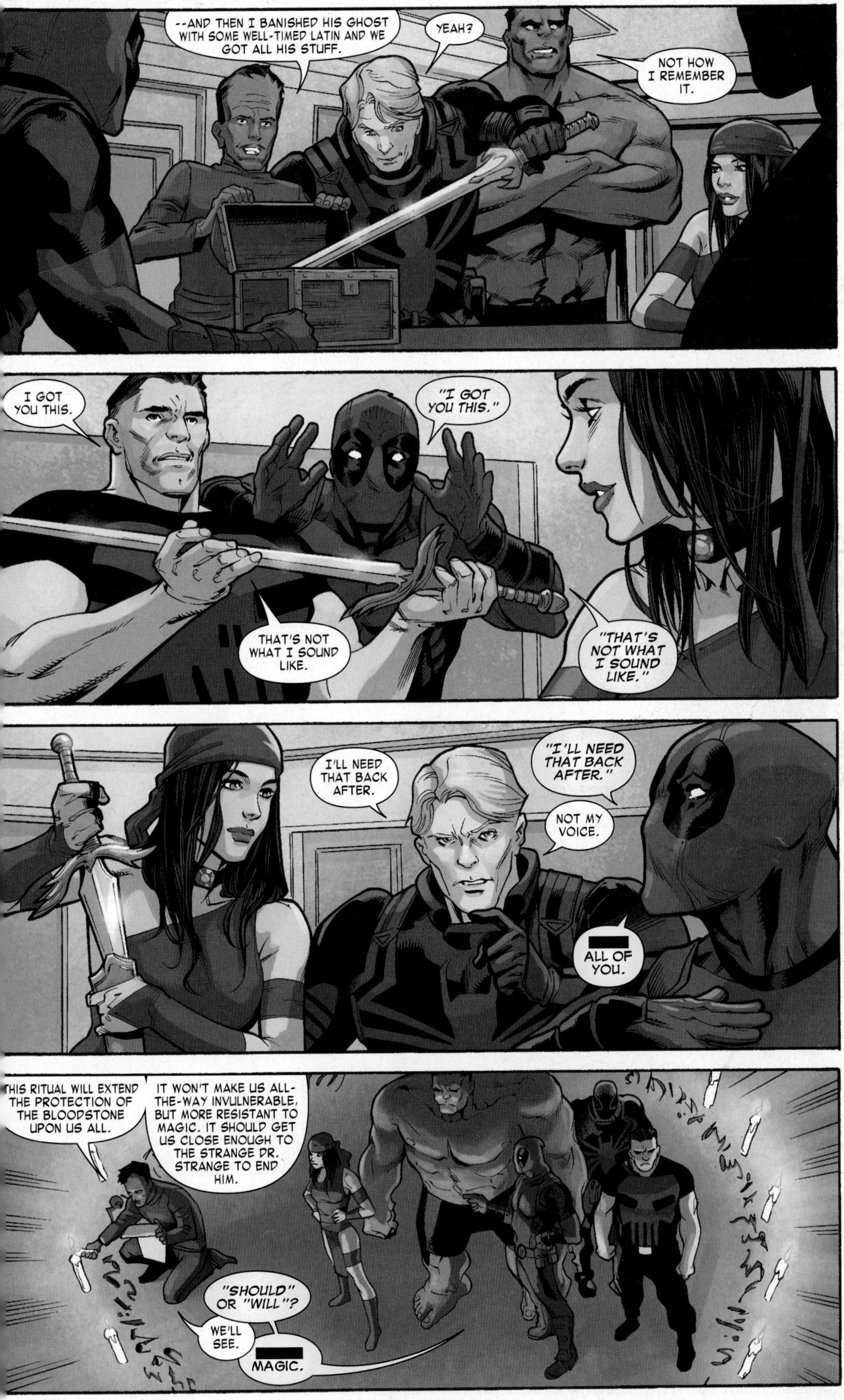
--AND THEN I BANISHED HIS GHOST WITH SOME WELL-TIMED LATIN AND WE GOT ALL HIS STUFF.
YEAH?
NOT HOW I REMEMBER IT.
I GOT YOU THIS.
"I GOT YOU THIS."
THAT'S NOT WHAT I SOUND LIKE.
"THAT'S NOT WHAT I SOUND LIKE."
I'LL NEED THAT BACK AFTER.
"I'LL NEED THAT BACK AFTER."
NOT MY VOICE.
[redacted] ALL OF YOU.
THIS RITUAL WILL EXTEND THE PROTECTION OF THE BLOODSTONE UPON US ALL.
IT WON'T MAKE US ALL-THE-WAY INVULNERABLE, BUT MORE RESISTANT TO MAGIC. IT SHOULD GET US CLOSE ENOUGH TO THE STRANGE DR. STRANGE TO END HIM.
"SHOULD" OR "WILL"?
WE'LL SEE.
[redacted] MAGIC.

ᒋᒃᔑᙿᔥᐁ
ᕥᒋᐤᒋᐦᐁᐤᒃᐁᐤ
ᔑᙿᒋᐤᒋᐦᐁᐤᑕᒃ
ᑲᐸᒋᐤᒃ

FORETOON'S DISPERSAL
FROM THE SCROLLS OF THE SLOR.

ᒋᒃᔑᙿᐁ
ᕥᒋᐤᒋᐦᐁᐤᒃ
ᔑᙿᒋᐤᒋᐦ ᐤᑕᐦ
ᔑᙿᒋᐤ

THAT'S NOT HOW YOU SAY THAT.

IT'S A "LONG A" SOUND IN THE WORD ᔑᙿᒋᐤᒋᐦ ᐤᑕᐦ. OTHER THAN THAT, YOU'RE NAILING IT.

STRANGE!

IN THE ASTRALLY PROJECTED NON-FLES JUST SAYING HI.

SORCERER *SUPREME*. SO. I KNOW WHAT YOU'RE UP TO. MORE THAN YO DO, PROBABLY. I'M FINE WITH IT. I WANT IT TO HAPPEN.

COME AT ME, BROS.

ELEKTRA.

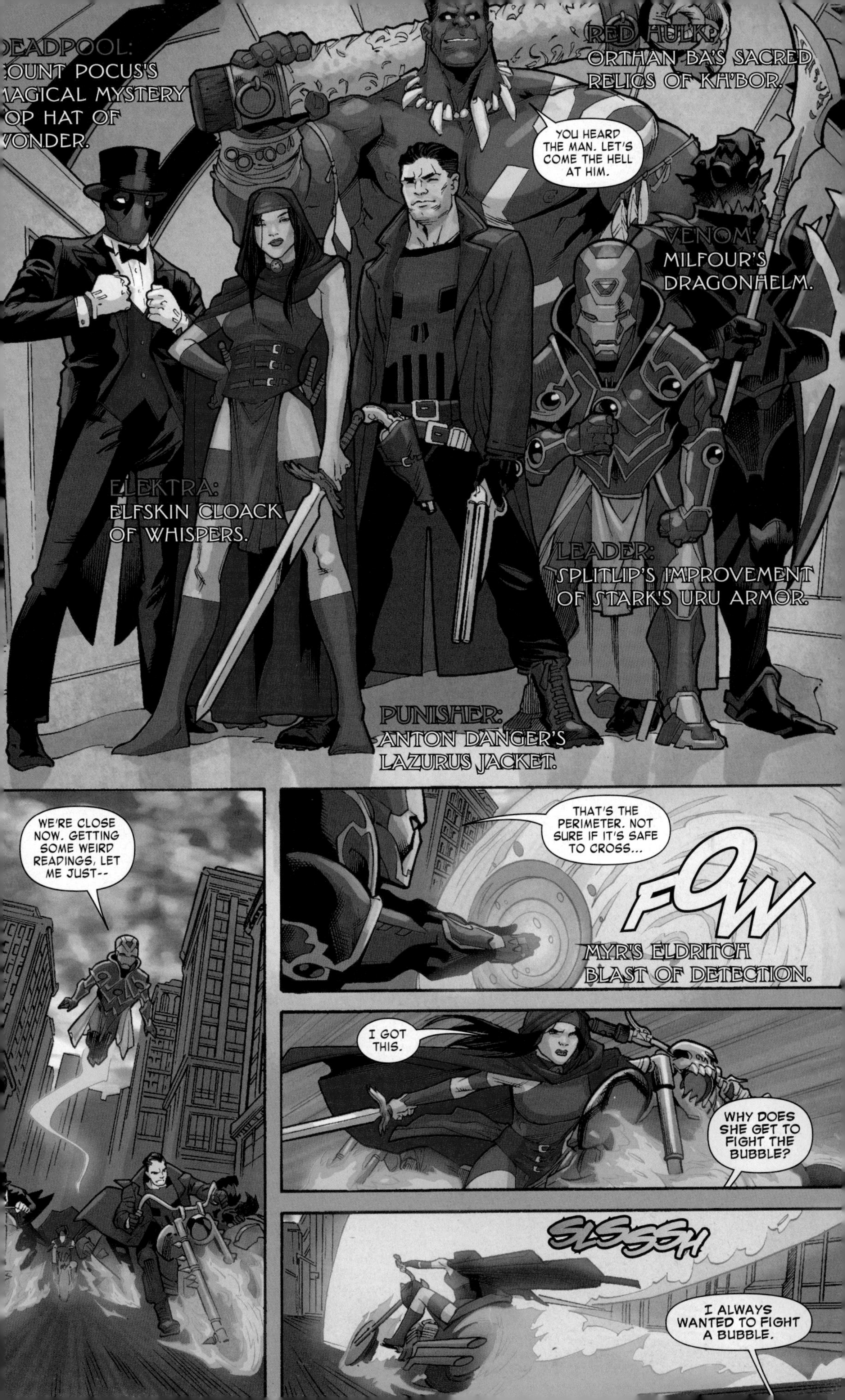
DEADPOOL:
COUNT POCUS'S MAGICAL MYSTERY TOP HAT OF WONDER.
RED HULK:
ORTHAN BA'S SACRED RELICS OF KH'BOR.
YOU HEARD THE MAN. LET'S COME THE HELL AT HIM.
VENOM:
MILFOUR'S DRAGONHELM.
ELEKTRA:
ELFSKIN CLOACK OF WHISPERS.
LEADER:
SPLITLIP'S IMPROVEMENT OF STARK'S URU ARMOR.
PUNISHER:
ANTON DANGER'S LAZURUS JACKET.
WE'RE CLOSE NOW. GETTING SOME WEIRD READINGS, LET ME JUST--
THAT'S THE PERIMETER. NOT SURE IF IT'S SAFE TO CROSS...
FOW
MYR'S ELDRITCH BLAST OF DETECTION.
I GOT THIS.
WHY DOES SHE GET TO FIGHT THE BUBBLE?
SLSSSH
I ALWAYS WANTED TO FIGHT A BUBBLE.

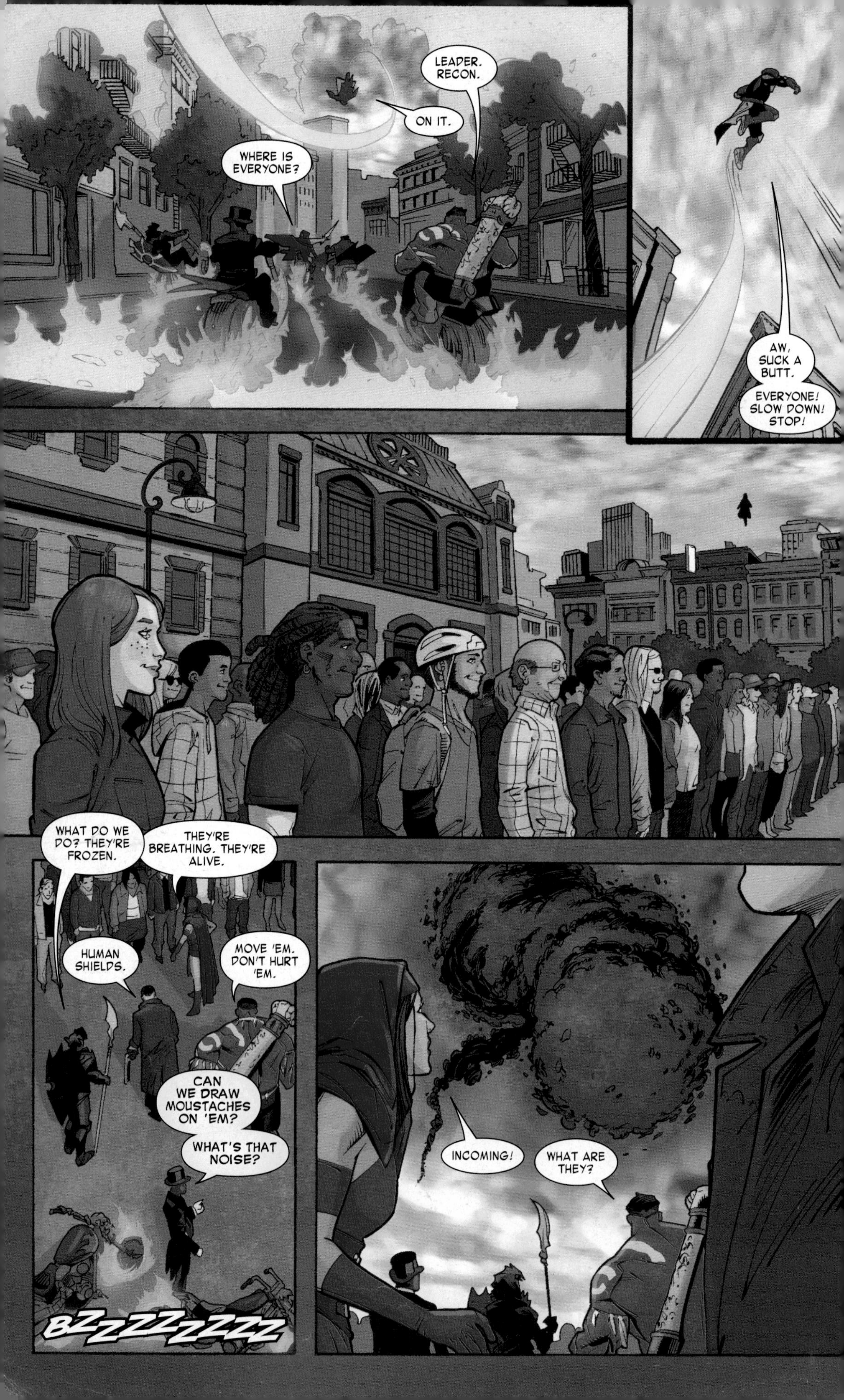
LEADER. RECON.
ON IT.
WHERE IS EVERYONE?
AW, SUCK A BUTT.
EVERYONE! SLOW DOWN! STOP!
WHAT DO WE DO? THEY'RE FROZEN.
THEY'RE BREATHING. THEY'RE ALIVE.
HUMAN SHIELDS.
MOVE 'EM. DON'T HURT 'EM.
CAN WE DRAW MOUSTACHES ON 'EM?
WHAT'S THAT NOISE?
BZZZZZZZZZZ
INCOMING!
WHAT ARE THEY?

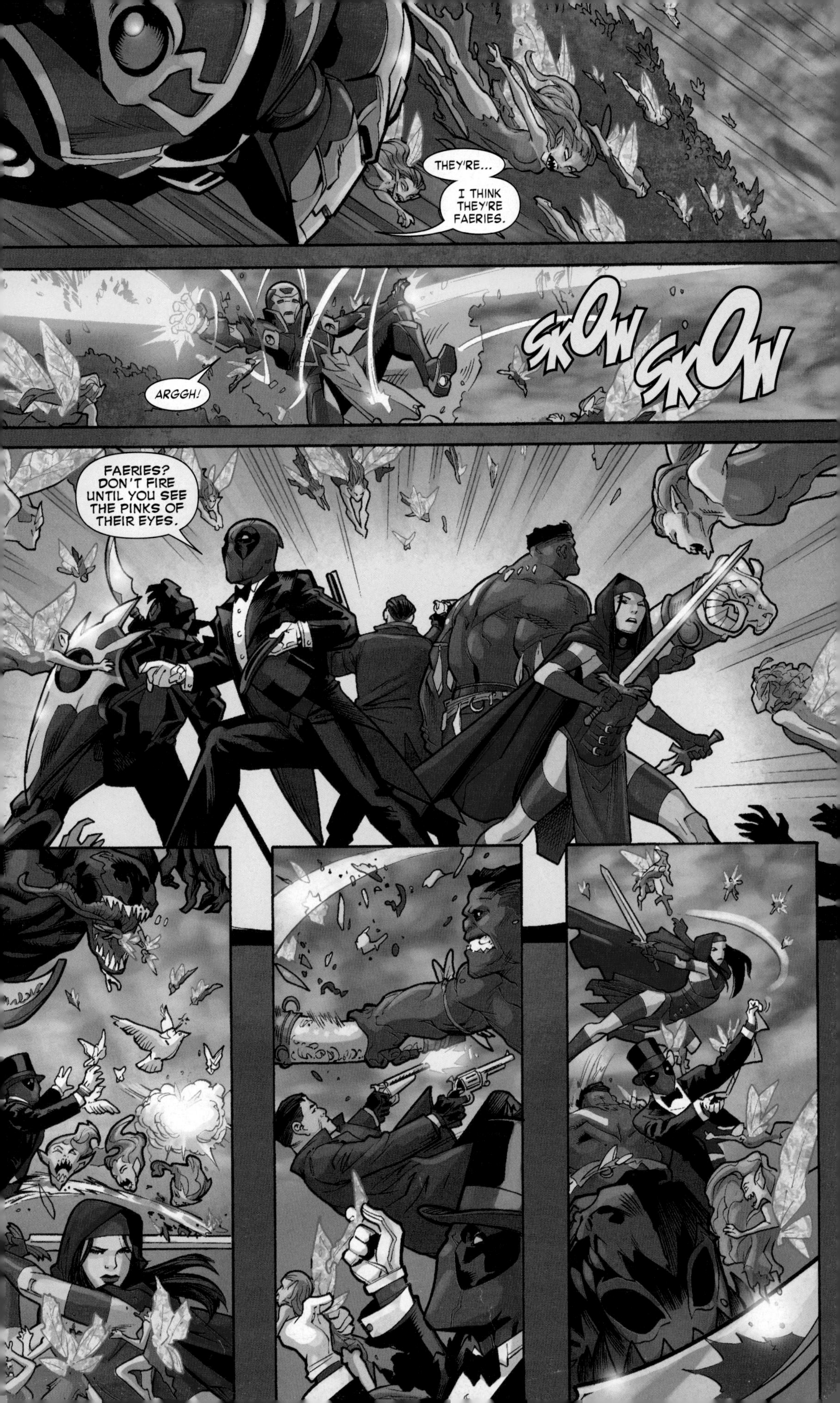
THEY'RE... I THINK THEY'RE FAERIES.
ARGGH!
SKOW SKOW
FAERIES? DON'T FIRE UNTIL YOU SEE THE PINKS OF THEIR EYES.

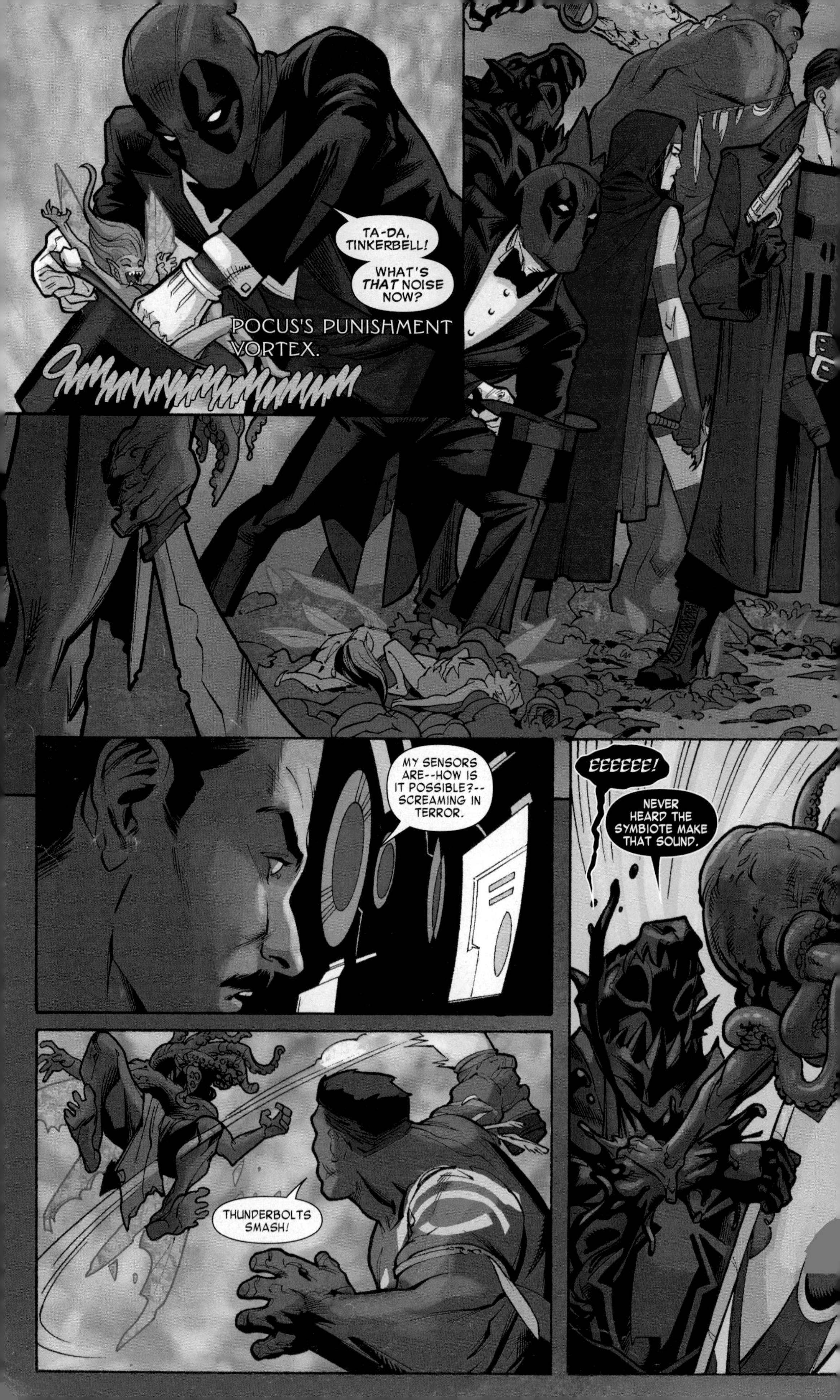

TA-DA, TINKERBELL!
WHAT'S *THAT* NOISE NOW?
POCUS'S PUNISHMENT VORTEX.
MY SENSORS ARE--HOW IS IT POSSIBLE?--SCREAMING IN TERROR.
EEEEEE!
NEVER HEARD THE SYMBIOTE MAKE THAT SOUND.
THUNDERBOLTS SMASH!

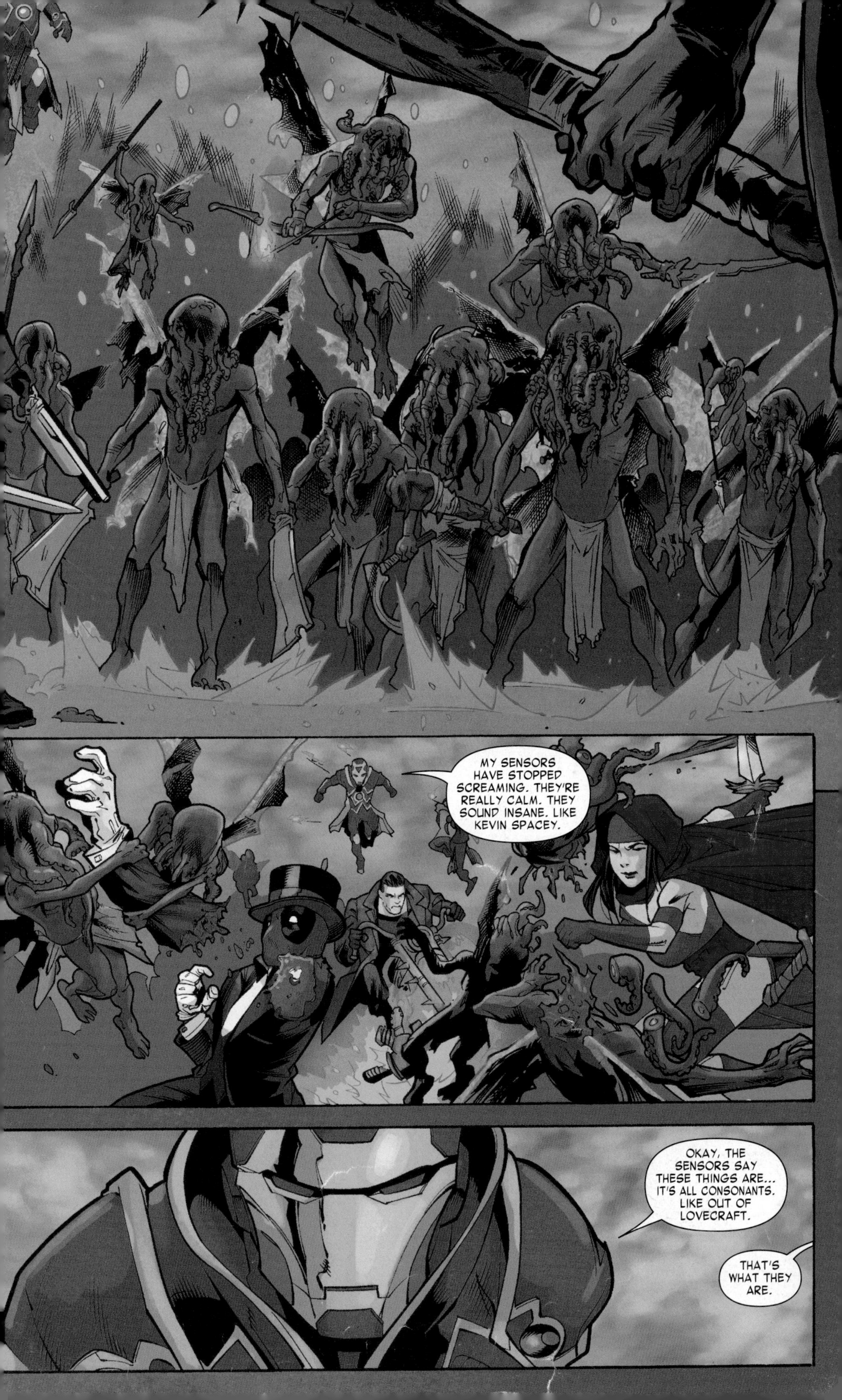

MY SENSORS HAVE STOPPED SCREAMING. THEY'RE REALLY CALM. THEY SOUND INSANE. LIKE KEVIN SPACEY.
OKAY, THE SENSORS SAY THESE THINGS ARE... IT'S ALL CONSONANTS. LIKE OUT OF LOVECRAFT.
THAT'S WHAT THEY ARE.

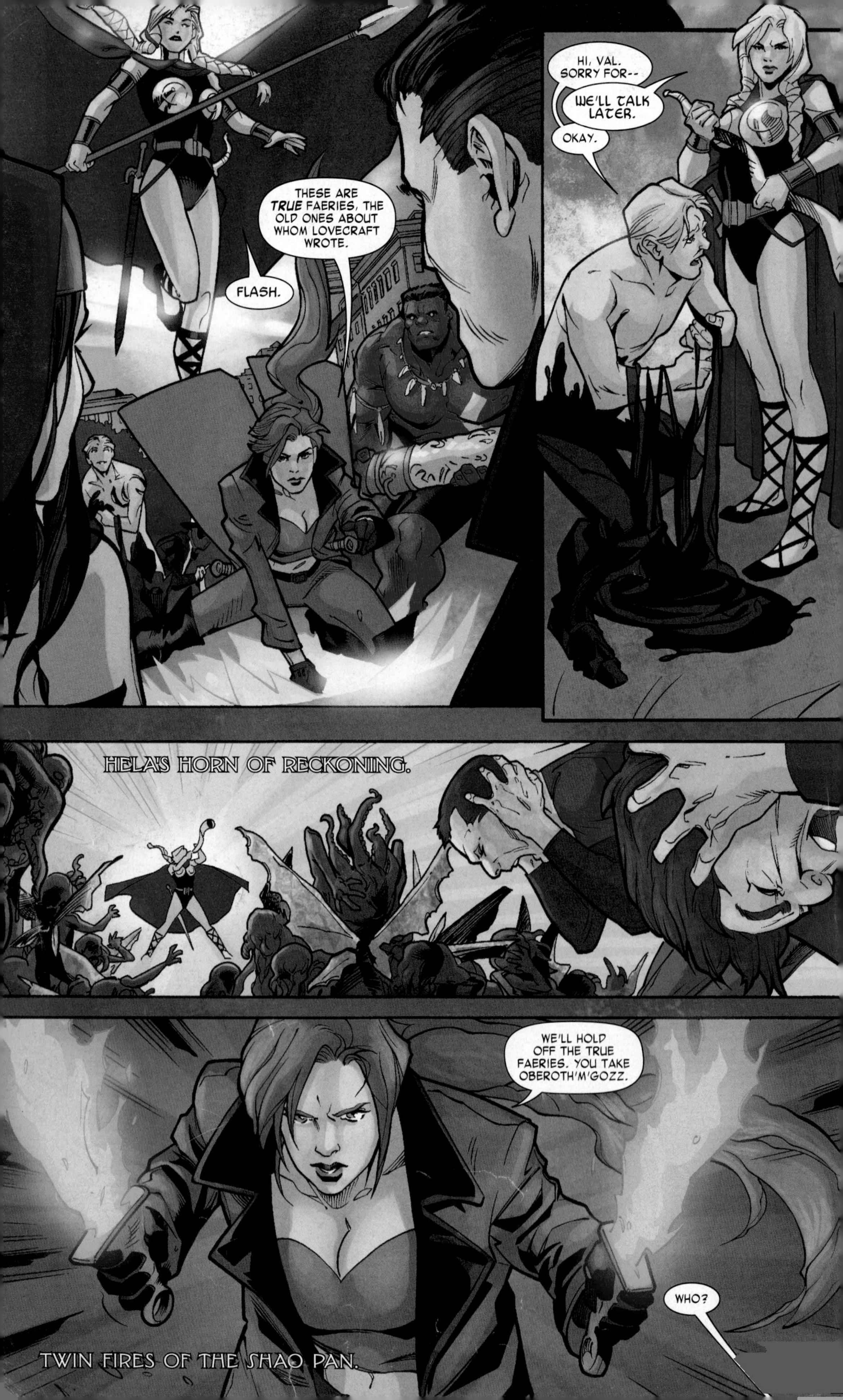
THESE ARE TRUE FAERIES, THE OLD ONES ABOUT WHOM LOVECRAFT WROTE.
FLASH.
HI, VAL. SORRY FOR--
WE'LL TALK LATER.
OKAY.
HELA'S HORN OF RECKONING.
WE'LL HOLD OFF THE TRUE FAERIES. YOU TAKE OBEROTH'M'GOZZ.
WHO?
TWIN FIRES OF THE SHAO PAN.

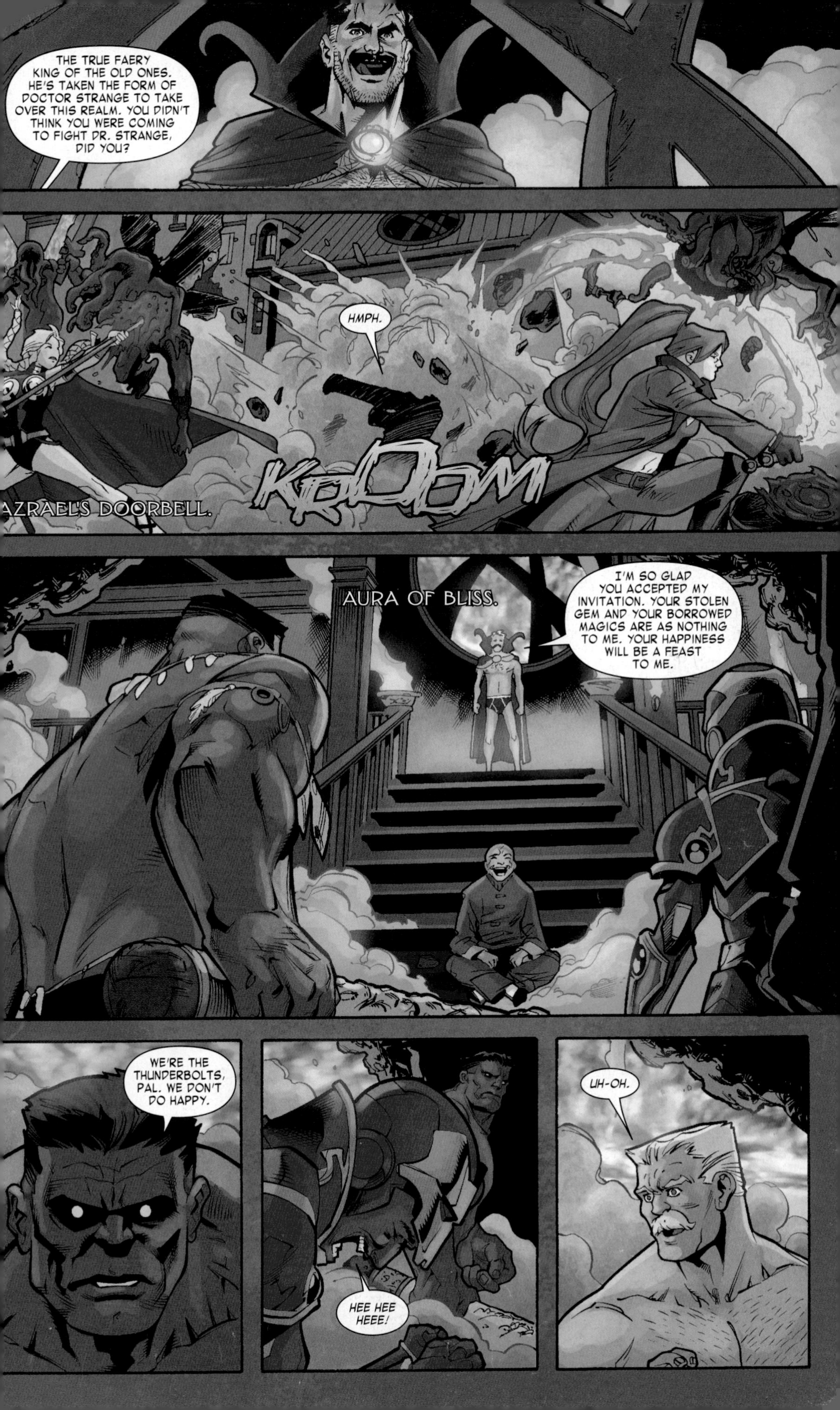
THE TRUE FAERY KING OF THE OLD ONES. HE'S TAKEN THE FORM OF DOCTOR STRANGE TO TAKE OVER THIS REALM. YOU DIDN'T THINK YOU WERE COMING TO FIGHT DR. STRANGE, DID YOU?
HMPH.
KROOOM
AZRAEL'S DOORBELL.
AURA OF BLISS.
I'M SO GLAD YOU ACCEPTED MY INVITATION. YOUR STOLEN GEM AND YOUR BORROWED MAGICS ARE AS NOTHING TO ME. YOUR HAPPINESS WILL BE A FEAST TO ME.
WE'RE THE THUNDERBOLTS, PAL. WE DON'T DO HAPPY.
HEE HEE HEEE!
UH-OH.

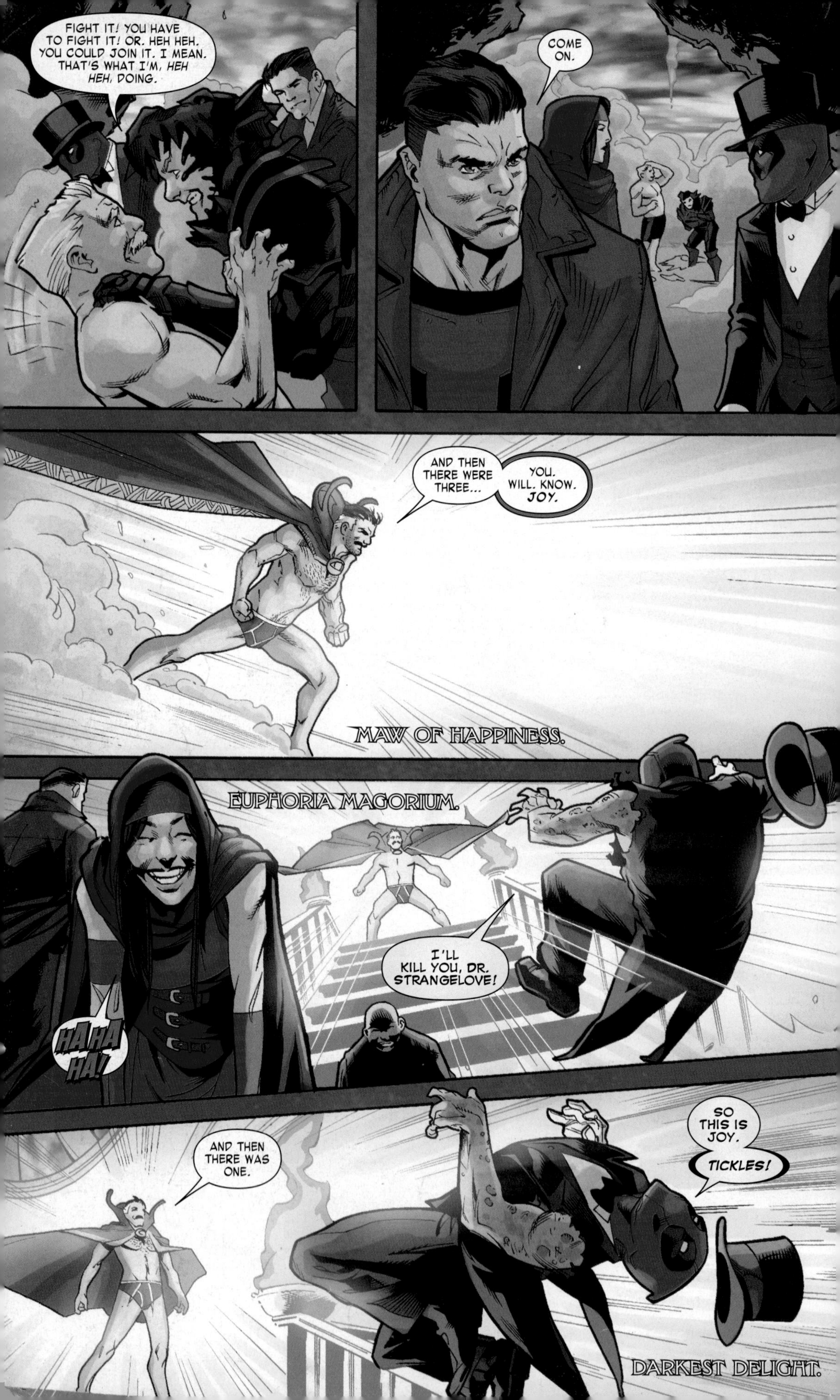
FIGHT IT! YOU HAVE TO FIGHT IT! OR. HEH HEH. YOU COULD JOIN IT. I MEAN. THAT'S WHAT I'M, *HEH HEH*, DOING.
COME ON.
AND THEN THERE WERE THREE...
YOU. WILL. KNOW. *JOY.*
MAW OF HAPPINESS.
EUPHORIA MAGORIUM.
I'LL KILL YOU, DR. STRANGELOVE!
HA HA HA!
AND THEN THERE WAS ONE.
SO THIS IS JOY.
TICKLES!
DARKEST DELIGHT.

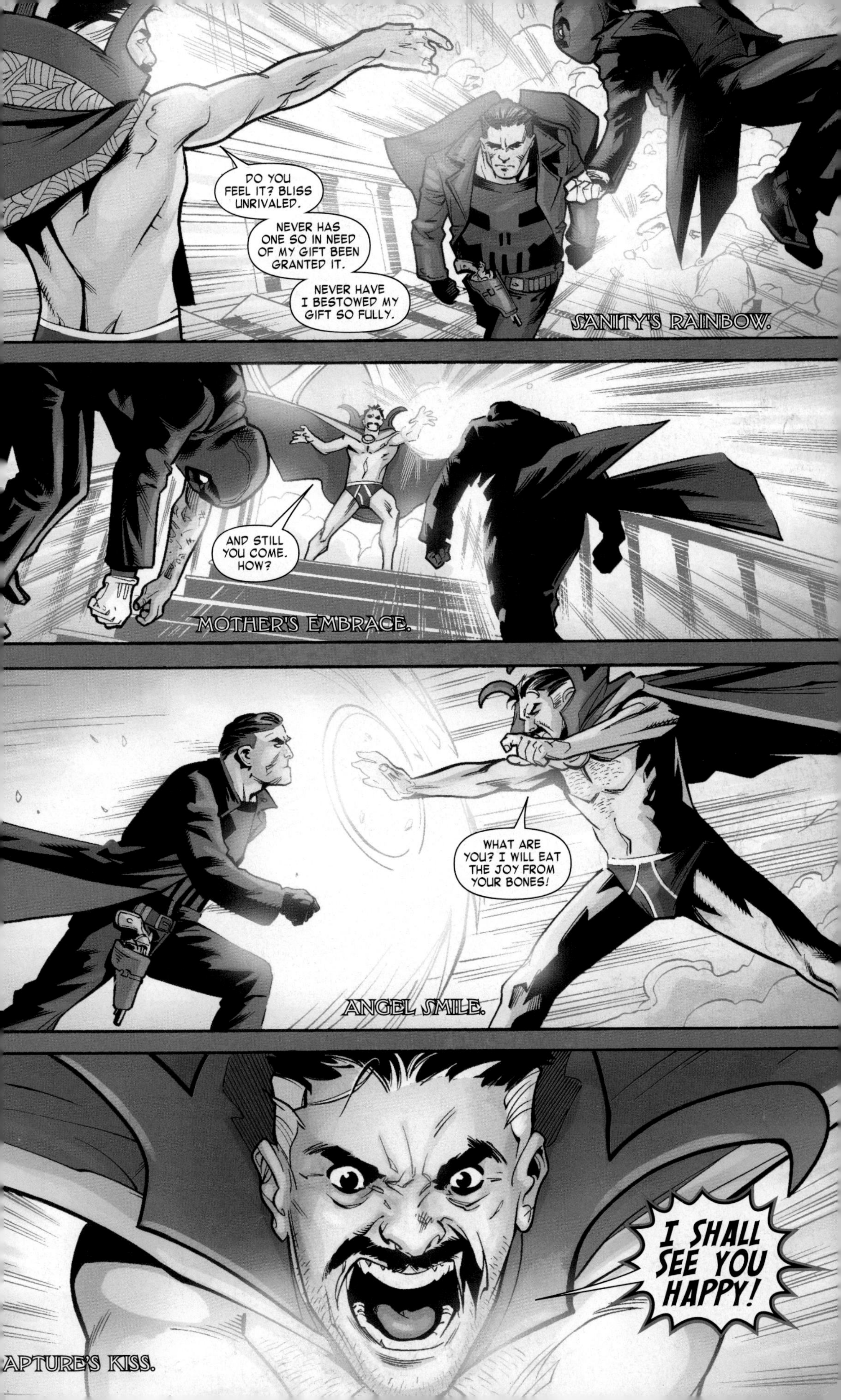
DO YOU FEEL IT? BLISS UNRIVALED.
NEVER HAS ONE SO IN NEED OF MY GIFT BEEN GRANTED IT.
NEVER HAVE I BESTOWED MY GIFT SO FULLY.
SANITY'S RAINBOW.
AND STILL YOU COME. HOW?
MOTHER'S EMBRACE.
WHAT ARE YOU? I WILL EAT THE JOY FROM YOUR BONES!
ANGEL SMILE.
I SHALL SEE YOU HAPPY!
APTURE'S KISS.

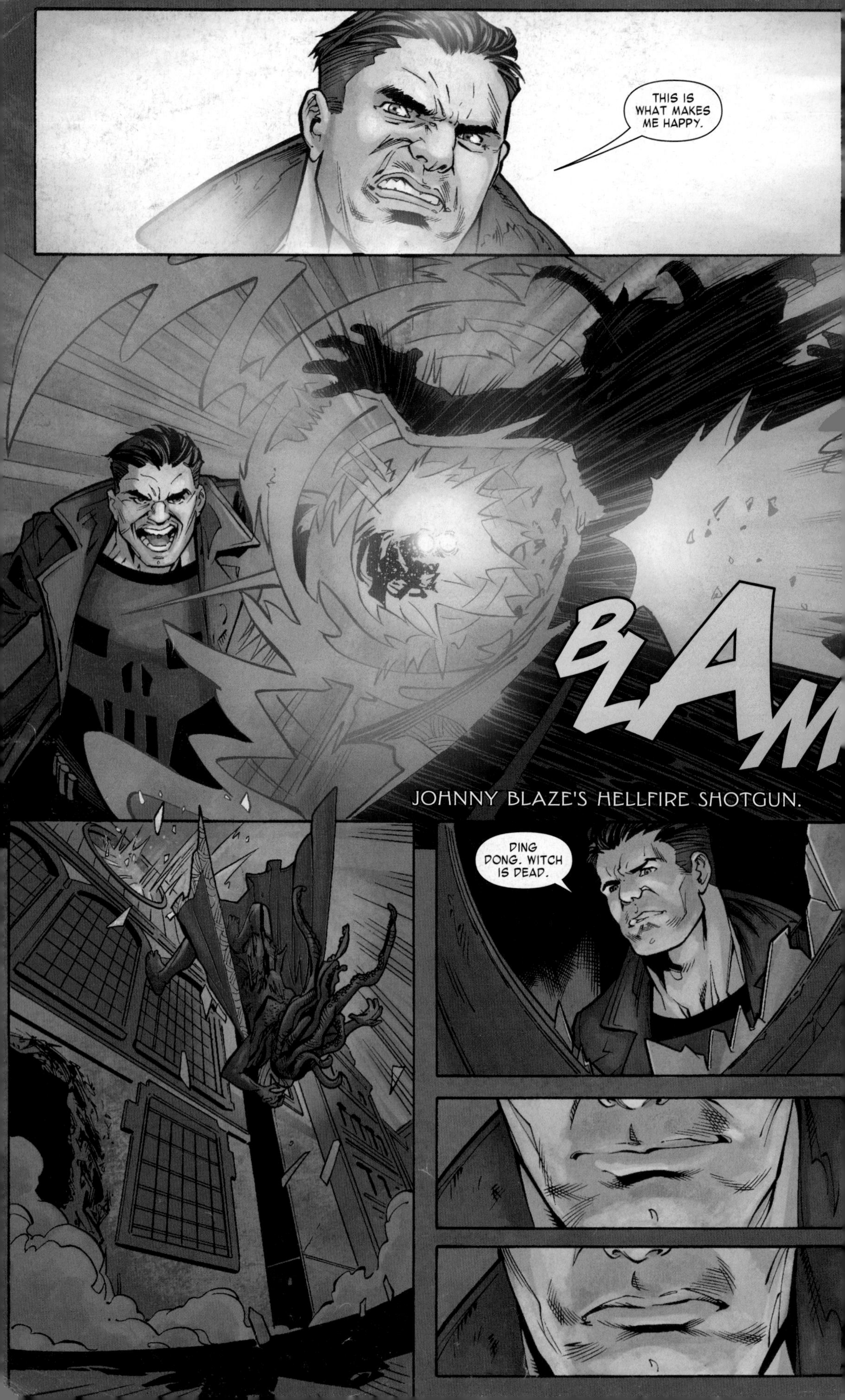
THIS IS WHAT MAKES ME HAPPY.
BLAM
JOHNNY BLAZE'S HELLFIRE SHOTGUN.
DING DONG. WITCH IS DEAD.

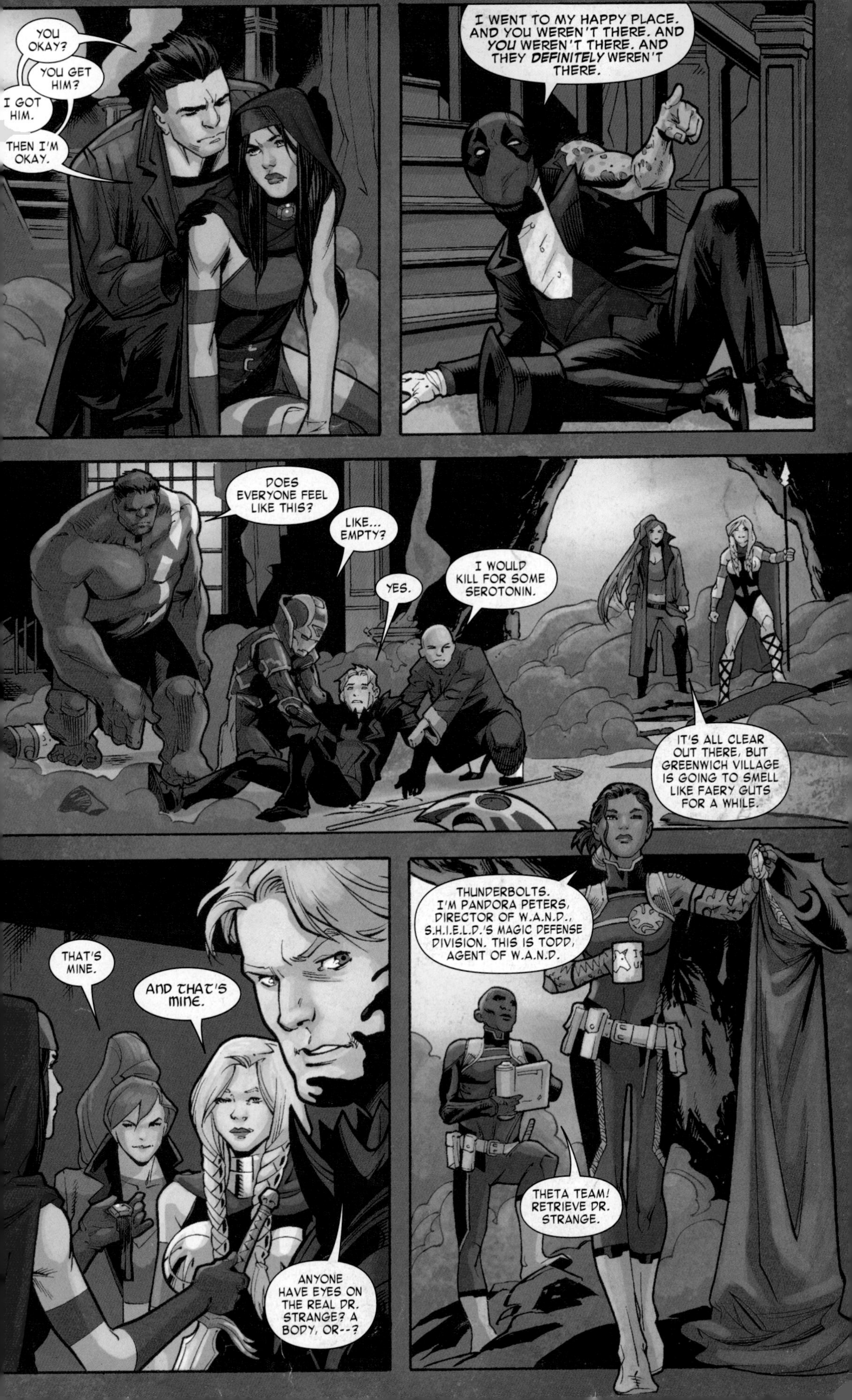
YOU OKAY?
YOU GET HIM?
I GOT HIM.
THEN I'M OKAY.
I WENT TO MY HAPPY PLACE. AND YOU WEREN'T THERE. AND YOU WEREN'T THERE. AND THEY DEFINITELY WEREN'T THERE.
DOES EVERYONE FEEL LIKE THIS?
LIKE... EMPTY?
YES.
I WOULD KILL FOR SOME SEROTONIN.
IT'S ALL CLEAR OUT THERE, BUT GREENWICH VILLAGE IS GOING TO SMELL LIKE FAERY GUTS FOR A WHILE.
THAT'S MINE.
AND THAT'S MINE.
ANYONE HAVE EYES ON THE REAL DR. STRANGE? A BODY, OR--?
THUNDERBOLTS. I'M PANDORA PETERS, DIRECTOR OF W.A.N.D., S.H.I.E.L.D.'S MAGIC DEFENSE DIVISION. THIS IS TODD, AGENT OF W.A.N.D.
THETA TEAM! RETRIEVE DR. STRANGE.

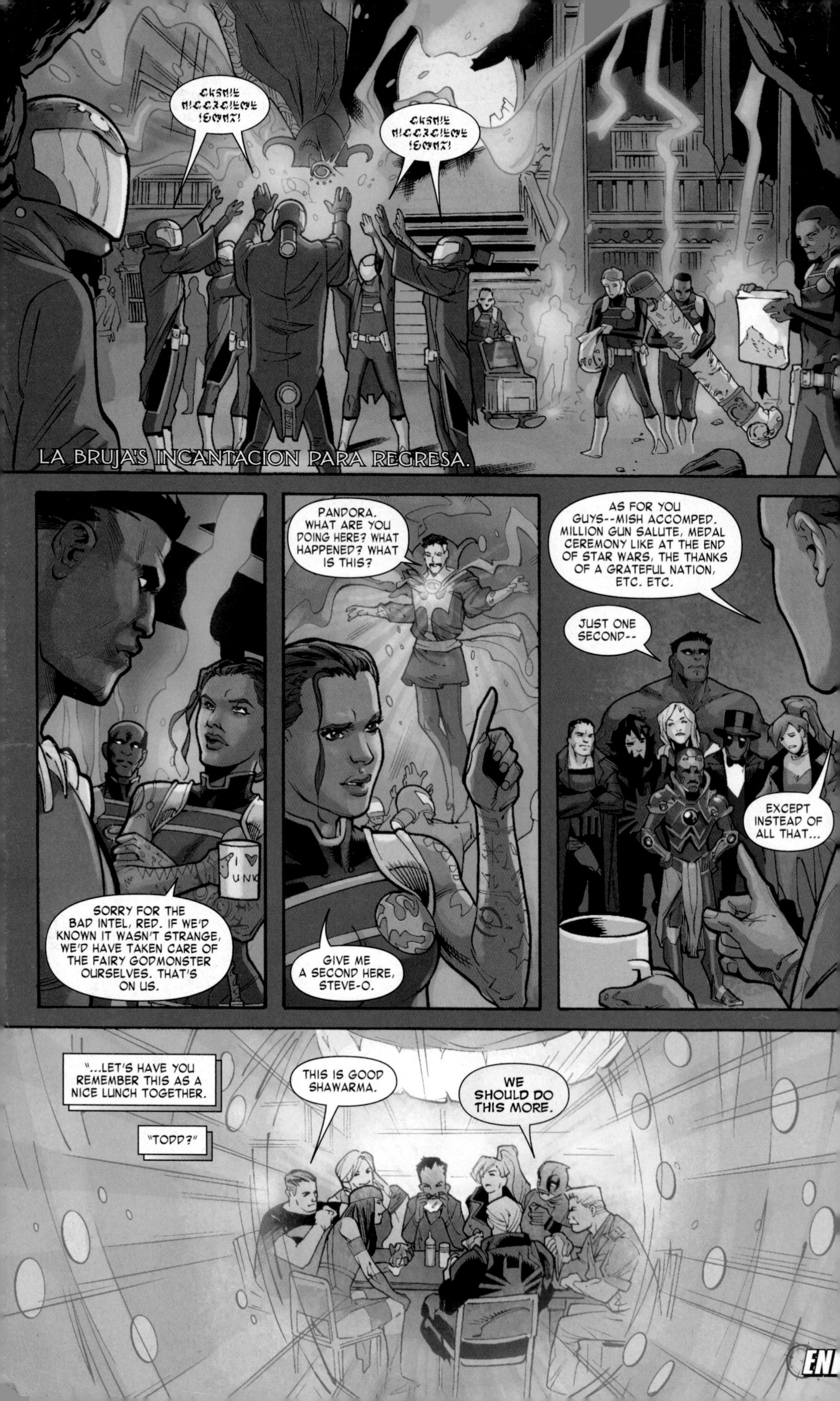
LA BRUJA'S INCANTACION PARA REGRESA.
SORRY FOR THE BAD INTEL, RED. IF WE'D KNOWN IT WASN'T STRANGE, WE'D HAVE TAKEN CARE OF THE FAIRY GODMONSTER OURSELVES. THAT'S ON US.
PANDORA. WHAT ARE YOU DOING HERE? WHAT HAPPENED? WHAT IS THIS?
GIVE ME A SECOND HERE, STEVE-O.
AS FOR YOU GUYS--MISH ACCOMPED. MILLION GUN SALUTE, MEDAL CEREMONY LIKE AT THE END OF STAR WARS, THE THANKS OF A GRATEFUL NATION, ETC. ETC.
JUST ONE SECOND--
EXCEPT INSTEAD OF ALL THAT...
"...LET'S HAVE YOU REMEMBER THIS AS A NICE LUNCH TOGETHER.
"TODD?"
THIS IS GOOD SHAWARMA.
WE SHOULD DO THIS MORE.

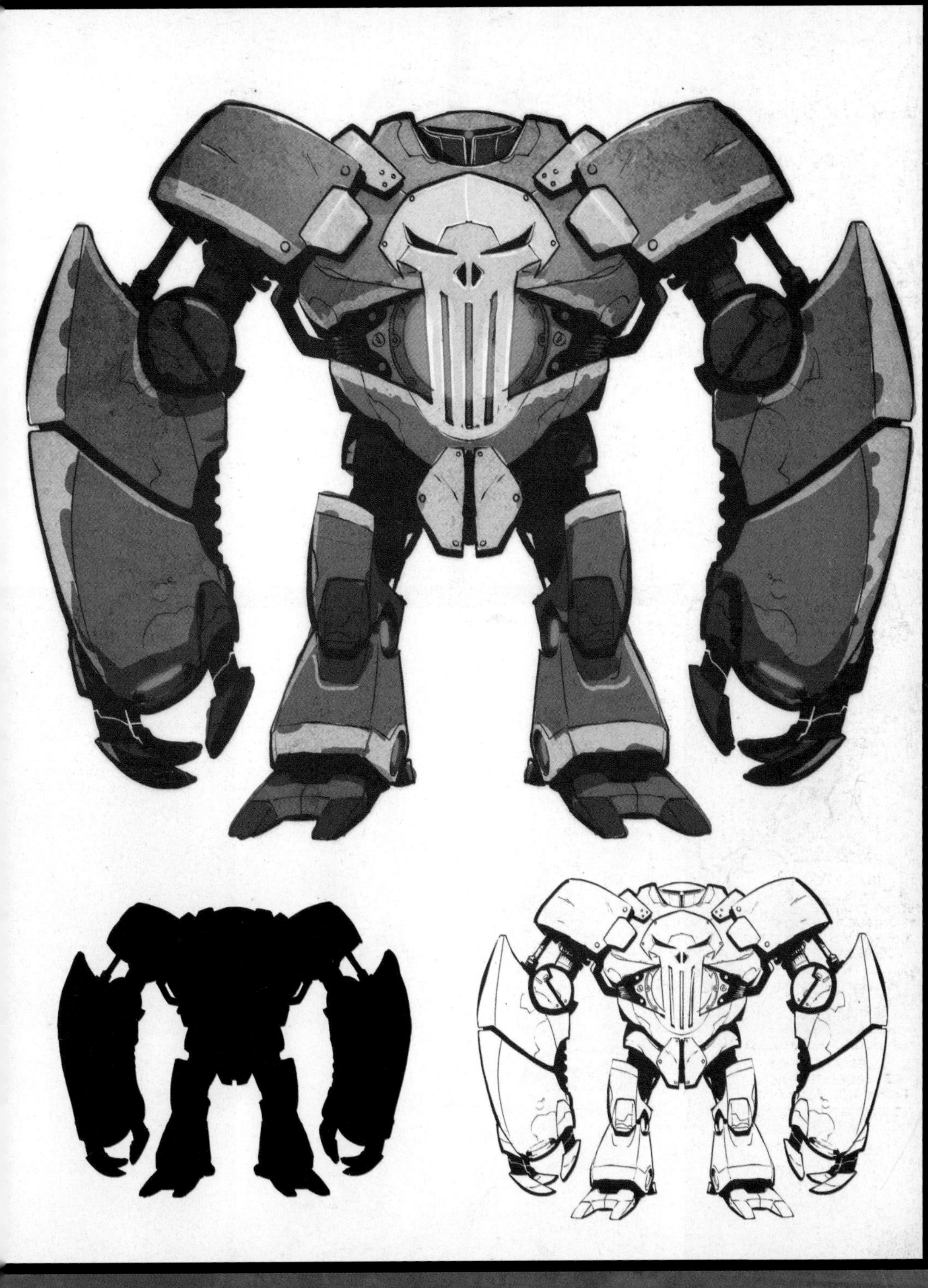

PUNISHER'S HULKBUSTER DESIGNS BY KIM JACINTO

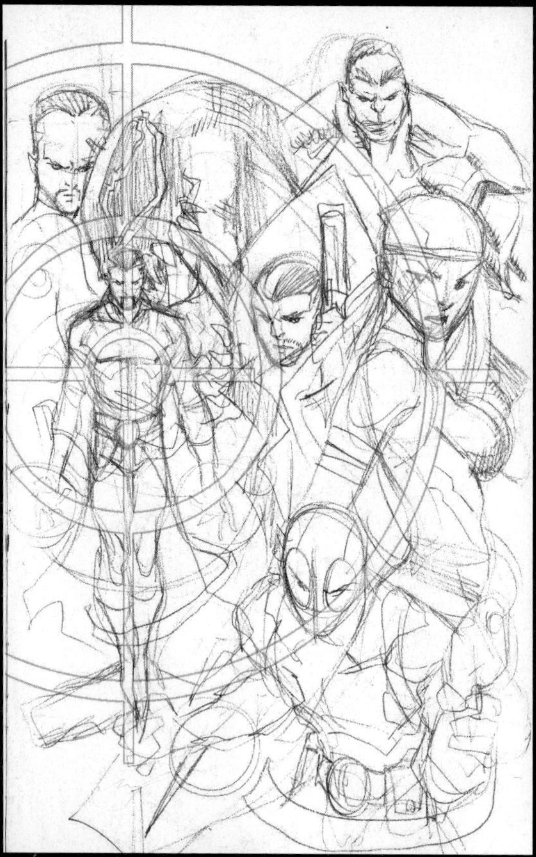

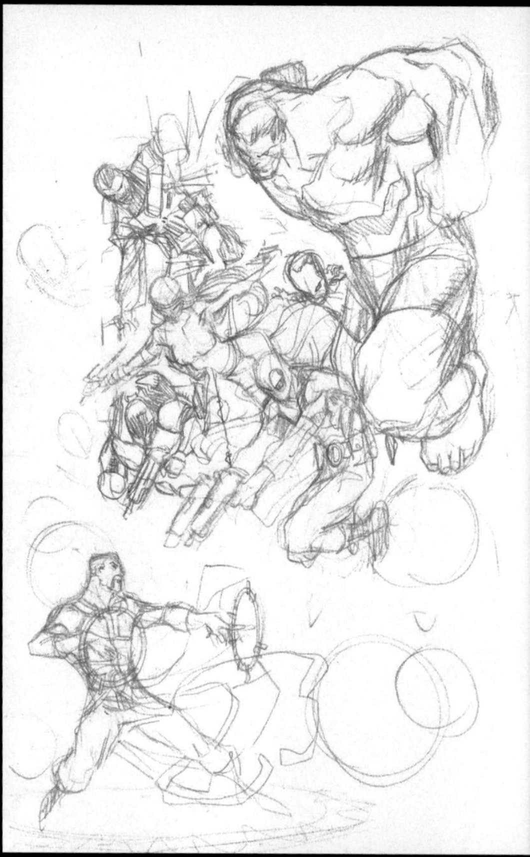

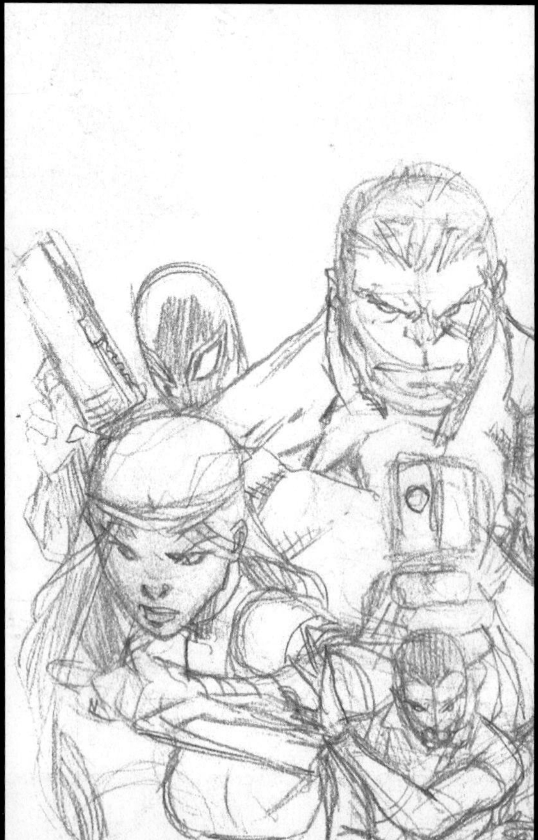

ANNUAL #1 COVER SKETCHES AND ART BY CARLO BARBERI

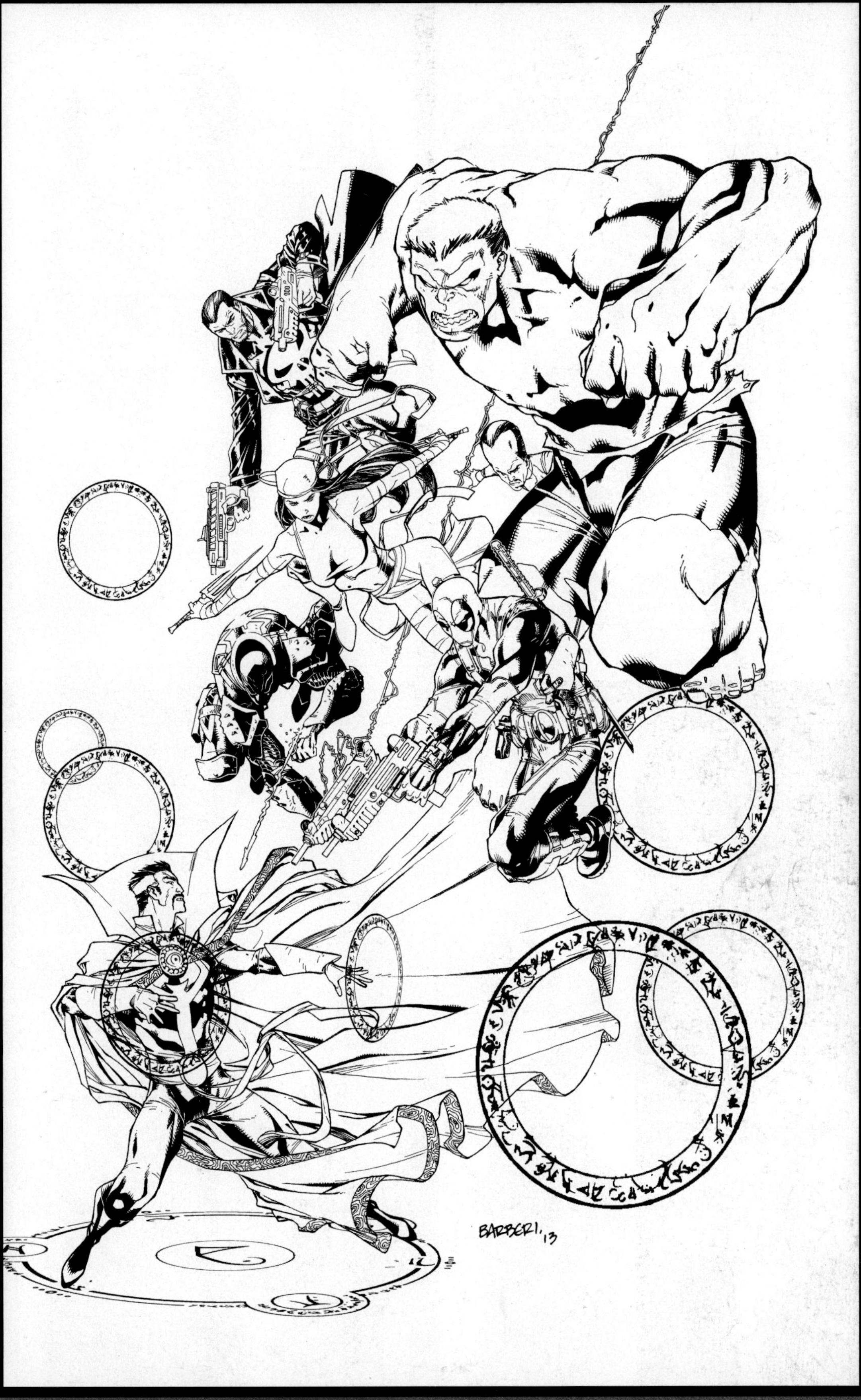
BARBERI, '13

MARVEL
NOW!
THUNDERBOLTS
RATED T
$4.99US/CAN
NEWSSTAND
MARVEL.COM
MARVEL ADVENTURES
DISPLAY UNTIL XX/XX/2012
1.1875" Full Bleed
0.25" TYPE SAFTEY
000

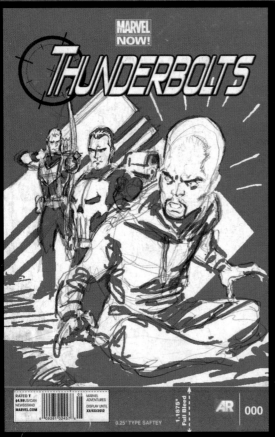

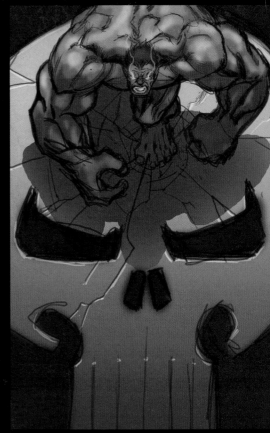

#28, #31 & #32 COVER SKETCHES BY DAVID YARDIN

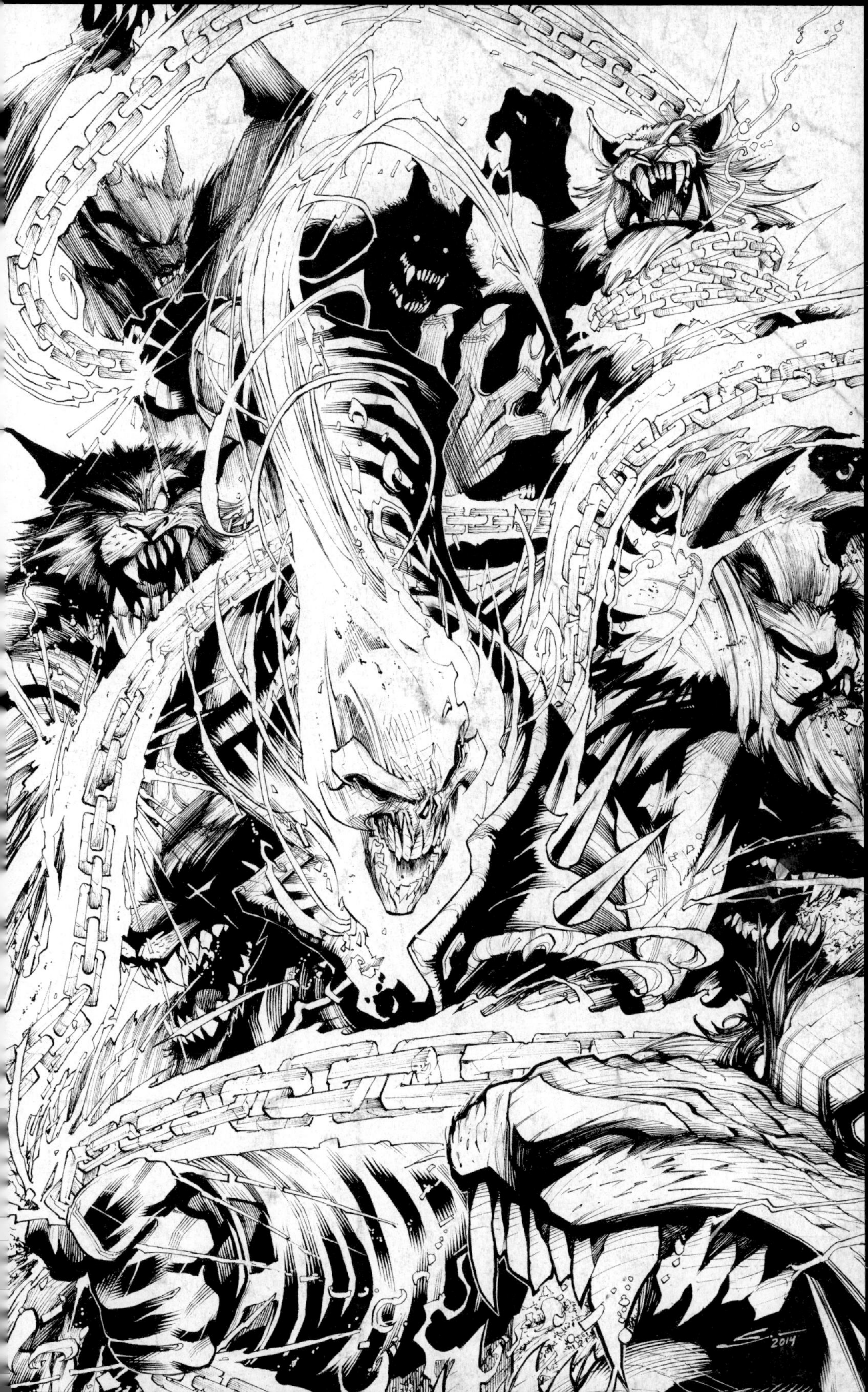
2014

#28 PAGE 8 ART BY GERARDO SANDOVAL

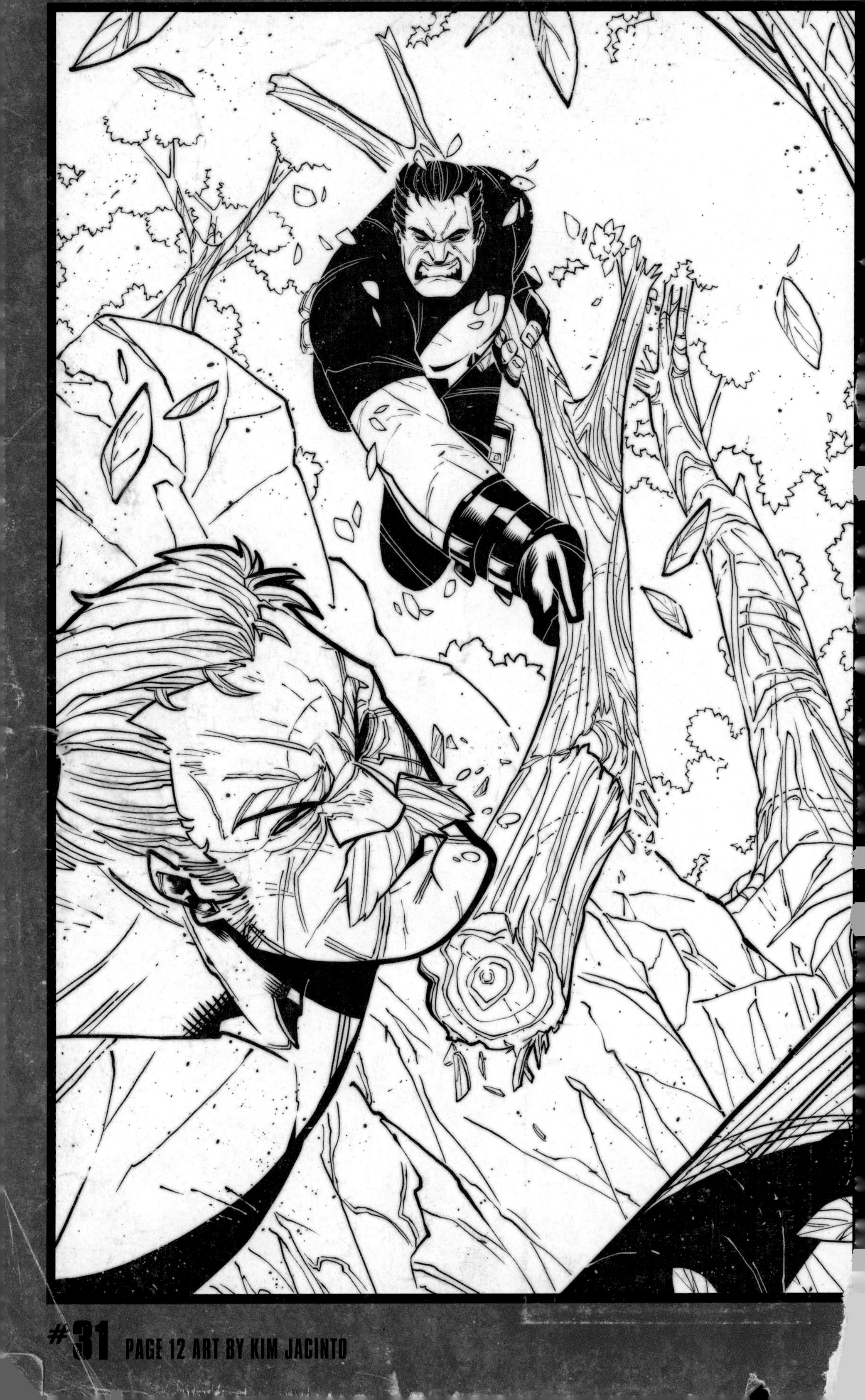

31 PAGE 12 ART BY KIM JACINTO